THE PYTHAGOREAN SOURCEBOOK AND LIBRARY

PYTHAGORAS.

THE PYTHAGOREAN SOURCEBOOK

AND LIBRARY

An Anthology of Ancient Writings
Which Relate to
Pythagoras and Pythagorean Philosophy

COMPILED AND TRANSLATED BY

KENNETH SYLVAN GUTHRIE

WITH ADDITIONAL TRANSLATIONS BY THOMAS TAYLOR
AND ARTHUR FAIRBANKS, JR.

INTRODUCED AND EDITED BY

DAVID R. FIDELER

WITH A FOREWORD BY

JOSCELYN GODWIN

PHANES PRESS
1987

© 1987, 1988 by Phanes Press

Published by Phanes Press, PO Box 6114, Grand Rapids, Michigan 49516, USA.

Designed by David R. Fideler
Typography by Phanes Press

Library of Congress Cataloging in Publication Data

Guthrie, Kenneth Sylvan, 1871-1940.
    The Pythagorean sourcebook and library.

    Bibliography p.
    Includes index.
    1. Pythagoras and Pythagorean school. I. Fideler, David R.   II. Title.
B243.G88   1987   182'.2   87-60459
ISBN 0-933999-50-X (alk. paper)
ISBN 0-933999-51-8 (pbk.: alk. paper)

This book is printed on alkaline paper which conforms to the permament paper standard developed by the National Information Standards Organization.

95   8 7 6 5

TABLE OF CONTENTS

PART II:
The Pythagorean Library

List of Figures

FOREWORD

IF WESTERN CIVILIZATION has taken, as it seems, not one but several wrong turnings between the time of Pythagoras (sixth century B.C.E.) and the present, it is because it has been unfaithful to him who should by rights have been its tutelary genius. Pythagoras is the very midwife of our epoch, ushering it to birth from the dusky, mythic past, sowing the seeds of a new consciousness, a new possibility for growth after the plan laid up in Heaven. His own story, accordingly, is part myth, part ascertainable history. Such divine figures as he inhabit both realms. His achievement is a prophetic one, for in his life and work he set forth the perfect framework for the unfoldment not only of Classical Greek culture but of the whole coming age up to our own time. The Pythagorean synthesis of religion with spiritual and natural philosophy would have been the ideal guide for a civilization whose destiny was to come to terms with the material world.

Pythagoras set the stage for this development with a careful system of checks and balances. In his emphasis on Number—the keystone of his doctrine—he revealed the secret without which modern technology would have been impossible. It is applied mathematics, after all, that has led to the so-called conquest of Nature. But at the same time, and much more importantly, Pythagoras taught the metaphysical and sacred aspect of Number as reflecting the One and its emanations. In this respect the Numbers, especially those from 1 to 10, are archetypal beings. To approach them as quantity alone is a denial of their nature verging on blasphemy. It is not the fault of Christianity that the idea of sacred number and geometry has vanished, along with any viable science based thereon: nowhere are these things more evident than in the scriptures and rituals of the Churches. It is the error of those who have forgotten the Pythagorean (and Christian) precept, to "honor first the Immortal Gods"—themselves Numbers—before embarking on any enterprise. Consequently number today carries not meaning and wisdom, but only information and power of a very dubious character.

The Pythagorean world view is a graduated, hierarchical one, with every stage filled by appropriate beings: Divinities, lesser Gods, daimons, heroes, geniuses. etc. It is in no way contrary to the Jewish, early Christian, and Islamic vision of rank upon rank of angels standing between God and the earth. Angels are unfashionable nowadays, and while in some respects it has been an advantage to bring the Absolute closer to man, it has lost most of its absoluteness in becoming a personal God. Far better to worship the One within, but to recognize and cooperate with those beings who have to maintain the world against mankind's best efforts to spoil it. Given this orderly hierarchical universe, Pythagoreanism has no need to blandly oppose spirit to matter: things are more subtle than that. Neither does it need to invent a Fall of angels or of man that violates the divine order. The *Golden Verses* say: "Men are children of the Gods, and sacred Nature

11

all things hid reveals.'' Everything proceeds according to a law that renders perfect justice to each, as surely as every physical action provokes an equal and opposite reaction. The One has no personality to make its favor or anger our concern. Since there is no Fall except the periodic one of soul into body, there is no vicarious salvation. Only one's own efforts and acquired wisdom can free one from this migration around the states of being. Nevertheless, there is every reason for piety towards the Gods, and for gratitude to Pythagoras and those others who have taught the means to attain freedom through rational conduct and the philosophic life.

Pythagoras' metaphysics enables the Intellect to approach and know the ultimate TRUTH. His moral precepts ensure conformity with the perfect GOODNESS. To complete the trinity, he also adored the supreme BEAUTY which inspires the Muses as they do our Arts. In the first place he seems to have used Music, both for the intellectual benefits of its speculative side and for the effects of practical music on psycho-physical health. Music is the art in which the Numbers penetrate directly to the heart; in Mathematics they occupy the brain. But it is not music alone that incarnates the transcendent virtues of Number. As it does so in time, so the visual arts do in space, depending no less for their beauty on harmony and correct proportion. It was this knowledge that enabled Classical Greek architecture and sculpture to attain such heights in the century after Pythagoras. Ever since then the high-points of Western and Islamic architecture have followed on the reapplication of harmonic principles, as one can prove by measurement of Gothic cathedrals, early Renaissance churches, and the masterpieces of Islamic architecture. Disobedience to harmonic laws leads to ugliness, which is a sin against the Muses and a denial of the divinely beautiful order of the cosmos. Obedience to them, on the other hand, presupposes a state of soul open also to Intelligible Beauty; music and architecture open our souls in the same way.

When he came to teach, Pythagoras recognized that people, too, are arranged in a hierarchy, and that they vary enormously in their receptivity to philosophy. Some are little more than animals, and require the same loving attentions, while others are little short of Gods. Consequently he reserved different degrees of teaching for the different levels. Much has been said about the secrecy of the most esoteric branch of his school, but like Plato and Jesus he also involved himself in public life, often to his cost. As a political reformer and giver of laws to several cities, he provided a field for the improvement of all, even of the lowest types—for that is what politics should be about. Within his school he went against contemporary custom in giving equal status to women, and his biographers are careful to record the names of his female disciples. I am sure that much evil would have been avoided had Western civilization not indulged in such parodies of the hierarchical principle as the simplistic division into Saved and Damned, and the restriction of public office and education to men alone.

Naturally Pythagoras did not invent his philosophy: it was not original except in the brilliance of his synthesis. Since Truth is perennial and invariable, to create an ''original'' philosophy is merely to hatch another untruth. Pythagoras' unique advantage was that he studied in every available school, philosophic and religious alike. Orphic by temperament, he also knew the early natural philosophers Thales and Anaximenes, but far from stopping with Greece he investigated the mysteries of Egypt, the science of Babylon, even the wisdom of the Hyperboreans (presumably the Ancient Britons). When he was in his fifties he began to teach the distillation of what he had learnt. Some of it, such as his mystery initiations, he could not pass on. He retained, in fact, only what would be useful to a coming age in which those mysteries would decline and disappear. The discovery of the Divine within oneself (the "Kingdom of Heaven within you") was to be its goal, aided by contemplation of that which "sacred Nature" reveals. There is no reason why this could not have been adapted to make an exoteric religion to serve the whole civilization. This actually seems to have been happening in the time of Caeser and the early Roman Empire, scene of so many religious might-have-beens. As it was, the Pythagorean strain survived only in its more esoteric cultivation by the Neoplatonic philosophers. Neoplatonism is to a very large degree Neopythagorean: it shares the typical interests in theosophy, cosmology, arithmology, speculative music, and exotic religion. In fact, just as Platonists regard Aristotle as a rather limited successor to their master, so Pythagoreans may well regard the Divine Plato.

Since the end of the Roman Empire Pythagoreans have periodically found shelter in the esoteric schools of Christianity and Islam. From time to time their presence has manifested, especially in architecture and the other arts. While I do not believe, as some do, that these schools can have been the motive force behind a history as disappointing as that of the West, one should mention some of those who have publicly carried the torch. Marsilio Ficino in the fifteenth century cast Pythagoras as a link in his genealogy of "prisci theologi": Hermes Trismegistus, Orpheus, Aglaophamus, Pythagoras, Philolaus, Plato. The astronomers Copernicus, Galileo and Kepler invoked the Pythagorean school as a precedent for their heliocentric astronomy; in Kepler's case there was much more, including his researches into the geometry and harmony of the spheres. Later there were two great "romantic" Pythagoreans, Thomas Taylor (1758-1835) and Fabre d'Olivet (1767-1825), perhaps the only ones up to their time who were not also Christians. Fabre published the *Golden Verses* in French, with his remarkable commentary, in 1813; Taylor published his *Theoretic Arithmetic* in 1816, his translation of Iamblichus's *Life of Pythagoras*, the basis of Guthrie's version, in 1818. Largely as a consequence of the work of these two men, the nineteenth century swarms with semi-Pythagoreans, great and small, but all of rather limited effect on the world in general. A stronger impetus was given by the Theosophical Society at the end of the nineteenth century, and by the various esoteric groups that surrounded and derived from it. Kenneth Sylvan Guthrie's work belongs in this context, as does the better-known achievement of Manly Palmer Hall.

Our civilization is now, quite unconsciously, more imbued with Pythagorean influences than it has ever been. The evidence is plain to see wherever one looks, in phenomena as various as vegetarianism and the whole-food movement; post-modernist architecture; the synthesis of religions; travelers in search of Oriental wisdom; researches into ancient Egypt and Babylon; the revivals of sacred geometry, arithmology and speculative music; reprints of Pythagorean literature; meditation; music therapy; the speculations of modern physicists; communes and spiritual communities; the widespread belief in reincarnation. Pythagoras is the center towards which all these scattered impulses point. If he failed as the avatar of the passing age, perhaps he is coming into his own as a new one dawns.

— JOSCELYN GODWIN

Preface to the Original Edition of 1920

THE REASON THAT PYTHAGOREANISM has been neglected, and often treated mythically, is that until this edition all the Pythagorean fragments have never been collected, in text or any translation. This book therefore marks an era in the study of philosophy, and is needed by every university and general library in the world, not to mention those of the students of philosophy.

But there is yet a wider group of people who will welcome it, the lovers of wisdom in general, who will be charmed by Hierocles' modern views about the family, inspired by Iamblichus' beautiful *Life of Pythagoras*, which has been inaccessible for over a century, and strengthened by the maxims of Sextus, which represent the religious facts of the future more perfectly than can easily be found elsewhere.

The universal culture of Pythagoras is faithfully portrayed by the manifold aspects of the teachings of Archytas, and Philolaus, and of many other Pythagoreans, among whose fragments we find dissertations on every possible subject: metaphysics, psychology, ethics, sociology, science, and art. Men of general culture, therefore, will feel the need of this encyclopedic information and study; and conversely, there is neither scientist, metaphysician, clergyman, litterateur or sociologist who will fail to discover herein something to his taste.

The Pythagorean fragments have been gathered from various sources. On Philolaus, the authority is Boeckh. The Archytas fragments have been taken from Chaignet; the minor works from Gale and Taylor, and the Maxims and Golden Verses from Dacier. The work by Timaeus was taken from Plato's works, among which it has been preserved.

This work was undertaken because of the great significance of these writings in the history of philosophy, which has been elsewhere more definitely been pointed out, and for the sake of which, no doubt, the book will be procured by all students, philosophers, and general lovers of wisdom. It was undertaken for no purpose other than the benefit of humanity that had for so long been deprived of this its precious heritage, and the editor will be satisfied if he succeeds in restoring these treasures of thought and inspiration to his day and generation.

— KENNETH SYLVAN GUTHRIE

PREFACE TO THE NEW EDITION

THIS ANTHOLOGY is based on Kenneth Sylvan Guthrie's *Pythagoras Source Book and Library,* issued in a very small printing by the Platonist Press between 1919 and 1920. Guthrie's edition contained his own translations of ancient Greek writings in addition to edited versions of writings initially translated by Thomas Taylor. In editing Taylor's translations, Guthrie carefully adhered to Taylor's renditions but greatly improved the readability of the style. Guthrie's original translations include Porphyry's *Life of Pythagoras,* the anonymous *Life of Pythagoras* from Photius, the biography from Diogenes Laeritus, and the fragments of Philolaus and Archytas. Most of the remaining works were translated by Taylor, and their sources are noted in the bibliography under "Pythagorean Texts." In editing this work I have repaired some awkward phrasings and have checked all of Guthrie's renditions against other translations including those of Taylor.

In addition to containing all the texts of Guthrie's original edition, much new material has been added as well: additional translations by Arthur Fairbanks, four new appendixes, illustrations, an index, a large bibliography, and a new foreword and introduction.

Throughout the production process a number of individuals have graciously provided assistance to whom thanks is due: Joscelyn Godwin, Steve Miller, Henry Morren, and Arthur Versluis were instrumental in helping with the proofreading, and Bob Tarte provided assistance with typography. I would also like to acknowledge the assistance of my father, Raymond E. Fideler (1912-1986), without whose help and generosity this project might not have been completed; unfortunately, he passed away before he could view the final results, so I would like to dedicate my introductory essay, with gratitude and affection, to his memory.

— DAVID R. FIDELER

INTRODUCTION

IT HAS BEEN SUGGESTED, by Alfred North Whitehead, that "the safest general characterization of the European philosophical tradition is that it consists of a series of footnotes to Plato." If such be the case, what might then be said of Pythagoras, to whose philosophy Plato was so greatly indebted? While no definitive answer will be attempted here, it might do well to note that not only did Pythagoras first employ the term *philosophy,* and define the discipline thereof in the classic sense, but that he bequeathed to his followers, and to the whole of Western civilization, many important studies and sciences which he was instrumental in either formulating or systematizing.

True as this may be, much mystery surrounds the figure of Pythagoras, despite the significant influence of Pythagorean thought in antiquity. Of course, many things can be precisely stated. He was both a natural philosopher and a spiritual philosopher, a scientist and a religious thinker. He was a political theorist, and was even involved in local government. While he may not have been the first to discover the ratios of the musical scale, with which he is credited, there can be no doubt that he did conduct extensive research into musical harmonics and tuning systems. Pythagoras is well known as a mathematician, but few realize that he was also a music therapist having, in fact, founded the discipline. Pythagoras taught the kinship of all living things; hence, he and his followers were vegetarians. Yet, while all these things may be safely stated, quite a bit of mystery still remains.[1] This is due in large part to the fact that Pythagoras left no writings, although it is said that he wrote some poems under the name of Orpheus.[2] Pythagoras' teaching was of an oral nature. While he seems to have made some speeches upon his arrival in southern Italy to the populace, the true fruits of his philosophic inquiries were presented only to those students who were equipped to assimilate them. Pythagoras no doubt felt, like his later admirer Plato, that philosophic doctrines of ultimate concern should never be published, seeing that philosophy is a process, and that books can never answer questions, nor engage in philosophical enquiry.[3]

Yet, despite the lack of first-hand writings by Pythagoras himself, we need not be deterred. There is an immense amount of material in the biographies of Pythagoras which goes back to a very early date, and it is certainly possible to sketch an accurate if not complete picture of early Pythagorean philosophy, even being quite specific on many points.[4] Let us then begin with Pythagoras himself.

Pythagoras

THE PRIMARY SOURCES of information about the life of Pythagoras are to be found in this anthology. In addition to containing quite a bit of information about Pythagoras which goes back to an early date, these four biographies also demonstrate in an admirable fashion the high esteem in which the philosopher was held.

Pythagoras was born around 570 B.C.E. to Mnesarchus of Samos, a gem-engraver, and his wife, Pythais.

The biographies of Pythagoras are unanimous that at an early age he travelled widely to assimilate the wisdom of the ancients wherever it might be found. He is said by Iamblichus to have spent some 22 years in Egypt studying there with the priests, and is also said to have studied the wisdom of the Chaldeans first-hand. These accounts are generally accepted by most scholars—as indeed they should be, owing to the high degree of contact between Asia Minor and other cultures—although it is doubtful, while not impossible, that he travelled to Persia to study the teachings of Zoroaster. In these distant lands Pythagoras not only studied the sciences there cultivated, including mathematical sciences we may safely presume, but was also initiated into the religious mysteries of the "barbarians." As Porphyry succinctly observes, "It was from his stay among these foreigners that Pythagoras acquired the greater part of his wisdom."[5]

After his studies abroad, Pythagoras returned home to the island of Samos, where he continued his philosophical researches. It is said that he outfitted a cave especially designed for the study of philosophy, and it was there that he made his home. About this time Pythagoras opened his first school, as we are told by Porphyry, yet it probably was not long-lived, as Pythagoras decided to leave Samos at the age of 40, owing to the tyranny of Polycrates which was then flourishing.

From Samos Pythagoras journeyed to South Italy, arriving at Croton, "conceiving that his real fatherland must be the country containing the greatest number of the most scholarly men."[6]

It would seem that his reputation preceeded the philosopher, for he was shortly asked to speak to the populace of Croton—men, women, and children—on the proper conduct of life. The essence of these speeches is to be found in the biography by Iamblichus. While obviously not recorded verbatim, it seems quite likely that the *content* of these talks is genuinely Pythagorean and goes back to Pythagoras himself.[7] According to the biographies, the populace was enthralled by the wisdom of this man, owing to which he was invited to become involved in local government.

Number, Kosmos, Harmonia

> ...and the ancients, who were superior to us and dwelt nearer to the Gods, have handed down a tradition that all things that are said to exist consist of a One and a Many and contain in themselves the connate principles of Limit and Unlimitedness.
>
> — Plato, *Philebus* 16c

WHERE PYTHAGORAS DEVELOPED his interest in Number we do not know, although it is likely that he was not the first to be concerned with its sacred or metaphysical dimension. What we do know is that a metaphysical philosophy of Number lay at the heart of his thought and teaching, permeating, as we shall see, even the domains of psychology, ethics and political philosophy.

The Pythagorean understanding of Number is quite different from the predominately quantitative understanding of today. For the Pythagoreans, Number is a living, qualitative reality which must be approached in an experiential manner. Whereas the typical modern usage of number is as a sign, to denote a specific quantity or amount, the Pythagorean usage is not, in a sense, even a usage at all: Number is not something to be *used;* rather, its nature is to be *discovered.* In other words, we use numbers as tokens to represent things, but for Pythagoreans Number is a universal principle, as real as light (electromagnetism) or sound. As modern physics has demonstrated, it is precisely the numeric, vibrational frequency of electromagnetic energy—the "wavelength"—which determines its particular manifestation. Pythagoras, of course, had already determined this in the case of sound.

Because Pythagorean science possessed a sacred dimension, Number is seen not only as a universal principle, it is a divine principle as well. The two, in fact, are synonymous: because Number is universal it is divine; but one could as easily say that because it is divine, it is universal. Hence, the aim of Pythagorean and later Platonic science is different from that of modern "Aristotelian" science: it is not so much involved with the investigation of things, as the investigation of principles. It should be very firmly emphasized, however, that for Pythagoras the scientific and religious dimensions of number were never at odds with each other. Moreover, the Pythagorean approach to Number, for the first time in Greece, elevated mathematics to a study worth pursuing above any purely utilitarian ends for which it had previously been employed.

The Pythagoreans believed that Number is "the principle, the source and the root of all things."[8] But to make things more explicit: the Monad, or Unity, is the principle of Number. In other words, the Pythagoreans did not see One as a number at all, but as the principle underlying number, which is to say that numbers—especially the first ten—may be seen as manifestations of diversity in a unified continuum.[9] To quote Theon of Smyrna:

> Unity is the principle of all things and the most dominant of all that is: all things emanate from it and it emanates from nothing. It is indivisible and it is everything in power. It is immutable and never departs from its own nature through multiplication ($1 \times 1 = 1$). Everything that is intelligible and not yet created exists in it; the nature of ideas, God himself, the soul, the beautiful and the good, and every intelligible essence, such as beauty itself, justice itself, equality itself, for we conceive each of these things as being one and as existing in itself.[10]

If One represents the principle of Unity from which all things arise, then Two, the Dyad, represents Duality, the beginning of multiplicity, the beginning of strife, yet also the possibility of *logos,* the relation of one thing to another:

> The first increase, the first change from unity is made by the doubling of unity which becomes 2, in which are seen matter and all this is perceptible, the generation of motion, multiplication and addition, composition and the relationship of one thing to another.[11]

With the Dyad arises the duality of subject and object, the knower and the known. With the advent of the Triad, however, the gulf of dualism is bridged, for it is through the third term that a Relation or Harmonia ("joining together") is obtained between the two extremes. While Two represents the first *possibility* of logos, the relation of one thing to another, the Triad achieves that relation in *actuality*. If this process of emergence is represented graphically as in figure 1, we can see that the Triad not only binds together the Two, but also, in the process, centrally reflects the nature of the One in a "microcosmic" and balanced fashion. (See figure 1.)

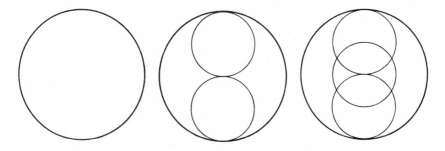

FIGURE 1. UNITY, DUALITY AND HARMONY

What we have seen in this example of Pythagorean paradigm, based on the universal principles of pure Number and Form, is the emergence of Duality out of Unity, and the subsequent unification of duality, which in turn results in a dynamic, differentiated image of the One in three parts—a continuum of beginning, middle and end, or of two extremes bound together with a mean term. This process, in fact, is the archaic and archetypal paradigm of cosmogenesis, the pattern of creation which results in the world. As F.M. Cornford has observed:

> The abstract formula which is common to the early cosmogonies is as follows:
> (1) There is an undifferentiated unity. (2) From this unity two opposite powers
> are separated out to form the world order. (3) The two opposites unite again
> to generate life.[12]

Cornford goes on to demonstrate how this universal pattern underlies not only the cosmogonies of Greek myth, but also those of the early Ionian scientific tradition.[13] It also underlies, as one may suspect, the Pythagorean view of the *kosmos,* literally "world-order" or "ordered-world," a term that Pythagoras is credited with first applying to the universe. The word *kosmos,* in addition to its primary meaning of order, also means ornament. The world, according to Pythagoras, is ornamented with order. This is another way of saying that the universe is *beautifully* ordered.

The idea of order is intimately connected with Limit (*peras*), the opposite of which is the Unlimited (*apeiron*), and these are the two most basic, and hence most universal, principles of Pythagorean cosmology. According to the Pythagoreans, the world or cosmos is compounded of these elements, summarized in the famous "Table of Opposites" which has been preserved by Aristotle in his *Metaphysics* (i. 5 986 a 23):

Limit	Unlimited
Odd	Even
One	Plurality
Right	Left
Male	Female
At rest	Moving
Straight	Crooked
Light	Darkness
Good	Bad
Square	Oblong

FIGURE 2. THE PYTHAGOREAN TABLE OF OPPOSITES

Limit is a definite boundary; the Unlimited is indefinite and is therefore in need of Limit. Apeiron also may be translated as Infinite, but it is infinite in a negative sense: that is, it is infinitely or indefinitely divisible, and hence *weak,* rather than the modern "positive" usage of the term, which is often synonymous with "powerful." To avoid any confusion between the ancient and modern meanings, Apeiron has been translated as either Indefinite or Unlimited in the writings which appear in this book, unless the context suggests otherwise.

Aristotle stated that the Pythagoreans made everything out to be created of numbers; what he means to say is that everything is created out of the *elements* of number, which include the Limited and the Indefinite, the Odd and the Even.

The Pythagoreans were in the habit of representing arithmetical numbers as geometrical forms, through which they arrived at some interesting insights. In fact, Aristotle makes reference to this very practice:

> The Pythagoreans identify the Unlimited with the Even. For this, they say, when it is enclosed and limited by the Odd provides things with the element of unlimitedness. An indication of this is what happens in numbers: if gnomons are placed around the unit and apart from the unit, in the latter case the resulting figure is always *other,* in the former it is always *one.* [14]

Aristotle is referring to the following figures:

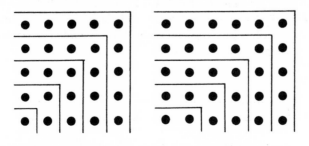

FIGURE 3.
SQUARE NUMBER

FIGURE 4.
OBLONG NUMBER

The Greek word *gnomon* signifies a "carpenter's square." In figure 3 gnomons have been placed around the One, in figure 4 around the Dyad. From this arrangement several patterns arise. In the case of figure 3, each gnomon or band of points is odd, in figure 4 each gnomon is even. From the above diagrams, we can easily see why the Pythagoreans, in the Table of Opposites, identified the Odd and Even with the Square and Oblong respectively. Moreover, the principles of Limit and the Unlimited are also most manifest in these representations, for figure 3 is limited by the stable form of the square, while figure 4 is infinitely variable: with each successive gnomon, the shape and its corresponding lateral to horizontal ratio changes each time, for it is the nature of the Unlimited to be eternally variable and multifarious.

According to the paradigms of ancient cosmology, Matter (the Indefinite) receives and is shaped by Form (Limit); hence, these two principles of *peras* and *apeiron* may be seen at the two most universal and essential elements which are absolutely necessary for the manifestation of phenomenal reality. From this perspective it becomes easy to see the logic behind the Pythagorean sentiment that the cosmos is created out of the elements of Number, namely the Limited and the Indefinite. Plato, in fact, takes over this Pythagorean cosmology to the letter. His only change, and a minor one at that, is that he referred to Limit as the One, the Unlimited as the Indefinite Dyad, terms which have even more Pythagorean implications than the originals.

In the Pythagorean and Platonic cosmology, Limit and the Indefinite, Form and Matter, are woven together through numerical harmony: their offspring, existing in the indefinite receptacle of space, is the phenomenal universe, in which every being is composed of universal constants and local variables. Hence, in his Pythagorean cosmogony of the *Timaeus,* Plato shows how the fabricator of the cosmos parcels out the stuff of the World Soul according to the numerical proportions of the musical scale.[15]

The Monochord: The Mathematics of Harmonic Mediation

> The musical proportions seem to me to be particularly correct natural proportions.
>
> — Novalis

PYTHAGORAS IS SAID to have discovered the musical intervals. While the story of the musical smithy is probably a Middle Eastern folk tale,[16] there can be no doubt that Pythagoras experimented with the monochord (figure 5), a one-stringed musical instrument with a moveable bridge, used to investigate the principles and problems of tuning theory.

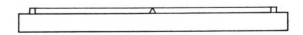

FIGURE 5. THE MONOCHORD. String, sounding box and moveable bridge.

The monochord affords an excellent example of how the primary principles of *peras* and *apeiron* underlie the realm of acoustic phenomena. Of course, the fact that numerical proportions underlie musical harmony has become a commonplace since the days of Pythagoras; yet there is something about the perfect beauty of these proportions, and their manifestations in the realm of sound, which will exercise a curious fascination over anyone who chooses to actually investigate them on the monochord.

The problem which the monochord presents is that the string can be divided at *any* point. The string represents an Indefinite continuum of tonal flux which may be infinitely divided. How, then, is it possible to "create" a musical scale at all? The solution, of course, resides in the limiting power of Number.

A curious phenomenon occurs when a string is plucked. First, the string vibrates as a unit. Then, in two parts, then in three parts, four, and so on. As the string vibrates in smaller parts higher tones are produced, this being the so-called harmonic overtone series.[17] While they are not as loud as the fundamental tone of the entire string vibrating, with practice the overtones can nonetheless be heard.

Through the power of Limit, the most formal manifestation of which is Number, harmonic nodal points naturally and innately exist on the string, dividing its length in halves, thirds, fourths, and so on, as shown in figure 6. Plucking the string at one end, and simultaneously touching one of the nodal points without the bridge, will produce the corresponding overtone vibration. In this fashion, one can play out the overtone series, as far as is practical. However, dampening the string at any other point will just deaden out the string. (See figure 6.)

The overtone series provides, as it were, the architectural foundation of the musical scale, the basic "field" of which is the octave, 1:2, or the doubling of the vibrational frequency, which inversely correlates with a halving of the string. Returning again to the basic question of how one bridges the tonal flux, we know the answer to be Number, but now we can see more clearly that the problem itself is one of *mediation* or *harmonia,* through the medium of numerical proportion or *logos.* The solution, in fact, can be seen as performing a marriage of opposites, linking together the upper and the lower (1:2), in a truly cosmic fashion, which is to say in a manner partaking of both order and beauty.

While the complete ratios of the scale are set out in Appendix IV, "The Ratios and Formation of the Pythagorean Scale," we shall here note the essentials.

In order to arrive at whole number solutions, we will use the octave of 6:12.

1) The first step is one of *arithmetic mediation.* To find the arithmetic mean we take the two extremes, add them together, and divide by 2. The result is a vibration of 9, which, in relation to 6, is in the ratio of 2:3. This is the *perfect fifth,* the most powerful musical relationship.

2) The second form of mediation is *harmonic.* It is arrived at by multiplying together the two extremes, doubling the sum, and dividing that result by the sum of the two extremes (i.e., 2AB / A+B). The harmonic mean linking together 6 and 12 then is 8. This proportion, 6:8 or 3:4, is the perfect fourth, which is actually the inverse of the perfect fifth.

3) Through only two operations we have arrived at the foundation of the musical scale, the so-called "musical" or "harmonic" proportion, 6:8 :: 9:12, the

discovery of which was attributed to Pythagoras. (See figure 7.)

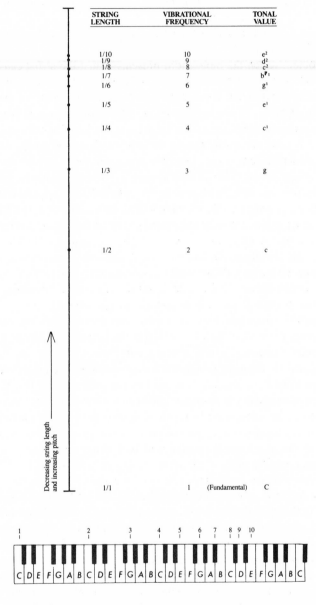

STRING LENGTH	VIBRATIONAL FREQUENCY	TONAL VALUE
1/10	10	e^2
1/9	9	d^2
1/8	8	c^2
1/7	7	$b^{\flat 1}$
1/6	6	g^1
1/5	5	e^1
1/4	4	c^1
1/3	3	g
1/2	2	c
1/1	1 (Fundamental)	C

Decreasing string length and increasing pitch

1   2   3   4   5   6   7   8 9   10

C D E F G A B C D E F G A B C D E F G A B C D E F G A B C

FIGURE 6. THE HARMONIC NODAL POINTS AND OVERTONE SERIES
ON THE MONOCHORD. The above figure illustrates the reciprocal
relation which exists between string length and vibrational frequency. By stopping the string at the geometrical nodal points the harmonic overtones may be individually emphasized.

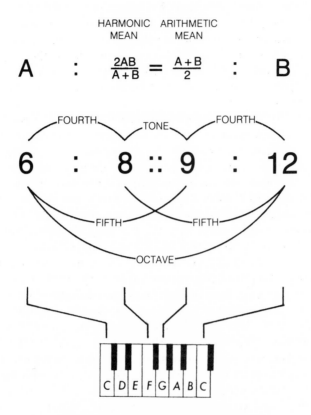

FIGURE 7. THE HARMONIC PROPORTION

This arrangement of the perfect consonances of the octave, fifth and fourth needs to be played out, preferably on the monochord, in order to fully appreciate its significance. While we have not "created" a complete musical scale, we have arrived at the architectural foundation on which it is based. By carefully observing the above arrangement, however, we shall discover enough information to complete the scale.

First of all, it would be well to notice the peculiar form of musical and mathematical "dialectic" which is occuring. That is to say, not only is 6:9 a perfect fifth, but 8:12 is as well; i.e., 6:9 :: 8:12. Nor is that all, for while 6:8 is a fourth, so too is 9:12; or, 6:8 :: 9:12. Again, the significance of this harmonic *symmetry* will be fully realized by playing these relations out.[18] However, not only are the fourth and fifth manifested in these multiple ways, but the ratio of 8:9 defines the *whole tone* as well.

The tone having been defined, the final creation of the scale is quite simple. The vibration of the tonic C is increased by the ratio 8:9 to arrive at D. D is increased by 8:9 to arrive at E. Now, if E were increased by that ratio, it would overshoot F; hence there we must stop. The ratio between E and F ends up being 243:256, called in Greek the *leimma*, or "left over," corresponding to our semitone.[19] Ascending from G, the same 8:9 ratio is used to fill up the remaining intervals. Likewise, the interval between B and C is the *leimma.*

While the fourth and fifth mediate between the two extremes via harmonic and arithmetic proportion, the scale is filled up through the continued *geometrical* proportion of 8:9; hence, the geometric mean between C and E would be D. All these forms of proportion interpenetrate, cooperate and harmonize with one another to produce the musical scale.

In summary, we can see the paramount importance of the musical scale and its formation in Pythagorean thought. First of all, the experiments conducted by the Pythagoreans on the monochord confirmed the importance of numerical *peras* as the limiting factor in the otherwise indefinite realm of manifestation. It also suggested for the first time that if a mathematical harmony underlies the realm of tone and music, that Number may account for other phenomena in the cosmic order—for example, planetary motion, which was also thought of being related to the mathematical *harmonia* of the scale, this being the famous "Music of the Spheres."[20] Moreover, the world is full of beings and phenomena which reflect the harmonic principle of dynamic *symmetry* present in the musical proportion as well. Through their investigation of musical harmony, the Pythagoreans shifted philosophic inquiry away from the materialistic cosmologies of the earlier Ionic tradition to the consideration of Form, which was now to be seen as constituting the world of First Principles. In addition to shifting emphasis from Matter to Form, the Pythagoreans also discovered the principle of *harmonia,* the fitting together of the high and the low, the hot and the cold, the moist and the dry. From then on, Health was seen as the perfect harmony of the elements comprising the body, disease as that state in which one of the elements becomes too weak or strong, destroying the proper symmetry of the arrangement. Indeed, it was Alcmaeon of Croton, a young man when Pythagoras was old, who first defined health as "the harmonious mixture of the qualities."[21] This had an inestimable effect on Hippocratic medicine. As is so apparent in their various cultural achievements, the ancient Greeks had a very special affinity with the principles of Form, Symmetry, and Harmony. The Pythagoreans were the inheritors of this affinity, and helped to articulate these principles in new, important ways which have profoundly influenced the arts and sciences of Western civilization.

The Tetraktys: Number as Paradigm

> I swear by the discoverer of the Tetraktys
> Which is the spring of all our wisdom
> The perennial fount and root of Nature.
> — Pythagorean Oath

THE PYTHAGOREANS PERCEIVED another principle of Number, in addition to seeing it as a formative agent active in nature. This is perhaps best exemplified in the figure of the Tetraktys which, as we might say in the present century, stood as a numerical paradigm of whole systems.

As we have observed, the Pythagoreans were accustomed to arranging numbers in geometrical shapes, and there are a variety of descriptions which have come down to us from antiquity of triangular, square, pentagonal, and other figured numbers and their properties.[22] This way of representing numbers may have well resulted in the discovery of geometrical theorems. Moreover, the observation that the relations between different types of "geometrical numbers" follow certain definite patterns surely furthered the Pythagorean contention that mathematical study is an important route leading to the perception of universal laws.

The most well known example of such a "figured number" is the famous Pythagorean Tetraktys ("Quaternary"), consisting of the first four integers arranged in a triangle of ten points:

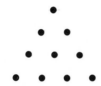

FIGURE 8. THE TETRAKTYS.

For the Pythagoreans the Tetraktys symbolized the perfection of Number and the elements which comprise it. In one sense it would be proper to say that the Tetraktys symbolize, like the musical scale, a differentiated image of Unity; in the case of the Tetraktys, it is an image of unity starting at One, proceeding through four levels of manifestation, and returning to unity, i.e., Ten. In the sphere of geometry, One represents the point • , Two represents the line •——• , Three represents the surface ▽ , and Four the tetrahedron ▽ , the first three-dimensional form. Hence, in the realm of space the Tetraktys represent the continuity linking the dimensionless point with the manifestation of the first body; the figure of the Tetraktys itself also represents the vertical hierarchy of relation between Unity and emerging Multiplicity. In the realm of music, it will be seen that the Tetraktys also contains the symphonic ratios which underlie the mathematical harmony of the musical scale: 1:2, the octave; 2:3, the perfect fifth; and 3:4, the perfect fourth.[23]

We might further note that the Tetraktys, being a Triangular number, is composed of consecutive integers, incorporating both the Odd and Even, whereas Square number (Limited) is composed of consecutive odd integers, and Oblong number of consecutive even integers (Indefinite). Since the universe is comprised of *peras* and *apeiron* woven together through mathematical *harmonia,* it is easy to see from these considerations why the Tetraktys, or the Decad, was called Kosmos (world-order), Ouranos (heaven), and Pan (the All). In Pythagorean thought the Tetraktys came to represent an inclusive paradigm of the four-fold pattern which underlies different classes of phenomena, as exemplified by Theon of Smyrna in Appendix I. Not only does a four-fold pattern underlie each class, but each level is in a certain fashion *analogous* or proportionately similar with that same level in every other class of phenomena. In many respects Pythagorean philosophy is a philosophy of *analogia.*

The Pythagoreans, then, were the first to use numerical and geometrical diagrams as models of cosmic wholeness and the celestial order. This use of arithmetic and geometrical paradigms of whole systems has a long and interesting history, extending from antiquity through Medieval times, through the Renaissance, up until the modern era.[24] If geometrical principles actually shape the phenomena of nature, why not use those same geometrical forms to illustrate the harmonies and symmetries which exist between natural phenomena? This is no doubt the reasoning behind this symbolic usage of number and geometry, and its appeal seems firmly rooted in the human imagination. In fact, it might be argued that such paradigms possess greater merit than more arbitrary typologies insofar that, being based on the principles of natural order, "Pythagorean" models have more intrinsically in common with the phenomena they seek to classify than other typologies which are of merely human invention. Whereas other models sometimes fail, Pythagorean cosmological symbolism seems particularly well suited in showing how parts relate to a larger whole, thus illustrating the principle of unity underlying diversity.

The Way of Philosophy and the Three Lives

ACCORDING TO A BEAUTIFUL and well known account, Pythagoras

> likened the entrance of men into the present life to the progression of a crowd to some public spectacle. There assemble men of all descriptions and views. One hastens to sell his wares for money and gain; another exhibits his bodily strength for renown; but the most liberal assemble to observe the landscape, the beautiful works of art, the specimens of valor, and the customary literary productions. So also in the present life men of manifold pursuits are assembled. Some are influenced by the desire of riches and luxury; others, by the love of power and dominion, or by insane ambition for glory. But the purest and most genuine character is that of the man who devotes himself to the contemplation of the most beautiful things, and he may properly be called a *philosopher*.[25]

Likewise, the story is told of how Pythagoras was indeed the first man to call himself a philosopher. Others before had called themselves wise (*sophos*), but Pythagoras was the first to call himself a philosopher, literally *a lover of wisdom*.

More importantly, for Pythagoras and his followers philosophy was not merely an intellectual pursuit, but *a way of life*, the aim of which was the assimilation to God. Even in the days of Plato the surviving Pythagoreans were noted for their distinctive *bios Pythagorikos*, or Pythagorean way of life, as Plato puts it in the *Republic* (600a-b).

The school of Pythagoras in Croton appears to have been a religious society centered around the Muses, the goddesses of learning and culture, and their leader Apollo.[26] Iamblichus' description of the school gives it something of a monastic flavor, and there was indeed a "rule" of life, but while the Pythagoreans gathered together at certain times of the day, most of them did not live together.

Apparently there were different levels within the school. One group, the *akousmatikoi* or "auditors" (from the verb *akouo*, to hear), went through a three year probationary period and were limited mainly to hearing lectures. A more advanced group, the *mathematikoi* or "students," went through a five year period of "silence,"[27] and held their property in common whereas the *akousmatikoi* did not; there is, however, nothing to indicate that the *mathematikoi* took anything like a vow of poverty. Rather, their property was managed by certain members of the society—the *politikoi*—and they received an adequate subsistence in return for its use.[28]

Pythagoras himself was heavily influenced by Orphism, an esoteric, private religion of ancient Greece, named after the legendary musician Orpheus, "the founder of initiations," which also featured a distinctive way of life. According to Orphism, the soul, a divine spark of Dionysus, is bound to the body (*soma*) as to a tomb (*sema*). Mankind is in a state of forgetfulness of its true, spiritual nature. The soul is immortal, but descends into the realm of generation, being bound to the "hard and deeply-grievous circle" of incarnations,[29] until it is released through a series of purifications and rites, regaining its true nature as a divine being.

Pythagoras fully accepted the Orphic belief in transmigration or "reincarnation"—in fact, he is said to have possessed the power to remember his previous lives, and the ability to remind his associates of theirs as well. Yet while Pythagoreanism remains closely related to the Orphic thought of the period,[30] the clearly distinguishing factor between the two is that for the Pythagoreans liberation from the wheel is obtained not through religious rite, but through *philosophy,* the contemplation of first principles. Hence, *philosophia* is a form of purification, a way to immortality. As others have observed, whereas the Eleusinian mysteries offered a single revelation, and Orphism a religious way of life, Pythagoras offered a way of life based on philosophy. Burnett notes that this conception lies at the heart of Plato's *Phaedo,* itself "dedicated, as it were, to a Pythagorean community at Phlious";[31] moreover, "This way of regarding philosophy is henceforth characteristic of the best Greek thought."[32]

One may well ask how assimilation to God is possible through philosophy. The answer is to be found in the nature of man:

> Pythagoras said that man is a microcosm, which means a compendium of the universe; not because, like other animals, even the least, he is constituted by the four elements, but because he contains all the powers of the cosmos. For the universe contains Gods, the four elements, animals and plants. All of these powers are contained in man. He has reason, which is a divine power; he has the nature of the elements, and the powers of moving, growing, and reproduction.[33]

Man, by comprising a world-order in miniature, contains all of those principles constituting the greater cosmos, of which he is a reflection, including the powers of divinity. The problem is not so much of becoming divine as becoming aware of the divine, universal principles within. It is this end, primarily, toward which the Pythagorean curriculum was focused. Plato alludes to the Pythagorean theory of philosophy in the *Republic* (500c) when he observes:

> a man should come to resemble that with which it delights him to associate...

> Hence the philosopher through the association with what is divine and orderly
> (*kosmios*) becomes divine and orderly (*kosmios*) insofar as a man may.

Man realizes the divine by knowing the universal and divine principles which constitute the cosmos—i.e., for the Pythagoreans, Number. To know the cosmos is to seek and know the divine element within, and one must become divine and harmonized since only like can know like. From this perspective it also becomes obvious that philosophy is nothing other, at least in one respect, than the *care of the soul.*

The Soul, its Nature and Care

ACCORDING TO SEVERAL ancient sources, it was from the Pythagoreans that Plato received his doctrine of the tripartite soul, a doctrine which underlies Pythagoras' parable of the three lives: one group of humanity is covetous, another ambitious, and the other curious. As J.L. Stocks has pointed out, "What the division specifies is the three typical motives of human action, and all three motives will be found in operation at different times in every normal human soul."[34] These motives are the desire for profit, honor, and knowledge.

Plato, apparently in line with the Pythagorean tradition, divides the soul into three parts: one part is reasoning, another part is "spirited," and the last desires the pleasures of nutrition and generation. Unlike certain schools of modern psychology, the Platonic division of the soul is hierarchical: the reasoning part is superior to the other two, and deserves more attention, for it is this dimension of the soul which makes us uniquely human. We might summarize the relation between the levels of the soul and their attendant virtues, or forms of excellence, as shown in figure 9.

THE THREE LIVES		THE "PLATONIC DIVISION"	
TYPES OF HUMANITY	HUMAN DESIRES	PARTS OF THE SOUL	CORRESPONDING VIRTUES
Curious	Knowledge	"Rational"	Wisdom
Ambitious	Honor	"Spirited"	Courage
Covetous	Profit	"Desirous"	Temperance

FIGURE 9. THE THREE LIVES

Seen in this perspective, it becomes plain that psychic health must result when the three "parts" of the soul are brought into a state of harmony, which is *not* to say a state of equality. Rather, this state of balance could be seen as a state of attunement, where each part receives what it is due. Psychic disturbance results when each part of the soul tries to go its own separate way; the psyche then becomes a house divided, resulting in dissociation and fragmentation, as opposed to the realization of psychic wholeness.

The grand project behind Plato's *Republic* is to define the nature of justice. We know that the Pythagoreans identified justice with proportion, especially geometrical proportion, because it is through proportion that "each part receives what it is due."[35] Following the Pythagorean tradition, Plato observes that in the realm of society justice exists when each part of society receives its due, and is able to achieve the function for which it is truly best suited. Justice, as a universal principle, operates in exactly the same fashion in the realm of the soul. There, "justice is produced in the soul, like health in the body, by establishing the elements concerned in their natural relations of control and subordination, whereas injustice is like disease and means that this natural order is inverted."[36] As Plato notes, in a magnificently Pythagorean passage:

> ...The just man does not allow the several elements in his soul to usurp one another's functions; he is indeed one who sets his house in order, by self-mastery and discipline coming to be at peace with himself, and *bringing into tune those three parts, like the terms in the proportion of a musical scale, the highest and lowest notes and the mean between them, with all the intermediate intervals.* Only when he has linked these parts together in *well-tempered harmony* and has made himself one man instead of many, will he be ready to go about whatever he may have to do, whether it be making money and satisfying bodily wants, or business transactions, or the affairs of state. In all these fields when he speaks of just and honorable conduct, he will mean the behavior that helps to produce and preserve this habit of mind; and by wisdom he will mean the knowledge which presides over such conduct. Any action which tends to break down this habit will be for him unjust; and the notions governing it he will call ignorance and folly. (My emphasis.)[37]

If Pythagorean philosophy, then, constitutes a care of the soul, of what precisely is that care comprised? The answer to this is to be found in the ethical and educational conceptions of the Pythagoreans, as well as in those special pursuits and studies for which they were renowned.

Pythagorean Educational Theory

WE HAVE SEEN that for Pythagoras philosophy represents a "purification," the aim of which is the assimilation to God. The universe is divine because of its order (*kosmos*), and the harmonies and symmetries which it contains and reflects. These principles make the universe divine for they are the characteristics of divinity, and they also innately subsist within the human soul. The Pythagoreans taught that the soul is a harmony.[38] If we are to become like God, then according to Pythagorean philosophy the soul must become aware of its harmonic origin, structure and content. Since the source of all harmony and order is the divine principle of Number, we can perhaps come to understand the initially enigmatic statement of Heracleides that, according to Pythagoras, true "happiness consists in knowledge of the perfection of the numbers of the soul."[39]

In the realm of epistemology the presence of Number is most evident: progress in rational thought depends on a fundamentally dyadic relationship between knower and known, subject and object. Moreover, as certainly as the principle of polarity underlies the world of phenomenal manifestation, so too does the mind depend on dualistic typologies, such as the Table of Opposites, in order to make intellectual progress.[40] Knowledge itself is the third, harmonic element which conjoins the two poles of subject and object. Knowledge then is unifying, much like the harmonic ratios of the musical scale or the central circle in figure 1. Moreover, as we shall see, to the Pythagoreans the knowledge of divine harmony can be either abstract or experiential or, indeed, both.

Even more immediately evident is the undeniable influence of Number on our psychic state through the medium of music, depending as it does on numerical proportion. Certain musical proportions express a sense of cheerfulness; others, such as the minor third, possess a bittersweet quality that can make us sad. The fact that Number can influence a person's emotional state is indeed mysterious and points toward a dimension of qualitative Number which transcends the merely quantitative.

Related to the question of music and harmony is the principle of *resonance:* two strings, tuned to the same frequency, will *both* vibrate if only one is pluck- ed, the unplucked string resonating in sympathy with the first. This, of course, is accomplished through the medium of the vibrating air, but the principle underly- ing the phenomenon is one of harmonic attunement. If, as the Pythagoreans held, man is a microcosm, and the soul is a harmony, perhaps it is through a form of resonance that we relate so intensely to the archetypal ratios of musical pro- portion.[41] Moreover, by experientially investigating and employing the principles of harmony in the external world, one comes to understand and activate those same principles within. This idea in fact underlies the Pythagorean approach to mathematical study.

The Pythagoreans divided the study of Number into four branches which may be analyzed in the following fashion:

> *Arithmetic* = Number in itself.
> *Geometry* = Number in space.
> *Music or Harmonics* = Number in time.
> *Astronomy* = Number in space and time.

Plato, of course, was heavily influenced by the Pythagorean study of number and incorporates the above quadrivium into his own educational curriculum set out in the *Republic,* adding another branch of study, *Stereometry,* the investiga- tion of Number in three-dimensional space, which probably relates to the regular "Platonic" solids and other polyhedra. For Plato—who believed that God geometrizes always[42]—"geometry is the knowledge of the eternally existent,"[43] and the emphasis that he placed on the study is well known from the legendary inscription above the Academy door, "Let no one ignorant of geometry enter here."[44]

Within the Platonic curriculum, the purpose of mathematical studies is to purify the eye of the intellect, for mathematical studies have the propensity "to draw the soul towards truth and to direct upwards the philosophic intelligence which is now wrongly turned earthwards."[45] Number, for Plato, is a transcendent Form to which we must intellectually ascend. For the earlier Pythagoreans, however, the emphasis was clearly on the *immanence* of Number.

While the Pythagoreans moved the direction of philosophical inquiry from the realm of matter to that of Form and principles, Plato took this movement even further than his predecessors. For Plato mathematical studies are a *preparation* for the contemplation of divine principles; for the Pythagoreans, mathematical studies *are* the contemplation of divine principles. As Cornelia de Vogel has lucidly observed, for the Pythagoreans

> The contemplation of divine Law, which was the content of the study of mathematics, was a direct contact with a divine Reality: Divinity immanent in the cosmos.
>
> It was different for Plato. He adopts the Pythagorean notion that number is the principle of order in the cosmos and life, but number as such to him is not yet a *theion* [divinity]. It points at a purely intelligible Number which is a 'Form' (*eidos*)—no immanent principle of order within the objects, but a transcendent Example. This is the basic difference between the Pythagorean doctrine of number and Plato's Theory of Forms. Plato's philosophy is a metaphysic of the transcendent; the Pythagorean philosophy is a metaphysic of the immanent order.[46]

This particular difference between the earlier Pythagoreans and Plato must have manifested itself in the sphere of *praxis*. For Plato it was, in a sense, best to pursue mathematical contemplation with as little reference to physical objects as possible: truth must be approached through intellect, and through intellect alone. For the Pythagoreans, truth manifests itself through the world of physical phenomena; for example, the Pythagoreans no doubt felt that through experimentation on the monochord one could experience the divine principles of harmony which underlie the structure of the cosmos.

The differing views between Plato and the earlier Pythagoreans can also be seen in the realm of music. Plato refers to different musical modes throughout his writings, and to the negative effects that some forms of music can have on the soul and on society. The Pythagoreans, however, actually *used* certain forms of music to pacify and harmonize the psychic state. In the same way that the music of Orpheus enchanted the wild beasts of the field, so too did the Pythagoreans use music to quell and harmonize the irrational passions.

While the Pythagoreans placed emphasis on the immanence of divine Number and Harmonia, they certainly did not ignore the transcendental dimension. This is made clear by their emphasis on *peras* and *apeiron,* the elements of Number, which they obviously took to be universal principles of the first order. It seems that, rather than focusing exclusively on either the immanent or transcendent levels of being, the Pythagoreans were intent on unifying all levels of human experience through the principles of harmony. The divine harmony can be grasped through the mind, yet can also be perceived through the senses. The experiential perception of harmony through the senses can lead to its intellectual apprehension. By means of *theoria* or contemplation the universal and abstract principles of harmony may be perceived, but through *praxis* they may be *felt* in the soul, itself a harmonic entity. Yet there is another level, that of *therapeia,* where harmonic principles can be *used* to effect changes in the psychic disposition.

Through the use of proper music, diet, and exercise, the early Pythagoreans sought to nurture and maintain the natural harmony of the psychic and somatic faculties. According to Iamblichus, "They took solitary morning walks to places which happened to be appropriately quiet, to temples or groves, or other suitable places. They thought it inadvisable to converse with anyone until they had gained inner serenity, focusing their reasoning powers. They considered it turbulent to mingle in a crowd as soon as they rose from bed, and that is the reason why these Pythagoreans always selected the most sacred spots to walk."[47] All of these practices can be seen as a form of philosophic "purification" (*catharsis*) or "practice"(*praxis*), designed to regulate the body and the emotions. On the intellectual and psychic levels, through their study of mathematics and the natural world, the Pythagoreans approached the principles of harmony experientially through the study of harmonics on the monochord and through geometrical constructions. The Pythagoreans also pursued the study of purely abstract mathematics.

Recalling that the end of all of these pursuits was to follow God, it is interesting to briefly contrast the Pythagorean approach to divinisation with the Christian mysticism of the late Hellenistic period and thereafter. The first stage of "the mystical ascent" consists of the ethical purification of the soul commonly known as *praxis*. The second stage is contemplation or *theoria;* in Christianity, however, the contemplation of Nature and universal principles, so characteristic of the Greek philosophic tradition, is replaced predominately by the contemplation of scripture. The final stage, *theosis,* is the union of the mystic with God. In Hellenistic Christian mysticism of the late antique world, however, the first two stages lose virtually all significance when the final stage is reached. *Catharsis* and *theoria* are merely the steps of a ladder; when the summit is reached, the ladder is oftentimes kicked away.

The ancient Pythagorean approach to divinisation would have *never* sanctioned kicking away the ladder. In early Pythagorean thought there nowhere appears an earnest desire to escape from the world. True, like the Orphics, the Pythagoreans believed in reincarnation, and looked upon the body as limiting the soul. But even so, there is no firm evidence that, like the Orphics, the Pythagoreans sought exemption from the Wheel of Generation. Rather than transcend the world, Pythagorean religiosity held as its goal to exist within the cosmos in a state of emotional repose and intellectual acuteness. Man, while possessing a soul which clearly transcends the limitations of the body, the realm of time and space, is nonetheless a reflection of the entire universe, a microcosm, and is linked together with nature, other living beings, and the Gods through harmony, justice, and proportion. The Pythagorean goal is not to leave the divinely beautiful cosmos behind for a realm of transcendent harmony, but rather to become aware of, and enhance the function of, transcendent harmony *in* the natural, psychological and social orders.[48]

Pythagorean Political and Ethical Theory

THE CENTRAL INSIGHTS of the Pythagoreans concerning the significance of *harmonia* were applied to political theory as well: in the same way that harmonic proportion underlies the health of the balanced soul, so too does the principle of justice underlie the living structure of a healthy state. In this regard Plato's

Republic, which is a study of justice in both the psychic and social realms, appears to be firmly based on earlier Pythagorean conceptions. Plato, via *analogia,* identifies the three parts of the soul with three different parts of society, and shows how both the soul and society attain their peak of excellence when "each part receives its due" and when each of the three parts fulfils the particular function for which it is best adapted. It is not possible to say whether Plato's tripartite division of society corresponds precisely with an earlier Pythagorean division, although it is known that the Pythagoreans identified justice with proportion, of which they viewed geometrical proportion as being the most perfect. Like Plato the early Pythagoreans were aristocrats, in the authentic sense of the word, believing that the best government will be composed of those best qualified to govern, as opposed to other political systems in which leadership is based on wealth, on power, or on the choice of the populace. Finally, it should be noted that the Pythagoreans were the first philosophical school to concern themselves with such social and political questions, which fell outside the natural philosophy of the earlier Ionian tradition.

As for Pythagorean ethics, little needs to be said, as the entire idea of "proper action" is tied up with the ideas of philosophy as a way of life, and the nature of the soul and the cosmos. As one discovers the structure and nature of the soul, and experiences and begins to understand the principles of harmony, it seems inevitable that such insight will leave a mark on one's personal conduct and dealings with others. Nonetheless, as the writings in this volume demonstrate, the Pythagoreans did not hesitate to make use of aphorisms and other explicit ethical teachings. At all events, however, it will be seen that these teachings reflect and spring from the more universal insights of Pythagorean thought. In short, because each part is linked to the whole through *harmonia,* every action has its repercussions, either beneficial or not, for which the individual is supremely responsible.

The Pythagorean Tradition and its Development

TO SURVEY THE INFLUENCE of Pythagorean thought would expand this introductory essay beyond reasonable boundaries, insofar as the basic conceptions of the Pythagoreans have influenced a long line of thinkers from antiquity reaching up until the present day. Nonetheless, something should be said about the thought of the early Pythagoreans and the Neopythagoreans of the first centuries B.C.E. and C.E., thus helping to place some of the writings here assembled into their proper context.

As the biographical accounts in this volume show, the downfall of the original Pythagorean school had much to do with anti-aristocratic sentiments amongst the populace of south Italy. A revolt was led against the Pythagoreans by Cylon in 500 B.C.E.—some say because he was rejected admission into the school—and a period of unrest followed. During the revolt led by Cylon, or during another revolt which followed, various meeting houses were attacked and a good number of Pythagoreans may have perished in the flames. This final attack seems to have been rather successful, and those Pythagoreans that remained alive seem to have migrated to mainland Greece with the exception of Archytas at Tarentum.

Unfortunately, the details concerning the attack on the school are sketchy and little more can be said than the above. The Pythagoreans did, however, carry on in mainland Greece where centers were established at Phlious and Thebes. Echecrates went to Phlious, Xenophilus went to Athens, and the names of Lysis and Philolaus are associated with Thebes, and it was there that Philolaus taught Simmias and Cebes who appear as characters in Plato's *Phaedo*. Philolaus, who was born around 474 B.C.E., was the first Pythagorean to actually record the teachings of the school in writing; hence his fragments, which are collected in this volume, possess an exceptional value.

Archytas (first half of the fourth century B.C.E.), who was the general of Tarentum and one of the Pythagorean *mathematikoi* like Philolaus, made contributions to mathematics, geometry, and harmonic theory. He was visited by Plato in 388 B.C.E. and it is possible that Archytas was Plato's model for the so-called "philosopher king."

This brings us to a discussion of Plato himself (428-348 B.C.E.) which is not a topic of minor significance for, as W.K.C. Guthrie has observed, "In general the separation of early Pythagoreanism from the teaching of Plato is one of the historian's most difficult tasks, to which he can scarcely avoid bringing a subjective bias of his own. If later Pythagoreanism was coloured by Platonic influences, it is equally undeniable that Plato himself was deeply affected by earlier Pythagorean belief."[49]

Many important Pythagorean influences have already been noted on the thought of Plato and perhaps it would be fair to view Plato as the most important Pythagorean thinker in the history of the West. There was quite a bit of interest in Pythagorean thought in the early Academy as well, and it has been suggested that the idea of the Academy was in part due to the inspiration of the earlier Pythagorean school. Whatever the case, some points of contact include the tripartite division of the soul;[50] Plato's usage of the One and the Indefinite Dyad;[51] the theory of education in the *Republic;*[52] the identification of the One and the Good in "the unwritten doctrine" referred to by Aristotle;[53] the Pythagorean character of Plato's lecture "On the Good" reported on by Aristotle;[54] the idea that the soul of the philosopher attains order by contemplating those things which possess order in nature;[55] the idea that "the goodness of anything is due to order and arrangement";[56] the idea that various beings are linked together through geometrical equality;[57] a doctrine of idea-numbers in the *dogmata agrapha* reported by Aristotle;[58] and various examples of Pythagorean musical symbolism.[59]

Following Plato in the leadership of the Academy was his nephew Speusippus (407-339 B.C.E.) who was also quite interested in Pythagorean thought: he suggested that there exists a One above being (an important teaching of later Neopythagorean and Neoplatonic thought), and also wrote a work *On Pythagorean Numbers* about the Tetraktys and numbers comprising the Decad.[60] This treatise was based on the writings of Philolaus and an interesting fragment of it survives.

Aristotle showed an interest in the Pythagorean school and even wrote an essay *On the Pythagoreans* which does not survive. One of his students, Aristoxenus of Tarentum, was a music theorist and was in touch with the last surviving generation of Pythagoreans at Phlious. Aristoxenus, who might have been one of the

Pythagorean *mathematikoi*, possessed an antiquarian interest in the school and wrote a biography of Pythagoras which is quoted from by Porphyry, Iamblichus and Diogenes Laertius.

After the time of Aristotle we are left with an uncomfortable gap in the history of Pythagorean thought until the Neopythagorean revival commencing in the first century B.C.E. Yet it is precisely during this period that most of the Pythagorean ethical and political tractates contained in the second section of this volume were probably composed. But the question remains, by whom were they written? And why?

Unfortunately, no one is certain even about the date or location of their composition. There now exists a tendency to see these writings as being somewhat earlier than previously thought, and Holger Thesleff suggests that the bulk of them were composed around the third century B.C.E. It will be noted that these writings are attributed to original members of the Pythagorean school, which in fact is actually not the case. This does not mean that these writings are "forgeries" in the modern sense of the word, for it was a fairly common practice in antiquity to publish writings as pseudepigrapha, attributing them to earlier, more-renowned individuals. It was probably out of reverence for their master—and also perhaps because they were discussing authoritative school traditions—that certain Pythagoreans who published writings attributed them directly to Pythagoras himself. Even Pythagoras is said to have attributed some poems of his to Orpheus. Other examples which might be cited include the many Jewish pseudepigrapha of the time, Orphic fragments, the Hermetic writings, and even a number of Pauline epistles from the New Testament.

A careful study of these writings will show that they are deeply imbued with many Pythagorean ideas—what, in fact, could be more Pythagorean than comparing the structure of the family or society to a well-tuned lyre?—a particularly beautiful and useful simile which appears more than once in the Pythagorica here collected. Yet, alongside the central Pythagorean core of these writings are found strong Academic and Peripatetic influences as well. Thesleff is probably correct in suggesting that these writings were composed as philosophical textbooks for laymen,[61] but it is unlikely that the exact date or locale of their composition will ever be decisively settled. However, as has been suggested, a careful study of these texts might well provide for some valuable insights into the thought of the early Academy.

The next phase of Pythagorean thought involves the so-called Neopythagorean revival at the beginning of the common era. Due to the Hellenization of the ancient world stemming from the conquests of Alexander the Great, interest in Greek philosophy was no longer limited to one small part of the world. This was especially true of the interest in Pythagorean and Platonic thought, and the names of many Pythagorean philosophers are known from the Hellenistic age. Unfortunately, for some of the most important thinkers the information concerning them is quite fragmentary, which is perhaps one reason why no one has attempted the kind of full scale study that the topic deserves: the study of the Neopythagorean thought of this period is not only significant for its own sake, but also for understanding the thought of Plotinus and the later Neoplatonists who were influenced by a range of Neopythagorean ideas. Actually, as John Dillon has succinctly observed, during this period "Middle Platonism" and "Neopythagoreanism" existed as something of a continuous tradition, with Neopythagoreanism representing "an attitude that might be taken up within Platonism."[62] Keeping this in mind, it might be useful to mention some of the thinkers during this period who were influenced by Pythagorean thought, for it is only through such a listing that one can get a true feeling for the creative ferment of this period.

The first word that we have concerning a renewed interest in Pythagorean thought comes from Cicero, regarding his friend Nigidius Figulus (98-45 B.C.E.), who was attempting to revive Neopythagoreanism in Rome. It appears however that Nigidius was less interested in abstract philosophy than in integrating astrological, ritual and a variety of occultist beliefs.

Eudorus of Alexandria (fl. 30 B.C.E.) appears to have been influenced by Pythagorean thought, and attempted to show that the Pythagoreans held that a Supreme Principle, the One, existed above the Monad and the Dyad. Whether or not the earlier Pythagoreans actually held such a belief is another question altogether, but the notion of a transcendent One surpassing the principles of Limited and Unlimited is important for the history of later philosophy.

Philo of Alexandria (20 B.C.E.-40 C.E.), a Hellenized Jew who interpreted Jewish scripture in light of Greek philosophy, shows a deep interest in Pythagorean thought, especially arithmology, in his voluminous writings. Philo was primarily a Platonist who subscribed to a emanationist cosmology which he tried to reconcile with Jewish thought, but it is interesting to note that he was referred to by Clement of Alexandria, an early church father, simply as "Philo the Pythagorean."[63]

We should not fail to mention Apollonius of Tyana, a colorful figure who flourished during the first half of the first century C.E. Apollonius was perhaps more of a Pythagorean wonderworking ascetic than a philosopher, who travelled through the ancient world as something of a pagan missionary, meeting with priests, performing marvels, and restituting cults of worship to their former purity. His life and exploits are chronicled in an entertaining historical novel by Philostratus. Whether or not this biography gives a well-rounded picture of Apollonius remains uncertain. It does seem, however, that Apollonius saw himself as a reincarnation of Pythagoras and also possessed much information on the life of the sage, which he used in compiling a biography, subsequently used by Porphyry and Iamblichus. In addition to the *Life* of Philostratus, several letters attributed to Apollonius are extant.[64]

Often overlooked as an important witness to Pythagorean thought is Plutarch of Chaeronea (45-125 C.E.), well known for his famous *Lives*. What is not so generally well known is that Plutarch was a Platonist with Neopythagorean leanings and was also a priest of Apollo at Delphi. In certain writings of his *Moralia* he displays a keen interest in the interpretation of myth, the religio-philosophical esoterism of the time, and various bits of Neopythagorean lore, including arithmology. His writings remain a vital resource for understanding the profound, inner dimensions of the contemporary spiritual universe and, like Plotinus, he refers to the Pythagorean interpretation of the name Apollo, which equates Apollo with the One (a = not; *pollon* = of many).[65]

About the same time as Plutarch we have Moderatus of Gades (fl. second half of the first century) who has been termed an "aggressive Pythagorean" for the severe criticism he applied to Plato, accusing him of using ideas of Pythagoras without giving proper credit where credit was due. In his cosmology Moderatus taught the existence of three unities: the first and highest, the One above being which he identified with the Good; secondly, a unified, active *logos,* identified with the intelligible realm; and thirdly, the realm of soul. Needless to say, the resemblance between these ideas and those of Plotinus are quite striking.

Theon of Smyrna brings us into the second century (fl. circa 125 C.E.). He was a Platonist and wrote a work *Mathematics Useful for Understanding Plato,* of which a good English translation exists, and which is equally useful for understanding aspects of Pythagorean thought.[66] In addition to discussing the principles of arithmetic, harmonics and astronomy, Theon also treats the symbolism of the first ten integers and various forms of the Tetraktys (see Appendix I). The work also dealt with the principles of geometry, but this section no longer survives.

Working in a similar vein, and not much later, was Nicomachus of Gerasa (active 140-150 C.E.), whose *Introduction to Arithmetic,*[67] translated into Latin by Apuleius and Boethius, remained a definitive handbook up until the Renaissance. Also surviving is Nichomachus' *Manual of Harmonics,* and fragments of his *Theology of Arithmetic,* a work on Pythagorean arithmology. He also wrote a *Life of Pythagoras* which was used by the later biographers and an *Introduction to Geometry* which did not survive. He is known to have been familiar with the practice of *gematria,*[68] and it has been suggested that Iamblichus' "Pythagorean encyclopedia" found its inspiration in the wide-ranging works of this scholar.

Numenius of Apamea in Syria (fl. 160 C.E.) was also a Platonist with Neopythagorean leanings. Some fragments of his works remain, but the majority have perished. He wrote *On the Good*; *On the Indestructibility of the Soul*; *On the Secret Doctrines of Plato*; a work called *Hoopoe,* after the bird of the same name; *On Numbers* (perhaps a work on arithmology); *On Place*; and *On the Divergence of the Academics from Plato.* He had an associate, Cronius, who flourished about the same date and wrote a work *On Reincarnation.*

With Numenius, the mixture of Middle Platonic and Neopythagorean thought begins to transform itself into Neoplatonism, of which philosophy the most brilliant and beautiful expositor was Plotinus. Plotinus seems to have been influenced to a certain extent by the thought of Numenius, and John Dillon sees Plotinus' direct teacher Ammonius Saccas (fl. *circa* 230 C.E.) as a being a Platonist of a strongly Neopythagorean cast.

The main feature which differentiates Neoplatonism from Middle Platonism is the Neoplatonic doctrine of the transcendent absolute, the One, which exists above the realm of Being. However, as we have seen, Plato's nephew Speusippus, Eudorus of Alexandria, and Moderatus of Gades all posited the existence of such a transcendent principle; even Plato himself, in the *Republic,* suggests that the Good, which he identified with the One, exists above being.[69] As is typical, the "clear cut" distinctions between various schools and periods are not always so sharp as one has been led to believe. This is especially true of the distinctions between Middle Platonism and Neopythagoreanism in the period outlined above.

In addition to the doctrine of the One above being, Plotinus (204-269 C.E.) also held that the intelligible realm, which he identified with *nous* or Mind, exists as a unity-diversity, as a differentiated "image" of the One. Hence, this world of Forms, which contains all the laws and principles of the universe, can be seen as the living union of the Monad and the Indefinite Dyad, with the Monad acting as the limiting and form-giving principle in the realm of *nous,* while the Indefinite Dyad acts as the "intelligible matter" upon which the Monad acts. The Indefinite Dyad also provides for the element of Infinity which allows for the existence of an unlimited number of forms and souls in the realm of Mind.

Henceforward, Pythagorean ideas played an important role in subsequent Neoplatonic thought. Porphyry (233-305 C.E.), Plotinus' successor, wrote a biography of Pythagoras which was part of his *History of Philosophy in Ten Books.* Iamblichus (d. *circa* 330), who was a student of Porphyry and thought of himself as something of a full-fledged Pythagorean, undertook the task of writing a multi-volume "Pythagorean encyclopedia" which included *The Life of Pythagoras* here reproduced and a number of other works: *The Exhortation to Philosophy, On the Common Mathematical Science, Commentary on Nichomachus' Introduction to Arithmetic,* three books *On the Natural, Ethical and Divine Conceptions which are Perceived in the Science of Numbers* (of which the anonymous *Theology of Arithmetic* is based on the third book); and three lost works on Pythagorean harmonics, geometry and astronomy, bringing the total number of volumes up to 10, the Pythagorean Perfect Number.

The Neopythagorean component of Neoplatonism did not end with Iamblichus but rather continued through to the closing of the school in Athens, only to resurface in Renaissance Florence with the thinkers associated with the Cosimo de' Medici's Platonic Academy, of which Marsilio Ficino was the head.

This is not to imply that only pagan thinkers were followers of Pythagorean thought. On the contrary, many of the early church fathers held Pythagoras and his teachings in high esteem. Not only that, it became quite fashionable, after the manner of Philo, to enlist the help of Pythagorean number symbolism in the interpretation of scripture. Justin Martyr (100-164 C.E.) was rejected by a Pythagorean teacher on account of his inadequate mathematical knowledge (recalling the words engraved above the Academy door); he turned to Platonism, and then to Christianity, but never gave up his admiration for the Greek sages. Clement of Alexandria (fl. *circa* 200 C.E.) was also an admirer of Hellenistic thought and even applied the ratios of the Harmonic Proportion to the exegesis of the holy writ.[70] Augustine (354-430), heavily influenced by Neoplatonism, also loved to indulge in numerical exegesis, and he was instrumental in helping to transmit an interest in number symbolism to the Middle Ages.

Also important in the transmission of the Pythagorean ideas to the following age were the pagan encyclopediasts of the late antique world. Macrobius (first part of the fifth century) discussed Pythagorean thought in his *Commentary on the Dream of Scipio,* and Martianus Capella (fl. 410-429) in his allegorical work on the seven liberal arts, *The Marriage of Philology and Mercury,* discussed arithmology in Book VII. Another important source for the medievals was Boethius (480-525), especially his works *On Arithmetic* and *On Music.*

Having arrived at the close of the ancient world we have also arrived at the end of our survey. Pythagorean ideas continued to be transmitted in the work of Christian thinkers and applied in the realm of sacred architecture by groups of medieval masons. Insofar as Pythagorean thought had been Christianized, it had been changed, yet nonetheless many important conceptions—such as the ideas of celestial harmony and the significance of Number as a cosmic paradigm—remained unaltered. There was a brief and beautiful Renaissance of Pythagorean thought at the cathedral school of Chartres in France during the 12th century, due in part to a Latin translation of Plato's *Timaeus,* and of course there was a renewed interest in Pythagorean thought with the rediscovery of classical writings during the rebirth of learning in Renaissance Italy.

A Philosophy of Whole Systems

IT SHOULD COME AS NO SURPRISE that the figure of Pythagoras appealed strongly to those scholars of Renaissance Italy, as he has invariably appealed to the more universal thinkers of every age. The appeal lies in his important and influential conceptions, which in many ways seem to directly reveal important principles existing at the sacred "root of Nature's fount," but also in the man's character, for Pythagoras himself seems to well represent the possibility of an integrated approach to the study of Nature as a philosophical way of life.

As we have seen, the central focus of Pythagorean thought is in many respects placed on the principle of *harmonia.* The Universe is One, but the phenomenal realm is a differentiated image of this unity—the world is a unity in multiplicity. What maintains the unity of the whole, even though it consists of many parts, is the hierarchical principle of harmony, the *logos* of relation, which enables every part to have its place in the fabric of the all.

Because of Pythagoras' approach, integrating mathematics, psychology, ethics, and political philosophy into one comprehensive whole, it would be quite inappropriate to end this essay without devoting a few words to the contemporary significance of the Pythagorean approach. Pythagoras would have never wished that his insights remain the focus of a merely antiquarian interest, and so we shall honor his intentions by inquiring into what value Pythagorean thought might possess in the contemporary world, addressing these matters in quite general terms.

Pythagoras, no doubt, would have disapproved of the radical split which occured between the sciences and philosophy during the 17th century "enlightenment" and which haunts the intellectual and social fabric of Western civilization to this day. In retrospect perhaps we can see that man is most happily at home in the universe as long as he can relate his experiences to both the universal and the particular, the eternal and the temporal levels of being.

Natural science takes an Aristotelian approach to the universe, delighting in the multiplicity of the phenomenal web. It is concerned with the individual parts as opposed to the whole, and its method is one of particularizing the universal. Natural science attempts to quantify the universal, through the reduction of living form and qualitative relations to mathematical and statistical formulations based on the classification of material artifacts.

By contrast, natural philosophy is primarily Platonic in that it is concerned with the whole as opposed to the part. Realizing that all things are essentially related to certain eternal forms and principles, the approach of the natural philosopher strives to understand the relation that the particular has with the universal. Through the language of natural philosophy, and through the Pythagorean approach to whole systems, it is possible to relate the temporal with the eternal and to know the organic relation between multiplicity and unity.

If the scientific spirit is seen as a desire to study the universe in its totality, it will be seen that both approaches are complementary and necessary in scientific inquiry, for an inclusive cosmology must be equally at home in dealing with the part or the whole. The great scientists of Western civilization—Kepler, Copernicus, Newton, Einstein, and those before and after—were able to combine both approaches in a valuable and fruitful way.

It is interesting that the split between science and philosophy coincides roughly with the industrial revolution—for once freed from the philosophical element, which anchors scientific inquiry to the whole of life and human values, science ceases to be science in a traditional sense, and is transformed into a servile nursemaid of *technology,* the development and employment of mechanization. Now machines are quite useful as long as they are subservient to human good, in all the ramifications of that word—but as it turned out, the industrial revolution also coincided with a mechanistic conceptualization of the natural order, which sought to increase material profit at the expense of the human spirit. This era, which gave rise to the nightmare of the modern factory—William Blake's "dark satanic mills"—gained its strength through the naive premise that the human spirit might be elevated and perfected through the agency of the machine.

Today, in many circles, to a large part fueled by the desire for economic reward, science has nearly become confused with and subservient to technology, and from this perspective it might be said that the ideal of a universal or inclusive science has been lost. This is because the ideal scientist is also a natural philosopher who is interested in relating his discoveries to a larger universal framework, whereas the dull-minded technologist, if he has any interest in universal principles at all, limits that interest to their specific mechanistic applications rather than their intrinsic worth of study. Yet, those who study universal principles as principles-in-themselves, often find that these principles have many applications in a wide variety of fields.

While Pythagoras would have taken a dim view of this artificial and dangerous split between science and philosophy, the negative consequences of this rupture have not gone unnoticed. Yet with his emphasis on the unity of all life, Pythagoras would have been in an excellent position to foresee the negative consequences: ecological imbalance, materialism, the varied effects of personal greed, the disintegration of human values, the decline of the arts, a lack of interest in personal excellence and achievement. In a sense these problems, not necessarily unique to this age, result from a lack of balance and an ability to see the parts in relation to the whole. As the poet Francis Thompson said, "You cannot move a flower without troubling a star," and so it is with every individual and collective action.

Pythagoras correctly observed that all things are linked together proportionately, by justice, harmony—call it what you will. By cultivating an awareness of harmonic forming principles and working within the bounds set by necessity, mankind possesses the potential to become a sacred steward of the earth and co-creator with Nature; but the inevitable corollary is that humanity also has every power to create and inhabit a hell of its own making. The simple fact remains that the scales of justice are inexorable—it is a principle of Nature, and not merely of human morals, that each should receive his due. If we poison our rivers, we poison ourselves; if we act in stupidity, it is only appropriate that we suffer the consequences. If there is a moral to the story it is simply that individuals and societies are far less likely to run into trouble should they possess an awareness of these principles and relationships. And if one would like to cultivate the innate human ability to see things as they are, in whole-part relations, there is scarcely a better guide than the Pythagorean sciences. There has been much talk among the avant garde of "whole systems," the "philosophy of holism," etc., but few have realized that it is actually Pythagoras who is the tutelary genius and founder of the philosophy of whole systems.

We have mentioned the split between science and philosophy because it is an easy and self-evident example. Yet Pythagoras would also have something to say about the structure of our educational system as well. It has become fashionable to create ever more specialized disciplines—a Ph.D. thesis is considered proportionately *better* the fewer the number of people that can understand it. This is not to imply that specialized knowledge lacks value, but rather to say that a danger exists in the self-inflicted alienation of academia and the sciences. Great things cannot fail to happen when minds get together and one mind fertilizes another—when disciplines inspire one another. Pythagoras would say that, from the standpoint of natural philosophy, a superfluous multiplicity of facts and compartmentalized data is useless in a higher sense unless one can determine their relation to the whole, or the universal patterns which underlie all creation.

Interestingly, it is the modern-day physicists who have come most closely to approximating Pythagorean conceptions. Hell-bent on proving the mechanistic notions of 18th-century materialism, physicists have discovered that the deeper they push into matter the more it looks like the cosmos of the Pythagoreans and Platonists. Each atom is a Pythagorean universe, the sight of eternity in a grain of sand, consisting of an arithmetic number of particles, geometrically distributed in space, dancing and vibrating like a miniature solar system to the music of the spheres. A modern physicist would have little difficulty comprehending the teaching of the Orphic theologians that "the essence of the Gods"—that is to say the formative principles—"is defined by Number."[71]

Matter and energy are but different aspects of one, underlying continuum. Advancing to the subatomic level, quantity becomes quality, energy becomes information. Many physicists, proceeding from particulars to universals, are now on the verge of recognizing the essential truth of the statement, common to all spiritual traditions, that "Through consciousness the universe is but one single thing; all is interdependent with all."[72] The science of physics, proceeding from matter to energy, from energy to intelligence (i.e., pattern, *logos*), and from intelligence to Nous, has all but discovered the *deus absconditus* of the alchemists, the God hidden in matter. If the alchemical poeticism be allowed, even matter, if properly tortured, slain and resurrected, contains the innate potentiality of revealing the Hermetic mercury of eternal being. With the atomic accelerator at their disposal, modern physicists indeed have the capability to change lead into gold. They have taught the world that flesh, coal and diamond are made of the same basic stuff (carbon), driving home the reality that soul and Form is the essential component of all things.

One important Pythagorean insight which possesses ramifications for both the sciences and human behavior is the observation that the phenomenal universe is a mixture, a synthesis of Limited and Unlimited elements. Plato, drawing upon this notion in the *Timaeus,* compares the limited world of the Forms to a father, and the unlimited Receptacle of Space to a mother, the "nurse of becoming" as he puts it.[73] From their conjunction is born an offspring: the visible, phenomenal universe, the world of eternal principles manifesting in time and space.

The significance of this observation lies in the fact that it paints a picture of the phenomenal realm existing as a manifestation of what might be called "ordered chaos"—we exist in an intermediate realm. Platonism, which posits the existence of an extratemporal and extraspatial world of perfect form, recognizes that the universe in which we live mirrors this perfection in an imperfect way. Hence Plato notes in the *Timaeus* that the receptacle of becoming, which we inhabit, was initially "filled with powers that were neither alike nor evenly balanced."[74] The receptacle might be compared to a sea, in which various currents provide for an ambient randomness. Stated in the terms of contemporary physics, one might observe that in the intelligible realm light, as principle, travels in a perfectly straight line, while in the realm of manifestation its path—and the fabric of space itself—is warped to a degree by gravitational mass.

While the Pythagoreans identified the principle of Limit with the Good, it should also be observed that without the principle of the Unlimited all manifestation would be impossible.[75] Moreover, working in conjunction with its partner, the principle of Unlimitedness is equally responsible for the organic beauty of the phenomenal realm. All trees of the same species more-or-less follow the same laws of growth, but at each juncture of growth there exists an indefinite number of possibilities. It is precisely the unlimited element which makes for the beauty of a forest, which would be much less beautiful if each tree were exactly the same. A musical composition also relies on order and randomness (change); should either element come to predominate it ceases to be beautiful.

Whereas the Platonism before the Renaissance possessed a tendency to focus on the transcendent world of forms, the first Pythagoreans seemed to concentrate more on the incarnate manifestations of universal principles. After all, not only did they study *harmonia* as a universal principle, seeing it reflected on all levels of the beautiful cosmos, they incorporated the principle into the fabric of their daily lives as well. But already with Aristotle we find a lack of insight into the Pythagorean view—he cannot understand how the Pythagoreans view Number as possessing "magnitude."[76] This could well represent a misunderstanding of the incarnationalist dimension of Pythagorean thought, and perhaps reveals an overly literalist interpretation on Aristotle's part as well.

The Pythagorean view of the universe as a living, harmonic mixture is not on-ly indispensable as a scientific concept, but it beautifully articulates the position of man in the cosmos as well. If, along with Plato, we view time as a moving image of eternity,[77] then each generation of humanity stands poised between the present moment and the timeless immensity of the eternal. Rather than being a worthless speck meaninglessly situated in the infinite expanse of space, each per-son, according to the Pythagorean view, is a microcosm, a complete image of the entire cosmos, with one foot located in the realm of eternal principles and the other foot rooted in a particular world of manifestation. Poised as he is bet-ween time and eternity, matter and spirit, man possesses an incredible freedom to learn, create and know, limited only by those principles on which creation is based. From this vantage point, humanity is engaged in a never-ceasing dialectic between time and eternity, possessing the ability to incarnate eternal principles in time (and in this sense mirror the creative work of Nature), yet also possess-ing the ability to elevate the particular to the universal through conscious understanding.

In relation to this theme, one final observation is in order: the creative endeavors of humanity seem to attain their peak of excellence precisely at that point when the intermediate nature of humanity is actively recognized. For with this recogni-tion comes the realization that one must actively integrate the particular and univer-sal aspects of being. Hence, the best science will once again embrace its sister, *philosophia*: both deal with universal principles and particular phenomena—and together they will not attempt to build up a system of thought either from "the top down," deduced from purely *a priori* formulations, nor will they dare to start exclusively from "the bottom up," abstracting observations only from particular phenomena while ignorning universal principles. This approach I believe is fun-damentally Pythagorean: the harmonic proportion, according to legend discovered by Pythagoras, exists as a purely universal principle, but it would have never been discovered without empirical experimentation on the monochord. The value of the harmonic proportion lies in *both* its universal nature as well as the significance and usefulness of its particular applications. Through the creative dialectic between the temporal and the eternal, there necessarily occurs a form of integration between otherwise purely theoretic and pragmatic approaches. Another benefit of this realization—the realization that all things are composed of constants and variables—is that, if seriously embraced, it actively encourages honest inquiry, rendering the twin dangers of Fundamentalism and Relativism equally impotent, for universal justice has its own means of dealing with individuals who mistakenly believe that they possess the Absolute Truth, or, conversely, think that "everything is relative."

One final point needs to be made about the Pythagorean approach, and that concerns the topic of value. There are many occasions where it is useful to take a divisive approach to Nature for the purposes of abstract analysis, yet there are also times when it becomes expedient to stress the unity of all being. For Aristo-tle Number was merely an abstraction as opposed to an innately existing *a priori* principle, so it is easy to see how he might become confused by the notion that abstract number possesses "magnitude." Yet, if Number acts as a geometrical forming principle in the sphere of natural phenomena, as some of the studies cited in the bibliography abundantly demonstrate, it seems unwise to deny its immanent efficacy. Likewise, Aristotle was equally bewildered by the Pythagorean symbolism which equated certain archetypal number forms with principles such as "justice." Yet the truth of the matter is that it is precisely through the Pythagorean approach that quantity (number) and quality are discovered to be integrally related. As Ernst Levy has pointed out in an important article, "The Pythagorean Concept of Measure," this is shown to be especially true in the realm of music where each tone is actually a number, yet also a qualitative phenomenon possessing *value*.[78] It is particularly true in the realms of music and what has been called "sacred geometry" that one can gain insight into the Pythagorean conception of Number as both creative paradigm and qualitative relation. Levy suggests that in order to once again benefit from a unified scientific and philosophical synthesis that "a new mental attitude is required which many among us will be reluctant to assume, because it is contrary to the scientifically determined mind. The definition of that attitude is simple enough. It consists in this, that we must be willing to ascribe equal reality and equal importance to quality and quantity."[79] It is worth observing that the Pythagorean approach, while realizing the necessity of employing antithetical pairs of opposites in a conceptual sense, always arrives at a position which emphasizes the unity of the all.

To conclude that Number, in the most Pythagorean sense of the term, and the cosmos itself possesses a dimension of *meaning* is, within the context of mechanistic "science" or modern reductionistic "philosophy," perhaps the ultimate heresy; yet, for the traditional scientist and philosopher such a realization is only the *starting point*. If Pythagoras had but one imperative for the present age—or any age—it would be, as F.M. Cornford has suggested, this:

Seek truth and beauty together; you will never find them apart.[80]

— DAVID R. FIDELER

NOTES TO THE INTRODUCTION

References to writings appearing in this volume follow Guthrie's chapter divisions.

1) It will not be my intention in this introductory essay to attempt to pierce through the various mysteries surrounding the figure of Pythagoras or to embark on the overwhelming task of textual criticism. Nor do I desire to write much about the life of Pythagoras, seeing that all of the primary source material is presented in this volume. Rather, I will attempt to briefly sketch out the history of the Pythagorean school and its influence, discussing those doctrines which are generally agreed upon, and to provide some type of context into which the writings of this sourcebook may be placed by the general reader. Indeed, I have tried to keep the general reader in mind throughout the introduction, and have limited more specialized comments to these notes, which also include references for further reading on topics which can only be touched upon here.

2) The source for this is Ion of Chios, quoted by Diogenes Laertius, *Life of Pythagoras,* chapter 5. For a discussion of Pythagorean Orphica see West, *The Orphic Poems,* Oxford University Press, 1984, 7-15.

3) For Plato's views on writing about matters of ultimate concern see his Seventh Letter.

4) Since Pythagoras left no writings, this presents the historian with some difficulties. What, in fact, can safely be attributed to Pythagoras? Moreover, what do we know about his life? At a very early date a body of legends grew up around Pythagoras; many of these beautiful and amusing stories are recorded in the biographies, which constitute the first part of this book. For a long time, due to the nearly miraculous accounts, certain scholars dismissed the biographies as "late" and "unreliable." However, Aristotle in his lost monograph *On the Pythagoreans* emphasized how Pythagoras was seen at two places at once, how he showed his golden thigh, how he was thought to be the Hyperborean Apollo, and how he was addressed by a certain river. Obviously these stories are not "late Neopythagorean inventions" but go back to the time of Plato or before. Another source of these accounts was *The Tripod* of Andron of Ephesus, who was roughly contemporary with Aristotle. While the *interpretive dimension* of Iamblichus' biography is certainly colored by later Neopythagorean and Neoplatonic influence, it is now taken for granted that the biographies contain a great deal of early information about Pythagoras and his school, and much of the information is taken from older authorities whose work has since perished. Some of the ealiest authorities include Timaeus of Tauromenium (*circa* 352-256 B.C.E.) who wrote a *History of Sicily* which contained information of the Pythagoreans and the speeches of Pythagoras, and Dicaearchus of Messina (fourth century B.C.E.), a pupil of Aristotle who wrote a comprehensive study of Greek history which also treated the Pythagoreans. Another student of Aristotle, Aristoxenus of Tarentum, wrote several works on the Pythagoreans, used by the later biographers, which drew on early sources and his first-hand contact with members of the Pythagorean school.

5) Porphyry, *Life of Pythagoras,* chapter 12.

6) Iamblichus, *Life of Pythagoras,* chapter 5. For all we know, Pythagoras may have been invited to go to Croton. While this, to my knowledge, has not been previously suggested, it seems unlikely that he would have moved his teaching activities to a distant city

without having some contact with and knowledge of the inhabitants. If this is correct, it would help explain his rapid acceptance by the populace.

7) See Vogel, *Pythagoras and Early Pythagoreanism,* for an analysis of these speeches. Iamblichus' source for these is Timaeus of Tauromenium.

8) Theon of Smyrna, *Mathematics Useful for Understanding Plato,* 12.

9) This concept—that the One or principle of unity is the source of all numbers—is easily grasped if one envisions "the One" as a circle in which various polygons are inscribed; the polygons, or numbers contained within the circle, may then be seen as various manifest *aspects* of the underlying unity. Another analogy is found in Pythagorean harmonics: the monochord, symbolizing unity (1/1), innately contains the entire overtone series (2/1, 3/1, 4/1, 5/1, etc.), which is manifested when the string is plucked.

10) Theon of Smyrna, *Mathematics Useful for Understanding Plato,* 66.

11) Ibid, 66.

12) Cornford, "Science and Mysticism in the Pythagorean Tradition," part 2, 3.

13) Ibid.

14) Aristotle, *Physics* 203 a 10.

15) Plato, *Timaeus* 35b f.

16) See Levin, *The Harmonics of Nichomachus and the Pythagorean Tradition,* chapter 6.

17) Different musical instruments emphasize different overtones. For example, the clarinet emphasizes the odd numbered overtones, thus accounting for its peculiar timbre.

18) This relation has been defined by Flora R. Levin in her *Harmonics of Nicomachus and the Pythagorean Tradition,* 1, as the "metaphysical octave," the characteristic feature of which is "a perfect fusion of parts (3:4 and 2:3) into a whole (2:1)." Richard L. Crocker in his article "Pythagorean Mathematics and Music," 330, observes: "This construction, dividing as it does the first consonance by the second and third in a curious, interlocking way, has every right to be called *the* harmony. Here the inner affinity of whole-number arithmetic and music finds its most congenial expression."

19) The *leimma* is the excess of the fourth over the double tone: $4/3 : 9/8 \times 9/8 = 4/3 \times 64/81 = 256/243$.

20) Needless to say, the "Music of the Spheres" is one of the most influential conceptions of Pythagoras. For a complete discussion which deals with its long and interesting history, as well as the significance of the concept as a poetic fact, see Joscelyn Godwin's *The Harmonies of Heaven and Earth.*

21) Alcmaeon of Croton in Freeman, *Ancilla to the Pre-Socratic Philosophers,* 41 (24 DK 4).

22) For more on figured numbers and their properties, see Heath, *A History of Greek Mathematics,* vol. 1, chapter 3, "Pythagorean Arithmetic." Also see the first volume of Ivor Thomas' *Greek Mathematical Fragments.*

23) Relating to the musical ratios of the Tetraktys is the Pythagorean saying "What is the Oracle at Delphi?" The answer is: "The Tetraktys, the very thing which is the Harmony of the Sirens" (Iamblichus, *Life of Pythagoras,* chapter 18). Nicomachus of Gerasa also identifies the harmonic ratio of 6:8::9:12 as a version of the Tetraktys in his *Manual of Harmonics,* vii, 10.

24) One modern proponent of this approach was Buckminster Fuller. Some important sources for the study of this approach and geometrical forming principles include Keith Critchlow's *Order in Space* and *Islamic Patterns,* Ghyka's *The Geometry of Art and Life,*

and *The Geometrical Basis of Natural Structure* by Robert Williams.

25) Iamblichus, *The Life of Pythagoras,* chapter 12.

26) Pythagoras was thought to be associated in some way with the God Apollo. This is only natural since Apollo is related to the celestial principles of harmonic order and *logos*, these being also the principles with which Pythagoras was most concerned. This connection is even made plain by the name of the philosopher—for Pythios is the name of Apollo at Delphi, his most sacred shrine from which his oracles were delivered. This obvious etymological connection led Diogenes Laertius to interpret the name as meaning that he spoke (*agoreuein*) the truth no less than Apollo (*Pythios*) at Delphi.

27) This period of silence may have only been a ritual matter required during the religious ceremonies of the society, not during everyday life. "The ceremonies are conducted by Pythagoras behind a veil or curtain. Those who have passed this five-year test may pass behind the curtain and see him face to face during the ceremonies; the others must merely listen." Minar, "Pythagorean Communism," 39.

28) This is Minar's analysis in "Pythagorean Communism."

29) From an Orphic gold funerary plate, translated in Freeman, *Ancilla to the Pre-Socratic Philosphers,* 5. (1 DK 18)

30) A fragment quoted by Iamblichus maintains that the nature of the Gods is related to Number (Iamblichus, *Life of Pythagoras,* chapter 28), and there was even an Orphic "Hymn to Number," portions of which are found in Kern, *Orphicorum Fragmenta,* Berlin, Weidemann, 1922.

Cameron, in his important study of Pythagorean thought observes that *harmonia* in Pythagorean thought inevitably possesses a religious dimension. He goes on to note that both *harmonia*—there is no "h" in the Greek spelling—and *arithmos* appear to be descended from the single root *ar*. This seems to "indicate that somewhere in the unrecorded past, the Number religion, which dealt in concepts of harmony or attunement, made itself felt in Greek lands. And it is probable that the religious element belonged to the *arithmos-harmonia* combination in prehistoric times, for we find that *ritus* in Latin comes from the same Indo-European root." (Alister Cameron, *The Pythagorean Background of Recollection,* 26.)

31) Burnet, *Early Greek Philosophy,* 83.

32) Ibid.

33) The *Life of Pythagoras* preserved by Photius, chapter 15.

34) Stocks, "Plato and the Tripartite Soul," 210-11.

35) For a good discussion of the Pythagorean view of justice as proportion see John Robinson, *An Introduction to Early Greek Philosophy,* 81-83.

36) Plato, *Republic* 444d (Cornford translation, 143).

37) Plato, *Republic* 443d f. (Cornford translation, 141-2).

38) For sources and a discussion of the soul as a *harmonia* see Guthrie, *A History of Early Greek Philosophy,* vol. 1, 307 f.

39) Quoted by Clement of Alexandria, *Stromateis* ii, 84.

40) Certain scholars, appealing primarily to the "Table of Opposites," have argued that the orientation of Pythagoreanism was essentially *dualistic*. Such a simplistic view overlooks the fact that every philosophical system employs dualistic typologies and that "as a religious philosophy, Pythagoreanism unquestionably attached central importance to the idea of unity, in particular the unity of all life, divine, human, and animal, implied

in the scheme of transmigration." (F.M. Cornford, *Plato and Parmenides*, 4.)

41) After writing this section I came across the observation of Viktor Goldschmidt: "Our capacity to apprehend the outside world may be explained thus, that there are processes in our mind (microcosm) which are analogous to those in nature. These psychological processes we call natural laws." (Quoted by Ernst Levy, "The Pythagorean Concept of Measure," 53.)

42) Heath, *A History of Greek Mathematics*, vol. 1, 10.

43) Plato, *Republic* 527b (Cornford translation, p. 244).

44) Tzetzes, *Chiliad*. viii. 972.

45) Plato, *Republic* 527b (Cornford translation, p. 244).

46) Vogel, *Pythagoras and Early Pythagoreanism*, 197.

47) Iamblichus, *Life of Pythagoras*, chapter 21.

48) Within this context it might be noted that Pythagorean metaphysics has, from ancient Greece to the present day, had an influence on the arts. The lesser can lead to the greater, and natural beauty, which is relative, can lead to the apprehension of transcendent Beauty which is absolute. This is, of course, a Platonic sentiment, but it is foreshadowed in the structure of Pythagorean thought. Perhaps, however, it would be more accurate in Pythagorean thought, with its immanent metaphysics, to suggest that the universal is realized through the particular. The use of mathematical and geometrical harmonies in sacred architecture, for example, can lead to the perception of, and resonance with, universal harmony. For example, through the medium of "Pythagorean geometry," a sacred edifice has the potential to become a celestial mediator: through the harmonic *nature* of its structure, the heavenly principles of harmonic form are reflected on earth; yet through the *effect* that this harmony has on those that are receptive to its beauty, the particular may be exalted to perceive the universal. This two-fold principle is applicable not only in architecture, however, but indeed in all the arts.

49) Guthrie, *A History of Early Greek Philosophy*, vol. 1, 170.

50) Plato, *Republic* 434d - 441c; also see J.L. Stocks, "Plato's Tripartite Soul."

51) Aristotle, *Metaphysics* i 6, 987 a 29 f.

52) Plato, *Republic*, particularly 398c - 403c and 521c - 531c.

53) This was stated in Plato's lecture "On the Good." See the note below.

54) Aristotle enjoyed telling a story about Plato's lecture "On the Good": "Everyone went there with the idea that he would be put in the way of getting one or other of the things in human life which are usually accounted good, such as Riches, Health, Strength, or, generally, any extraordinary gift of fortune. But when they found that Plato discoursed about mathematics, arithmetic, geometry, and astronomy, and finally declared the One to be the Good, no wonder they were altogether taken by surprise; insomuch that in the end some of the audience were inclined to scoff at the whole thing, while others objected to it altogether." (Aristoxenus, *Harmonica* ii ad init., quoted by Heath, *A History of Greek Mathematics*, vol. 1, 24.)

55) *Republic* 500c.

56) *Gorgias* 506e.

57) *Gorgias* 508a.

58) Aristotle, *Metaphysics* xiii 7; see also the discussion in Dillon and Vogel (below).

59) For Pythagorean musical symbolism in Plato see Ernest McClain, *The Pythagorean Plato*. For more on similarities and differences between Plato and the Pythagoreans, and

the characteristics of post-Platonic Pythagoreanism, see the valuable discussion in chapter 8 of Vogel's *Pythagoras and Early Pythagoreanism*. For a brief discussion of the *dogmata agrapha* and the early Academy see Dillon, *The Middle Platonists*, chapter 1.

60) A translation of the fragment appears in volume 1 of Ivor Thomas' *Greek Mathematical Fragments*. Dillon gives a succinct overview of the thought of Speusippus in chapter 1 of *The Middle Platonists;* Taran's *Speusippus of Athens* is a comprehensive study of the remaining Greek fragments and the thought of Speusippus.

61) Holger Thesleff, *An Introduction to the Pythagorean Writings of the Hellenistic Period*, 72.

62) Dillon in A.H. Armstrong, ed., *Classical Mediterranean Spirituality*, NY, Crossroad, 1987, 226.

63) Clement of Alexandria, *Stromateis*, i, 15.

64) Philostratus' *Life of Apollonius of Tyana*, which includes the letters, appears in the Loeb Classical Library.

65) For the equation of Apollo with the One see Plutarch, *Moralia* 270f, 393c and 436b. For his Pythagorizing tendencies see "On the Mysteries of Isis and Osiris" and his Delphic essays, collected in volume 5 of Plutarch's *Moralia*, Harvard, 1936.

66) Theon of Smyrna, *Mathematics Useful for Understanding Plato*, translated by Robert and Deborah Lawlor, San Diego, Wizards Bookshelf, 1979.

67) Nicomachus of Gerasa, *Introduction to Arithmetic*, translated by M.L. D'Ooge. New York, MacMillan, 1926.

68) Dillon, *The Middle Platonists*, 359. Each letter of the Greek alphabet possesses a numerical value and hence each word may also be represented as a number. The science of *gematria* involves the conscious use of this numerical symbolism and is not to be confused with either arithmology or numerology. A well known example is found in the name of the Gnostic divinity Abraxas, the numerical value of which is 365, the number of days in a solar year. The Babylonian divinities were represented by whole numbers and a Babylonian clay tablet indicates that Sargon II (fl. 720 B.C.E.) ordered that the wall of Khorsabad be constructed to have a length of 16,283 cubits, the numerical value of his name. The present writer has researched the history of *gematria* in some depth and has discovered an extremely strong body of evidence that *gematria* was utilized in Greece prior to the Hellenistic period.

69) Plato, *Republic* 509b.

70) In book ix, chapter 11 of the *Stromateis*, which deals with "The Mystical Meanings in the Proportions of Number, Geometrical Ratios, and Music." Clement also refers to the sage from Samos as "Pythagoras the great." (*Stromateis* i, 21.)

71) Iamblichus, *The Life of Pythagoras*, chapter 28.

72) R.A. Schwaller de Lubicz, *Nature Word*, West Stockbridge, MA, Lindisfarne Press, 1982, 99.

73) Plato, *Timaeus* 49.

74) Plato, *Timaeus* 52e.

75) Plato's nephew Speusippus thought that it was inappropriate to apply ethical values to the principles of *peras* and *apeiron*.

76) Aristotle, *Metaphysics* 1080 b 16; 1080 b 31; 1083 b 9; and 1090 a 20.

77) Plato, *Timaeus* 37d. Plato adds that time is a moving image of eternity "according to number."

78) Ernest Levy, "The Pythagorean Concept of Measure," 53.
79) Ibid.
80) Francis M. Cornford, "The Harmony of the Spheres," 27.

PART I:
THE PYTHAGORAS SOURCEBOOK

FIGURE 10. IAMBLICHUS

Iamblichus:

The Life of Pythagoras

OR

On the Pythagorean Life

IAMBLICHUS (c. 250 - c. 325 C.E.) was an important Neoplatonic philosopher and a student of Porphyry, whose *Life of Pythagoras* also appears in this volume. Iamblichus was very interested in the philosophical dimension of then current religious practices which he interpreted in light of Neoplatonism. He was also quite an original thinker and highly influenced later Neoplatonism with his triadic metaphysics. In addition to being a Platonist, Iamblichus thought of himself as a Pythagorean philosopher.

Iamblichus attempted to write a ten volume 'encyclopedia' of Pythagorean thought, the first volume of which is his *Life of Pythagoras*. The second volume of this work was entitled *Concerning Pythagorean Explanations, Including an Exhortation to Philosophy*, often called simply the *Exhortation to Philosophy*. The *Exhortation*, in addition to outlining the benefits of the philosophic life, contains a detailed commentary on the 39 Pythagorean Symbols. Other volumes in Iamblichus' Pythagorean *corpus* of works include *On the Common Mathematical Science, On the Introduction to the Arithmetic of Nichomachus*, and *The Theology of Numbers*.

Iamblichus saw Pythagoras as the Father of Philosophy who revealed to his disciples the principles of the philosophic life as well as all those studies which lead to the purification of the intellect. While Iamblichus has a tendency to personally interpret Pythagoras through the eyes of Neoplatonism, many of the sources on which he draws, which are often quoted verbatim, are quite ancient. Actually, Neoplatonism was in many ways heavily influenced by Pythagorean and Neopythagorean thought.

For a complete biography of Iamblichus and a listing of his various writings see the introduction to the *Exhortation to Philosophy*, Phanes Press, 1988.

THE LIFE OF PYTHAGORAS

1. The Importance of the Subject

SINCE WISE PEOPLE are in the habit of invoking the divinities at the beginning of any philosophic consideration, this is all the more necessary on studying that one which is justly named after the divine Pythagoras. Inasmuch as it emanated from the divinities it cannot be apprehended without their inspiration and assistance. Besides, its beauty and majesty so surpasses human capacity that it cannot be comprehended all in one glance. Only gradually can some details of it be mastered when, under divine guidance, we approach the subject with a quiet mind. Having therefore invoked the divine guidance, and adapted ourselves and our style to the divine circumstances, we shall acquiesce in all the suggestions that come to us. Therefore we shall not begin with any excuses for the long neglect of this sect, or with any explanations about its having been concealed by foreign disciplines, or by mystic symbols, nor insist that it has been obscured by false and spurious writings, nor make apologies for any special hindrances to it progress. For us it is sufficient that this is the will of the Gods, which will enable us to undertake tasks even more arduous than these. Having thus acknowledged our primary submission to the divinities, our secondary devotion shall be to the prince and father of this philosophy as a leader. We shall, however, have to begin by a study of his descent and nationality.

2. Youth, Education, Travels

IT IS REPORTED that Ancaeus, who dwelt in Samos in Cephallenia, was descended from Zeus, the fame of which honorable descent might have been derived from his virtue, or from a certain magnanimity. In any case, he surpassed the remainder of the Cephallenians in wisdom and renown. This Ancaeus was, by the Pythian oracle, bidden to form a colony from Arcadia and Thessaly; and besides leading with him some inhabitants of Athens, Epidaurus, and Chalcis, he was to render habitable an island which, from the virtue of the soil and vegetation was to be called Black-leaved (*Melamphyllos*), while the city was to be called Samos, after Same, in Cephallenia. The oracle ran thus: "I bid you, Ancaeus, to colonize the maritime island of Same, and to call it Phyllas." That the colony originated from these places is proved first from the divinities, and their sacrifices, which were imported by the inhabitants, second by the relationships of the families, and by their Samian gatherings.

From the family and alliance of this Ancaeus, founder of the colony, were therefore descended Pythagoras' parents Mnesarchus and Pythais. That Pythagoras was the son of Apollo is a legend due to a certain Samian poet, who thus described the popular recognition of his noble birth. Sang he,

> Pythais, the fairest of the Samian race
> From the embraces of the God Apollo
> Bore Pythagoras, the friend of Zeus.

It might be worthwhile to relate the circumstances of this prevalent report. Mnesarchus had gone to Delphi on a business trip, leaving his wife without any signs of pregnancy. He enquired of the oracle about the event of his return voyage to Syria, and he was informed that his trip would be lucrative, and most conformable to his wishes, but that his wife was new with child, and would present him with a son who would surpass all others who had ever lived in beauty and wisdom, and that he would be of the greatest benefit to the human race in everything pertaining to human achievements. But when Mnesarchus realized that the God, without waiting for any question about a son, had by an oracle informed him that he would possess an illustrious prerogative, and a truly divine gift, he immediately changed his wife's former name Parthenis to one reminiscent of the Delphic prophet and her son, naming her Pythais, and the infant, who was soon after born at Sidon in Phoenicia, Pythagoras, by this name commemorating that such an offspring had been promised him by the Pythian Apollo. The assertions of Epimenides, Eudoxus and Xenocrates, that Apollo having at that time already had actual connection with Parthenis, causing her pregnancy, had regularized that fact by predicting the birth of Pythagoras, are by no means to be admitted. However, no one will deny that the soul of Pythagoras was sent to mankind from Apollo's domain, having either been one of his attendants, or more intimate associates, which may be inferred both from his birth and his versatile wisdom.

After Mnesarchus had returned from Syria to Samos, with great wealth derived from a favorable sea voyage, he built a temple to Apollo, inscribed to Pythius. He took care that his son should enjoy the best possible education, studying under Creophilus, then under Pherecydes the Syrian, and then under almost all who presided over sacred concerns, to whom he especially recommended his son, that he might be as expert as possible in divinity. Thus by education and good fortune he became the most beautiful and godlike of all those who have been celebrated in the annals of history. After his father's death, though he was still but a youth, his aspect was so venerable, and his habits so temperate that he was honored and even reverenced by elderly men, attracting the attention of all who saw and heard him speak, creating the most profound impression. That is the reason that many plausibly asserted that he was a child of the divinity. Enjoying the privilege of such a renown, of an education so thorough from infancy, and of so impressive a natural appearance, he showed that he deserved all these advantages, by the adornment of piety and discipline, by exquisite habits, by firmness of soul, and by a body duly subjected to the mandates of reason. An inimitable quiet and serenity marked all his words and actions, soaring above all laughter, emulation, contention, or any other irregularity or eccentricity; his influence, at Samos, was that of some beneficent divinity. His great renown, while yet a youth, reached not only men as illustrious for their wisdom as Thales at Miletus, and Bias at Priene, but also extended to the neighboring cities. He was celebrated everywhere as the "long-haired Samian," and by the multitude was given credit for being under divine inspiration.

When he had attained his eighteenth year, there arose the tyranny of Polycrates; and Pythagoras foresaw that under such a government his studies might be impeded, as they engrossed the whole of his attention. So by night he privately departed with one Hermodamas—who was surnamed Creophilus, and was the grandson of the host, friend and general preceptor of the poet Homer—going to Pherecydes, to Anaximander the natural philosopher, and to Thales at Miletus. He successively associated with each of these philosophers in a manner such that they all loved him, admired his natural endowments, and admitted him to the best of their doctrines. Thales especially, on gladly admitting him to the intimacies of his confidence, admired the great difference between him and other young men, who were in every accomplishment surpassed by Pythagoras. After increasing the reputation Pythagoras had already acquired, by communicating to him the utmost he was able to impart to him, Thales, laying stress on his advanced age and the infirmities of his body, advised him to go to Egypt, to get in touch with the priests of Memphis and Zeus. Thales confessed that the instruction of these priests was the source of his own reputation for wisdom, while neither his own endowments nor achievements equalled those which were so evident in Pythagoras. Thales insisted that, in view of all this, if Pythagoras should study with those priests, he was certain of becoming the wisest and most divine of men.

3. Journey to Egypt

PYTHAGORAS HAD BENEFITED by the instruction of Thales in many respects, but his greatest lesson had been to learn the value of saving time, which led him to abstain entirely from wine and animal food, avoiding greediness, confining himself to nutriments of easy preparation and digestion. As a result, his sleep was short, his soul pure and vigilant, and the general health of his body was invariable.

Enjoying such advantages, therefore, he sailed to Sidon, both because it was his native country, and because it was on his way to Egypt. In Phoenicia he conversed with the prophets who were the descendents of Moschus the physiologist,* and with many others, as well as with the local hierophants. He was also initiated into all the mysteries of Byblos and Tyre, and in the sacred function performed in many parts of Syria. He was led to all this not from any hankering after superstition, as might easily by supposed, but rather from a desire and love for contemplation, and from an anxiety to miss nothing of the mysteries of the divinities which deserved to be learned.

After gaining all he could from the Phoenician mysteries, he found that they had originated from the sacred rites of Egypt, forming as it were an Egyptian colony. This led him to hope that in Egypt itself he might find monuments of erudition still more genuine, beautiful and divine. Therefore following the advice of his teacher Thales, he left, as soon as possible, through the agency of some Egyptian sailors, who very opportunely happened to land on the Phoenician coast under Mount Carmel where, in the temple on the peak, Pythagoras for the most part had dwelt in solitude. He was gladly received by the sailors, who intended to make a great profit by selling him into slavery. But they changed their mind in his favor during the voyage, when they perceived the chastened venerability of the mode of life he had undertaken. They began to reflect that there was something supernatural in the youth's modesty, and in the manner in which he had unexpectedly appeared to them on their landing, when, from the summit of Mount Carmel, which they knew to be more sacred than other mountains, and quite inaccessible to the vulgar, he had leisurely descended without looking back, avoiding all delay from precipices or difficult rocks; and that when he came to the boat, he said nothing more than, "Are you bound for Egypt?" What is more, on their answering affirmatively he had gone aboard and had, during the whole trip, sat silent where he would be least likely to inconvenience them at their tasks.

For two nights and three days Pythagoras had remained in the same unmoved position, without food, drink, or sleep, except that, unnoticed by the sailors, he might have dozed while sitting upright. Moreover, the sailors considered that contrary to their expectations, their voyage had proceeded without interruptions, as if some deity had been on board. From all these circumstances they concluded that a veritable divinity had passed over with them from Syria into Egypt. Addressing Pythagoras and each other with a gentleness and propriety that was un-

*That is, Moses.

common, they completed the remainder of their voyage through a halcyon sea, and at length happily landed on the Egyptian coast. Reverently the sailors here assisted him to disembark; and after they had seen him safe onto a firm beach, they raised before him a temporary altar, heaped on it the now abundant fruits of trees, as if these were the first fruits of their freight, presented them to him and departed hastily to their destination. Pythagoras, however, whose body had become emaciated through the severity of so long a fast, did not refuse the sailors' help on landing, and as soon as they had left partook as much of the fruits as was requisite to restore his physical vigor. Then he went inland, in entire safety, preserving his usual tranquility and modesty.

4. Studies in Egypt and Babylonia

HERE IN EGYPT he frequented all the temples with the greatest diligence, and most studious research, during which time he won the esteem and admiration of all the priests and prophets with whom he associated. Having most solicitously familiarized himself with every detail, he did not, nevertheless, neglect any contemporary celebrity, whether a sage renowned for wisdom, or a peculiarly performed mystery. He did not fail to visit any place where he thought he might discover something worthwhile. That is how he visted all of the Egyptian priests, acquiring all the wisdom each possessed. He thus passed twenty-two years in the sanctuaries of temples, studying astronomy and geometry, and being initiated in no casual or superficial manner in all the mysteries of the Gods. At length, however, he was taken captive by the soldiers of Cambyses, and carried off to Babylon. Here he was overjoyed to be associated with the Magi, who instructed him in their venerable knowledge, and in the most perfect worship of the Gods. Through their assistance, likewise, he studied and completed arithmetic, music and all the other sciences. After twelve years, about the fifty-sixth year of his age, he returned to Samos.

5. Travels in Greece; Settlement at Croton

ON HIS RETURN to Samos, he was recognized by some of the older inhabitants, who found that he had gained in beauty and wisdom, and had achieved a divine graciousness, wherefore they admired him all the more. He was officially invited to benefit all men, by imparting his knowledge publicly. To this he was not averse; but the method of teaching he wished to introduce was the symbolical one, in a manner similar to that in which he had been instructed in Egypt. This mode of teaching, however, did not please the Samians, whose attention lacked perseverance. Not one proved genuinely desirous of those mathematical disciplines which he was so anxious to introduce among the Greeks, and soon he was left entirely alone. This, however, did not embitter him to the point of neglecting or despising Samos. Because it was his home town, he desired to give his fellow-citizens a taste of the sweetness of the mathematical disciplines, in spite of their refusal to learn. To overcome this he devised and executed the following strategem. In the gymnasium he happened to observe the unusually skillful and masterful ball-playing of a youth who was greatly devoted to physical culture, but financially lacking and in difficult circumstances. Pythagoras wondered whether this youth, if supplied with the necessities of life, and freed from the anxiety of supplying them, could be induced to study with him. Pythagoras therefore called the youth, as he was leaving the bath, and proposed furnishing him the means to continue his physical training, on the condition that he would study with him easily and gradually, but continuously, so as to avoid confusion and distraction, certain disciplines which he claimed to have learned from the Barbarians in his youth, but which were now beginning to desert him in consequence of the inroads of the forgetfulness of old age. Moved by hopes of financial support, the youth took up the proposition without delay. Pythagoras then introduced him to the rudiments of arithmetic and geometry, illustrating them objectively on an abacus, paying him three oboli as fee for the learning of every figure. This was continued for a long time, the youth being incited to the study of geometry by the desire for honor, with diligence, and in the best order. But when the sage observed that the youth had become so captivated by the logic, ingeniousness and style of those demonstrations to which he had been led in an orderly way, that he would no longer neglect their pursuit merely because of the sufferings of poverty, Pythagoras pretended poverty, and consequent inability to continue payment of the three oboli fee. On hearing this, the youth replied that even without the fee he could go on learning and receiving this instruction. Then Pythagoras said, "But even I myself am lacking the means to procure food!" As he would have to work to earn his living, he ought not to be distracted by the abacus and other trifling occupations. The youth, however, loath to discontinue his studies, replied, "In the future, it is I who will provide for you, and repay your kindness in a way resembling that of the stork; for in my turn, I will give you three oboli for every figure." From this time on he was so captivated by these disciplines, that, of all the Samians, he alone elected to leave home to follow Pythagoras, being a namesake of his, though differing in patronymic, being the son of Eratocles. It is probably to him that should be ascribed three books *On Athletics*, in which he recommends a diet of flesh, instead of dry figs, which of course would hardly have been written by the Mnesarchian Pythagoras.

About this time Pythagoras went to Delos, where he was much admired as he approached the so-called bloodless altar of Father Apollo, and worshipped at it. Then Pythagoras visited all the oracles. He dwelt for some time in Crete and Sparta, to learn their laws, and on acquiring proficiency therein he returned home to complete his former omissions.

On his arrival in Samos, he first established a school, which is even now called the Semicircle of Pythagoras, in which the Samians now consult about public affairs, feeling the fitness of dispensing justice and promoting profit in the place constructed by him who promoted the welfare of all mankind. Outside of the city he fashioned a cave, adapted to the practices of his philosophy, in which he spent the greater part of day and night, ever busied with scientific research, and meditating as did Minos, the son of Zeus. Indeed he surpassed those who later practiced his disciplines chiefly in this: that they advertised themselves for the knowledge of theorems of minute importance, while Pythagoras unfolded a complete science of the celestial orbs, founding it on arithmetical and geometrical demonstrations.

Still more than for all this, he is to be admired for what he accomplished later. His philosophy now gained great importance, and his fame spread to all Greece, so that the best students visited Samos on his account, to share in his erudition. But his fellow-citizens insisted on employing him in all their embassies, and compelling him to take part in the administration of public affairs. Pythagoras began to realize the impossibility of complying with the claims of his country while remaining at home to advance his philosophy, and observing that all earlier philosophers had passed their lives in foreign countries, he was determined to resign all political occupations. Besides, according to contemporary testimony, he was disgusted at the Samians' scorn for education.

Therefore, he went to Italy, conceiving that his real fatherland must be the country containing the greatest number of the most scholarly men. Such was the success of his journey that on his arrival at Croton, the noblest city in Italy, that he gathered as many as six hundred followers, who by his discourses were moved, not only to philosophical study, but to an amicable sharing of their worldly goods, whence they derived the name of *Cenobites.* *

6. The Pythagorean Community

THE CENOBITES were students that philosophized; but the greater part of his followers were called Hearers (*akousmatikoi*) of whom, according to Nicomachus, there were two thousand that had been captivated by a single oration on his arrival in Italy. These, with their wives and children, gathered into one immense auditory, called the Auditorium (*Homacoion*), which was so great as to resemble a city, thus founding a place universally called Greater Greece (*Magna Graecia*). This great multitude of people, receiving from Pythagoras laws and mandates as so many divine precepts, without which they declined to engage in any occupation, dwelt together in the greatest general concord, estimated and celebrated by their neighbors as among the number of the blessed, who, as was already observed, shared all their possessions.

Such was their reverence for Pythagoras that they ranked him with the Gods, as a genial beneficent divinity. While some celebrated him as the Pythian, others called him the Hyperborean Apollo. Others considered him Paeon,† others, one of the divinities that inhabit the moon; yet others considered that he was one of the Olympian Gods, who, in order to correct and improve terrestrial existence, appeared to their contemporaries in human form, to extend to them the salutary light of philosophy and felicity. Never indeed came, nor, for the matter of that, ever will come to mankind a greater good than that which was imparted to the Greeks through this Pythagoras. Hence, even now, the nickname of "long-haired Samian" is still applied to the most venerable among men.

In his treatise *On the Pythagoric Philosophy*, Aristotle relates that among the principle arcana of the Pythagoreans was preserved this distinction among rational animals: Gods, men, and beings like Pythagoras. Well indeed may they have done so, inasmuch as he introduced so just and apt a generalization as Gods,

*Greek for "common life."
†A form of Apollo as the physician of the Gods.

heroes and daimons; of the world, of the manifold motions of the spheres and stars, their oppositions, eclipses, inequalities, eccentricites and epicycles; and of all the natures contained in heaven and earth, together with the intermediate ones, whether apparent or occult. Nor was there, in all this variety of information, anything contrary to the phenomena, or to the conceptions of the mind. Besides all this, Pythagoras unfolded to the Greeks all the disciplines, theories and researches that would purify the intellect from the blindness introduced by studies of a different kind, so as to enable it to perceive the true principles and causes of the universe.

In addition, the best polity, popular concord, community of possessions among friends, worship of the Gods, piety to the dead, legislation, erudition, silence, abstinence from eating the flesh of animals, continence, temperance, sagacity, divinity, and in brief, whatever is anxiously desired by the scholarly, was brought to light by Pythagoras.

It was on account of all this, as we have already observed, that Pythagoras was so much admired.

7. Italian Political Achievements

NOW WE MUST RELATE HOW HE TRAVELLED, what places he first visited, and what discourses he made, on what subjects, and to whom addressed, for this would illustrate his contemporary relations. His first task, on arriving in Italy and Sicily, was to inspire with a love of liberty those cities which he understood had more or less recently oppressed each other with slavery. Then, by means of his auditors, he liberated and restored to independence Croton, Sybaris, Catanes, Rhegium, Himaera, Agrigentum, Tauromenas, and some other cities. Through Charondas the Catanaean, and Zaleucus the Locrian, he established laws which caused the cities to flourish, and become models for others in their proximity. Partisanship, discord and sedition, and that for several generations, he entirely rooted out, as history testifies, from all the Italian and Sicilian lands, which at that time were disturbed by inner and outer contentions. Everywhere, in private and in public, he would repeat, as an epitome of his own opinions, and as a persuasive oracle of divinity, that by any means whatsoever, strategem, fire, or sword, we should amputate from the body, disease; from the soul, ignorance; from a household, discord; and from all things whatsoever, lack of moderation; through which he brought home to his disciples the quintessence of all teachings, and that with a most paternal affection.

For the sake of accuracy, we may state that the year of his arrival in Italy was that one of the Olympic victory in the stadium of Eryxidas of Chalcis, in the sixty-second Olympiad. He became conspicuous and celebrated as soon as he arrived, just as formerly he achieved instant recognition at Delos, when he performed his adorations at the bloodless altar of Father Apollo.

8. Intuition, Reverence, Temperance and Studiousness

ONE DAY, during a trip from Sybaris to Croton, by the sea-shore, he happened to meet some fishermen engaged in drawing up from the deep their heavily-laden fish-nets. He told them he knew the exact number of fish they had caught.

The surprised fishermen declared that if he was right they would do anything he said. He then ordered them, after counting the fish accurately, to return them alive to the sea, and what is more wonderful, while he stood on the shore, not one of them died, though they had remained out of their natural element quite a little while. Pythagoras then paid the fishermen the price of their fish, and departed for Croton. The fishermen divulged the occurrence, and on discovering his name from some children, spread it abroad publicly. Everybody wanted to see the stranger, which was easy enough to do. They were deeply impressed on beholding his countenance, which indeed betrayed his real nature.

A few days later, on entering in the gymnasium, he was surrounded by a crowd of young men, and he embraced this opportunity to address them, exhorting them to attend to their elders, pointing out to them the general preeminence of the early over the late. He instanced that the east was more important than the west, the morning than the evening, the beginning than the end, growth than decay; natives than strangers, city-planners than city-builders; and in general, that Gods were more worthy of honor than daimons, daimons than demigods, and heroes than men; and that among these the authors of birth in importance excelled their progeny. All this, however, he said only to prove by induction, that children should honor their parents, to whom, he asserted, they were as much indebted for gratitude as would be a dead man to him who should bring him back to life, and light. He continued to observe that it was no more than just to avoid paining, and to love preeminently those who had benefitted us first and most. Prior to the children's birth, these are benefitted by their parents exclusively, being the springs of their offspring's righteous conduct. In any case, it is impossible for children to err by not allowing themselves to be outdistanced in reciprocation of benefits towards their parents. Besides, since from our parents we learn to honor divinity, no doubt the Gods will pardon those who honor their parents no less than those who honor the Gods (thus making common cause with them). Homer even applied the paternal name to the King of the Gods, calling Him the father of Gods and men. Many other mythologists informed us that the chiefs of the Gods even were anxious to claim for themselves that superlative affection which, through marriage, binds children to their parents. That is why they introduced among the Gods the terms father and mother, Zeus begetting Athena, while Hera produced Hephaestus, the nature of which offspring is contrary, so as to unite the most remote through friendship.

As this argument about the immortals proved convincing to the Crotonians, Pythagoras continued to enforce voluntary obedience to the parental wishes, by the example of Hercules, who had been the founder of the Crotonian colony. Tradition indeed informs us that that divinity had undertaken labors so great out of obedience to the commands of a senior, and that after his victories therein, he instituted the Olympic games in honor of his father. Their mutual association should never result in hostility to friends, but in transforming their own hostility into friendship. Their benevolent filial disposition should manifest as modesty, while their universal philanthropy should take the form of fraternal consideration and affection.

Temperance was the next topic of his discourses. Since the desires are most flourishing during youth, this is the time when control must be effective. While temperance alone is universal in its application to all ages, boy, virgin, woman, or the aged, yet this special virtue is particularly applicable to youth. Moreover, this virtue alone applies universally to all goods, those of body and soul, preserving both the health, and studiousness. This may be proved conversely. When the Greeks and Barbarians warred over Troy, each of them fell into the most dreadful calamities, both during the war, and the return home, and all this through the incontinence of a single individual. Moreover, the divinity ordained that the punishment of this single injustice should last over a thousand and ten years, by an oracle predicting the capture of Troy, and ordering that annually the Locrians should send virgins into the Temple of Athena in Troy.

Cultivation of learning was the next topic Pythagoras urged upon the young men. He invited them to observe how absurd it would be to rate the reasoning power as the chief of their faculties, and indeed consult about all other things by its means, and yet bestow no time or labor on its exercise. Attention to the body might be compared to fostering unworthy friends, and is liable to rapid failure; while erudition lasts till death, and for some procures post-mortem renown, and may be likened to good, reliable friends. Pythagoras continued to draw illustrations from history and philosophy, demonstrating that erudition enables a naturally excellent disposition to share in the achievements of the leaders of the race. For others share in their discoveries by erudition.

[Erudition possesses four great advantages over all other goods.] First, some advantages, such as strength, beauty, health and fortitude, cannot be exercised except by the cooperation of somebody else. Moreover, wealth, dominion, and many other goods do not remain with him who imparts them to somebody else. Third, some kinds of goods cannot be possessed by some men, but all are susceptible to instruction, according to their individual choice. Moreover, an instructed man will naturally, and without any impudence, be led to take part in the administration of the affairs of his home country (as does not occur with more wealth). One great advantage of erudition is that it may be imparted to another person without in the least diminishing the store of the giver. For it is education which makes the difference between a man and a wild beast, a Greek and a Barbarian, a free man and a slave, and a philosopher and a boor. In short, erudition has so great an advantage over those who do not possess it, that in one whole city and during one whole Olympiad seven men only were found to be eminent winners in racing, and that in the whole habitable globe those that excelled in wisdom amounted to no more than seven. But in subsequent times it was generally agreed that Pythagoras alone surpassed all others in philosophy; for instead of calling himself a wise man, he called himself a *philosopher* (a lover of wisdom).

9. Community and Chastity

WHAT PYTHAGORAS said to the youths in the gymnasium, these reported to their elders. Hereupon these latter, a thousand strong, called him into the senate house, praised him for what he had said to their sons, and desired him to unfold to the public administration any thoughts which he might have advantageous to the Crotonians.

His first advice was to build a temple to the Muses, which would preserve the already existing concord. He observed to them that all of these divinities were grouped together by their common names, that they subsisted only in conjunction with each other, that they specially rejoiced in social honors, and that [in spite of all changes] the choir of the Muses subsisted always one and the same. They comprehended symphony, harmony, rhythm, and all things breeding concord. Not only to beautiful theorems does their power extend, but to the general symphonious harmony.

Justice was the next desideratum. Their common country was [not to be victimized selfishly, but] to be received as a common deposit from the multitude of citizens. They should therefore govern it in a manner such that, as a hereditary possession they might transmit it to their posterity. This could best be effected if the members of the administration realized their equality with the citizens, with the only supereminence of justice. From the common recognition that justice is required in every place came the fables that Themis is seated in the same order with Zeus, and that Dike, or Justice, is seated by Hades, and that Law is established in all cities, so that whoever is unjust in things required of him by his position in society may concurrently appear unjust towards the whole world. Moreover, senators should not make use of any of the Gods for the purpose of an oath, inasmuch as their language should make them credible even without any oaths.

As to their domestic affairs, their government should be the object of deliberate choice. They should show genuine affection to their own offspring, remembering that those, from among all creatures, were the only ones who could appreciate this affection. Their associations with their partners in life, their wives, should be such as to be mindful that while other compacts are engraved on tables and pillars, the marital ones are incarnated in children. They should moreover make an effort to win the affection of their children, not merely in a natural, involuntary manner, but through deliberate choice, which alone constitutes beneficence.

He further besought them to avoid connexion with any but their wives lest, angered by their husbands' neglect and vice, these should not get even by adulterating the race. They should also consider that they received their wives from the Vestal hearth with libations, and brought them home in the presence of the Gods themselves, as suppliants would have done. By orderly conduct and temperance they should become models not only for their family, but also for their community.

Again, they should minimize public vice, lest offenders indulge in secret sins to escape the punishment of the laws, but should rather be impelled to justice from reverence for beauty and propriety. Procrastination also should be ended, inasmuch as opportuneness is the best part of any deed. The separation of parents from their children Pythagoras considered the greatest of evils. While he who is able to discern what is advantageous to himself may be considered the best man, next to him in excellence should be ranked he who can see the utility in what happens to others, while the worst man is he who waits till he himself is afflicted before understanding where true advantage lies. Seekers of honor might well imitate racers, who do not injure their antagonists, but limit themselves to trying to achieve the victory themselves. Administrators of public affairs should not betray offense at being contradicted, but on the other hand benefit those they lead. Seekers of true glory should strive really to become what they wished to seem; for counsel is not as sacred as praise, the former being useful only among men, while the latter mostly refers to the divinities.

In closing, he reminded them that their city happened to have been founded by Hercules, at a time when, having been injured by Lacinius, he drove the oxen through Italy; when, rendering assistance to Croton by night, mistaking him for an enemy, he slew him unintentionally. Wherefore Hercules promised that a city should be built over the sepulchre of Croton; from him the city derives its name, thus endowing him with immortality. Therefore, said Pythagoras to the rulers of the city, those should justly render thanks for the benefits they had received.

The Crotonians, on hearing his words, built a temple to the Muses, and drove away their concubines, and requested Pythagoras to address the young men in the temple of Pythian Apollo, and the women in the temple of Hera.

10. Advice to Youths

TO BOYS PYTHAGORAS, complying with their parents' request, gave the following advice. They should neither revile any one, nor revenge themselves on those who did. They should devote themselves diligently to learning, which in Greek derives its name from their age.* A youth who started out modestly would find it easy to preserve probity for the remainder of his life, which would be a difficult task for one who at that age was not well disposed; nay, for one who begins his course from a bad impulse, to run well to the end is almost impossible.

Pythagoras pointed out that boys were most dear to the divinities; and he pointed out that, in times of great drought, cities would send boys as ambassadors to implore rain from the Gods, in the persuasion that divinity is especially attentive to children, although such as are permitted to take part in sacred ceremonies continuously hardly ever arrive at perfect purification. That is also the reason why the most philanthropic of the Gods, Apollo and Love, are, in pictures, universally represented as having the ages of boys. It is similarly recognized that some of the [athletic] games in which the victors are crowned were instituted for the behoof of boys; the Pythian, in consequence of the serpent Python having been slain by a boy, and the Nemean and Isthmian, because of the death of Archemorus and Nelicerta. Moreover, while the city of Croton was building, Apollo promised to the founder that he would give him a progeny, if he brought a colony into Italy, inferring therefrom that Apollo presided over their development, and that inasmuch as all the divinities protected their age, it was no more than fair that they should render themselves worthy of their friendship.

He added that they should practice hearing, so that they might learn to speak. Further, he said that as soon as they had entered on the path along which they intended to proceed for the remainder of their existence, they should imitate their predecessors, never contradicting those who were their seniors. For later on, when they themselves will have grown, they will justly expect not to be injured by their

*In Greek, *pais* = a child; *paideia* = education.

juniors.

Because of these moral teachings, Pythagoras deserved no longer to be called by his own name, but deserved to be called divine.

11. Advice to Women

TO THE WOMEN Pythagoras spoke as follows about sacrifices. To begin with, inasmuch as it was no more than natural that they would wish that some other person who intended to pray for them should be worthy, nay, excellent, because the Gods attend to these particularly, so also it is advisable that they themselves should most highly esteem equity and modesty, so that the divinities may be the more inclined to grant their requests.

Further, they should offer to the divinities such things as they themselves have with their own hands produced, such as cakes, honey-combs, and perfumes, and should bring them to the altars without the assistance of servants. They should not worship divinities with blood and dead bodies, nor offer so many things at one time that it might seem they meant never to sacrifice again.

Concerning their association with men, they should remember that their female nature had by their parents been granted the license to love their husbands more excessively than even the authors of their existence. Consequently they should take care neither to oppose their husbands, nor consider that they have subjected their husbands should these latter yield to them in any detail.

It was in the same assembly that Pythagoras is said to have made the celebrated suggestion that, after a woman has had congress with her husband, it is holy for her to perform sacred rites on the same day, which would be inadmissible had the connection been with any man other than her husband.

He also advised the women that their conversation should always be cheerful, and to endeavor that others may speak good things of them. He further admonished them to care for their good reputation, and to try not to blame the fable writer who, observing the justice of women, accused three women of using a single eye in common, so great is their mutual willingness to accomodate each other with the loan of garments and ornaments, without a witness, when some one of them has special need thereof, returning them without arguments or obligation.

Further, Pythagoras observed that he who is called the wisest of all (i.e., Hermes),* who arranged the human voice, and in short, was the inventor of names, whether he was a God, or a divinity, or a certain divine man, or in special animals such as the ibis, ape, or dogs, perceiving that the female sex was most given to devotion, gave to each of their ages the name of one divinity. So an unmarried woman was called Kore (maiden), or Persephone, a bride, Nympha; a matron, Mother; and a grandmother, in the Doric dialect, Maia. Consequently, the oracles at Dodona and Delphi are brought to light by a woman.

---

*Hermes was the God of *logos,* reason or speech, the naming power. He was identified with the Egyptian deity Thoth, the lord of scribes, whose symbolic animals were the ibis and the ape, and who was said to have invented writing. Compare this passage with the early Christian writer Theodotus: "Pythagoras thought that he who gave things their names, ought to be regarded not only the most intelligent, but the oldest of the wise men..." He then goes on to discuss the investigation of names contained in scripture. *Excerpts of Theodotus,* 32.

By this praise of female piety Pythagoras is said to have affected so great a change in popular female attire, that some no longer dared to dress up in costly raiment, consecrating thousands of their garments in the temple of Hera.

This discourse had effect also on marital fidelity to an extent such that in the Crotonian region connubial faithfulness became proverbial, [thus imitating] Ulysses who, rather than abandon Penelope, considered immortality well lost. Pythagoras encouraged the Crotonian women to also emulate Ulysses, by exhibiting their probity to their husbands.

In short, through these discourses Pythagoras acquired great fame both in Croton, and in the rest of Italy.

12. Why Pythagoras Called Himself a Philosopher

PYTHAGORAS is said to have been the first to call himself a philosopher, a word which heretofore had not been an appellation, but a description. He likened the entrance of men into the present life to the progression of a crowd to some public spectacle. There assemble men of all descriptions and views. One hastens to sell his wares for money and gain; another exhibits his bodily strength for renown; but the most liberal assemble to observe the landscape, the beautiful works of art, the specimens of valor, and the customary literary productions. So also in the present life men of manifold pursuits are assembled. Some are influenced by the desire of riches and luxury; others, by the love of power and dominion, or by insane ambition for glory. But the purest and most genuine character is that of the man who devotes himself to the contemplation of the most beautiful things, and he may properly be called a philosopher.

Pythagoras adds that the survey of the whole heaven, and of the stars that revolve therein, is indeed beautiful, when we consider their order, which is derived from participation in the first and intelligible essence. But that first essence is the nature of Number and "reasons"* which pervades everything, and according to which all those [celestial] bodies are arranged elegantly, and adorned fittingly. Now veritable wisdom is a science conversant with the first beautiful objects which subsist in invariable sameness, being undecaying and divine, by the participation in which other things also may well be called beautiful. The desire for something like this is philosophy. Similarly beautiful is devotion to erudition, and this notion Pythagoras extended, in order to effect the improvement of the human race.

13. How He Shared Orpheus' Control Over Animals

ACCORDING TO CREDIBLE HISTORIANS, his words possessed an admonitory quality that prevailed even with animals, which confirms that in intelligent men learning tames even wild or irrational beasts. The Daunian bear, who had severely injured the inhabitants, was by Pythagoras detained. After long stroking it gently, feeding it on maize and acorns, and compelling it by an oath to leave alone living beings, he sent it away. It hid itself in the mountains and forest, and was never since known to injure any irrational animal.

At Tarentum he saw an ox feeding in a pasture, where he ate green beans.

---

* "Reasons" = *logoi*, productive principles, ratios, patterns, etc.

He advised the herdsman to tell the ox to abstain from this food. The herdsman laughed at him, remarking he did not know the language of oxen; but that if Pythagoras did, he had better tell him so himself. Pythagoras approached the ox's ear and whispered into it for a long time, whereafter the ox not only refrained from them, but never even tasted them. This ox lived a long while at Tarentum, near the temple of Hera, and was fed on human food by visitors till very old, being considered sacred.

Once happening to be talking to his intimates about birds, symbols and prodigies, and observing that all these are messengers of the Gods, sent by them to men truly dear to them, he brought down an eagle flying over Olympia, which he gently stroked, and dismissed.

Through such and similar occurrences, Pythagoras demonstrated that he possessed the same dominion as Orpheus over savage animals, and that he allured and detained them by the power of his voice.

14. On Pythagoras' Preexistence

PYTHAGORAS used to make the very best possible approach to men by teaching them what would prepare them to learn the truth in other matters. For by the clearest and surest indications he would remind many of his intimates of the former life lived by their soul before it was bound to their body. He would demonstrate by indubitable arguments that he had once been Euphorbus, son of Panthus, conqueror of Patroclus. He would especially praise the following funeral Homeric verses pertaining to himself, which he would sing to the lyre most elegantly, frequently repeating them.

> The shining circlets of his golden hair,
> Which even the Graces might be proud to wear,
> Instarred with gems and gold, bestrew the shore
> With dust dishonored, and deformed with gore.
> As the young olive, in some sylvan scene,
> Crowned by fresh fountains with eternal green,
> Lifts the gay head, in snowy flowerets fair,
> And plays and dances to the gentle air;
> When lo, a whirlwind from high heaven invades
> The tender plant, and withers all its shades;
> It lies uprooted from its genial bed,
> A lovely ruin now defaced and dead;
> Thus young, thus beautiful Euphorbus lay,
> While the fierce Spartan tore his arms away.
> (Homer, *Iliad*, 17, Pope's translation.)

We shall, however, omit the reports about the shield of this Phrygian Euphorbus, which, among other Trojan spoils, was dedicated to Hera of Argive, as being too popular in nature. What Pythagoras, however, wished to indicate by all these particulars was that he knew the former lives he had lived, which enabled him to originate his providential attention to others, in which he reminded them of their former existences.

15. How Pythagoras Cured by Music

PYTHAGORAS CONCEIVED that the first attention that should be given to men should be addressed to the senses, as when one perceives beautiful figures and forms, or hears beautiful rhythms and melodies. Consequently he laid down that the first erudition was that which subsists through music's melodies and rhythms, and from these he obtained remedies of human manners and passions, and restored the pristine harmony of the faculties of the soul. Moreover, he devised medicines calculated to repress and cure the diseases of both bodies and souls. Here is also, by Zeus, something which deserves to be mentioned above all: namely, that for his disciples he arranged and adjusted what might be called "preparations" and "touchings," divinely contriving mingling of certain diatonic, chromatic and enharmonic melodies, through which he easily switched and circulated the passions of the soul in a contrary direction, whenever they had accumulated recently, irrationally, or clandestinely—such as sorrow, rage, pity, over-emulation, fear, manifold desires, angers, appetites, pride, collapse or spasms. Each of these he corrected by the rule of virtue, attempering them through appropriate melodies, as through some salutary medicine.

In the evening, likewise, when his disciples were retiring to sleep, he would thus liberate them from the day's perturbations and tumults, purifying their intellective powers from the influxive and effluxive waves of corporeal nature, quieting their sleep, and rendering their dreams pleasing and prophetic. But when they arose again in the morning, he would free them from the night's heaviness, coma and torpor through certain peculiar chords and modulations, produced by either simply striking the lyre, or adapting the voice. Not through instruments or physical voice-organs did Pythagoras effect this; but by the employment of a certain indescribable divinity, difficult of apprehension, through which he extended his powers of hearing, fixing his intellect on the sublime symphonies of the world, he alone apparently hearing and grasping the universal harmony and consonance of the spheres, and the stars that are moved through them, producing a melody fuller and more intense than anything effected by mortal sounds.

This melody was also the result of dissimilar and varying sounds, speeds, magnitudes and intervals arranged with reference to each other in a certain musical ratio, producing a convoluted motion most musical and gentle. Irrigated therefore with this melody, his intellect ordered and exercised thereby, he would, to the best of his ability exhibit certain symbols of these things to his disciples, especially through imitations thereof through instruments or the physical organs of voice. For he conceived that, of all the inhabitants of earth, by him alone were these celestial sounds understood and heard, as if coming from the central spring and root of nature. He therefore thought himself worthy to be taught, and to learn something about the celestial orbs, and to be assimilated to them by desire and imitation, inasmuch as his body alone had been well enough conformed thereto by the divinity who had given birth to him. As to other men, he thought they should be satisfied with looking to him and the gifts he possessed, and in being benefited and corrected through images and examples, in consequence of their inability truly to comprehend the first and genuine archetypes of things. Just as to those who are unable to look intently at the sun, we contrive to show its eclipses in either the reflections of some still water, or in melted pitch, or some smoked glass, or well brazen mirror, so we spare the weakness of their eyes devising a method of representing light that is reflective, though less intense than its archetype, to those who are interested in this sort of thing.

This peculiar organization of Pythagoras' body, far finer than that of any other man, seems to be what Empedocles was obscurely driving at in his enigmatical verses:

> Among the Pythagoreans was a man transcendent in knowledge;
> Who possessed the most ample stores of intellectual wealth,
> And in the most eminent degree assisted in the works of the wise.
> When he extended all the powers of his intellect,
> He easily beheld everything,
> As far as ten or twenty ages of the human race!

These words "transcendent," "he beheld every detail of all beings," and "the wealth of intellect," and so on, describe as accurately as possible his peculiar and exceptionally accurate method of hearing, seeing and understanding.

16. Pythagorean Asceticism

MUSIC THEREFORE performed this Pythagorean soul-adjustment. But another kind of purification of the discursive reason, and also of the whole soul, through various studies, was effected [by asceticism]. He had a general notion that disciplines and studies should imply some form of labor; and therefore, like a legislator, he decreed trials of the most varied nature, punishments, and restraints by fire and sword for innate intemperance, or an ineradicable desire for possessions, which the depraved should neither suffer nor sustain. Moreover, his intimates were ordered to abstain from all animal food, and any others that are hostile to the reasoning power by impeding its genuine energies. On them he likewise enjoined suppression of speech, and perfect silence, exercising them for years at a time in the subjugation of the tongue, while strenuously and assiduously investigating and ruminating over the most difficult theorems. Hence also he ordered them to abstain from wine, to be sparing in their food, to sleep little, and to cultivate an unstudied contempt of and hostility to fame, wealth, and the like; unfeignedly to reverence those to whom reverence is due, genuinely to exercise democratic assimilation and benevolence towards their fellows in age, and towards their juniors courtesy and encouragement without envy.

Moreover, Pythagoras is generally acknowledged to have been the inventor and legislator of friendship, under its many various forms, such as universal amity of all towards all, of God towards men through their piety and scientific theories, or of the mutual interrelation of teachings, or universally of the soul towards the body, and of the rational to the irrational part, through philosophy and its underlying theories; or whether it be that of men towards each other, of citizens indeed through sound legislation, but of strangers through a correct physiology; or of the husband to the wife, or of brothers and kindred, through unperverted communion; or whether, in short, it be of all things towards all, and still farther, of certain irrational animals through justice, and a physical connexion and association; or whether it be the pacification and conciliation of the body which of itself is mortal, and of its latent conflicting powers, through health, and a temperate diet conformable to this, in imitation of the salubrious condition of the mundane elements.

In short, Pythagoras procured his disciples the most appropriate converse with the Gods, both waking and sleeping—something which never occurs in a soul disturbed by anger, pain, or pleasure, and surely all the more by any base desire, or defiled by ignorance, which is the most noxious and unholy of all the rest. By all these inventions, therefore, he divinely purified and healed the soul, resuscitating and saving its divine part, and directing to the intelligible its divine eye, which, as Plato says, is more worth saving than ten thousand corporeal eyes, for when it is strengthened and clarified by appropriate aids, when we look through this, we perceive the truth about all being.* In this particular respect, therefore, Pythagoras purified the discursive power of the soul. This is the [practical] form that erudition took with him, and such were the objects of his interest.

17. Tests of Pythagorean Initiation

AS HE THEREFORE thus prepared his disciples for culture, he did not immediately receive as an associate any who came to him for that purpose until he had tested them and examined them judiciously. To begin with he inquired about their relation to their parents and kinsfolk. Next he surveyed their laughter, speech or silence, as to whether it was unseasonable; further, about their desires, their associates, their conversation, how they employed their leisure, and what were the subjects of their joy or grief. He observed their form, their gait, and the whole motions of their body. He considered their frame's natural indications physiognomically, rating them as visible exponents of the invisible tendencies of the soul.

After subjecting a candidate to such trials, he allowed him to be neglected for three years, still covertly observing his disposition towards stability, and genuine studiousness, and whether he was sufficiently averse to glory, and ready to despise popular honors.

After this the candidate was compelled to observe silence for five years, so as to have made definite experiments in continence of speech, inasmuch as the subjugation of the tongue is the most difficult of all victories, as has indeed been unfolded by those who have instituted the mysteries.

During this probation, however, the property of each was disposed of in common, being committed to trustees, who were called politicians, economizers, or legislators. Of these probationers, after the five-year silence, those who by modest dignity had won his approval as worthy to share in his doctrines, then became *esoterics*, and within the veil both heard and saw Pythagoras. Prior to this they participated in his words through the hearing alone, without seeing him who remained within the veil, and themselves offering to him a specimen of their manners.

*Cf. Plato, *Republic*, 527e.

If rejected, they were given the double of the wealth they had brought, but the *homacoi* raised to them a tomb, as if they were dead, the disciples being generally called Hearers. Should these later happen to meet the rejected candidate, the would treat him as a stranger, declaring that he whom they had by education modelled had died, inasmuch as the object of these disciplines had been to turn out good and honest men.

Those who were slow in the acquisition of knowledge were considered to be badly organized, or, we may say, deficient and sterile.

If, however, after Pythagoras had studied them physiognomically, their gait, motions and state of health, he conceived good hopes of them; and if, after the five years' silence, and the emotions and initiations from so many disciplines together with the ablutions of the soul, and so many and so great purifications produced by such various theorems, through which sagacity and sanctity is ingrained into the soul—if, after all this even, some one was found to be still sluggish and dull, they would raise to such a candidate within the school a pillar or monument, such as was said to have been done to Perialus the Thurian, and Cylon the prince of the Sybarites, who were rejected. They expelled them from the auditorium, loading them down with silver and gold. This wealth had by them been deposited in common, in the care of certain custodians, aptly called Economics. Should any of the Pythagoreans later meet with the reject, they did not recognize him who they accounted dead. Hence, also Lysis, blaming a certain Hipparchus for having revealed the Pythagorean doctrines to the profane, and to such as accepted them without disciplines or theory, said, "It is reported that you philosophize indiscriminately and publicly, which is opposed to the customs of Pythagoras. With assiduity you did indeed learn them, O Hipparchus; but you have not preserved them. My dear fellow, you have tasted Sicilian tidbits, which you should not have repeated. If you give them up, I shall be delighted; but if you do not, you will to me be dead. For it would be pious to recall the human and divine precepts of Pythagoras, and not to communicate the treasures of wisdom to those who have not purified their souls, even in a dream. It is unlawful to give away things obtained with labors so great, and with assiduity so diligent to the first person you meet, quite as much as to divulge the mysteries of the Eleusinian goddesses to the profane. Either thing would be unjust and impious. We should consider how long a time was needed to efface the stains that had insinuated themselves in our breasts, before we became worthy to receive the doctrines of Pythagoras. Unless the dyers previously purified the garments in which the desired colors were to be fixed, the dye would either fade, or be washed away entirely. Similarly, that divine man prepared the souls of lovers of philosophy, so that they might not disappoint him in any of these beautiful qualities which he hoped they would possess. He did not impart spurious doctrines, nor stratagems, in which most of the Sophists, who are at leisure for no good purpose, entangle young men; but his knowledge of things human and divine was scientific. These Sophists, however, use his doctrines as a mere pretext to commit dreadful atrocities, sweeping the youths away as in a dragnet most disgracefully, making their auditors become rash nuisances. They infuse theorems and divine doctrines into hearts whose manners are confused and agitated, just as if pure, clear water should be poured into a deep well full of mud, which would stir up the sediment and destroy the clearness of the water. Such a mutual misfortune occurs between such teachers and disciples. The intellect and heart of those whose initiation has not proceeded by disciplines, are surrounded by thickets dense and thorny, which obscure the mild, tranquil and reasoning power of the soul, and impede the development and elevation of the intellective part. These thickets are produced by intemperance and avarice, both of which are prolific.

"Intemperance produces lawless marriages, lusts, intoxications, unnatural enjoyments, and passionate impulsions which drive headlong into pits and abysses. The unbridling of desires has removed the barriers against incest with even mothers or daughters, and just as a tyrant would violate city regulations, or a country's laws, with their hands bound behind them, like slaves, they have been dragged to the depths of degradation. On the other hand, avarice produces rapine, robbery, parricide, sacrilege, sorcery, and kindred evils. Such being the case, these surrounding thickets, infested with passions, will have to be cleared out with systematic disciplines, as if with fire and sword; and when the reason will have been liberated from so many and great evils, we are in a position to offer to it, and implant within it something useful and good."

So great and necessary was the attention which, according to Pythagoras, should be paid to disciplines as introductions to philosophy.

Moreover, inasmuch as he devoted so much care to the examination of the mental attitudes of prospective disciples, he insisted that the teaching and communication of his doctrines should be distinguished by great honor.

18. Organization of the Pythagorean School

THE NEXT STEP is to set forth how, after admission to discipleship, followed distribution into several classes according to individual merit. As the disciples were naturally dissimilar, it was impractical for them to participate in all things equally, nor would it have been fair for some to share in the deepest revelations, while others might get excluded therefrom, or others from everything; such discrimination would be unjust. While he communicated some suitable portion of his discourses to all, he sought to benefit everybody, preserving the proportion of justice, by making every man's merit the index of the extent of his teachings. He carried this method so far as to call some Pythagoreans, and others Pythagorists, just as we discriminate poets from versifiers. According to this distinction of names, some of his disciples he considered genuine, and to be models of the others. The Pythagoreans' possessions were to be shared in common, inasmuch as they were to live together, while Pythagorists should continue to manage their own property, though by assembling frequently they might all be at leisure to pursue the same activities. These two modes of life which originated from Pythagoras were transmitted to his successors.

Among the Pythagoreans there were also two forms of philosophy, pursued by two classes, the Hearers (*akousmatikoi*) and the Students (*mathematikoi*). The latter were universally recognized as Pythagoreans, by all the rest, though the Students did not admit as much for the Hearers, insisting that these derived their instructions not from Pythagoras, but from Hippasus, who was variously described as either a Crotonian or Metapontine.

The philosophy of the Hearers consisted in lectures without demonstrations or conferences or arguments, merely directing something to be done in a certain way, unquestioningly preserving them as so many divine dogmas, non-discussable, and which they promised not to reveal, esteeming as most wise those who more than others retained them.

Of the lectures there were three kinds: the first merely announced certain facts, others expressed what it was especially, and the third, what should, or should not be done about it. The objective lectures studied such questions as:

What are the islands of the Blessed?
The sun and moon.

What is the oracle at Delphi?
The Tetraktys, the very thing which is the Harmony of the Sirens.

The subjective lectures studied the special nature of an object, such as:

What is the most just thing?
To sacrifice.

What is the wisest thing?
Number. The next wisest is the naming power.

What is the wisest human thing?
Medicine.

What is the most beautiful?
Harmony.

What is the most powerful?
Mental decision.

What is the most excellent?
Felicity.

Which is the most unquestioned proposition?
That all men are depraved.

That is why Pythagoras was said to have praised the Salaminian poet Hippodomas, for singing:

> Tell, O ye Gods, the source from whence ye came,
> And ye, O Men, how evil ye became.

Such were these subjective lectures, which taught the distinctive nature of everything.

This sort of study really constitutes the wisdom of the so-called Seven Sages. For these also did not investigate what was simply good, but especially good, nor what is difficult, but what is particularly so—namely, for a man to know himself. So also they considered not what was easy, but what was most so, namely, to continue following out your habits. Such studies resembled and followed those of the sages who preceded Pythagoras.

The practice lectures, which studied what should or should not be done, considered questions such as the necessity of begetting children, inasmuch as we must leave after us successors who may worship the divinities; or whether we should put the shoe on the right foot first; or whether it is proper or not to parade on the public streets, or to dip into a sprinkling vessel, or to wash in a public bath, for in all these cases the cleanliness of the agents is uncertain.

Other maxims include the following: Do not assist a man in laying down a burden, which encourages him to loiter, but to assist him in undertaking something. Do not hope to beget children from a woman who is rich. Speak not about Pythagoric affairs without light. Perform libations to the Gods from the handle of the cup, to make the omen auspicious and to avoid drinking from the same part [from which the liquor was poured out]. Wear not the image of a God on a ring, for fear of defiling it, as such resemblances should be protected in a house. Use no woman ill, for she is a suppliant, wherefore, indeed, we bring her from the Vestal hearth, and take her by the right hand. Nor is it proper to sacrifice a white cock, who also is a suppliant, being sacred to the moon, and announces the hours. To him who asks for counsel, give none but the best, for counsel is a sacrament. The most laborious path is the best, just as the pleasurable one is mostly the worst, inasmuch as we entered into the present life for the sake of education, which best proceeds by chastening. It is proper to sacrifice, and to take off one's shoes on entering into a temple. In going to a temple, one should not turn out of the way; for divinity should not be worshipped carelessly. It is well to sustain, and show wounds, if they are in the breast, but not if they are behind. The soul of man incarnates in the bodies of all animals, except in those which it is lawful to kill; hence we should eat none but those whom it is proper to slay. Such were the subjects of these ethical lectures.

The most extended lectures, however, were those concerning sacrifices, both at the time when migrating from the present life, and at other times; also, about the proper manner of sepulture.

For some of these propositions the reason is assigned—such as for instance that we must beget children to leave successors to worship the Gods. But no justification is assigned for the others, although in some cases they are implied proximately or remotely, such as that bread is not to be broken, because it contributes to the judgment of Hades. Such merely probable reasons, that are additional, are not Pythagoric, but were devised by non-Pythagoreans who wished to add weight to the statement. Thus for instance, in respect to the last statement, that bread is not to be broken, some add the reason that we should not [unnecessarily] distribute what has been assembled, inasmuch as in barbarian times a whole friendly group would together pounce upon a single piece. Others again explain that precept on the grounds that it is inauspicious, at the beginning of an undertaking, to make an omen of fracture or diminution. Moreover, all these precepts are based on one single underlying principle, the end of divinity, so that the whole of every life may result in following God, which is the principle and doctrine of philosophy. For it is absurd to search for good in any direction other than from the Gods. Those who do so resemble a man who, in a country governed by a king, should do honor to one of his fellow-citizens who is a magistrate, while neglecting him who is the ruler of them all. Indeed, this is what the Pythagoreans thought of people who searched for good elsewhere than from God. For since He exists as the lord of all things, it must be self-evident that good must be requested of Him alone. For even men impart good to those they love and enjoy, and do the opposite to those they dislike. Such indeed was the wisdom of those precepts.

There was, however, a certain Aegean named Hippomedon, one of the Pythagorean Hearers, who insisted that Pythagoras himself gave the reasons for, and demonstrations of these precepts himself; but that in consequence of their being delivered to many, some of whom were slow, the demonstrations were removed, leaving the bare propositions. The Pythagorean Students, however, insist that the reasons and demonstrations were added by Pythagoras himself, explaining that the difference arose [between the Students and Hearers] as follows. According to them, Pythagoras hailed from Ionia and Samos, to Italy then flourishing under the tyranny of Polycrates, and he attracted as associates the very most prominent men of the city. But the more elderly of these who were busied with politics, and therefore had no leisure, needed the discourses of Pythagoras dissociated from reasonings, as they would have found it difficult to follow his meanings through disciplines and demonstrations, while nevertheless Pythagoras realized that they would be benefited by knowing what ought to be done, even though lacking the underlying reason, just as physicians' patients obtain their health without hearing the reasons of every detail of the treatment. But Pythagoras conversed through disciplines and demonstrations with the younger associates, who were able both to act and learn. Such then are the differing explanations of the Hearers and Students.

As to Hippasus, however, they acknowledge that he was one of the Pythagoreans, but that he met the doom of the impious in the sea in consequence of having divulged and explained the method of forming a sphere from twelve pentagons; but nevertheless he [unjustly] obtained the renown of having made the discovery. In reality, however, this, just as everything else pertaining to geometry, was the invention of *that man*, as they referred to Pythagoras. But the Pythagoreans say that geometry was divulged under the following circumstance: A certain Pythagorean happened to lose his fortune, to recoup which he was permitted to teach that science which, by Pythagoras, was called *historia* [or inquiry].

So much then concerning the difference of each mode of philosophizing, and the classes of Pythagoras' disciples. For those who heard him either within or without the veil, and those who heard him accompanied with seeing, or without seeing him, and who are classified as internal of external auditors, were none other than these. Under these can be classified the Political, Economic, and

Legislative Pythagoreans.

19. *Abaris the Hyperborean*

GENERALLY, however, it should be known that Pythagoras discovered many paths of erudition, but that he communicated to each only that part of wisdom which was appropriate to the recipients' nature and power, of which the following is an appropriate striking illustration. When Abaris the Scythian came from the Hyperboreans, he was already of an advanced age, and unskilled and uninitiated in the Greek learning. Pythagoras did not compel him to wade through introductory theorems, the period of silence, and long lectures, not to mention other trials, but considered him to be fit as an immediate listener to his doctrines, and instructed him in the shortest way, in his treatise *On Nature,* and one *On the Gods.*

This Hyperborean Abaris was elderly, and most wise in sacred concerns, being a priest of the Apollo there worshipped. At that time he was returning from Greece to his country, in order to consecrate the gold which he had collected to the God in his temple among the Hyperboreans. As therefore he was passing through Italy, he saw Pythagoras, and identified him as the God of whom he was the priest.

Believing that Pythagoras resembled no man, but was none other than the God himself, Apollo, both from the venerable indications he saw around him, and from those the priest already knew, he paid him homage by giving him a sacred dart. This dart he had taken with him when he had left his temple, as an implement that would stand him in good stead in the difficulties that might befall him in so long a journey: for in passing through inaccessible places, such as rivers, lakes, marshes, mountains, and the like, it carried him, and by it he was said to have performed lustrations and expelled winds and pestilences from the cities that requested him to liberate them from such evils. For instance, it was said that Lacedaemon, after having been by him purified, was no longer infected with pestilence, which formerly had been endemic, through the noxious nature of the ground, in the suffocating heat produced by the overhanging mountain Taygetus, just as happens with Cnossus in Crete. Many other similar circumstances were reported of Abaris.

Pythagoras, however, accepted the dart, without expressing any amazement at the novelty of the thing, nor asking why the dart was presented to him, as if he really was a God. Then he took Abaris aside, and showed him his golden thigh, as an indication that he was not wholly mistaken [in his estimate of his real nature]. Then Pythagoras described to him several details of his distant Hyperborean temple, as proof of deserving being considered divine. Pythagoras also added that he came [into the regions of mortality] to remedy and improve the condition of the human race, having assumed human form lest men, disturbed by the novelty of his transcendency should avoid the discipline he advised. He advised Abaris to stay with him, to aid him in correcting [the manners and morals] of those they might meet, and to share the common resources of himself and his associates, whose reason led them to practice the precept that the possessions of friends are common.

So Abaris stayed with him, and was compendiously taught physiology and theology; and instead of divining by the entrails of beasts, he revealed to him the art of prognosticating by numbers, conceiving this to be a method purer, more divine, and more kindred to the celestial numbers of the Gods. Also he taught Abaris other studies for which he was fit.

Returning, however, to the purpose of the present treatise, Pythagoras endeavored to correct and amend different persons according to their individual abilities. Unfortunately most of these particulars have neither been publicly transmitted, nor is it easy to describe that which has been transmitted to us concerning him.

20. *Psychological Requirements*

WE MUST NOW set forth a few of the most celebrated points of the Pythagoric discipline and landmarks of their distinctive studies.

When Pythagoras tested a novice, he considered the latter's ability to hold his counsel, *echemuthein* being his technical term for this, referring to whether they could reserve and preserve what they had heard and learned. Next, he examined their modesty, for he was much more anxious that they should be silent than that they should speak. Further, he tested every other quality—for instance, whether they were astonished by the energies of any immoderate desire or passion. His examination of how they were affected by desire or anger, their contentiousness or ambition, their inclination to friendship or discord, was by no means superficial. If then after an accurate survey these novices were approved as of worthy manners, he then directed his attention to their facility in learning and their memory. He examined their ability to follow what was said, with rapidity and perspicuity; and then, whether they were impelled to the disciplines taught them by temperance and love. For he laid stress on natural gentleness, and this he called culture. Ferocity he considered hostile to such a kind of education. For savage manners are attended by impudence, shamelessness, intemperance, sloth, stupidity, licentiousness, disgrace, and the like, while the opposite attends mildness and gentleness.

These things then he considered in making trial of those that came to him, and in these the Learners were exercised. Those that were adapted to receive the goods of the wisdom he possessed, he admitted to discipleship, endeavoring to elevate them to scientific knowledge; but if he perceived that any novice was unadapted to them, he expelled him as a stranger and a barbarian.

21. *The Daily Program*

THE STUDIES which he delivered to his associates were as follows, for those who committed themselves to the guidance of his doctrine acted thus.

They took solitary morning walks to places which happened to be appropriately quiet, to temples or groves, or other suitable places. They thought it inadvisable to converse with any one until they had gained inner serenity, focusing their reasoning powers. They considered it turbulent to mingle in a crowd as soon as they rose from bed, and that is the reason why these Pythagoreans always selected the most sacred spots to walk.

After their morning walk they associated with each other, especially in temples, or, if this was not possible, in similar places. This time was employed in the discussion of disciplines and doctrines, and in the correction of manners.

After an association so holy they turned their attention to the health of the body. Most of them were rubbed down and raced; fewer wrestled, in gardens or groves; others exercised in leaping with leaden weights on their hands, or in oratorical gesticulations, with a view to the strengthening of the body, studiously selecting for this purpose alternating exercises.

They lunched on bread and honey, or on the honey-comb, avoiding wine. Afterwards, they held receptions to guests and strangers, conformably to the mandates of the laws, which receptions were restricted to this time of day.

In the afternoon they once more betook themselves to walking, yet not alone, as in the morning walk, but in parties of two or three, rehearsing the disciplines they had learned, and exercising themselves in attractive studies.

After the walk, they patronized the bath; and after ablutions they gathered in the common dining room, which accommodated no more than a group of ten. Then were performed libations and sacrifices, with fumigations and incense. Then followed supper, which closed before the setting of the sun. They ate herbs, raw and boiled, maize, wine, and every food that is eaten with bread. Of any animals lawful to immolate, they ate the flesh; but they rarely partook of fish, which was not useful to them, for certain causes. Animals not naturally noxious were neither to be injured, nor slain. This supper was followed by libations, succeeded by readings. The youngest read what the eldest advised, and as they suggested.

When they were about to depart, the cupbearer poured out a libation for them, after which the eldest would announce precepts, like the following: that a mild and fruitful plant should neither be injured nor corrupted, nor should any harmless animal. It was further enjoined that we should speak piously, forming suitable conceptions of divine, tutelary and heroic beings, and similarly, of parents and benefactors; and that we should aid, and not obstruct the enforcement of laws. Whereafter, all separated to go home.

They wore a white garment that was pure. They also lay on white and pure beds, the coverlets of which were made of linen, not wool. They did not hunt, nor undertake any similar exercise. Such were the precepts delivered daily to the disciples of Pythagoras, in respect to eating and living.

22. On Pythagorean Friendship

TRADITION tells of another kind of teaching, by Pythagorean maxims pertaining to human opinions and practices, some examples of which may here be mentioned. It is advised to remove strife from true friendship. If possible, this should apply to all friendship; but at all events to that towards parents, elders, and benefactors. Existing friendships with such as these would not be preserved [but destroyed] by rivalry, contention, anger, and subsequent graver passions. The scars and ulcers which their advice sometimes cause should be minimized as much as possible, which will be effected if especially the younger of the two should learn how to yield, and subdue his angry emotions. On the other hand, the so-called *paedartases*, or corrections and admonitions of the elder towards the younger, should be made with much suavity of manners, and great caution; also with much solicitude and tact, which makes the reproof all the more graceful and useful.

Faith should never be separated from friendship, whether seriously or in jest. Existing friendship cannot survive the insinuation of deceit between professors of friendship.

Nor should friendship be affected by misfortune or other human vicissitude, and the only rejection of friendship which is commendable is that which follows definite and incurable vice.

Such is an example of the Pythagorean exhortatory maxims, which extended to all the virtues, and to the whole of life.

23. The Use of Symbols in Instruction

PYTHAGORAS considered most necessary the use of symbols in instruction. Most of the Greeks had adopted it, as the most ancient, and it had been both preferentially and in principle employed by the Egyptians, who had developed it in the most varied manner. In harmony with this it will be found that Pythagoras attended to it sedulously, if from the Pythagoric symbols we unfold their significance and arcane intentions, developing their content of rectitude and truth, liberating them from their enigmatic form. When, according to straightforward and uniform tradition, they are accommodated to the sublime intelligence of these philosophers, they deify beyond human conception.

Those who came from this school, not only the most ancient Pythagoreans, but also those who during his old age were still young, such as Philolaus, and Eurytus, Charondas and Zaleucus, Brysson and the elder Archytas, Aristaeus, Lysis and Empedocles, Zalmoxis and Epimenides, Milo and Leucippus, Alcmaeon and Hippasus, and Thymaridas were all of that age, a multitude of savants, incomparably excellent—all these adopted this mode of teaching, both in their conversations, commentaries and annotations. Their writings also, and all the books which they published, most of which have been preserved to our times, were not composed in popular or vulgar diction, or in a manner usual to all other writers, so as to be immediately understood, but in a way not to be easily apprehended by their readers. For they adopted Pythagoras' law of reserve, in an arcane manner concealing divine mysteries from the uninitiated, obscuring their writings and mutual conversations.

The result is that they who present these symbols without unfolding their meaning by a suitable exposition, run the danger of exposing them to the charge of being ridiculous and inane, trifling and garrulous. When, however, the meanings are expounded according to these symbols, and made clear and obvious even to the crowds, then they will be found analogous to prophetic sayings, such as the oracles of the Pythian Apollo. Their admirable meaning will inspire those who unite intellect and scholarliness.

It might be well to mention a few of them in order to explain this mode of discipline: Do not negligently enter into a temple, nor adore carelessly, even if only at the doors. Sacrifice and adore unshod. Shunning public roads, walk in unfrequented paths. Do not without light speak about Pythagoric affairs.

Such is a sketch of the symbolic mode of teaching adopted by Pythagoras.

24. Dietary Suggestions

SINCE FOOD, used properly and regularly, greatly contributes to the best discipline, it may be interesting to consider Pythagoras' precepts on the subject. Forbidden was generally all food causing flatulence or indigestion, while he recommended the contrary kinds of food that preserve and are astringent. Wherefore he recommended the nutritious qualities of millet. Rejected was all food foreign to the Gods, as withdrawing us from communion with them. On the other hand, he forbade to his disciples all food that was sacred, as too honorable to subserve common utility. He exhorted his disciples to abstain from such things as are an impediment to prophecy, or to the purity and chastity of the soul, or to the habit of temperance, and virtue. Lastly, he rejected all things that are an impediment to sanctity, and disturb or obscure the other purities of the soul, and the phantasms which occur in sleep. Such were the general regulations about food.

Specially, however, the most contemplative of the philosophers, who had arrived at the summit of philosophic attainments, were forbidden superfluous food such as wine, or unjustifiable food, such as was animated, and not to sacrifice animals to the Gods, nor by any means to injure animals, but to observe most solicitous justice towards them. He himself lived after this manner, abstaining from animal food, and adoring altars undefiled with blood. He was likewise careful to prevent others from destroying animals of a nature kindred to ours, and rather corrected and instructed savage animals, than injuring them as punishment. Further, he ordered abstaining from animal food even to politicians; for as they desired to act justly to the highest degree, they must certainly not injure any kindred animals. How indeed could they persuade others to act justly, if they themselves were detected in an insatiable avidity in devouring animals allied to us? These are conjoined to us by a fraternal alliance through the communion of life, and the same elements, and the co-mingling of these. Eating of the flesh of certain animals was, however, permitted to those whose lives were not entirely purified, philosophic and sacred; but even for these was appointed a definite time of abstinence. Besides, these were not to eat the heart, nor the brain, which were entirely forbidden to all Pythagoreans. For these organs are predominant, and are as it were ladders and seats of wisdom and life.

Food other than animal was by him also considered sacred, due to the nature of divine reason. Thus his disciples were to abstain from mallows, because this plant is the first messenger and signal of the sympathy of celestial with terrestrial gods. Moreover, the fish *melanurus* was interdicted because it was sacred to the terrestrial Gods. Likewise, the *erythinus*. Beans also were interdicted, due to many causes, physical, psychic and sacred.

Many other similar precepts were enjoined, in the attempt to lead men to virtue through their food.

25. Music and Poetry

PYTHAGORAS was likewise of the opinion that music, if properly used, greatly contributed to health. For he was wont to use it in no careless way, but as a *purification*. Indeed, he restricted this word to signify music used as medicine.

About the vernal season he used a melody in this manner. In the middle was placed a person who played on the lyre, and seated around him in a circle were those able to sing. Then the lyrist in the center struck up, and the singers raised certain paeans, through which they were evidently so overjoyed that their manners became elegant and orderly. This music instead of medicines was also used at certain other times.

Certain melodies were devised as remedies against the passions of the soul, as also against despondency and lamentation, which were invented by Pythagoras specifically for this. Further, he employed other melodies against anger and rage, and all other aberrations of the soul. Another kind of modulation was invented against desires. He likewise used dancing, which was accompanied by the lyre, instead of the pipe, which he conceived to have an influence towards insolence, being theatrical, and by no means liberal. For the purpose of correcting the soul, he also used select verses of Homer and Hesiod.

It is related among the deeds of Pythagoras that once, through a spondaic song, he extinguished the rage of a Tauromenian lad who, after feasting by night, intended to burn the vestibule of the house of his mistress, on seeing her issuing from the house of a rival. [To this rash attempt] the lad had been inflamed by a Phrygian song, which however Pythagoras at once suppressed. As Pythagoras was astronomizing he happened to meet this Phrygian piper at an unseasonable time of night, and persuaded him to change his Phrygian song for a spondaic one. Through this the fury of the lad was immediately repressed, and he returned home in an orderly manner, although but a little while before he had stupidly insulted Pythagoras on meeting him, and would bear no admonition, and could not be restrained.

Here is another instance. Anchitus, the host of Empedocles, had, as judge, condemned to death the father of a youth, who rushed on Anchitus with drawn sword, intending to slay him. Empedocles changed the youth's intention by singing, to his lyre, that verse of Homer (*Odyssey*, 4):

> Nepenthe, without gall, o'er every ill
> Oblivion spreads,—

thus saving his host Anchitus from death, and the youth from committing murder. It is said that from that time on the youth became one of the most faithful disciples of Pythagoras.

The Pythagoreans distinguished three states of mind, called *exartysis*, or readiness; *synarmoge,* or fitness, and *epaphe,* or contact, which converted souls to contrary passions, and these could be produced by certain appropriate songs.

When they retired, they purified their reasoning powers from the noises and perturbations to which they had been exposed during the day, by certain odes and hymns which produced tranquil sleep, and few, but good dreams. But when they arose from slumbers, they again liberated themselves from the dazedness and torpor of sleep by songs of another kind. Sometimes the passions of the soul and certain diseases were, as they said, genuinely lured by enchantments, by musical sounds alone, without words. This is indeed probably the origin of the general use of this word *epode* or enchantment.

Thus through music Pythagoras produced the most beneficial correction of manners and lives.

26. Theoretical Music*

WHILE DESCRIBING PYTHAGORAS' WISDOM in instructing his disciples, we must not fail to note that he discovered the harmonic science and ratios. But to explain this we must go a little backwards in time. Once as he was intently considering music, and reasoning with himself whether it would be possible to devise some instrumental assistance to the sense of hearing, so as to systematize it, as sight is made precise by the compass, rule, and telescope, or touch is made reckonable by balance and measures—so thinking of these things Pythagoras happened to pass by a brazier's shop where he heard the hammers beating out a piece of iron on anvil, producing sounds that harmonized, except one. But he recognized in these sounds the concord of the octave, the fifth, and the fourth. He saw that the sound between the fourth and the fifth, taken by itself, was a dissonance, and yet completed the greater sound among them.

Delighted, therefore, to find that the thing he was anxious to discover had by divine assistance succeeded, he went into the smithy, and by various experiments discovered that the difference of sound arose from the magnitude of the hammers, but not from the force of the strokes, nor from the shape of the hammers, nor from the change of position of the beaten iron. Having then accurately examined the weights and the swing of the hammers, he returned home, and fixed one stake diagonally to the walls, lest some difference should arise from there being several of them, or from some difference in the material of the stakes.

From this stake he then suspended four gut-strings, of similar materials, size, thickness, and twist. A weight was suspended from the bottom of each. When the strings were equal in length, he struck two of them simultaneously, he reproduced the former intervals, forming different pairs. He discovered that the string stretched by the greatest weight, when compared with that stretched by the smallest weight, had the interval of an octave. The weight of the first was twelve pounds, and that of the latter, six. Being therefore in a double ratio, it formed the octave, which was made plain by the weights themselves. Then he found that the string from which the greatest weight was suspended compared with that from which was suspended the weight next to the smallest, and which weight was eight pounds, produced the interval known as the fifth. Hence he discovered that this interval is in a ratio of one and a half to one, or three to two, in which ratio the weights also were to each other. Then he found that the string stretched by the greatest weight produced, when compared with that which was next to it, in weight, namely, nine pounds, the interval called the fourth, analogous to the weights. This ratio, therefore, he discovered to be in the ratio of one and a third to one, or four to three; while that of the string from which a weight of nine pounds was suspended, to the string which had the smallest weight,

---

*This chapter is based on the account given in Nichomachus' *Manual of Harmonics*. While the ratios given do indeed correspond to the musical intervals described, the method of obtaining them here related, using weights, is spurious. See Levin, *The Harmonics of Nichomachus and the Pythagorean Tradition,* chapter 6, for a discussion of this account.

was again in a ratio of three to two, which is 9 to 6. In like manner, the string next to that from which the smallest weight was suspended, was to that which had the smallest weight, in the ratio of 4 to 3 (being 8 to 6), but to the string which had the greatest weight, in a ratio of 3 to 2, being 12 to 8. Hence that which is between the fifth and the fourth, and by which the fifth exceeds the fourth, is proved to be as nine is to eight. But either way it may be proved that the octave is a system consisting of the fifth in conjunction with the fourth, just as the double ratio consists of three to two, and four to three; as for instance 12, 8, and 6; or, conversely, of the fourth and the fifth, as in the double ratio of four to three and three to two, as for instance, 12, 9, and 6.

Thus therefore, and in this order, having conformed both his hand and hearing to the suspended weights, and having established according to them the ratio of the proportions, by an easy artifice he transferred the common suspension of the strings from the diagonal stake to the head of instrument which he called *chordotonon* or string-stretcher. Then by the aid of pegs he produced a tension of the strings analogous to that effected by the weights.

Employing this method, therefore, as a basis, and as it were an infallible rule, he afterwards extended the experiment to other instruments, namely, the striking of pans, to pipes and to monochords, triangles, and the like, in all of which he found the same ratio of numbers to obtain. Then he named the sound which participates in the number 6, tonic; that which participates in the number 8, and is four to three, subdominant; that which participates in the number 9, and is one tone higher than the subdominant, he called dominant, and 9 to 8; but that which participates of the number 12, octave.

Then he filled up the middle spaces with analogous sounds in diatonic order, and formed an octochord from symmetric numbers: from the double, the three to two, the four to three, and from the difference of these, the 8 to 9. Thus he discovered the harmonic progression, which tends by a certain physical necessity from the lowest to the most acute sound, diatonically.

Later, from the diatonic he progressed to the chromatic and enharmonic orders, as we shall later show when we treat of music. This diatonic scale, however, seems to have the following progression: a semi-tone, a tone, and a tone; and this is the fourth, being a system consisting of two tones, and of what is called a semi-tone. Afterwards, adding another tone, we produce the fifth, which is a system consisting of three tones and a semi-tone. Next to this is the system of a semi-tone, a tone, and a tone, forming another fourth, that is, another four to three ratio. Thus in the more ancient octave indeed, all the sounds from the lowest pitch which are with respect to each other fourths, produce everywhere with each other fourths; the semi-tone, by transition, receives the first, middle and third place, according to that tetrachord. Now in the Pythagoric octave, however, which by conjunction is a system of the tetrachord and pentachord, but if disjoined is a system of two tetrachords separated from each other, the progression is from the gravest to the most acute sound. Hence all sounds that by their distance from each other are fifths, with each other produce the interval of the fifth. The semitone successively proceeds into four places, the first, second, third, and fourth. This is the way in which music was said to have been discovered by Pythagoras.

Having reduced it to a system, he delivered it to his disciples as being subservient to everything that is most beautiful.

27. *Mutual Political Assistance*

MANY DEEDS OF THE PYTHAGOREANS in the political sphere are deservedly praised. At one time the Crotonians were in the habit of making funerals and internments too sumptuous. Thereupon one of them said to the people that once he had heard Pythagoras converse about divine natures, during which he had observed that the Olympian divinities attended to the dispositions of the sacrificers, and not to the multitude of the offerings. The terrestrial Gods, on the contrary, as being interested in less important matters, rejoiced in lamentations and banquets, libations, delicacies, and luxurious expense; and as proof thereof, the divinity of Hades is called Pluto (*plutos* = wealth), from his wish to receive. Those that honor him slenderly [he does not much care for], and permits to stay quite a little while in the upper world; but he hastens to draw down those disposed to spend profusely on funeral solemnities, that he may obtain the honors offered in commemoration of the dead. The result was that the Crotonians who heard this advice were persuaded that if they conducted themselves moderately in misfortunes, they would be promoting their own salvation, but would die prematurely if immoderate in such expenses.

A certain difference arose about an affair in which there was no witness. Pythagoras was made arbitrator, and he led both litigants to a certain monument, announcing that the man buried was exceedingly equitable. The one prayed that he might receive much reward for his good life, while the other declared that the defunct was no better off for his opponent's prayers. Pythagoras condemned the latter, confirming that he who praised the dead man for his worth had earned credibility.

At another time, in a case of great moment, he decided that one of the two who had agreed to settle the affair by arbitration, should pay four talents, but that the other should receive two. Afterwards, he condemned the defendant to pay three talents, and thus he appeared to have given a talent to each of them.*

Two persons had fraudulently deposited a garment with a woman who belonged to a court of justice, and told her that she was not to give it to either of them unless both were present. Later, with intent to defraud, one claimed and got the common deposit, saying he had the consent of the other party. The other one turned informer and related the compact made at the beginning to the magistrates. A certain Pythagorean, however, as arbitrator, decided that the woman was guiltless, construing the claimed assent as constructive presence.

Two other persons, who had seemed to be great friends, had gotten to suspect each other through calumnies of a flatterer, who told one that the other had taken undue liberties with his wife. A Pythagorean, however, happened to enter the smithy where the injured party was finding fault with the blacksmith for not having sufficiently sharpened a sword he had brought him for that purpose. The Pythagorean suspecting the use to which the sword was to be put said, ''The sword

*The text here is confused.

is sharper than all things except calumny.'' This caused the prospective avenger to consider that he should not rashly sin against a friend who was within an invitation.

A stranger in the temple of Asklepius accidentally dropped his belt, on which were gold ornaments. When he tried to pick it up, he was informed that the temple regulations forbade picking up anything on the floor. He was indignant, and a Pythagorean advised him to remove the golden ornaments which were not touching the floor, leaving the belt which was.

During a public spectacle, some cranes flew over the theatre. One sailor said to his companion, "Do you see the witnesses?" A Pythagorean nearby summoned the sailors into a court presided over by a thousand magistrates where, being examined, they confessed to having thrown certain boys into the sea, who on drowning had called on the cranes, flying above them, to witness the deed. This story is mistakenly located elsewhere, but it really happened at Croton.

Certain recent disciples of Pythagoras were at variance with each other, and the junior came to the senior, declaring there was no reason to refer the matter to an arbitrator, inasmuch as all they needed to do was to dismiss their anger. The elder agreed, but regretted he had not been the first to make that proposition.

We might relate here the story of Damon and Phintias, of Plato and Archytas, and of Clinias and Prorus.* At present, however, we shall limit ourselves to that of Eubulus the Messenian, who, when sailing homeward, was taken captive by the Tyrrhenians, where he was recognized by a Pythagorean named Nausithus, who redeemed him from the pirates, and sent him home in safety.

When the Carthaginians were about to send five thousand soldiers into a desert island, the Carthaginian Miltiades saw among them the Argive Possiden, [both of whom were Pythagoreans]. Approaching him, and without revealing his intentions, he advised him to return home with all possible haste. He placed him in a ship then sailing near the shore, supplied him with the travel necessities, and thus saved him from the impending danger.

He who would try to relate all the fine deeds that beautified the mutual relations of the Pythagoreans would find the task exceeding space and patience. I shall therefore pass on to show that some of the Pythagoreans were competent administrators, adapted to rule. Many were custodians of the laws, and ruled over certain Italian cities, unfolding to them and advising them to adopt the most salutary measures, while themselves refusing all pay. Though greatly calumniated, their probity and the desire of the citizens prevailed to make them administrators. At this time the best governed states seem to have been in Italy and Sicily. One of the best legislators, Charondas the Catanean, was a Pythagorean, and so were the celebrated Locrian legislators Zaleucus and Timares. Pythagoreans also established those Rheginic polities, called the Gymnasiarchic, named after Theocles. Excelling in studies and manners which were then adopted by their fellow-citizens, were Phytius, Theocles, Elecaon, and Aristocrates. Indeed, it is said that Pythagoras was the originator of all political erudition, when he said that nothing existent is pure, inasmuch as earth participates of fire, fire of air,

*The accounts about Damon and Phintias, Clinias and Prorus, are related by Iamblichus in chapter 33.

and air of water, and water of spirit. Likewise the beautiful participates in the deformed, the just of the unjust, and so on; so that from this principle human impulse may (by proper direction) be turned in either direction. He also said that there were two motions: one of the body, which is irrational, and one of the soul, which is the result of deliberate choice. He also said polities might be likened to three lines whose extremities join, forming a right angle, the lines being 4, 3, 2; so that one of them is as 4 to 3, another as 3 to 2, and the other [3] is the arithmetical medium between 2 and 4. Now when, by reasoning we study the mutual relations of these lines, and the places under them, we shall find that they represent the best image of a polity. Plato plagiarized, for in his *Republic* he clearly says, "That the result of the 4 to 3 ratio, conjoined with the 5 ratio, produces two harmonies." [This means that] he cultivated the moderation of the passions, and the middle path between extremes, rendering happy the life of his disciples by relating them to ideals of the good.

We are also told that he persuaded the Crotonians to give up associations with courtesans and prostitutes. Crotonian wives came to the wife of the Pythagorean Brontinus, who was a wise and splendid woman, the author of the maxim that "It is proper for women to sacrifice on the same day they have risen from the embraces of their husbands"—which some ascribe to Pythagoras' wife Theano— and entreated her to persuade Pythagoras to discourse to them on their continence as due to their husbands. This she did, and Pythagoras accordingly made an address to the Crotonians, which successfully ended the then prevalent incontinence.

When ambassadors came from Sybaris to Croton to demand the return of the exiles, Pythagoras, seeing one of the ambassadors who with his own hand had slain one of Pythagoras' friends, made no answer whatever. But when this man insisted on an explanation, and addressed Pythagoras, the latter said it was unlawful to converse with murderers. This induced many to believe he was Apollo.

All these stories, together with what we mentioned above about the destruction of tyrants, and the democratization of the cities of Italy and Sicily, and many other circumstances, are eloquent of the benefits conferred on mankind by Pythagoras in political respects.

28. Divinity of Pythagoras

HENCEFORWARD we shall confine ourselves to the works flowing from Pythagoras' virtues. As usual, we shall begin from the divinities, endeavoring to exhibit his piety, and marvelous deeds. Of his piety, let this be a specimen: that he knew what his soul was, whence it came into the body, and also its former lives, of this giving the most evident indications. Again, once passing over the river Nessus along with many associates, he addressed the river, which, in a distinct and clear voice, in the hearing of all his associates, answered, "Hail, Pythagoras!"

Further, all his biographers insist that during the same day he was present in Metapontum in Italy, and at Tauromenium in Sicily, discoursing with his disciples in both places, although these cities are separated, both by land and sea by many stadia, the travelling over which consumes many days.

It is also a matter of common report that he showed his golden thigh to the

Hyperborean Abaris, who said that he resembled the Apollo worshipped among the Hyperboreans, of whom Abaris was the priest; and that he had done this so that Abaris might be certified thereof, and that he was not deceived therein.

Many other more admirable and divine particulars are likewise unanimously and uniformly related of *the man*, such as infallible predictions of earthquakes, rapid expulsions of pestilences, and hurricanes, instantaneous cessations of hail, and tranquilizations of the waves of rivers and seas, in order that his disciples might the more easily pass over them. The power of effecting miracles of this kind was achieved by Empedocles of Agrigentum, Epimenides the Cretan, and Abaris the Hyperborean, and these they performed in many places. Their deeds were so manifest that Empedocles was surnamed a *wind-stiller*, Epimenides an *expiator*, and Abaris an *air-walker*, because, carried on the dart given him by the Hyperborean Apollo, he passed over rivers, and seas and inaccessible places like one carried on air. Many think that Pythagoras did the same thing, when in the same day he discoursed with his disciples at Metapontum and Tauromenium. It is also said that he predicted there would be an earthquake from the water of a well which he had tasted; and that a ship sailing with a prosperous wind would be submerged in the sea. These are sufficient proofs of his piety.

Pitching my thoughts on a higher key, I wish to exhibit the principle of the worship of the Gods, established by Pythagoras and his disciples, that the mark aimed at by all plans, with respect to undertaking or not undertaking something, is consent with the divinity. The principle of their piety, and indeed their whole life is arranged with a view to follow God. Their philosophy explicitly asserts that men act ridiculously in searching for good from any source other than God; and that in this respect the conduct of most men resembles that of a man who, in a country governed by a king, should reverence one of the city magistrates, neglecting him who is the ruler of all of them. Since God exists as the lord of all things, it is evident and acknowledged that good must be requested of him. All men impart good to those they love, and admire, and the contrary to those they dislike. Evidently we should do those things in which God delights. Not easy, however, is it for a man to know which these are, unless he obtains this knowledge from one who has heard God, or has heard God himself, or procures it through divine art. Hence also, the Pythagoreans were studious of divination, which is an interpretation of the benevolence of the Gods. That such an employment is worthwhile will be admitted by one who believes in the Gods; but he who thinks that either of these is folly will also believe that both are foolish. Many of the precepts of the Pythagoreans were derived from the Mysteries, which were not the fruits of arrogance, in their estimation, but were derived from divinity.

Indeed, Pythagoreans give full belief to mythological stories such as are related of Aristeas the Proconesian, and Abaris the Hyperborean, and such like. To them every such thing seems credible, and worthy of being tried out. They also frequently recollect apparently fabulous particulars, not disbelieving anything which may be referred to the divinity. For instance, it is said that the Pythagorean Eurytus, a disciple of Philolaus, related that a shepherd feeding his flock near Philolaus' tomb heard someone singing. His interlocutor, instead of disbelieving the story, asked what kind of harmony it was. Again, a certain person told Pythagoras that

he once seemed to be conversing with his deceased father, in his dreams, and
asked Pythagoras what this might signify. The answer was "Nothing," even
though the conversation with his father was genuine. "As therefore," said he,
"nothing is signified by my conversing with you, neither is anything signified
by your conversing with your father."

In all these matters they considered that the stupidity lay with the sceptics, rather
than with themselves; for they did not conceive that some things, and not others,
are possible with the Gods, as fancy the Sophists; they thought that with the Gods
all things are possible. This very assertion is the beginning of some verses attributed to Linus:

> All things may be the objects of our hopes,
> Since nothing hopeless anywhere is found;
> All things with ease Divinity effects,
> And naught can frustrate his almighty power.

They thought that their opinions deserved to be believed, because he who first
promulgated them was not some chance person, but a divinity. This indeed was
one of their pet puzzlers: "What was Pythagoras?" For they say he was the Hyperborean Apollo, of which this was an indication: that rising up, while at the Olympian games, he showed his golden thigh; and also that he received the Hyperborean Abaris as his guest, and was presented by him with the dart on which
he rode through the air. But it is said that this Abaris came from the Hyperborean
regions to collect gold for his temple, and that he predicted a pestilence. He also
dwelt in temples, and was never seen to eat or drink. It is likewise said that rites
[of his] are performed by the Lacedaemonians, and that on this account
Lacedaemon is never infested with pestilence. Pythagoras therefore caused this
Abaris to acknowledge [that he was more than man], receiving from him at the
same time the golden dart, without which it was not possible for him to find his
way. In Metapontum also, certain persons praying that they might obtain what
a ship contained that was sailing into port, Pythagoras said to them, "You will
then have a dead body." In Sybaris, too, he caught a deadly serpent and drove
it away. In Tyrrhenia also he caught a small serpent, whose bite was fatal. In
Croton it is said that a white eagle allowed Pythagoras to stroke it. When a certain person wished to hear him converse, Pythagoras said it was impossible until
some sign appeared. Later a white bear was seen in Cauconia, whose death he
declared to a person who came to announce to him its death. He likewise reminded
Myllias the Crotonian that he had formerly lived as Midas the son of Gordius,
and Myllias journeyed to Asia to perform at the sepulchre of Midas such rites
as Pythagoras had commanded him. The person who purchased Pythagoras'
residence dug up what had been buried in it, but did not dare to tell anyone what
he saw [on this occasion]. Although he did not suffer [any divine vengeance] for
this offence, he was seized and executed for the sacrilege of taking a golden beard
that had fallen from a statue. The fact that these stories and other such are related
by the Pythagoreans lend authority to their opinions. As their veracity is generally acknowledged, and as they could not possibly have happened to a mere man,
they consequently think it is clear that the stories about Pythagoras should be

received as referring not to a mere man, but to a super-man. This also is what is meant by their maxim that *man, bird, and another thing are bipeds,* thereby referring to Pythagoras. Such, therefore, on account of his piety, was Pythagoras, and such he was truly thought to be.

Oaths were religiously observed by the Pythagoreans, who were mindful of that precept of theirs,

> As duly by law, thy homage pay first to the immortal Gods;
> Then to thy oath, and last to the heroes illustrious.

For instance, a certain Pythagorean was in court and asked to take an oath. Rather than to disobey this principle, although the oath would have been a religiously permitted one, he preferred to pay to the defendant a fine of three talents.

Pythagoras taught that no occurrence happened by chance or luck, but rather conformably to divine Providence, and especially so to good and pious men. This is well illustrated by a story from Androcydes' treatise *On Pythagoric Symbols,* about the Tarentine Pythagorean Thymaridas. For when he was sailing away from his country, his friends were all present to embrace him and bid him farewell. He had already embarked when someone cried to him, ''O Thymaridas, I pray that the Gods may shape all your circumstances according to your wishes!'' But he retorted, ''Predict me better things; namely, that what may happen to me may be conformable to the will of the Gods!'' For he thought it more scientific and prudent to not resist or grumble against divine providence.

If asked about the source whence these men derived so much piety, we must acknowledge that the Pythagorean number theology was clearly foreshadowed, to some extent, in the Orphic writings. Nor is it to be doubted that when Pythagoras composed his treatise *Concerning the Gods,* he received assistance from Orpheus, on which account also he called it *The Sacred Discourse,* because it contains the flower of the most mystical place in Orpheus. [It is uncertain] whether this work was in reality written by Pythagoras, as by most authors it is said to have been, or as some of the Pythagorean school assert, was composed by Telauges, being taken by him from the commentaries which were left by Pythagoras himself to his daughter Damo, the sister of Telauges, and which it is said after her death were given to Bitale the daughter of Damo, and to Telauges the son of Pythagoras, and also to the husband of Bitale, when he was of a mature age. For when Pythagoras died, Telauges was left very young with his mother Theano. In this *Sacred Discourse* also, or treatise *Concerning the Gods* (for it has both these inscriptions), who it was that delivered to Pythagoras what is there said concerning the Gods is rendered manifest. For we read:

> Pythagoras, the son of Mnesarchus, was instructed in what pertains to the Gods when he celebrated rites in the Thracian Libethra, being therein initiated by Aglaophemus; and that Orpheus, the son of Calliope, having learned wisdom from his mother in the mountain Pangaeus, said that the eternal essence of Number is the most providential principle of the universe, of heaven and earth, and of the intermediate nature; and further still, that it is the root of the permanency of divine natures, of Gods, and daimons.

From this it is evident that he learned from the Orphic writers that the essence of the Gods is defined by Number. Through the same numbers also, he produced a wonderful prognostication and worship of the Gods, both of which are particularly allied to numbers.

As conviction is best produced by an objective fact, the above principle may be proved as follows. When Abaris performed sacred rites according to his customs, he procured a foreknowledge of events, which is studiously cultivated by all the Barbarians, by sacrificing animals, especially birds; for they think that the entrails of such animals are particularly adapted to this purpose. Pythagoras, however, not wishing to suppress his ardent pursuit of the truth, but to guide it into a safer way, without blood and slaughter, and also because he thought that a cock was sacred to the sun, furnished him with a consummate knowledge of all truth, through arithmetical science. From piety, also, he derived faith concerning the Gods. For Pythagoras always insisted that nothing marvelous concerning Gods or divine teachings should be disbelieved, inasmuch as the Gods are competent to effect anything. But the divine teachings in which we must believe are those delivered by Pythagoras. The Pythagoreans therefore assumed and believed what they taught [on the *a priori* ground that] they were not the offspring of false opinion. Hence Eurytus the Crotonian, the disciple of Philolaus, said that a shepherd feeding his sheep near Philolaus' tomb had heard someone singing. But the person to whom this was related did not at all question this, merely asking what kind of harmony it was. Pythagoras himself also, being asked by a certain person the significance of a conversation with his defunct father in sleep, answered that it meant nothing. "For neither is anything portended by your speaking with me," said he.

Pythagoras wore clean white garments, and used clean white sheets, avoiding the woolen ones. This custom he enjoined on his disciples.

In speaking of superior natures, he used honorable appellations, and words of good omen, on every occasion mentioning and reverencing the Gods; so, while at supper, he performed libations to the divinities, and taught his disciples daily to celebrate the superior beings with hymns. He attended likewise to rumors and omens, prophecies and lots, and in short to all unexpected circumstances. Moreover, he sacrificed to the Gods with millet, cakes, honey-combs, and fumigations. But he did not sacrifice animals, nor did any of the contemplative philosophers. His other disciples, however, the Hearers and the Politicians, were by him ordered to sacrifice animals such as a cock, or a lamb, or some other young animal, but not frequently; but they were prohibited from sacrificing oxen.

Another indication of the honor he paid the Gods was his teaching that his disciples must never use the names of the divinities uselessly in swearing. For instance, Syllus, one of the Crotonian Pythagoreans, paid a fine rather than swear, though he could have done so without violating the truth. Just as the Pythagoreans abstained from using the names of the Gods, so also, through reverence, they were unwilling to name Pythagoras, indicating him whom they meant as the inventor of the Tetraktys. Such is the form of an oath ascribed to them:

I swear by the discoverer of the Tetraktys,
Which is the spring of all our wisdom,
The perennial root of Nature's fount.

In short, Pythagoras imitated the Orphic mode of writing, and [pious] disposition, and the way they honored the Gods, representing them in images and in brass not resembling our [human] form, but the divine receptacle [of the Sphere], because they comprehend and provide for all things, being of nature and form similar to the universe.

But his divine philosophy and worship was compound, having learned much from the Orphic followers, but much also from the Egyptian priests, the Chaldeans and Magi, the mysteries of Eleusis, Imbrus, Samothracia, and Delos, and even the Celtic and Iberian. It is also said that Pythagoras' *Sacred Discourse* is current among the Latins, not being read to or by all, but only by those who are disposed to learn the best things, avoiding all that is base.

He ordered that libations should be made thrice, observing that Apollo delivered oracles from the tripod, the triad being the first number. Sacrifices to Venus were to be made on the sixth day, because this number is the first to partake of every number, and when divided in every possible way, receives the power of the numbers subtracted, and those that remain. Sacrifices to Hercules, however, should be made on the eighth day of the month, counting from the beginning, commemorating his birth in the seventh month.

He ordained that those who entered into a temple should be clothed in a clean garment, in which no one had slept; because sleep, just as black and brown, indicates sluggishness, while cleanliness is a sign of equality and justice in reasoning.

If blood should be found unintentionally spilled in a temple, there should be made a lustration, either in a golden vessel, or with seawater, gold being the most beautiful of all things, and the measure of exchange of everything else, while the latter is derived from the principle of moistness, the food of the first and more common matter. Also, children should not be born in a temple, where the divine part of the soul should not be bound to the body. On a festal day neither should the hair be cut, nor the nails pared, as it is unworthy to disturb the worship of the Gods to attend to our own advantage. Nor should lice be killed in a temple, as divine power should not participate in anything superfluous or degrading.

The Gods should be honored with cedar, laurel, cypress, oak and myrtle; nor should the body be purified with these; nor should any of them be cut with the teeth.

He also ordered that what is boiled should not be roasted, signifying hereby that mildness has no need of anger.

The bodies of the dead he did not suffer to be burned, herein following the Magi, being unwilling that anything [so] divine [as fire] should be mingled with mortal nature. He thought it holy for the dead to be carried out in white garments, thereby obscurely prefiguring the simple and first nature, according to Number, and the principle of all things.

Above all, he ordained that an oath should be taken religiously, since that which is behind [i.e., the futurity of punishment] is long.

He said that it is much more holy to be injured than to kill a man, for judgment is pronounced in Hades, where the soul and its essence, and the first nature of things is correctly appraised.

He ordered that coffins should not be made of cypress, either because the sceptre of Zeus was made of this wood, or for some other mystic reason.

Libations were to be performed before the altar of Zeus the Savior, of Hercules, and the Dioscuri, thus celebrating Zeus as the presiding cause and leader of the meal, Hercules as the power of Nature, and the Dioscuri, as the symphony of all things. Libations should not be offered with closed eyes, as nothing beautiful should be undertaken with bashfulness and shame.

When it thundered, he said one ought to touch the earth, in remembrance of the generation of things.

Temples should be entered from places on the right hand, and exited from the left hand; for the right hand is the principle of what is called the odd number, and is divine; while the left hand is a symbol of the even number, and of dissolution.

Such are many of the injunctions he is said to have adopted in the pursuance of piety. Other particulars which have been omitted may be inferred from what has been given. Hence the subject may be closed.

29. Sciences and Maxims

THE PYTHAGOREANS' COMMENTARIES best express his wisdom, being accurate, concise, savoring of the ancient elegance of style, and deducing the conclusions exquisitely. They contain the most condensed conceptions, and are diversified in form and matter. They are both accurate and eloquent, full of clear and indubitable arguments, accompanied by scientific demonstration, in syllogistic form, as indeed will be discovered by any careful reader.

In his writings, Pythagoras, from a supernal source, delivers the science of intelligible natures and the Gods. Afterwards, he teaches the whole of physics, completely unfolding ethics and logic. Then come various disciplines and other excellent sciences. There is nothing pertaining to human knowledge which is not discussed in these encyclopedic writings. If therefore it is acknowledged that of the [Pythagorean] writings which are now in circulation, some were written by Pythagoras himself, while others consist of what he was heard to say, and on this account are anonymous, though of Pythagoric origin—if all this be so, it is evident that he was abundantly skilled in all wisdom.

It is said that while he was in Egypt he very much applied himself to geometry. For Egyptian life bristles with geometrical problems since, from remote periods, when the Gods were fabulously said to have reigned in Egypt, on account of the rising and falling of Nile, the skillful have been compelled to measure all the Egyptian land which they cultivated, wherefrom indeed the science's name, geometry (i.e., "earth measure"), was derived. Besides, the Egyptians studied the theories of the celestial orbs, in which Pythagoras also was skilled. All theorems about lines also seem to have been derived from that country.

All that relates to numbers and computation is said to have been discovered

in Phoenicia. The theorems about the heavenly bodies have by some been referred to the Egyptians and Chaldeans in common. Whatever Pythagoras received,
however, he developed further, he arranged them for learners, and personally
demonstrated them with perspicuity and elegance. He was the first to give a name
to philosophy, describing it as a desire for and love of wisdom, which later he
defined as the science of objectified truth. Beings he defined as immaterial and
eternal natures, alone possessing a power that is efficacious, as are incorporeal
essences. The rest of things are beings only figuratively, and considered such
only through the participation of real beings; such are corporeal and material
forms, which arise and decay without ever truly existing. Now wisdom is the
science of things which are truly existing beings, but not of the mere figurative
entities. Corporeal natures are neither the objects of science, nor admit of a stable
knowledge, since they are indefinite, and by science incomprehensible; and when
compared with universals resemble non-beings, and are in a genuine sense indeterminate. Indeed it is impossible to conceive that there should be a science
of things not naturally the objects of science; nor could a science of non-existent
things prove attractive to any one. Far more desirable will be things which are
genuine beings, existing in invariable permanency, and always answering to their
description. For the perception of objects existing only figuratively, never truly
being what they seem to be, follows the apprehension of real beings, just as the
knowledge of particulars is posterior to the science of universals. For, as said
Archytas, he who properly knows universals will also have a clear perception
of the nature of particulars. That is why beings are not alone, only-begotten, nor
simple, but various and multiform. For those genuine beings are intelligible and
incorporeal natures, while others are corporeal, falling under the perception of
sense, communicating with that which is really existent only by participation.
Concerning all these Pythagoras formed the most appropriate sciences, leaving
nothing uninvestigated. Besides, he developed the master sciences of method,
common to all of them, such as logic, definitions, and analysis, as may be gathered
from the Pythagorean commentaries.

To his intimates he was wont to utter symbolically oracular sentences, wherein
the smallest number of words were pregnant with the most multifarious
significance, not unlike certain oracles of the Pythian Apollo, or like Nature herself
in tiny seeds, the former exhibiting conceptions, and the latter effects innumerable
in multitude, and difficult to understand. Such was Pythagoras' own maxim, "The
beginning is the half of the whole." In this and similar utterances the most divine
Pythagoras concealed the sparks of truth, as in a treasury, for those capable of
being kindled thereby. In this brevity of diction he deposited an extension of theory
most ample and difficult to grasp, as in the maxim, "All things accord in number,"
which he frequently repeated to his disciples. Another one was, "Friendship is
equality; equality is friendship." He even used single words, such as *kosmos* or
"adorned world;" or, by Zeus, *philosophia*, or further, *Tetraktys*!

All these and many other similar inventions were by Pythagoras devised for
the benefit and amendment of his associates; and by those that understood them,
they were considered to be so worthy of veneration, and so divinely inspired,
that those who dwelt in the common auditorium adopted this oath:

I swear by the discoverer of the Tetraktys,
Which is the spring of all our wisdom,
The perennial root of Nature's fount.

This was the form of his so admirable wisdom.

Of the sciences honored by the Pythagoreans not the least were music, medicine and divination.

Of medicine, the most emphasized part was dietetics, and they were most scrupulous in its exercise. First they sought to understand the physical symptoms of symmetry, labor, eating and repose. They were nearly the first to make a business of the preparation of food, and to describe its methods. More frequently than their predecessors the Pythagoreans used poultices, disapproving more of medicated ointments, which they chiefly limited to the cure of ulcerations. Most of all they disapproved of cuts and cauterizations. Some diseases they cured by incantations. Music, if used in a proper manner, was by Pythagoras supposed to contribute greatly to health. The Pythagoreans likewise employed select sentences of Homer and Hesiod for the amendment of souls.

The Pythagoreans were habitually silent and prompt to hear, and he won praise who listened [most effectively]. But that which they had learned and heard was supposed to be retained and preserved in memory. Indeed this ability of learning and remembering determined the amount of disciplines and lectures, inasmuch as learning is the power by which knowledge is obtained, and remembering that by which it is preserved. Hence memory was greatly honored, abundantly exercised, and given much attention. In learning also it was understood that they were not to dismiss what they were taught, till its first rudiments had been entirely mastered. This was their method of recalling what they daily heard. No Pythagorean rose from his bed till he had first recollected the transactions of the day before; and he accomplished this by endeavoring to remember what he first said, or heard, or ordered done by his domestics before rising, or what was the second or third thing he had said, heard or commanded. The same method was employed for the remainder of the day. He would try to remember the identity of the first person he had met on leaving home, and who was the second, and with whom he had discoursed first, second or third. So also he did with everything else, endeavoring to resume in his memory all the events of the whole day, and in the very same order in which each of them had occurred. If, however, after rising there was enough leisure to do so, the Pythagorean reminisced about the day before yesterday. Thus they made it a point to exercise their memories systematically, considering that the ability of remembering was most important for experience, science and wisdom.

This Pythagorean school filled Italy with philosophers; and this place which before was unknown, was later, on account of Pythagoras, called Greater Greece, which became famous for its philosophers, poets and legislators. Indeed the rhetorical arts, demonstrative reasonings and legislation was entirely transferred from Greece. As to physics, we might mention the principal natural philosophers, Empedocles and Parmenides of Elea. As to ethical maxims, there is Epicharmus, whose conceptions are used by almost all philosophers.

Thus much concerning the wisdom of Pythagoras, how in a certain respect he very much impelled all his hearers to its pursuit, so far as they were adapted to its participation, and how perfectly he delivered it.

30. Justice and Politics

HOW HE CULTIVATED and delivered justice to humanity we shall best understand if we trace it to its first principle, and ultimate cause. Also we must investigate the ultimate cause of injustice, which will show us how he avoided it, and what methods he adopted to make justice fructify in his soul.

The principle of justice is mutuality and equality, through which, in a way most nearly approximating union of body and soul, all men become cooperative, and distinguish the mine from the thine, as is also testified by Plato, who learned this from Pythagoras. Pythagoras effected this in the best possible manner, by erasing from common life everything private, while increasing everything held in common, so far as ultimate possessions, which after all are the causes of tumult and sedition. For among his disciples everything was common, and the same to all, no one possessing anything private. He himself, indeed, who most approved of this communion, made use of common possessions in the most just manner; but disciples who changed their minds were given back their original contribution, with an addition, and left. Thus Pythagoras established justice in the best possible manner, beginning at its very first principle.

In the next place, justice is introduced by association with other people, while injustice is produced by unsociability and neglect of other people. Wishing therefore to spread this sociability as far as possible among men, he ordered his disciples to extend it to the most kindred animal races, considering these as their intimates and friends, and would forbid injuring, slaying or eating any of them. He who recognizes the community of element and life between men and animals will in much greater degree establish fellowship with those who share a kindred and rational soul. This also shows that Pythagoras promoted justice beginning from its very root principle. Since lack of money often compels men sometimes to act contrary to justice, he tried to avoid this by practicing such economy that his necessary expenses might be liberal, and yet retain a just sufficiency. For as cities are only magnified households, so the arrangement of domestic concerns is the principle of all good order in cities. For instance, it was said that he himself was the heir to the property of Alcaeus, who died after completing an embassy to the Lacedaemonians; but that in spite of this Pythagoras was admired for his economy no less than for his philosophy. Also when he married he so educated the daughter that was born to him, and who afterwards married the Crotonian Meno, that while unmarried she was a choir-leader, while as wife she held the first place among those who worshipped at altars. It is also said that the Metapontines preserved Pythagoras' memory by turning his house into a temple of Demeter, and the street on which he lived a place sacred to the Muses.

Because injustice also frequently results from insolence, luxury, and lawlessness, he daily exhorted his disciples to support the laws, and shun lawlessness. He considered luxury the first evil that usually glides into houses and cities, the second insolence, the third destruction. Luxury therefore should by all possible means be excluded and expelled, and men from birth should be accustomed to living temperately, and in a manly fashion. He also added the necessity of purification from bad language, whether it be piteous, or provocative, reviling, insolent or scurrilous.

Besides these household justices, he added another and most beautiful kind, the legislative, which both orders what to do and what not to do. Legislative justice is more beautiful than the judicial kind, resembling medicine which heals the diseased, but differs in that it is preventive, planning the health of the soul from afar.

That is why the best of all legislators graduated from the school of Pythagoras: first, Charondas the Catanean, and next Zaleucus and Timaratus, who legislated for the Locrians. Besides these were Theaetetus and Helicaon, Aristocrates and Phytius, who legislated for the Rhegini. All these aroused from the citizens honors comparable to those offered to divinities. For Pythagoras did not act like Heraclitus, who agreed to write laws for the Ephesians, but also petulantly added that in those laws he would order the citizens to hang themselves. What laws Pythagoras endeavored to establish were benevolent and scientific.

Nor need we specially admire those [above-mentioned professional] legislators. For Pythagoras had a slave by the name of Zalmoxis, hailing from Thrace. After hearing Pythagoras' discourses, and obtaining his freedom, he returned to the Getae, and there, as has already been mentioned at the beginning of this work, exhorted the citizens to fortitude, persuading them that the soul is immortal. So much is this true that even at present all the Galatians and Trallians, and many others of the Barbarians, persuade their children that the soul cannot be destroyed, but survives death, so that the latter is not to be feared, and that [ordinary] danger is to be met with a firm and manly mind. For instructing the Getae in these things, and for having written laws for them, Zalmoxis was by them considered as the greatest of the Gods.*

Further, Pythagoras conceived that the dominion of the divinities was most efficacious for establishing justice; and from this principle he deduced a whole polity, particular laws and a principle of justice. Thus his basic theology was that we should realize God's existence, and that his disposition towards the human race is such that he inspects and does not neglect it. This theology was very useful: for we require an inspection that we would not be disposed to resist, such as the inspective government of the divinity, for if divine nature is of this nature, it deserves the empire of the universe. For the Pythagoreans rightly taught that [the natural] man is an animal naturally insolent, and changeable in impulse, desire and passions. He therefore requires an extraordinary inspectionary government of this kind, which may produce some chastening and ordering. They therefore thought that any who recognizes the changeableness of their nature should never be forgetful of piety towards and worship of Divinity, ever keeping Him before the eye of the mind, as watching and inspecting the conduct of mankind. Everyone should pay heed, beneath the divine nature, and that of the genii, to his parents

---

*Zalmoxis was a deity of the Getae in Thrace, associated with a doctrine of the immortality of the soul. See Eliade, *A History of Religious Ideas,* II, p. 175 ff.

and the laws, and obey them unfeignedly and faithfully. In general, they thought it necessary to believe that there is no evil greater than anarchy, since the human race is not naturally adapted to salvation without some guidance.

The Pythagoreans also considered it advisable to adhere to the customs and laws of their ancestors, even though somewhat inferior to other regulations. For it is unprofitable and not salutary to evade existing laws, or to be studious of innovation. Pythagoras, therefore, to evince that his life was conformable to his doctrines gave many other specimens of piety to the Gods.

It may be quite suitable to mention one of these, as example of the rest. I will relate what Pythagoras said and did relative to the embassy from Sybaris to Croton, relative to the return of the exiles. By order of the ambassadors, some of his associates had been slain, a part of them, indeed, by one of the ambassadors himself, while another one of them was the son of one of those who had excited the sedition, and had died of disease. When the Crotonians therefore were deliberating how they should act in this affair, Pythagoras told his disciples he was displeased that the Crotonians should be so much at odds over the matter, and that in his opinion the ambassadors should not even be permitted to lead victims to the altar, let alone drag thence the suppliant exiles. When the Sybarites came to him with their complaints, and the man who had slain some of his disciples with his own hands, was defending his conduct, Pythagoras declared he would make no answer [to a murderer]. Another [ambassador] accused him of asserting that he was Apollo, because when, in the past, some person had asked him about a certain subject, why the thing was so, and he had retorted, ''Would he think it sensible, when Apollo was delivering oracles to him, to ask Apollo why he did so?'' Another one of the ambassadors derided his school, wherein he taught the return of souls to this world, saying that as Pythagoras was about to descend into Hades, the ambassador would give Pythagoras an epistle to his father, and begged him to bring back an answer when he returned. Pythagoras responded that he was not about to descend into the abode of the impious, where he clearly knew that murderers were punished. As the rest of the ambassadors reviled him, Pythagoras, followed by many people, went to the sea-shore, and sprinkled himself with water. After reviling the rest of the ambassadors, one of the Crotonian counsellors observed that he understood they had defamed Pythagoras, whom not even a brute would dare to blaspheme, though all animals should again utter the same voice as men, as prehistoric fables relate.

Pythagoras discovered another method of restraining men from injustice, namely the fear of judgment. He knew that this method could be taught, but also that fear was often able to suppress justice. He asserted therefore that it is much better to be injured than to kill a man, for judgment is dispensed in Hades, where the soul and its essence and the first nature of beings are accurately appraised.

Desiring to exhibit among human unequal, indefinite and unsymmetrical affairs the equality, definiteness and symmetry of justice, and to show how it ought to be exercised, he likened justice to a diagram [of a right-angled triangle], the only one among geometrical forms which, though having an infinite diversity of adjustments of indeed unequal parts [the length of the sides], yet has equal powers [for the square on the hypotenuse is equal to the squares on the other two sides].

Since all associations imply relations with some other person and therefore entail justice, the Pythagoreans declared that there were two kinds of associations: the seasonable, and the unseasonable, according to age, merit, familiarity, philanthropy, and so forth. For instance, the association of a younger person with an elderly one is unseasonable, while that of two young persons is seasonable. No kind of anger, threatening or boldness is becoming in a younger towards an elderly man, all which unseasonable conduct should be cautiously avoided. So also with respect to merit; for, towards a man who has arrived at the true dignity of consummate virtue, neither an unrestrained form of speech, nor any other of the above manners of conduct is seasonable.

Not unlike this was what he taught about the relations towards parents and benefactors. He said that the use of the opportune time was various. For of those who are angry or enraged, some are so seasonably, and some unseasonably. The same distinction obtains with desires, impulses and passions, actions, dispositions, associations and meetings. He further observed that to a certain extent opportuneness is to be taught, and also that the unexpected might be analyzed artificially, while none of the above qualifications obtain when applied universally, and simply. Nevertheless its results are very similar to those of opportuneness, namely elegance, propriety, congruence, and the like.

Reminding us that unity is the principal of the universe, being its principle element, so also is it in science, experiment, and growth. However, twofoldness is most honorable in houses, cities, camps, and suchlike organizations. For in sciences we learn and judge not by any single hasty glance, but by a thorough examination of every detail. There is therefore grave danger of entire misapprehension of things, when the principle has been mistaken; for while the true principle remains unknown no consequent conclusions can be final. The same situation obtains in things of another kind. Neither a city nor a house can be well organized unless each has an effective ruler who governs voluntary servants. For voluntariness is as necessary for the ruler to govern as in the ruled to obey. So also must there be a concurrence of will between teacher and learner, for no satisfactory progress can be made while there obtains resistance on either side. Thus he demonstrated the beauty of being persuaded by rulers, and being obedient to preceptors.

This was the greatest objective illustration of this argument. Pherecydes the Syrian had been his teacher, but now was afflicted with the *morbus pedicularis*. Pythagoras therefore went from Italy to Delos, to nurse him, tending him until he died, and piously performing whatever funeral rites were due to his former teacher. That is how diligent was he in the discharge of his duties towards those from whom he had received instruction.

Pythagoras insisted strenuously with his disciples on the fulfillment of mutual agreements. Lysis had once completed his worship in the temple of Hera, and was leaving as he met in the vestibule with Euryphamus the Syracusan, one of his fellow-disciples, who was then entering into the temple. Euryphamus asked Lysis to wait for him, till he had finished his worship also. So Lysis sat down on a stone seat there and waited. Euryphamus went in, finished his worship, but,

having become absorbed in some profound considerations, forgot his appointment, and passed out of the temple by another gate. Lysis, however, continued
to wait, without leaving his seat, the remainder of that day, and the following
night, and also the greater part of the next day. He might have stayed there still
longer, perhaps, unless, the following day, in the auditorium, Euryphamus had
heard that Lysis' associates were missing him. Recollecting his appointment, he
hastened to Lysis, relieved him of the engagement, telling him the cause of his
forgetfulness as follows: "Some God produced this oblivion in me, as a trial of
your firmness in keeping your engagements."

Pythagoras also ordained abstinence from animal food, for many reasons besides
the chief one that it is conducive to peaceableness. Those who are trained to
abominate the slaughter of animals as iniquitous and unnatural will think it much
more unlawful to kill a man, or engage in war. For war promotes slaughter, and
legalizes it, increasing it, and strengthening it.

Pythagoras' maxim "Touch not the balance above the beam" is in itself an
exhortation to justice, demanding the cultivation of everything that is just, as will
be shown when we study the Pythagorean symbols. In all these particulars,
therefore, Pythagoras paid great attention to the practice of justice, and to its
preachment to men, both in deeds and words.

31. Temperance and Self-Control

TEMPERANCE is our next topic, cultivated as it was by Pythagoras and taught
to his associates. The common precepts about it have already been detailed, in
which we learned that everything irregular should be cut off with fire and sword.
A similar precept is the abstaining from animal food, and also from anything
likely to produce intemperance and lull the vigilance and genuine energies of the
reasoning powers. A further step in this direction is the precept to introduce,
at a banquet, sumptuous fare, which is to be shortly sent away, and given to the
servants, having been exhibited merely to chasten the desires. Another one was
that none but courtesans should wear gold, and not the free women. Further the
practice of taciturnity, and even entire silence, for the purpose of governing the
tongue. Next, the intensive and continuous puzzling out of the most difficult
speculations, for the sake of which wine, food and sleep would be minimized.
Then would come genuine discrediting of notoriety, wealth, and the like; a sincere
reverence towards those to whom reverence is due; joined with an unassumed
democratic geniality towards one's equals in age, and towards the juniors guidance
and counsel, free from envy, and everything similar which is to be deduced from
temperance.

The temperance of the Pythagoreans, and how Pythagoras taught this virtue,
may be learned from what Hippobotus and Neanthes narrate of Myllias and
Timycha, who were Pythagoreans. It seems that Dionysius the tyrant could not
obtain the friendship of any one of the Pythagoreans, though he did everything
possible to accomplish that purpose; for they had noted, and condemned his monarchical leanings. He therefore sent a troop of thirty soldiers, under the command
of Eurymenes the Syracusan, who was the brother of Dion, through [whose]
treachery he hoped to take advantage of the Pythagoreans' usual annual migra-

tion to catch some of them; for they were in the habit of changing their abode at different seasons of the year, and they selected places suitable to such a migration.

Therefore in Phalae, a rugged part of Tarentum, through which the Pythagoreans were scheduled to pass, Eurymenes insidiously concealed his troop; and when the unsuspecting Pythagoreans reached there about noon, the soldiers rushed upon them with shouts, after the manner of robbers. Disturbed and terrified at an attack so unexpected, at the superior number of their enemies—the Pythagoreans amounting to no more than ten, and being unarmed against regularly equipped soldiery—the Pythagoreans saw that they would inevitably be taken captive, so they decided that their only safety lay in flight, which they did not consider inadmissible to virtue. For they knew that, according to right reason, courage is the art of avoiding as well as enduring. So they would have escaped, and their pursuit would have been given up by Eurymenes' soldiers, who were heavily armed, had their flight not led them up against a field sown with beans, which were already flowering. Unwilling to violate their principle not to touch beans, they stood still, and driven to desperation turned, and attacked their pursuers with stones and sticks, and whatever they found at hand, till they had wounded many, and slain some. But [numbers told and] all the Pythagoreans were slain by the spearmen, as none of them would suffer himself to be taken captive, preferring death, according to the Pythagorean teachings.

As Eurymenes and his soldiers had been sent for the express purpose of taking some of the Pythagoreans alive to Dionysius, they were much crest-fallen; and having thrown the corpses in a common sepulchre, and piled earth thereupon, they turned homewards. But as they were returning they met two of the Pythagoreans who had lagged behind, Myllias the Crotonian, and his Lacedaemonian wife Timycha, who had not been able to keep up with the others, being in the sixth month of pregnancy. These therefore the soldiers gladly made captive, and led to the tyrant with every precaution, so as to insure their arrival alive. On learning what had happened, the tyrant was very much disheartened, and said to the two Pythagoreans, "You shall obtain from me honors of unusual dignity if you shall be willing to reign in partnership with me." All his offers, however, were by Myllias and Timycha rejected. Then said he, "I will release you with a safe-guard if you will me one thing only." On Myllias asking what he wished to learn, Dionysius replied: "Tell me only why your companions chose to die rather than to tread on beans?" But Myllias at once answered, "My companions did indeed prefer death to treading on beans; but I had rather do that than tell you the reason." Astonished at this answer, Dionysius ordered him forcibly removed, and Timycha tortured, for he thought that a pregnant woman, deprived of her husband, would weaken before the torments, and easily tell him all he wanted to know. The heroic woman, however, with her teeth bit her tongue until it was separated, and spat it out at the tyrant, thus demonstrating that the offending member should be entirely cut off, even if her female nature, vanquished by the torments, should be compelled to disclose something that should be reserved in silence. Such difficulties did they make to the admission of outside friendships, even though they happened to be royal.

Similar to these also were the precepts concerning silence, which tended to the practice of temperance, for of all continence, the subjugation of the tongue is the most difficult. The same virtue is illustrated by Pythagoras' persuading the Crotonians to relinquish all sacrilegious and questionable commerce with courtesans. Moreover Pythagoras restored to temperance a youth who had become wild with amatory passion, through music. Exhortations against lascivious insolence promote the same virtue.

Such things were delivered to the Pythagoreans by Pythagoras himself, who was their cause. They took such care of their bodies that they remained in the same condition, not being at one time lean, and at another stout, which changes they considered anomalous. With respect to their mind also, they managed to remain uniformly mildly joyful, and not at one time hilarious, and at another sad, which could be achieved only by expelling perturbations, despondency or rage.

It was a precept of theirs that no human casualties ought to be unexpected by the intelligent, expecting everything which it is not in their power to prevent. If however at any time any one of them fell into a rage, or into despondency, he would withdraw from his associates' company, and seeking solitude, endeavor to digest and heal the passion.

Of the Pythagoreans it is also reported that none of them punished a servant or admonished a free man during anger, but waited until he had recovered his wonted serenity. They use a special word, *paidartan,* to signify such [self-controlled] rebukes, effecting this calming by silence and quiet. So Spintharus relates of Archytas the Tarentine, that on returning after a certain time from the war against the Messenians waged by the Tarentines, to inspect some land belonging to him, and finding that the bailiff and the other servants had not properly cultivated it, greatly neglecting it, he became enraged, and was so furious that he told his servants that it was well for them that he was angry, for otherwise they would not have escaped the punishment due to so great an offence. A similar anecdote is related of Clinias, according to Spintharus, for he also was wont to defer all admonitions and punishments until his mind was restored to tranquility.

Of the Pythagoreans it is further related that they restrained themselves from all lamentation, weeping, and the like; and that neither gain, desire, anger or ambition, or anything of the like, ever became the cause of dissension among them, all Pythagoreans being disposed towards each other as parents towards their offspring.

Another beautiful trait of theirs was that they gave credit to Pythagoras for everything, naming it after him, not claiming the glory of their own inventions, except very rarely. Few there are who acknowledged their own works.

Admirable too is the careful secrecy with which they preserved the mystery of their writings. For during so many centuries, prior to the times of Philolaus, none of the Pythagorean commentaries appeared publicly. Philolaus first published those three celebrated books which, at the request of Plato, Dion of Syracuse is said to have bought for a hundred minae. For Philolaus had been overtaken by sudden severe poverty, and he capitalized the writings of which he was partaker through his alliance with the Pythagoreans.

As to the value of opinion, such were their views: a stupid man should defer to the opinion of everyone, especially to that of the crowds. Only a very few are qualified to apprehend and opine rightly; for evidently this is limited to the intelligent, who are very few. To the crowds, such a qualification of course does not extend. But to despise the opinion of everyone is also stupid, for such a person will remain unlearned and incorrigible. The unscientific should study that of which he is ignorant, or lacks scientific knowledge. A learner should also defer to the opinion of the scientific, and who is able to teach. Generally, youths who wish to be saved should attend to the opinion of their elders, or of those who have lived well.

During the course of human life there are certain ages, by them called *endedasmenae*, which cannot be connected by the power of any chance person. Unless a man from his very birth is trained in a beautiful and upright manner, these ages antagonize each other. A well-educated child, formed to temperance and fortitude, should be given a great part of his education during the stage of adolescence. Similarly, when the adolescent is trained to temperance and fortitude, he should focus his education on the next age of manhood. Nothing could be more absurd than the way in which the general public treats this subject. They fancy that boys should be orderly and temperate, abstaining from everything troublesome or indecorous; but as soon as they have arrived at the age of adolescence, they may do anything they please. In this age, therefore, there is a combination of both kinds of errors, puerile and virile. To speak plainly, they avoid anything that demands diligence and good order, while following anything that has the appearance of sport, intemperance and petulance, being familiar only with boyish affairs. Their desires should be developed from the boyish stage into the next one. In the meanwhile ambition and the rest of the more serious and turbulent inclinations and desires of the virile age prematurely invade adolescence wherefore this adolescence demands the greatest care.

In general, no man ought to be allowed to do whatever he pleases, for there is always need of a certain inspection, or legal and cultured government, to which each of the citizens is responsible. For animals, when left to themselves and neglected, rapidly degenerate into vice and depravity.

The Pythagoreans [who did not approve of men being intemperate], would often compel answers from, and puzzle [such intemperate people] by asking them why boys are generally trained to take food in an orderly and moderate manner, being compelled to learn that order and decency are beautiful, and that their contraries, disorder and intemperance are base, while drunkards and gormandizers are held in great disgrace. For if no one of these is useful to us when we have arrived at the age of virility, it was in vain that we were accustomed, when boys, to an order of this kind. The same argument holds good in respect to other good habits to which children are trained. Such a reversal of training is not seen in the case of the education of other lower animals. From the very first a whelp and a colt are trained, and learn those tricks which they are to exercise when arrived at maturity.

The Pythagoreans are generally reported to have exhorted not only their intimates, but also to whomsoever they happened to meet, to avoid pleasure as a danger demanding the utmost caution. More than anything else does this passion deceive us, and mislead us into error. They contended that it was wiser never to do anything whose end was pleasure, whose results are usually shameful and harmful. They asserted we should adopt the beautiful and fair, and do our duty. Only secondarily should we consider the useful and advantageous. In these matters there is need for special consideration.

Of desire, the Pythagoreans said that desire itself is a certain tendency, impulse and appetite of the soul, wishing to be filled with something, or to enjoy the presence of something, or to be disposed according to some sense-enjoyment. There are also contrary desires, of evacuation and repulsion, and to terminate some sensation. This passion is manifold, and is almost the most Protean of human experiences. However, many human desires are artificially acquired, and self-prepared. That is why this passion demands the utmost care and watchfulness, and physical exercise that is more than casual. That when the body is empty it should desire food is no more than natural; and then it is just as natural that when it is full it should desire appropriate evacuation. But to desire superfluous food, or luxurious garments or coverlets, or residences, is artificial. The Pythagoreans applied this argument also to furniture, dishes, servants and cattle raised for butchering. Besides, human passions are never permanent, but are ever changing, even to infinity. That is why education of the youth should begin at the earliest moment possible, that their aspirations may be directed towards ends that are proper, avoiding those that are vain and unnecessary, so as to be undisturbed by, and remain pure from such undesireable passions; and may despise those who are objects of contempt, because they are subjected to [myriad] fleeting desires. Yet it must be observed that senseless, harmful, superfluous and insolent desires subsist in the souls of such individuals who are the most powerful; for there is nothing so absurd that the soul of such boys, men and women would not lead them to perform.

Indeed, the variety of food eaten is beyond description. The kinds of fruits and roots which the human race eats is nothing less than infinite. The kinds of flesh eaten are innumerable; there is no terrestrial, aerial, or aquatic animal which has not been partaken of. Besides, in the preparation of these, the contrivances used are endless, and they are seasoned with manifold mixtures of juices. Hence, according to the motions of the human soul, it is no more than natural that the human race should be so various as to include those actually insane; for each kind of food that is introduced into the human body becomes the cause of a certain peculiar disposition.

[Quantity] is as important as quality; for sometimes a slight change in quantity produces a great change in quality, as with wine. First it makes men more cheerful, later it undermines morals and sanity. This difference is generally ignored in things in which the result is not so pronounced, although everything eaten is the cause of a certain peculiar disposition. Hence it requires great wisdom to know and perceive what quality and quantity of food to eat. This science, first unfolded by Apollo and Paeon, was later developed by Asklepius and his followers.

About propagation the Pythagoreans taught as follows. First, they prevented untimely birth. Not even among plants or animals is prematurity good. To produce good fruit there is need of maturation for a certain time to give strong and perfect bodies to fruits and seeds. Boys and girls should therefore be trained to work and exercise, with endurance, and they should eat foods adapted to a life of labor and temperance with endurance. There are many things in human life which it is better to learn at a late period in life, and the use of sex is one of them. It is therefore advisable that a boy should be educated so as not to begin sex-connection before the twentieth year, and even then rarely. This will take place if he holds high ideals of a good habit for the body. Bodily hygiene and intemperance are not likely to subsist in the same individual. The Pythagoreans praised the earlier Greek laws forbidding intercourse with a woman who is a mother, daughter or sister in a temple or other public place. It is advisable that there be many impediments to the practice of this energy. The Pythagoreans forbade entirely intercourse that was unnatural, or resulting from wanton insolence, allowing only the natural and temperate forms, which occur in the course of chaste and recognized procreation of children.

Parents should make circumstancial provision for their offspring. The first precaution is a healthful and temperate life, not unseasonably filling oneself with food, nor using foods which create bad body-habits, above all avoiding intoxication. The Pythagoreans thought that an evil, discordant, trouble-making character produced depraved sperma. They insisted that none but an indolent or inconsiderate person would attempt to produce an animal, and introduce it to existence, without most diligently providing for it a pleasing and even elegant ingress into this world. Lovers of dogs pay the utmost possible attention to the breeding of their puppies, knowing that goodness of the offspring depends on goodness of parents, at the right season, and in proper surroundings. Lovers of birds pay no less attention to the matter; procreators of generous animals therefore should by all possible means manage that their efforts be fruitful. It is therefore absurd for men to pay no attention to their own offspring, begetting casually and carelessly, and after birth, feeding and educating them negligently. This is the most powerful and manifest cause of the vice and depravity of the greater part of mankind, for the multitude undertake procreation on impulse, like beasts.

Such were the Pythagoreans' teachings about temperance, which they defended by work and practiced in deed. They had originally received them from Pythagoras himself, as if they had been oracles delivered by the Pythian Apollo.

32. Courage or Fortitude

FORTITUDE, the subject of this chapter, has already been illustrated, by the heroism of Timycha, and those Pythagoreans who preferred death to transgression of Pythagoras' prohibition to touch beans, and other instances. Pythagoras himself showed it in the generous deeds he performed when travelling everywhere alone, undergoing heart-breaking labors and serious dangers, and in choosing to leave his country and to live among strangers. Likewise when he dissolved tyrannies, ordered confused commonwealths, and emancipated cities, he ended illegalities, and impeded the activities of insolent and tyrannical men. As a leader, he showed himself benignant to the just and mild, but expelled rough and licentious men from his society, refusing even to answer them, resisting them with all his might, although he assisted the former.

Of these courageous deeds, as well as of many upright actions, many instances could be adduced; but the greatest of these is the prevailing freedom of speech he employed towards the tyrant Phalaris, the most cruel of those who detained him in captivity. A Hyperborean sage named Abaris visited him, to converse with him on many topics, especially sacred ones, respecting statues and worship, the divine Providence, natures terrestrial and célestial, and the like. Pythagoras, under divine inspiration, answered him boldly, sincerely and persuasively, so that he converted all listeners. This roused Phalaris' anger against Abaris for praising Pythagoras, and increased the tyrant's resentment against Pythagoras. Phalaris swore proudly as was his wont, and uttered blasphemies against the Gods themselves. Abaris however was grateful to Pythagoras, and learned from him that all things are suspended from, and governed by the heavens, which he proved from many considerations, but especially from the potency of sacred rites. For teaching him these things, so far was Abaris from thinking Pythagoras an enchanter, that his reverence for him increased till he considered him a God. Phalaris tried to counteract this by discrediting divination, and publicly denying there was any efficacy of the sacraments performed in sacred rites. Abaris, however, guided the controversy towards such things as are granted by all men, seeking to persuade him of the existence of a divine providence, from circumstances that lie above human influence, such as immense wars, incurable diseases, the decay of fruits, incursions of pestilence, or the like, which are hard to endure, and are deplorable, arising from the beneficent [purifying] energy of the powers celestial and divine.

Shamelessly and boldly Phalaris opposed all this. Then Pythagoras, suspecting that Phalaris intended to put him to death, but knowing he was not destined to die through Phalaris, retorted with great freedom of speech. Looking at Abaris, he said that from the heavens to aerial and terrestrial beings there was a certain descending communication. Then from instances generally known he showed that all things follow the heavens. Then he demonstrated the existence of an indisputable power of freedom of will in the soul, proceeding further to amply discuss the perfect energy of reason and intellect. With his [usual] freedom of will he even dared to discuss tyranny, and all the prerogatives of fortune, concerning injustice and human avarice, solidly teaching that all these are of no value. Further, he gave Phalaris a divine admonition concerning the most excellent life, earnestly comparing it with the most depraved. He likewise clearly unfolded the manner of subsistence of the soul, its powers and passions; and, what was the most beautiful of all, demonstrated to him that the Gods are not the authors of evils, and that diseases and bodily calamities are the results of intemperance, at the same time finding fault with the poets and mythologists for the unadvisedness of many of their fables.

Then he directly confuted Phalaris, and admonished him, experimentally demonstrating to him the power and magnitude of heaven, and by many arguments demonstrated to him that reason dictates that punishments should be legal. He demonstrated to him the difference between men and other animals, scientifically demonstrating the difference between internal and external speech. Then he expounded the nature of the intellect, and the knowledge that is derived therefrom, with its ethical corollaries. He discoursed about most beneficial of useful things, adding the mildest possible admonitions of what ought not to be done. Most important of all, he unfolded to him the distinction between the productions of fate and intellect, and the difference between the results of destiny and fate. Then he reasoned about the divinities, and the immortality of the soul.

All this, really, belongs to some other chapter, the present one's topic being the development of courage or fortitude. But if, when situated in the midst of the most dreadful circumstances Pythagoras philosophized with firmness of decision, if on all sides he resisted fortune, and repelled it, enduring its attacks strenuously, if he employed the greatest boldness of speech towards him who threatened his life, it must be evident that he entirely despised those things generally considered dreadful, rating them as unworthy of attention. If also he despised execution, when this appeared imminent, and was not moved by its imminence, it is evident that he was perfectly free from the fear of death.

But he did something still more generous, effecting the dissolution of the tyranny, restraining the tyrant when he was about to bring the most deplorable calamities on mankind, and liberating Sicily from the most cruel and imperious power. That it was Pythagoras who accomplished this, is evident from the oracles of Apollo, which had predicted that the dominion of Phalaris would come to an end when his subjects would become better men, and cooperate, which also happened through the presence of Pythagoras, by his imparting to them instruction and good principles. The best proof of this may be found in the time when it happened. For on the very day that Phalaris condemned Pythagoras and Abaris to death, he himself was by stratagem slain.

Another argument for the truth of this are the adventures of Epimenides. He was a disciple of Pythagoras; and when certain persons planned to destroy him, he invoked the Furies and the avenging divinities, and thereby caused those who had attempted his life to destroy each other. In the same way Pythagoras, who assisted mankind, imitating both the manner and fortitude of Hercules for the benefit of men, punished and occasioned the death of him who had behaved insolently and in a disorderly manner towards others—and this through the very oracles of Apollo, in the class of which divinity both he and Epimenides had naturally since birth belonged. This admirable and strenuous deed was the effect of his fortitude.

We shall present another example of preservation of lawful opinion; for following it out, he did what to him seemed just and dictated by right reason, without permitting himself to be diverted from his intention by pleasure, labor, passion or danger. His disciples also preferred death to transgression of any precept of his. They preserved their manners unchanged under the most varying fortunes. Being involved in myriad calamities could not cause them to deviate from his rules. They never ceased exhorting each other to support the laws, to oppose lawlessness, and from birth to train themselves to a life of temperance and fortitude, so as to restrain and oppose luxury. They also used certain original melodies which Pythagoras had invented as remedies against the passions of the soul, against lamentation and despondency, as affording the greatest relief in these maladies.

Other melodies they employed against anger and rage, through which they could increase or diminish those passions, till they reduced them to moderation, and compatibility with fortitude. The thought which afforded them the greatest support in generous endurance was the conviction that no human casualty should be unexpected by men of intellect, but that they must resign themselves to all vicissitudes beyond human control.

Moreover, whenever overwhelmed by grief or anger, they immediately forsook the company of their associates, and in solitude endeavored to digest and heal the oppressing passion. They took it for granted that studies and disciplines implied labor, and that they must expect severe tests of different kinds, and be restrained and punished even by fire and sword, so as to exorcise innate intemperance and greediness, for which purpose no labor or endurance should be spared. Further to accomplish this, they unselfishly abstained from animal food, and also some other kinds. This also was the cause of their slowing of speech and complete silence, as means to the entire subjugation of the tongue, which demanded a year-long exercise of fortitude. In addition, their strenuous and assiduous investigation and resolution of the most difficult theorems, their abstinence from wine, food and sleep, and their contempt of wealth and glory, were means by which they trained themselves to fortitude.

But this is not all. They restrained themselves from lamentations and tears. They abstained from entreaty, supplication, and adulation, as being effeminate and abject. To the same practice of fortitude must be referred their peculiarity of absolute reserve concerning the arcana of the first principles of their discipline, preserving them from being divulged to strangers, committing them unwritten to memory, and transmitting them orally to their successors as if they were the mysteries of the Gods. That is why nothing worth mentioning of their philosophy was ever made public, and though it had been taught and learned for a long while, it was not known beyond their walls. Those outside, whom I might call the profane, sometimes happened to be present; and under such circumstances the Pythagoreans would communicate only obscurely, through symbols, a vestige of which is retained by celebrated precepts still in circulation, such as, "Fire should not be poked with a sword," and other like ones which, taken literally, resemble old wives' tales, but which, when properly unfolded, are to the recipients admirable and venerable.

That precept which, of all others, was of the greatest efficacy in the achievement of fortitude, is that one which helps defend and liberate from the life-long bonds that retain the intellect in captivity, and without which no one can perceive or learn anything rational or genuine, whatever be the sense in activity. Thus they said,

> 'Tis mind that sees all things, and hears them all;
> All else is deaf and blind.

The next most efficacious precept is that which exhorts one excessively to be studious of purifying the intellect, and by various methods adapting it through mathematical disciplines to receive something divinely beneficial, so as neither to fear a separation from the body, nor, when directed towards incorporeal natures, through their most refulgent splendor to be compelled to turn away the eyes, nor to be converted to those passions which fasten and even nail the soul to the body, and makes her rebellious to all those passions which are the progeny of procreation, degrading her to a lower level. The training of ascent through all these is the study of the most perfect fortitude. Such are important instances of the fortitude of Pythagoras and his followers.

33. Universal Friendship

FRIENDSHIP of all things towards all was most clearly unfolded by Pythagoras. Indeed, the friendship of Gods towards men he explained through piety and scientific cultivation; but that of teachings towards each other, and generally of the soul to the body, of the rational towards the irrational part he unfolded, through philosophy and its teachings. That of men towards each other, and of citizens, he justified through proper legislation; that of strangers, through the common possession of a body; that between man and wife, children, brothers or kindred, through the unperverted ties of nature. In short, he taught the friendship of all for all; and still further, of certain animals, through justice, and common physical experiences. But the pacification and conciliation of the body, which is mortal by itself, and of its latent immortal powers, he enforced through health, and a temperate diet suitable thereto, in imitation of the ever-healthy condition of the mundane elements.

In all these, Pythagoras is recognized as the inventor and summarizer of them in a single name, that *friendship.* So admirable was his friendship to his associates, that even now when people are extremely benevolent mutually, people call them Pythagoreans. We should therefore narrate Pythagoras' discipline related thereto, and the precepts he taught his disciples.

The Pythagoreans therefore exhorted the effacing of all rivalry and contention from true friendship; and if not from all friendship, at least from parental friendship, and generally from all gratitude towards seniors and benefactors. To strive or contend with such, out of anger or some other passion, is not the way to preserve existing friendship. Scars and ulcers in friendship should be the least possible; and this will be the case if those that are friends know how to subdue their anger. If indeed both of them know this, or rather the younger of the two, and who ranks in some one of the above-mentioned orders [their friendship will be the more easily preserved]. They also taught that corrections and admonitions, which they called *paidartases,* should take place from the elder to the younger, and with much suavity and caution; and likewise that much careful and considerate attention should be manifested in admonitions. For thus they will be persuasive and helpful. They also said that confidence should never be separated from friendship, whether in earnest, or in jest. Existing friendship cannot survive, when once falsehood insinuates itself into the habits of professed friends. According to them, friendship should not be abandoned on account of misfortune, or any other human vicissitude; the only permissible rejection of friend or friendship is the result of great and incorrigible vice. Hatred should not be entertained voluntarily against those who are not perfectly bad, but when once formed, it should be strenuously and firmly maintained, unless its object should change his morals, so as to become a better man. Hostility should not consist in words, but in deeds, and such war is commendable and legitimate when conducted in a manly manner.

No one should ever permit himself to become the cause of contention, and we should so far as possible avoid its source. In a friendship which is intended to be pure, the greater part of the things pertaining to it should be definite and legitimate. These should be properly distinguished, and not be casual; and moreover our conversation should never grow casual or negligent, but remain orderly, modest and benevolent. So also with the remaining passions and dispositions.

We should not decline foreign friendships carelessly, but accept and guard them with the greatest care.

That the Pythagoreans preserved friendship towards each other for many ages may be inferred from what Aristoxenus, in his treatise *On the Pythagoric Life*, says he heard from Dionysius the tyrant of Sicily when, having been deposed, he taught language at Corinth. Here are the words of Aristoxenus:

"So far as they could these men avoided lamentations and tears, and the like; also adulation, entreaty, supplication and other emotions. Dionysius, therefore, having fallen from his tyranny and come to Corinth, told us the detailed story about the Pythagoreans Phintias and Damon, who were sponsors for each other's death.

"This is how it was: certain intimates of his had often mentioned the Pythagoreans, defaming and reviling them, calling them arrogant, and asserting that their gravity, their pretended fidelity, and stoicism would disappear on falling into some calamity. Others contradicted this; and as contention arose on the subject, it was decided to settle the matter by an experiment. One man accused Phintias, before Dionysius, of having conspired with others against his life. Others corroborated the charges, which looked probable, though Phintias was astonished at the accusation. When Dionysius had unequivocally said that he had verified the charges, and that Phintias must die, the latter replied that if Dionysius thought that this was necessary, he requested the delay of the remainder of the day, to settle the affairs of himself and Damon, as these two men lived together and had all things in common; but as Phintias was the elder, he mostly undertook the management of the household affairs. He therefore requested that Dionysius allow him to depart for this purpose, and that he would appoint Damon as his surety.

Dionysius claimed surprise at such a request, and asked him if any man existed who would stand surety for the death of another. Phintias asserted that there was, and Damon was sent for; and on hearing what had happened, agreed to become the sponsor, and that he would remain there until Phintias' return. Dionysius declared astonishment at these circumstances, and they who had proposed the experiment derided Damon as the one who would be caught, sneering at him as the 'vicarious stag.' When, however, sunset approached, Phintias came to die, at which all present were astonished and subdued. Dionysius, having embraced and kissed the men, requested that they would receive him as a third into their friendship. They however would by no means consent to anything of the kind, though he entreated them to comply with his request." These words are related by Aristoxenus, who received them from Dionysius himself.

It is also said that the Pythagoreans endeavored to perform the offices of friendship to those of their sect, though they were unknown, and had never seen each other, on receiving a sure indication of participation in the same doctrines; so that judging from such friendly offices it may be believed, as is generally reported, that worthy men, even though they should dwell in the remotest parts of the earth, are mutually friends, and this before they become known to, and salute each other.

The story runs that a certain Pythagorean, travelling through a long and solitary road on foot, came to an inn; and there from over exertion, or other causes, fell into a long and severe disease, so as at length to want the necessities of life. The innkeeper, however, whether from pity or benevolence, supplied him with everything requisite, sparing neither personal service, nor expense. Feeling the end near, the Pythagorean wrote a certain symbol on a tablet, and desired the innkeeper, in event of his death, to hang the tablet near the road, and observe whether any traveller read the symbol. "For that person," said he, "will repay you what you have spent on me, and will also thank you for your kindness." On the Pythagorean's death the innkeeper buried him, and attended to the funeral details without any expectation of being repaid, nor of receiving any remuneration from anybody who might read from the tablet. However, struck with the Pythagorean's request, he was induced to expose the writing in the public road. A long time thereafter a Pythagorean passed that way, and on understanding the symbol, found out who had placed the tablet there, and having also investigated every particular, paid the innkeeper a sum very much greater than he had disbursed.

It is also related that Clinias the Tarentine, when he learned that the Cyrenaean Prorus, who was a zealous Pythagorean, was in danger of losing all his property, sailed to Cyrene, and after having collected a sum of money, restored the affairs of Prorus to a better condition, though thereby he diminished his own estate, and risked the peril of the sea-voyage.

Similarly, Thestor Posidoniates, having from mere report heard that the Pythagorean Thymaridas Parius had fallen from great wealth into abject poverty, is said to have sailed to Paros, and after having collected a large sum of money, reinstated Thymaridas in affluence. These are beautiful instances of friendship.

But much more admirable than the above examples were the Pythagoreans' teachings respecting the communion of divine goods, the agreement of intellect, and their doctrines about the divine soul. They were ever exhorting each other not to tear apart the divine soul within them. The significance of their friendship both in words and in deeds was an effort to achieve a certain divine union, or communion of intellect with the divine soul. Anything better than this, either in what is uttered in words, or performed by deeds, is not possible to find. For I am of opinion that in this all the goods of friendship are united. In this, as a climax, we have collected all the blessings of Pythagorean friendship; there is nothing left to say.

34. Miscellaneous Topics

HAVING THUS, according to plan, discussed Pythagoras and Pythagoreanism, we may be interested in scattered points which do not fall under any of the former topics.

[First, as to language]. It is said that each Greek novice was ordered to use his native language, as they did not approve of the use of a foreign language. Foreigners also joined the Pythagoreans: Messenians, Lucani, Picentini, and Romans. Metrodorus, the son of Thyrsus, the father of Epicharmus, who specialized in medicine, in explaining his father's writings to his brother, says that Epicharmus, and prior to him Pythagoras, conceived that the best and most musical dialect was the Doric. The Ionic and Aeolic relate to chromatic harmony, which however is still more evident in the Attic. The Doric, consisting of pronounced letters, is enharmonic.

Myths also bear witness to the antiquity of this dialect. Nereus was said to have married Doris, the daughter of Ocean, by whom he had fifty daughters, one of whom was the mother of Achilles. Metrodorus also says that some insist that Helen was the offspring of Deucalion, who was the son of Prometheus and Pyrrha, the daughter of Epimetheus; and from him descended Dorus and Aeolus. Further he observes that from the Babylonian sacred rites he had learned that Helen was the offspring of Jupiter, and that the sons of Helen were Dorus, Xuthus, and Aeolus, with which Herodotus also agrees. Accuracy in particulars so ancient is difficult for moderns, to enable them to decide which of the accounts is most trustworthy. But either of them claim that the Doric dialect is the most ancient, that the Aeolic, whose name derives from Aeolus, is the next in age, and that the third is the Ionic, derived from Ion, the son of Xuthus. Fourth is the Attic, named from Creusa, the daughter of Erechtheus, and it is three generations younger than the others, for it existed about the time of the Thracians, and the rape of Orithyia, as is evident from the testimony of most histories. The Doric dialect was also used by the most ancient of the poets, Orpheus.

Of medicine, the most emphasized part was dietetics, and they were most scrupulous in its exercise. First they sought to understand the physical symptoms of symmetry, labor, eating and repose. They were nearly the first to make a business of the preparation of food, and to describe its methods. More frequently than their predecessors the Pythagoreans used poultices, disapproving more of medicated ointments, which they chiefly limited to the cure of ulcerations. Most of all they disapproved of cuts and cauterizations. Some diseases they cured by incantations. Music, if used in a proper manner, was by Pythagoras supposed to contribute greatly to health. The Pythagoreans likewise employed select sentences of Homer and Hesiod for the amendment of souls.

The Pythagoreans objected to those who offered disciplines for sale, who open their souls like the gates of an inn to every man that approaches them; and who, if they do not thus get buyers, diffuse themselves through the cities, and in short, hire gymnasia, and require a reward from young men for those things that are without price. Pythagoras indeed hid the meaning of much that was said by him, in order that those who were genuinely instructed might clearly be partakers of it; but that others, as Homer says of Tantalus, might be pained in the midst of what they heard, in consequence of receiving no delight therefrom.

The Pythagoreans thought that those who teach for the sake of reward show themselves worse than sculptors, or artists who perform their work sitting. For these, when someone orders them to make a statue of Hermes, search for wood suited to receive the proper form; while those pretend that they can readily produce the works of virtue from every nature.

The Pythagoreans likewise said that it is more necessary to pay attention to philosophy, than to parents or to agriculture; for no doubt it is owing to the latter that we live, but philosophers and preceptors are the causes of our living well, and becoming wise, on discovering the right mode of discipline and instruction.

Nor did they think fit either to speak or to write in such a way that their conceptions might be obvious to the first comer; for the very first thing Pythagoras is said to have taught is that, being purified from all intemperance, his disciples should preserve the doctrines they had heard in silence. It is accordingly reported that he who first divulged the theory of commensurable and incommensurable quantities to those unworthy to receive it, was by the Pythagoreans so hated that they not only expelled him from their common association, and from living with him, but also for him constructed a [symbolic] tomb, as for one who had migrated from the human into another life. It is also reported that the Divine Power was so indignant with him who divulged the teachings of Pythagoras that he perished at sea, as an impious person who divulged the method of inscribing in a sphere the dodecahedron, one of the so-called solid figures, the composition of the *icostagonus*. But according to others this is what happened to him who revealed the doctrine of irrational and incommensurable quantities.

All Pythagoric discipline was symbolic, resembling riddles and puzzles, and consisting of maxims, in the style of the ancients. Likewise the truly divine Pythian oracles seem to be somewhat difficult of understanding and explanation to those who carelessly receive the answers given. These are the indications about Pythagoras and the Pythagoreans collected from tradition.

35. The Attack on Pythagoreanism

THERE WERE, however, certain persons who were hostile to the Pythagoreans, and who rose against them. That stratagems were employed to destroy them, during Pythagoras' absence, is universally acknowledged; but the historians differ in their account of the journey which he then undertook. Some say that he went to Pherecydes the Syrian, and others, to Metapontum. Many causes of the stratagems are assigned. One of them, which is said to have originated from the men called Cylonians, is as follows: Cylon of Croton was one of the most prominent citizens, in birth, renown and wealth; but in manners he was severe, turbulent, violent, tyrannical. His greatest desire was to become a partaker of the Pythagoric life, and he made application to Pythagoras who was now advanced in age, but was rejected for the above reasons. Consequently he and his friends became violent enemies of the brotherhood. Cylon's ambition was so vehement and immoderate that, with his associates, he persecuted the very last of the Pythagoreans. That is why Pythagoras moved to Metapontum, where he ended his existence.

Those who were called Cylonians continued to plot against the Pythagoreans, and to exhibit the most virulent malevolence. Nevertheless, for a time this enmity was subdued by the Pythagoreans' probity, and also by the vote of the citizens, who entrusted the whole of the city affairs to their management.

At length, however, the Cylonians became so hostile to "the men," as they were called, that they set fire to Milo's residence, where were assembled all the Pythagoreans, holding a council of war. All were burnt, except two, Archippus and Lysis, who escaped through their bodily vigor. As no public notice was taken of this calamity, the Pythagoreans ceased to pay any further attention to public affairs, which was due to two causes: the cities' negligence, and through the loss of those men most qualified to govern.

Both of the saved Pythagoreans were Tarentines, and Archippus returned home. Lysis, resenting the public neglect, went into Greece, residing in the Achaian Peloponnesus. Stimulated by an ardent desire, he migrated to Thebes, where he had as disciple Epaminondas, who spoke of his teacher as his father. There Lysis died.

Except Archytas of Tarentum, the rest of the Pythagoreans departed from Italy, and dwelt together in Rhegium. The most celebrated were Phanto, Echecrates, Polymnastus, and Diocles, who were Phlyasians, and Xenophilus Chalcidensis of Thrace. But in course of time, as the administration of public affairs went from bad to worse, these Pythagoreans nevertheless preserved their pristine manners and disciplines; yet soon the sect began to fail, till they nobly perished. This is the account by Aristoxenus.

Nicomachus agrees with Aristoxenus, except that he dates the plot against the Pythagoreans during Pythagoras' journey to Delos, to nurse his preceptor Pherecydes the Syrian, who was then afflicted with *morbus pedicularis*, and after his death performed the funeral rites. Then those who had been rejected by the Pythagoreans, and to whom monuments had been raised, as if they were dead, attacked them, and committed them all to the flames. Afterwards they were overwhelmed by the Italians with stones, and thrown out of the house unburied. Then science died in the breasts of its possessors, having by them been preserved as something mystic and incommunicable. Only such things as were difficult to be understood, and which were not expounded, were preserved in the memory of those who were outside the sect—except a few things, which certain Pythagoreans, who at that time happened to be in foreign lands, preserved as sparks of science very obscure, and of difficult investigation. These men being solitary, and dejected at this calamity, were scattered in different places, retaining no longer any public influence. They lived alone in solitary places, wherever they found any, and each preferred association with himself to that with any other person.

Fearing however, lest the name of philosophy should be entirely exterminated from among mankind, and that they should, on this account, incur the indignation of the Gods by suffering so great a gift of theirs to perish, they made a collection of certain commentaries and symbols, gathered the writings of the more ancient Pythagoreans, and of such things as they remembered. These relics each left at his death to his son, or daughter, or wife, with a strict injunction not to divulge them outside the family. This was carried out for some time, and the relics were transmitted in succession to their posterity.

Since Apollonius dissents in a certain place regarding these particulars, and adds many things that we have not mentioned, we must record his account of the plot against the Pythagoreans. He says that from childhood Pythagoras had aroused envy. So long as he conversed with all that came to him, he was pleasing to all; but when he restricted his intercourse to his disciples the general peoples' good opinion of him was altered. They did indeed permit him to pay more attention to strangers than to themselves, but they were indignant at his preferring some of their fellow-citizens before others, and they suspected that his disciples assembled with intentions hostile to themselves. In the next place, as the young men that were indignant with him were of high rank, and surpassed others in wealth—and when they arrived at the proper age, not only held the first honors in their own families, but also managed the affairs of the city in common—they, being more than three hundred in number, formed a large body, so that there remained but a small part of the city which was not conversant with their habits and pursuits.

Moreover, so long as the Crotonians confined themselves to their own country, and Pythagoras dwelt among them, the original form of government continued; but the people had changed, and they were no longer satisfied with it, and were therefore seeking a pretext for a change. When they captured Sybaris, and the land was not divided by lot, according to the desire of the multitude, this veiled hatred against the Pythagoreans burst forth, and the populace forsook them.

The leaders of this dissension were those that were nearest to the Pythagoreans, both by kindred and intercourse. These leaders as well as the common folk were offended by the Pythagoreans' actions, which were unusual, and the people interpreted that peculiarity as a reflection on them.

[None of the Pythagoreans called Pythagoras by his name. While alive, they referred to him as *divine*; after his death as *that man*, just as Homer makes Eumaeus refer to Ulysses thus:

> Though absent he may be, O guest, I fear
> To name him; so great is my love and care.

Such were some of his precepts: They were to get up before sunrise, and never to wear a ring on which the image of God was engraved, lest that image be defiled by being worn at funerals, or other impure places. They were to adore the rising sun. Pythagoras ordered them never to do anything without previous deliberation and discussion, in the morning forming a plan of what was to be done later, and at night to review the day's actions, which served the double purpose of strengthening the memory, and considering their conduct. If any one of their associates appointed to meet them at some particular place and time, they should stay there till he came, regardless of the length of time, for Pythagoreans should not speak carelessly, but remember what was said, and regard order and method. At death they were not to blaspheme, but to die uttering propitious words, such as are used by those who sail out of the port into the Adriatic Sea.]*

The Pythagoreans' kindred were indignant that they associated with none, their parents excepted; that they shared in common their possessions to the exclusion

---

*This section seems to be out of place in the received text.

of their kindred, whom they treated as strangers. These personal motives turned the general opposition into active hostility. Hippasus, Diodorus, and Theages united in insisting that the assembly and the magistracy should be opened to every citizen, and that the rulers should be responsible to elected representatives of the people. This was opposed by the Pythagoreans Alcimachus, Dimachus, and Meton and Democedes, who disagreed with changes in the inherited constitution. They were, however, defeated, and were formally accused in a popular assemby by two orators, the aristocrat Cylon and the plebeian Ninon. These two planned their speeches together, the first and longer one being made by Cylon, while Ninon concluded by pretending that he had penetrated the Pythagorean mysteries, and that he had gathered and written out such particulars as were calculated to incriminate the Pythagoreans, and to a scribe he gave to read a book which was entitled the *Sacred Discourse.*

Friends, it was said in the book, are to be venerated in the same manner as Gods; but others are to be treated as brutes. This very sentiment is ascribed to Pythagoras himself, but in verse, such as,

> Like the blessed Gods, his friends he e'er revered,
> But reckoned others as of no account.

Pythagoras considered that Homer deserved to be praised for calling a king the shepherd of the people, which implied approval of aristocracy, in which the rulers are few, while the implication is that the rest of men are like cattle. Beans should be scorned, because they are used in voting, inasmuch as the Pythagoreans selected office-holders by appointment. To rule should be an object of desire, for it is better to be a bull for one day only, than for all one's life to be an ox. While other states' constitutions might be laudable, yet it would be advisable to use only that which is known to oneself.

In short, Ninon showed that their philosophy was a conspiracy against democracy. He advised the people not even to listen to the defendants, considering that they would never have been admitted into the assembly if the Pythagoreans' council had had to depend for admission on the session of a thousand men, and said that they should not allow speech to those who had used their utmost power to prevent the speech of others. The people must remember that when they raised their right hands to vote, or even counted their votes, that their right hand was constructively rejected by the Pythagoreans, who were aristocrats. It was also disgraceful that the Crotonian masses who had conquered thirty myriads of men at the river Tracis should be outweighed by a thousandth part of the same number through sedition in the city itself.

Through these calumnies Ninon so exasperated his hearers that a few days later a great multitude assembled, intending to attack the Pythagoreans as they were sacrificing to the Muses in a house near the temple of Apollo. Foreseeing this, the Pythagoreans fled to an inn, while Democedes with the youths retired to Plataea. The partisans of the new constitution decreed an accusation against Democedes of inciting the youths to capture power, putting a price of thirty talents on his head, dead or alive. A battle ensued, and the victor Theages was given the thirty talents promised by the city. The city's evils were spread to the whole region, and the exiles were arrested in Tarentum, Metapontum, and Caulonia.

The envoys from these cities that came to Croton to get the charges were, according to the Crotonian record, bribed, with the result that the exiles were condemned as guilty, and driven out further. The Crotonians then expelled from the city all who were dissatisfied with the existing regime, banishing along with them all their families, on the two-fold pretext that impiety was unbearable and that the children should not be separated from their parents. They then repudiated the debts, and redistributed the lands.

Many years after, when Dinarchus and his associates had been slain in another battle, and when Litagus, the chief leader of the sedition, was dead, pity and repentance induced the citizens to recall from exile what remained of the Pythagoreans. They therefore sent for messengers from Achaia, who were to come to an agreement with the exiles, and file their oaths at Delphi. The Pythagoreans who returned from exile were about sixty in number, not to mention the aged, among whom were some physicians and dieticians who worked along original lines. When these Pythagoreans returned, they were welcomed by the crowds, who silenced dissenters by announcing that the Ninon regime was ended. Then the Thurians invaded the country, and the Pythagoreans were sent to procure assistance; but they perished in battle, mutually defending each other. So thoroughly had the city become Pythagoreanized that beside the public praise, they performed a public sacrifice in the temple of the Muses which had originally been built at the instigation of Pythagoras.

That is all concerning the attack made on the Pythagoreans.

36. The Pythagorean Succession

PYTHAGORAS' acknowledged successor was Aristaeus, the son of the Crotonian Damophon, who was Pythagoras' contemporary, and lived seven ages before Plato. Being exceedingly skillful in Pythagoric dogmas, he carried on the school, educated Pythagoras' children, and married his wife Theano. Pythagoras was said to have taught his school 39 years, and to have lived a century. Aristaeus, growing old, relinquished the school to Pythagoras' son Mnesarchus. He was followed by Bulagoras, in whose time Croton was plundered. After the war, Gartydas the Crotonian who had been absent on a journey, returned, and took up the school; but he so grieved about his country's calamity that he died prematurely. But the Pythagoreans who became very old were accustomed to liberate themselves from the body, as from a prison.

Later, being saved through certain strangers, Aresas Lucanus undertook the school, and to him came Diodorus Aspendius, who was received into the school because of the small number of genuine Pythagoreans.

Clinias and Philolaus were at Heraclea, Theorides and Eurytus at Metapontum, and at Tarentum, Archytas. Epicharmus was also said to have been one of the foreign Hearers, but he was not one of the school. However, having arrived at Syracuse, he refrained from public philosophizing in consideration of the tyranny of Hiero. But he wrote the Pythagorean views in metre, and published the occult Pythagorean dogmas in comedies.

It is probable that the majority of the Pythagoreans were anonymous, and remain unknown. But the following names are known and celebrated:

Of the Crotonians, Hippostratus, Dymas, Aegon, Aemon, Sillus, Cleosthenes, Agelas, Episylus, Phyciadas, Ecphantus, Timaeus, Buthius, Eratus, Itmaeus, Rhodippus, Bryas, Evandrus, Myllias, Antimedon, Ageas, Leophron, Agylus, Onatus, Hipposthenes, Cleophron, Alcmaeon, Damocles, Milon and Menon.

At Metapontum resided Brontinus, Parmiseus, Orestadas, Leon, Damarmenus, Aeneas, Chilas, Melisias, Aristeas, Laphion, Evandrus, Agesidamus, Xenocades, Euryphemus, Aristomenes, Agesarchus, Alceas, Xenophantes, Thraseus, Arytus, Epiphron, Eiriscus, Megistias, Leocydes, Thrasymedes, Euphemus, Procles, Antimenes, Lacritus, Damotages, Pyrrho, Rhexibius, Alopecus, Astylus, Dacidas, Aliochus, Lacrates and Glycinus.

Of the Agrigentines was Empedocles.

Of the Eleatae, was Parmenides.

Of the Tarentines were Philolaus, Eurytus, Archytas, Theodorus, Aristippus, Lycon, Hestiaeus, Polemarchus, Asteas, Clinias, Cleon, Eurymedon, Arceas, Clinagoras, Archippus, Zopyrus, Euthynus, Dicaearchus, Philonidas, Phrontidas, Lysis, Lysibius, Dinocrates, Echecrates, Paction, Acusiladas, Icmus, Pisicrates, and Clearatus.

Of the Leontines were Phrynichus, Smichias, Aristoclidas, Clinias, Abroteles, Pisyrrhydus, Bryas, Evandrus, Archemachus, Mimnomachus, Achmonidas, Dicas, and Carophantidas.

Of the Sybarites were Metopus, Hippasus, Proxenus, Evanor, Deanax, Menestor, Diocles, Empedus, Timasius, Polemaeus, Evaeus, and Tyrsenus.

Of the Carthaginians were Miltiades, Anthen, Odius and Leocritus.

Of the Parians, Aeetius, Phaenecles, Dexitheus, Alcimachus, Dinarchus, Meton, Timaeus, Timesianax, Amaerus, and Thymaridas.

Of the Locrians, Gyptius, Xenon, Philodamus, Evetes, Adicus, Sthenonidas, Sosistratus, Euthynus, Zaleucus, and Timares.

Of the Posidonians, Athamas, Simus, Proxenus, Cranous, Myes, Bathylaus, Phaedon.

Of the Lucani, Ocellus, and his brother Occillus, Oresandrus, Cerambus, Dardaneus, and Malion.

Of the Aegeans, Hippomedon, Timosthenes, Euelthon, Thrasydamus, Crito, and Polyctor.

Of the Lacones, Autocharidas, Cleanor, Eurycrates.

Of the Hyperboreans, Abaris.

Of the Rheginenses, Aristides, Demosthenes, Aristocrates, Phytius, Helicaon, Mnesibulus, Hipparchides, Athosion, Euthycles, Opsimus.

Of the Selinuntians, Calais.

Of the Syracusans, Leptines, Phintias, and Damon.

Of the Samians, Melissus, Lacon, Archippus, Glorippus, Heloris, Hippon.

Of the Caulonienses, Callibrotus, Dicon, Nastas, Drymon, and Xentas.

Of the Phliasians, Diocles, Echecrates, Phanton and Polymnastus.

Of the Sicyonians, Poliades, Demon, Sostratius, and Sosthenes.

Of the Cyrenaeans, Prorus, Melanippus, Aristangelus, and Theodorus.

Of the Cyziceni, Pythodorus, Hipposthenes, Butherus, and Xenophilus.

Of the Catanaei, Charondas and Lysiades.

Of the Corinthians, Chrysippus.

Of the Tyrrhenians, Nausitheus.

Of the Athenians, Neocritus.

Of the Pontians, Lyramnus.

In all, two hundred and eighteen.

The most illustrious Pythagorean women include the following: Timycha, the wife of Myllias the Crotonian. Philtis, the daughter of Theophrius the Crotonian. Byndacis, the sister of Ocellus and Occillus, Lucanians. Chilonis, the daughter of Chilon the Lacedaemonian. Cratesiclea the Lacedaemonian, the wife of the Lacedaemonian Cleanor. Theano, the wife of Brontinus of Metapontum. Mya, the wife of Milon the Crotonian. Lasthenia the Arcadian. Abrotelia, the daughter of Abroteles the Tarentine. Echecratia the Phliasian. Tyrsenis the Sybarite. Pisirrhonde, the Tarentine. Nisleadusa, the Lacedaemonian. Bryo, the Argive. Babelyma the Argive, and Cleaechmas, the sister of Autocharidas the Lacedaemonian. In all, seventeen.

PORPHYRY:

THE LIFE OF PYTHAGORAS

PORPHYRY'S *Life of Pythagoras* is the only surviving fragment of his *History of Philosophy* in four books. Porphyry (c. 233—c. 305 C.E.), the brilliant student of Plotinus, was an important Neoplatonic philosopher who wrote over 70 works dealing with metaphysics, literary criticism, history, the allegorical interpretation of myth, and so on. Porphyry's biography of Pythagoras is short, enjoyable and informative, causing one to wish that his entire *History of Philosophy* had survived.

Kenneth Sylvan Guthrie was the first person to translate Porphyry's *Life of Pythagoras* into English. Since then the work has been translated by Morton Smith and appears in Hadas and Smith, *Heroes and Gods: Spiritual Biographies in Antiquity,* New York, 1965.

For an account of the life and work of Porphyry see the introduction to *Porphyry's Letter to His Wife Marcella*, Phanes Press, 1985. For a complete listing of his known writings see the appendix in Porphyry's *Launching Points to the Realm of Mind*, Phanes Press, 1988.

THE LIFE OF PYTHAGORAS

MANY THINK THAT PYTHAGORAS was the son of Mnesarchus, but they differ as to the latter's race; some thinking him a Samian, while Neanthes, in the fifth book of his *Fables* states that he was a Syrian, from the city of Tyre. As a famine has arisen in Samos, Mnesarchus went thither to trade, and was naturalized there. There was also born his son Pythagoras, who early manifested studiousness, but was later taken to Tyre, and there entrusted to the Chaldeans, whose doctrines he imbibed. Thence he returned to Ionia, where he first studied under the Syrian Pherecydes, then also under Hermodamas the son of Creophylius, who as that time was an old man, residing in Samos.

2. Neanthes says that others hold that his father was a Tyrrhenian [or Etruscan], of those who inhabit Lemnos, and that while on a trading trip to Samos was there naturalized. On sailing to Italy, Mnesarchus took the youth Pythagoras with him. Just at this time this country was greatly flourishing. Neanthes adds that Pythagoras had two older brothers, Eunostus and Tyrrhenus. But Apollonius [of Tyana], in his book about Pythagoras affirms that his mother was Pythais, a descendant of Ancaeus, the founder of Samos. Apollonius adds that he was said to be the offspring of Apollo and Pythais, on the authority of Mnesarchus; and a Samian poet sings:

> Pythais, of all Samians the most fair,
> Zeus-loved Pythagoras to Phoebus bare!

Apollonius says that Pythagoras studied not only under Pherecydes and Hermodamas, but also under Anaximander.

3. Duris of Samos, in the second book of his *Chronicles*, writes that his son was Arimnestus, that he was a teacher of Democritus and that on returning from banishment he suspended a brazen pillar in the temple of Hera, a pillar two cubits

[three feet] in diameter, bearing this inscription:

> Me, Arimnestus, who many proportions traced,
> Pythagoras's beloved son here placed.

This tablet was removed by Simus, a musician, who claimed the harmonic canon graven thereon, and published it as his own. Seven proportions were engraved, but when Simus took away one, the others were destroyed.

4. It is said that by Theano, a Cretan, the daughter of Pythenax, Pythagoras had a son, Telauges, and a daughter, Myia; to whom some add Arignota, whose Pythagorean writings are still extant. Timaeus relates that Pythagoras' daughter, while a maiden, took precedence among the maidens in Croton, and when a wife, among married women. The Crotonians made Pythagoras' house a temple of Demeter, and the neighboring street they called Museum Street.

5. Lycus, in the fourth book of his *Histories*, noting different opinions about his country says, "Unless you happen to know the country and the city of which Pythagoras was a citizen, it will remain a mere matter of conjecture. Some say he was a Samian, others from Phlious [in the Peloponnesus], others from Metapontum [in southern Italy]."

6. As to his knowledge, it is said that he learned the mathematical sciences from the Egyptians, Chaldeans, and Phoenicians; for of old the Egyptians excelled in geometry, the Phoenicians in numbers and proportions, and the Chaldeans in astronomical theorems, divine rites, and worship of the Gods; other secrets concerning the course of life he received and learned from the Magi.

7. These accomplishments are the more generally known, but the rest are less celebrated. Moreover, Eudoxus, in the second book of his *Description of the Earth*, writes that Pythagoras practiced the greatest purity, and was shocked at all bloodshedding and killing; that he not only abstained from animal food, but never in any way approached butchers or hunters. Antiphon, in his book *On Illustrious Virtuous Men*, praises his perseverance while he was in Egypt, saying that Pythagoras, desiring to become acquainted with the institutions of the Egyptian priests, and diligently endeavoring to participate therein, requested the Tyrant Polycrates [of Samos] to write to Amasis, the King of Egypt, his friend and former host, to procure him initiation. Coming to Amasis, he was given letters to the priests, but the priests of Heliopolis sent him on to those at Memphis, on the pretense that they were the more ancient. On the same pretense, he was sent on from Memphis to Diospolis [or ancient Thebes].

8. From fear of the King, the latter priests dared not make excuses [to initiate Pythagoras], but thinking that he would desist from his purpose as a result of great difficulties, they enjoined on him very hard precepts, entirely different from the institutions of the Greeks. These he performed so readily that he won their admiration, and they permitted him to sacrifice to the Gods, and to acquaint himself with all their sciences, a favor never previously granted to a foreigner.

9. Returning to Ionia, he opened in his own country a school which is even now called Pythagoras' Semicircle, and in which the Samians meet to deliberate about matters of common interest. Outside the city he adapted a cave to the study of his philosophy, in which he lived day and night, discoursing with a few of

his associates. He was now forty years old, says Aristoxenus. Seeing that Polycrates' government was becoming so violent that soon a free man would become a victim of his tyranny, he journeyed towards Italy.

10. Diogenes, in his treatise *On the Incredible Things Beyond Thule*, has treated Pythagoras' affairs so carefully that I think his account should not be omitted. He says that Mnesarchus was of the race of the Etruscans who inhabited Lemnos, Imbros, and Scyrus, and that he departed thence to visit many cities and various lands. During his journeys he found an infant lying under a large, tall poplar tree. On approaching, he observed it laying on its back, looking steadily without blinking at the sun. In its mouth was a little slender reed, like a pipe, through which the child was being nourished by the dew-drops that fell from the tree. This great wonder prevailed upon him to take the child, believing it to be of a divine origin. The child was fostered by a native of that country, named Androcles, who later on adopted him, and entrusted to him the management of his affairs. On becoming wealthy, Mnesarchus educated the boy whom Androcles adopted, naming him Astraeus, and rearing him with his own three sons, Eunostus, Tyrrhenus, and Pythagoras.

11. He sent the boy to a lyre player, a gymnast and a painter. Later he sent him to Anaximander at Miletus, to learn geometry and astronomy. Then Pythagoras visited the Egyptians, the Arabians, the Chaldeans and the Hebrews, from whom he acquired expertise in the interpretation of dreams, and acquired the use of frankincense in the worship of divinities.

12. In Egypt he lived with the priests, and learned the language and wisdom of the Egyptians, and their three kinds of letters, the epistolographic, the hieroglyphic, and symbolic, whereof one imitates the common way of speaking, while the others express the sense of allegory and parable. In Arabia he conferred with the king. In Babylon he associated with the other Chaldeans, especially attaching himself to Zaratus [=Zoroaster], by whom he was purified from the pollutions of his past life, and taught the things from which a virtuous man ought to be free. Likewise he heard lectures about Nature, and the principles of wholes. It was from his stay among these foreigners that Pythagoras acquired the greater part of his wisdom.

13. Astraeus was by Mnesarchus entrusted to Pythagoras, who received him, and after studying his physiognomy and the motions of his body, instructed him. He first accurately investigated the science about the nature of man, discerning the disposition of every one he met. None was allowed to become his friend or associate without being examined in facial expression and disposition.

14. Pythagoras had another youthful disciple, from Thrace. Zalmoxis was his name because he was born wrapped in a bear's skin, in Thracian called *zalmon*. Pythagoras loved him and instructed him in sublime speculations concerning sacred rites, and the worship of the Gods. Some say this youth was also named Thales, and that the barbarians worshipped him as Hercules.

15. Dionysophanes says that he was a servant of Pythagoras, who fell into the hands of thieves and by them was branded when Pythagoras was persecuted and banished, and bound up his forehead on account of the scars. Others say that the name Zalmoxis signifies a stranger or foreigner.

Pherecydes, in Delos, fell sick; and Pythagoras attended him until he died, and performed his funeral rites. Pythagoras then, longing to be with Hermodamas the son of Creophylus, returned to Samos. After enjoying his society, Pythagoras trained the Samian athlete Eurymenes, who though he was of small stature, conquered at Olympia through his surpassing knowledge of Pythagoras' wisdom. While according to ancient custom the other athletes fed on cheese and figs, Eurymenes, by the advice of Pythagoras, fed daily on meat, which endued his body with great strength. Pythagoras gradually imbued him with his wisdom, exhorting him to go into the struggle not for the sake of victory, but for the exercise, that he should gain by the training, avoiding the envy resulting from victory. For the victors, though decked with leafy crowns, are not always pure.

16. Later, when the Samians were oppressed with the tyranny of Polycrates, Pythagoras saw that life in such a state was unsuitable for a philosopher, and so planned to travel to Italy. At Delphi he inscribed an elegy on the tomb of Apollo, declaring that Apollo was the son of Silenus, but was slain by Pytho, and buried in the place called "Tripod," so named from the local mourning for Apollo by the three daughters of Triopas.

17. Going to Crete, Pythagoras besought initiation from the priests of Morgos, one of the Idaean Dactyls, by whom he was purified with the meteoric thunderstone, during which he lay, at dawn, stretched upon his face by the seaside, and at night, beside a river, crowned with a black lamb's woolen wreath. Descending into the Idaean cave, wrapped in black wool, he stayed there twenty-seven days, according to the custom; he sacrificed to Zeus, and saw the couch which there is yearly made for him. On Zeus' tomb Pythagoras inscribed an epigram, "Pythagoras to Zeus," which begins: "Zan deceased here lies, whom men call Zeus."

18. When he reached Italy, he stopped at Croton. His presence was that of a free man, tall, graceful in speech and in gesture, and in everything else. Dicaearchus relates that the arrival of this great traveller, endowed with all the advantages of nature, and prosperously guided by fortune, produced on the Crotonians so great an impression, that he won the esteem of the older magistrates by his many and excellent discourses. They ordered him to deliver exhortations to the young men, and then to the boys who flocked out of the school to hear him, and then to the women, who came together for this purpose.

19. Through this he achieved great reputation, and he drew great audiences from the city, not only of men, but also of women, among whom was a specially illustrious person named Theano. He also drew audiences from among the neighboring barbarians, among whom were magnates and kings. What he told his audiences cannot be said with certainty, for he enjoined silence upon his hearers. But the following is a matter of general information. He taught that the soul is immortal, and that after death it transmigrates into other animated bodies. After certain specified periods, he said, the same events occur again, for nothing is entirely new; all animated beings are kin, he taught, and should be considered as belonging to one great family. Pythagoras was the first one to introduce these teachings into Greece.

20. His speech was so persuasive that, according to Nicomachus, in one ad-

dress made on first landing in Italy, he made more than two thousand adherents. Out of desire to live with him, these built a large auditorium, to which both women and boys were admitted. [Foreign visitors were so many that] they built whole cities, settling that whole region of Italy now known as Magna Graecia. His ordinances and laws were by them received as divine precepts, and they would do nothing to transgress them. Indeed, they ranked him among the divinities and held all property in common; and whenever they communicated to each other some choice bit of his philosophy, from which physical truths could always be deduced, they would swear by the Tetraktys, adjuring Pythagoras as a divine witness, in the words,

> I call to witness him who to our souls expressed the
> Tetraktys, eternal Nature's fountain-spring.

21. During his travels in Italy and Sicily he found various cities subjected one to another, both of long standing and recently. By his disciples, some of whom were found in every city, he infused into them an aspiration for liberty, thus restoring to freedom Croton, Sybaris, Catana, Regium, Himera, Agrigentum, Tauromenium, and others, on whom he imposed laws through Charondas of Catana, and Zaleucus of Locri, which resulted in a long era of good government, emulated by all their neighbors. Simicus the tyrant of Centoripae, on hearing Pythagoras' discourse, abdicated his rule, and divided his property between his sister and the citizens.

22. According to Aristoxenus, some Lucanians, Messapians, Peucetians, and Romans came to him. He rooted out all dissensions, not only among his disciples and their successors, for many ages, but among all the cities of Italy and Sicily, both internally and externally. For he would continuously say, "We ought to the best of our ability avoid, and even with fire and sword eradicate from the body, sickness; from the soul, ignorance; from the belly, luxury; from a city, sedition; from a family, discord; and from all things, excess."

23. If we may credit what ancient and trustworthy writers have related of him, he exerted an influence even over irrational animals. The Daunian bear, who had committed extensive depredations in the neighborhood, he seized; and after having patted her for awhile, and given her barley and fruits, he made her swear never again to touch a living creature, and then released her. She immediately took herself into the woods and the hills, and from that time on never attacked any irrational animal.

24. At Tarentum, in a pasture, seeing an ox cropping beans, he went to the herdsman, and advised him to tell the ox to abstain from beans. The countryman mocked him, proclaiming his ignorance of the ox-language. So Pythagoras himself went and whispered in the ox's ear. Not only did the bovine at once desist from his diet of beans, but would never touch any thenceforward, though he survived many years near Hera's temple at Tarentum, until very old, being called the sacred ox, and eating any food given him.

25. While at the Olympic games, he was discoursing with his friends about auguries, omens, and divine signs, and how men of true piety do receive messages from the Gods. Flying over his head was an eagle, who stopped, and came down

to Pythagoras. After stroking her awhile he released her.

Meeting with some fishermen who were drawing in their nets heavily laden with fishes from the deep, he predicted the exact number of fish they had caught. The fishermen said that if his estimate was accurate they would do whatever he commanded. They counted them accurately, and found the number correct. He then bade them to return the fish alive into the sea; and, what is more wonderful, not one of them died, although they had been out of the water a considerable time.

26. Many of his associates he reminded of the lives lived by their souls before they were bound to their present body, and by irrefutable arguments demonstrated that he had been Euphorbus, the son of Panothus. He specially praised the following Homeric verses about himself, and sang them to the lyre most elegantly:

> The shining circlets of his golden hair,
> Which even the Graces might be proud to wear,
> Instarred with gems and gold, bestrew the shore,
> With dust dishonored, and deformed with gore,
> As the young olive, in some sylvan scene,
> Crowned by fresh fountains with celestial green,
> Lifts the gay head in snowy flowerets fair,
> And plays and dances to the gentle air,
> When lo, a whirlwind from high heaven invades,
> The tender plant, and withers all its shades;
> It lies uprooted from its genial head,
> A lovely ruin, now defaced and dead.
> Thus young, the beautiful Euphorbus lay,
> While the fierce Spartan tore his shield away.
>   (*Iliad*, 17. 51-66.)

27. The stories about the shield of this Phrygian Euphorbus being at Mycenae dedicated to Hera of Argive, along with other Trojan spoils, shall here be omitted as being of too generally known a nature.

It is said that the river Caucasus, while he, with many of his associates was passing over it, said to him very clearly, "Hail, Pythagoras!"

Almost unanimous is the report that on one and the same day he was present at Metapontum in Italy, and at Tauromenium in Sicily, in each place conversing with his friends, though the places are separated by many miles, both at sea and land, demanding a journey of many days.

28. It is well known that he showed his golden thigh to Abaris the Hyperborean, to confirm him in the opinion that he was the Hyperborean Apollo, whose priest Abaris was.

A ship was coming into the harbor, and his friends expressed the wish to own the goods it contained. "Then," said Pythagoras, "you would own a corpse!" On the ship's arrival this was found to be the true state of affairs.

Of Pythagoras many other more wonderful and divine things are persistently and unanimously related, so that we have no hesitation in saying never was more attributed to any man, nor was any more eminent.

29. Verified predictions of earthquakes are handed down, also, that he immediately chased away a pestilence, suppressed violent winds and hail, calmed

storms both on rivers and on seas, for the comfort and safe passage of his friends. As their poems attest, the like was often performed by Empedocles, Epimenides and Abaris, who had learned the art of doing these things from him. Empedocles, indeed, was surnamed Alexanemos, "the chaser of winds," Epimenides, Cathartes, "the purifyer," Abaris was called Aethrobates, the "air-walker," for he was carried in the air on an arrow of the Hyperborean Apollo, over rivers, seas, and inaccessible places. It is believed that this was the method employed by Pythagoras when on the same day he discoursed with his friends at Metapontum and Tauromenium.

30. He soothed the passions of the soul and body by rhythms, songs, and incantations. These he adapted and applied to his friends. He himself could hear the Harmony of the Universe, and understood the universal music of the spheres, and of the stars which move in concert with them, and which we cannot hear because of the limitations of our weak nature. This is testified to by these characteristic verses of Empedocles:

> Amongst these was one in things sublimest skilled,
> His mind with all the wealth of learning filled.
> Whatever sages did invent, he sought;
> And whilst his thoughts were on this work intent,
> All things existent, easily he viewed,
> Through ten or twenty ages making search.

31. The words "sublimest things," and "he surveyed all existent things," and "the wealth of the mind," and the like, are indicative of Pythagoras' constitution of body, mind, seeing, hearing and understanding, which was exquisite, and surpassingly accurate.

Pythagoras affirmed that the Nine Muses were constituted by the sounds made by the seven planets, the sphere of the fixed stars, and that which is opposed to our earth, called the "counter-earth."* He called Mnemosyne, or Memory, the composition, symphony and connexion of them all, which is eternal and unbegotten as being composed of all of them.

32. Diogenes, setting forth his daily routine of living, relates that he advised all men to avoid ambition and vainglory, which chiefly excite envy, and to shun the presence of crowds. He himself held morning conferences at his residence, composing his soul with the music of the lyre, and singing certain ancient paeans of Thales. He also sang verses of Homer and Hesiod, which seemed to soothe the mind. He danced certain dances which he thought conferred on the body agility and health. Walks he took not too promiscuously, but only in company of one or two companions, in temples of sacred groves, selecting the most quiet and beautiful places.

33. His friends he loved exceedingly, being the first to declare that "The goods of friends are common," and that "A friend is another self." While they were

---

*According to the cosmology of the Pythagorean Philolaus, *antichthon,* the counter-earth, revolves in time with the earth opposite the central fire. Aristotle assumes that the counter-earth was introduced to bring the number of the celestial bodies up to ten, the Pythagorean perfect number.

in good health he always conversed with them; if they were sick, he nursed them; if they were afflicted in mind, he solaced them, some by incantations and magic charms, others by music. He had prepared songs for the diseases of the body, by singing which he cured the sick. He had also some that caused forgetfulness of sorrow, mitigation of anger, and destruction of lust.

34. As to food, his breakfast was chiefly of honey; at dinner he used bread made of millet, barley or herbs, raw and boiled. Only rarely did he eat the flesh of sacrificial victims, nor did he take this from every part of the anatomy. When he intended to sojourn in the sanctuaries of the divinities, he would eat no more than was necessary to still hunger and thirst. To quiet hunger he made a mixture of poppy seed and sesame, the skin of a sea-onion, well washed until entirely drained of the outward juices, of the flowers of the daffodil, and the leaves of mallows, of paste of barley and chick peas, taking an equal weight of which, and chopping it small, with honey of Hymettus he made it into a mass. Against thirst he took the seed of cucumbers, and the best dried raisins, extracting the seeds, and coriander flowers, and the seeds of mallows, purslane, scraped cheese, wheat meal and cream, all of which he mixed up with wild honey.

35. He claimed that this diet had, by Demeter, been taught to Hercules, when he was sent into the Libyan deserts. This preserved his body in an unchanging condition, not at one time well, and at another time sick, nor at one time fat, and at another lean. Pythagoras' countenance showed the same constancy that was also in his soul. For he was neither more elated by pleasure, nor dejected by grief, and no one ever saw him either rejoicing or mourning.

36. When Pythagoras sacrificed to the Gods, he did not use offensive profusion, but offered no more than barley bread, cakes and myrrh, least of all animals, unless perhaps cocks and pigs. When he discovered the proposition that the square of the hypotenuse of a right-angled triangle was equal to the squares on the sides containing the right angle, he is said to have sacrificed an ox, although the more accurate say that this ox was made of flour.

37. His utterances were of two kinds, plain or symbolical. His teaching was twofold: of his disciples some were called Students (*mathematikoi*), and others Hearers (*akousmatikoi*). The Students learned the fuller and more exactly elaborate reasons of science, while the Hearers heard only the summarized instructions of learning, without more detailed explanations.

38. He ordained that his disciples should speak well and think reverently of the Gods, daimons, and heroes, and likewise of parents and benefactors; that they should obey the laws; that they should not relegate the worship of the Gods to a secondary position, but should perform it eagerly, even at home; that to the celestial divinities they should sacrifice uncommon offerings, and ordinary ones to the inferior deities. [The world he divided into] opposite powers: the better is the Monad, light, right, equal, stable and straight; while the worse is an inferior Dyad, darkness, left, unequal, unstable and curved.

39. Moreover, he taught the following. A cultivated and fruit-bearing plant, harmless to man and beast, should be neither injured nor destroyed. A deposit of money or of teachings should be faithfully preserved by the trustee. There are three kinds of things that deserve to be pursued and acquired:

honorable and virtuous things, those that conduce to the use of life, and those that bring pleasures of the blameless, secure and solemn kind, and not the vulgar intoxicating kinds. Of pleasures there are two kinds: one that indulges the stomach and lusts by a profusion of wealth, which he compared to the murderous songs of the Sirens; the other kind consists of things honest, just, and necessary to life, which are just as sweet as the first, without being followed by repentance, and these pleasures he compared to the harmony of the Muses.

40. He advised that special regard should be given to two times of the day: the one when we go to sleep, and the other when we awake. At each of these we should consider our past actions, and those that are to come. We ought to require of ourselves an account of our past deeds, while of the future we should have a providential care. Therefore he advised everybody to repeat to himself the following verses before he fell asleep:

> Nor suffer sleep to close thine eyes
> Till thrice thy acts that day thou has run o'er;
> How slip? What deeds? What duty left undone?

And on rising, the following:

> As soon as ere thou wakest, in order lay
> The actions to be done that following day.

41. Such things taught he, though advising above all things to speak the truth, for this alone deifies men. For as he had learned from the Magi, who call God Horomazda, God's body is like light, and his soul is like truth. He taught much else, which he claimed to have learned from Aristokleia at Delphi. Certain things he declared mystically, symbolically, most of which were collected by Aristotle, as when he called the sea a tear of Kronos, the Great and Little Bear the hands of Rhea, the Pleiades the lyre of the Muses, and the planets the dogs of Persephone. He called the sound caused by striking on brass the voice of a daimon enclosed in the brass.

42. He had also another kind of symbols, such as *pass not over a balance*, that is, shun avarice; *poke not the fire with a sword*, that is, we ought not to excite a man full of fire and answer with sharp language; *pluck not a crown* meant not to violate the laws, which are the crowns of cities.

Moreover, *Eat not the heart* signified not to afflict ourselves with sorrows. *Do not sit upon a bushel basket* meant not to live ignobly. *On starting a journey, do not turn back*, meant that this life should not be regretted when near its end. *Do not walk in the public way* meant to avoid the opinions of the multitude, adopting those of the learned and the few. *Receive not swallows into your house* meant not to admit under the same roof garrulous and intemperate men. *Help a man to take up a burden, but not to lay it down*, meant to encourage no one to be indolent, but to apply oneself to labor and virtue. *Do not carry the images of the Gods in rings*, signifies that one should not at once to the vulgar reveal one's opinons about the Gods, or discourse about them. *Offer libations to the Gods, just to the ears of the cup*, meant that we ought to worship and celebrate the Gods with music, for that penetrates through the ears. *Do not eat those things that are unlawful—beginning, increase, source nor end—nor the first basis of all things.*

43. He thereby taught abstention from the loins, testicles, genitals, brains, feet and heads of sacrificial victims. The loins he called a foundation, because on them as on foundations living beings are settled. Testicles and genitals he called beginning for no one is engendered without the help of these. The brain he called increase, as it is the cause of growth in living beings. The source was the feet, and the head the end, since it has the most power in the government of the body. He likewise advised abstention from beans, as if from human flesh.

44. Beans were forbidden, it is said, because the particular plants grow and individualize only after that which is the principle and origin of things is mixed together, so that many things underground are confused, and coalesce, after which everything rots together. Then living creatures were produced together with plants, so that both men and beans arose out of putrefaction, whereof he alleged many manifest arguments. For if any one should chew a bean, and having ground it to a pulp with his teeth, and should expose that pulp to the warm sun, for a short while, and then return to it, he will perceive the scent of human blood. Moreover, if at the time when beans bloom, one should take a little of the flower, which is then black, and should put it into an earthen vessel, and cover it closely, and bury it in the ground for ninety days, and at the end thereof take it up, and uncover it, instead of the bean he will find that either the head of an infant or the vagina of a woman has developed.

45. He also wished men to abstain from other things, such as sea-wombs, red mullet, and a sea-fish called a "nettle" (anemone), and from nearly all other marine animals. He referred his origin to those of past ages, affirming that he was first Euphorbus, then Aethalides, then Hermotimus, then Pyrrhus, and last, Pythagoras. He showed to his disciples that the soul is immortal, and to those who were rightly purified he brought back the memory of the acts of their former lives.

46. He cultivated philosophy, the scope of which is to free the mind implanted within us from the impediments and fetters within which it is confined, without whose freedom none can learn anything sound or true, or perceive the unsoundness in the operation of sense. Pythagoras thought that mind alone sees and hears, while all the rest are blind and deaf. The purified mind should be applied to the discovery of beneficial things, which can be effected by certain arts, which by degrees induce it to the contemplation of eternal and incorporeal things which never vary. This orderliness of perception should begin from consideration of the most minute things, lest by any change the mind should be jarred and withdraw itself, through the failure of continuousness in its subject-matter.

47. That is the reason he made so much use of the mathematical disciplines and speculations, which are intermediate between the physical and the incorporeal realm, for the reason that, like bodies, they have a three-fold dimension, and yet share the impassibility of incorporeals. [These disciplines he used] as degrees of preparation to the contemplation of the really existent things, by an artistic principle diverting the eyes of the mind from corporeal things, whose manner and state never remain in the same condition, to a desire for true [spiritual] food. By means of these mathematical sciences therefore, Pythagoras rendered men

truly happy, by this artistic introduction of truly existent things.

48. Among others, Moderatus of Gades, who learnedly treated of the qualities of numbers in eleven books, states that the Pythagoreans specialized in the study of numbers to explain their teachings symbolically, as do geometricians, inasmuch as the primary forms and principles are hard to understand and express otherwise in plain discourse. A similar case is the representation of sounds by letters, which are known by marks, which are called the first elements of learning; later, they inform us these are not the true elements, which they only signify.

49. As the geometricians cannot express incorporeal forms in words, and have recourse to the drawings of figures, saying "This is a triangle," and yet do not mean that the actually seen lines are *the* triangle, but only what they represent, the knowledge in the mind, so the Pythagoreans used the same objective method in respect to first reasons and forms. As these incorporeal forms and first principles could not be expressed in words, they had recourse to demonstration by numbers. Number One denoted to them the reason of Unity, Identity, Equality, the purpose of friendship, sympathy, and conservation of the Universe, which results from persistence in Sameness. For unity in the details harmonizes all the parts of a whole, as by the participation of the First Cause.

50. Number Two, or Dyad, signified the dual reason of diversity and inequality, of everything that is divisible, or mutable, existing at one time in one way, and at another time in another way. After all, these methods were not confined to the Pythagoreans, being used by other philosophers to denote unitive powers, which contain all things in the universe, among which are certain reasons of equality, dissimilitude and diversity. These reasons are what they meant by the terms Monad and Dyad, or by the words uniform, biform, or diversiform.

51. The same reasons apply to their use of other numbers, which were ranked according to certain powers. Things that had a beginning, middle and end they denoted by the number Three, saying that anything that has a middle is triform, which was applied to every perfect thing. They said that if anything was perfect it would make use of this principle, and be adorned according to it; and as they had no other name for it, they invented the form, Triad, and whenever they tried to bring us to the knowledge of what is perfect they led us to that by the form of this Triad. So also with the other numbers, where were ranked according to the same reasons.

52. All other things were comprehended under a single form and power, which they called Decad, explaining it by a pun, as *dechada* ("receptacle"), meaning comprehension. That is why they call Ten a perfect number, the most perfect of all, as comprehending all difference of numbers, reasons, species and proportions. For if the nature of the universe be defined according to the reasons (*logoi*) and proportions of numbers, and if that which is produced, increased and perfected, proceed according to the reason of numbers and since the Decad comprehends every reason [or ratio] of numbers, every proportion, and every species—why should Nature herself not be denoted by the most perfect number, Ten? Such was the use of numbers among the Pythagoreans.

53. This primary philosophy of the Pythagoreans finally died out, first because it was enigmatical, and then because their commentaries were written in Doric

[Greek], which dialect itself is somewhat obscure, so that Doric teachings were not fully understood, and they became misapprehended and finally suspect as spurious when later those who published them no longer were Pythagoreans. The Pythagoreans affirm that Plato, Aristotle, [and their followers] Speusippus, Aristoxenus and Xenocrates appropriated the best of them, making but minor changes, but later collected and delivered as characteristic Pythagorean doctrines whatever had been invented by envious and malicious persons, to cast contempt on Pythagoreanism.

54. Pythagoras and his associates were long held in such admiration in Italy. that many cities invited them to undertake their administration. At last, however, they incurred envy, and a conspiracy was formed against them as follows. Cylon, a Crotonian, who in race, nobility and wealth was the most preeminent, was of a severe, violent and tyrannical disposition, and did not hesitate to use the multitude of his followers to achieve his ends. As he esteemed himself worthy of whatever was best, he considered it his right to be admitted to Pythagorean fellowship. He therefore went to Pythagoras, extolled himself, and desired his conversation. Pythagoras, however, who was accustomed to read in the nature and manners of human bodies the disposition of the man, bade him to depart, and go about his business. Cylon, being of a rough and violent disposition, took it as a great affront, and became furious.

55. He therefore assembled his friends, began to accuse Pythagoras, and conspired against him and his disciples. Pythagoras then went to Delos, to visit the Syrian Pherecydes, formerly his teacher, who was dangerously sick, to nurse him. Pythagoras' friends than gathered together in the house of Milo the athlete, and were all stoned and burned when Cylon's followers set the house on fire. Only two escaped—Archippus and Lysis—according to the account of Neanthes. Lysis took refuge in Greece and settled in Thebes with Epaminodas, of whom he became the teacher.

56. But Dicaearchus and other more accurate historians relate that Pythagoras himself was present when this conspiracy bore fruit, for Pherecydes had died before he left Samos. Of his friends, forty who were gathered together in a house were slain; while others were gradually slain as they came to the city. As his friends were taken, Pythagoras himself first escaped to the harbor of Caulonia, and thence to Locri. Hearing of his coming, the Locrians sent some old men to their frontiers to intercept him. They said, "Pythagoras, you are wise and of great worth, but as our laws contain nothing reprehensible, we will preserve them intact. Go to some other place, and we will furnish you with any needed necessities of travel." Pythagoras turned back, and sailed to Tarentum, where, receiving the same treatment as at Croton, he went to Metapontum. Everywhere arose great mobs against him, of which even now the inhabitants make mention, calling them the Pythagorean riots, as his followers were called Pythagoreans.

57. Pythagoras fled to the temple of the Muses in Metapontum. There he abode forty days and, starving, died. Others, however, state that his death was due to grief at loss of all his friends who, when the house in which they were gathered was burned, in order to make a way for their master, threw themselves into the flames and made a bridge of safety for him with their own bodies, whereby in-

deed he escaped. When the Pythagoreans died, with them also died their knowledge, which till then they had kept secret, except for a few obscure things which were commonly repeated by those who did not understand them. Pythagoras himself left no book; but some little sparks of his philosophy, obscure and difficult to grasp, were preserved by the few who were preserved by being scattered, like Lysis and Archippus.

58. The Pythagoreans now avoided human society, being lonely, saddened and dispersed. Fearing nevertheless that among men the name of philosophy would be entirely extinguished, and that therefore the Gods would be angry with them, they made abstracts and commentaries. Each man made his own collection of written authorities and his own memories, leaving them wherever he happened to die, charging their wives, sons and daughters to preserve them within their families. This mandate of transmission within each family was obeyed for a long time.

59. Nicomachus says that this was the reason why the Pythagoreans studiously avoided friendship with strangers, preserving a constant friendship among each other.

Aristoxenus, in his book on *The Life of Pythagoras*, says he heard many things from Dionysius, the tyrant of Sicily, who, after his abdication, taught letters at Corinth. Among these were that they abstained from lamentations and grieving, and tears; also from adulation, entreaty, supplication and the like.

60. It is said that Dionysius at one time wanted to test their mutual fidelity under imprisonment. He contrived this plan. Phintias was arrested, and taken before the tyrant, and charged with plotting against the tyrant, convicted, and condemned to death. Phintias, accepting the situation, asked to be given the rest of the day to arrange his own affairs, and those of Damon, his friend and associate, who now would have to assume the management. He therefore asked for a temporary release, leaving Damon as security for his appearance. Dionysius granted the request, and they sent for Damon, who agreed to remain until Phintias should return.

61. The novelty of this deed astonished Dionysius, but those who had first suggested the experiment scoffed at Damon, saying he was in danger of losing his life. But to the general surprise, near sunset Phintias came to die. Dionysius then expressed his admiration, embraced them both, and asked to be received as a third in their friendship. Though he earnestly besought this, they refused this, though assigning no reason therefore. Aristoxenus states that he heard this from Dionysius himself.

Hippobotus and Neanthes relate about Myllia and Timycha...

[Here the manuscript ends.]

FIGURE 11. COIN FROM CROTON

ANONYMOUS:

THE LIFE OF PYTHAGORAS
PRESERVED BY PHOTIUS

THE ANONYMOUS BIOGRAPHY here reproduced was preserved in the writings of
Photius (c. 820-891 C.E.), a Byzantine patriarch and professor of philosophy at the Im-
perial Academy in Constantinople. Little can be said about its unidentified author except
that he, in turn, may preserve some parts of Aristotle's lost treatise *On the Pythagoreans.*

This work discusses briefly the family of Pythagoras and touches upon some elements
of Pythagorean metaphysics and traditional cosmology. This tractate is particularly interesting in that it discusses the ancient Pythagorean idea that man is a microcosm, reflecting all of the elements that make up the universe.

Guthrie was the first translator to render this text into English.

THE LIFE OF PYTHAGORAS

PLATO WAS THE PUPIL of Archytas, and thus the ninth in succession from
Pythagoras; the tenth was Aristotle. Those of Pythagoras' disciples that were
devoted to contemplation were called *sebastici,* the reverend, while those who
were engaged in business were called politicians (*politikoi*). Those who cultivated
the disciplines of geometry and astronomy were called students (*mathematikoi*).
Those who associated personally with Pythagoras were called Pythagoreans
(*Pythagorikoi*), while those who merely imitated his teachings were called
Pythagoristians (*Pythagoristai*). All these generally abstained from the flesh of
animals; at a certain time they tasted the flesh of sacrificial animals only.

2. Pythagoras is said to have lived 104 years; and Mnesarchus, one of his sons,
died a young man. Telauges was another son, and Sara and Myia were his
daughters. Theano, it is said, was not only his disciple, but practically his daughter.

3. The Pythagoreans preach a difference between the Monad, and the One;
the Monad dwells in the intelligible realm, while the One dwells among numbers.
Likewise, the Two exists among numerable things, while the Dyad is
indeterminate.

4. The Monad expresses equality and measure, the Dyad expresses excess and
defect. Mean and measure cannot admit of more or less, while excess and defect,
which proceed to infinity, admit it; that is why the Dyad is called indeterminate.
Since, because of the all-inclusion of the Monad and Dyad, all things refer to
number, they call all things numbers; and the number is perfected in the decad. Ten
is reached by adding in order the first four figures; that is why the Ten is called
the Quaternary [or Tetraktys].

5. They affirm that man may improve in three ways: first, by conversation
with the Gods, for to them none can approach unless he abstain from all evil,
imitating the divinity, even unto assimilation; second, by well-doing, which is
a characteristic of the divinity; third by dying, for if the slight soul-separation
from the body resulting from discipline improves the soul so that she begins to

divine, in dreams—and if the deliria of illness produces visions—then the soul must surely improve far more when entirely separated from the body by death.

6. The Pythagoreans abstained from eating animals on account of their foolish belief in transmigration, and also because flesh-food engages digestion too much, and is too fattening. Beans they also avoided, because they produce flatulency, over-satiety, and for other reasons.

7. The Pythagoreans considered the Monad as the origin (*arche*) of all things, just as a point is the beginning of a line, a line of a surface, and a surface of a solid, which constitutes a body. A point implies a preceding Monad, so that it is really the principle of bodies, and all of them arise from the Monad.

8. The Pythagoreans are said to have predicted many things, and Pythagoras' predictions always came true.

9. Plato is said to have learned his speculative and physical doctrines from the Italian Pythagoreans, his ethics from Socrates, and his logic from Zeno, Parmenides and the Eleatics. But all of these teachings descended from Pythagoras.

10. According to Pythagoras, Plato and Aristotle, sight is the judge of the ten colors, white and black being the extremes of all others between: yellow, tawny, pale, red, blue, green, light blue, and grey. Hearing is the judge of the voice, sharp and flat. Smell is the judge of odors, good and bad, and putridity, humidity, liquidness and evaporation. Taste is the judge of tastes, sweet and bitter, and between them five: sharp, acid, fresh, salt and hot. Touch judges many things between the extremes of heaviness and lightness, such as heat and cold; and those between them, hardness and softness; and those between them, dryness and moistness, and those between them. While the four main senses are confined to their special senses in the head, touch is diffused throughout the head and the whole body, and is common to all the senses, but is specialized in the hands.

11. Pythagoras taught that in heaven there are twelve orders, the first and outermost being the fixed sphere where, according to Aristotle, dwelt the highest God, and the intelligible deities, and where Plato located his Ideas. Next are the seven planets: Saturn, Jupiter, Mars, Venus, Mercury, Sun and Moon. Then comes the sphere of Fire, that of Air, Water, and last, Earth. In the fixed sphere dwells the First Cause, and whatever is nearest thereto is the best organized, and most excellent; while that which is furthest therefrom is the worst. Constant order is preserved as low as the Moon, while all things sublunary are disorderly.

Evil, therefore, must necessarily exist in the neighborhood of the Earth, which has been arranged as the lowest, as a basis for the world, and as a receptacle for the lowest things. All superlunary things are governed in firm order, and Providentially by the decree of God, which they follow; while beneath the moon operate four causes: God, Fate, our election, and Fortune. For instance, to go aboard a ship, or not, is in our power; but the storms and tempests that may arise out of a calm, are the result of Fortune; and the preservation of the ship, sailing through the waters, is in the hands of Providence, of God. There are many different modes of Fate. There is a distinction to be made between Fate, which is determined, orderly and consequent, while Fortune is spontaneous and casual. For example, it is one mode of Fate that guides the growth of a boy through all the sequential ages to manhood.

12. Aristotle, who was a diligent investigator, agreed with the Pythagoreans that the Zodiac runs obliquely, on account of the generations of those earthly things which become complements to the universe. For if these moved evenly, there would be no change of seasons, of any kind. Now the passage of the sun and the other planets from one sign to another effect the four seasons of the year, which determine the growth of plants, and the generation of animals.

13. Others thought that the sun's size exceeded that of the earth by no more than thirty times; but Pythagoras, as I think correctly, taught it was more than a hundred times as great.

14. Pythagoras called the revolution of Saturn the great year, inasmuch as the other planets run their course in a shorter time; Saturn, thirty years, Jupiter, twelve, Mars, two; the Sun in one; Mercury and Venus the same as the Sun. The moon, being nearest to the Earth, has the smallest cycle, that of a month.

15. It was Pythagoras who first called heaven *kosmos*, because it is perfect, and "adorned" with infinite beauty and living beings.

With Pythagoras agreed Plato and Aristotle that the soul is immortal, although some who did not understand Aristotle claimed he thought the soul was mortal.

Pythagoras said that man was a *microcosm*, which means a compendium of the universe; not because, like other animals, even the least, he is constituted by the four elements, but because he contains all the powers of the cosmos. For the universe contains Gods, the four elements, animals and plants. All of these powers are contained in man. He has reason, which is a divine power; he has the nature of the elements, and the powers of moving, growing, and reproduction. However, in each of these he is inferior to the others. For example, an athlete who practices five kinds of sports, diverting his powers into five channels, is inferior to the athlete who practices a single sport well; so man, having all of the powers, is inferior in each. We have less reasoning powers than the Gods, and less of each of the elements than the elements themselves. Our anger and desire are inferior to those passions in the irrational animals, while our powers of nutrition and growth are inferior to those in plants. Constituted therefore of different powers, we have a difficult life to lead.

16. While all other things are ruled by one nature only, we are drawn by different powers; as for instance, when by God we are drawn to better things, or when we are drawn to evil courses by the prevailing of the lower powers. He who, like a vigilant and expert charioteer,* within himself cultivates the divine element, will be able to utilize the other powers by a mingling of the elements, by anger, desire and habit, just as far as may be necessary. Though it seems easy to *know yourself*, this is the most difficult of all things. This is said to derive from the Pythian Apollo, though it is also attributed to Chilo, one of the Seven Sages. Its message is, in any event, to discover our own power, which amounts to learning the nature of the whole extant world which, as God advises us, is impossible without philosophy.

17. There are eight organs of knowledge: sense, imagination, art, opinion, deliberation, science, wisdom and mind. Art, prudence, science and mind we

---

*Cf. Plato, *Phaedrus,* for the myth of the charioteer.

share with the Gods; sense and imagination, with the irrational animals; while opinion alone is our characteristic. Sense is a fallacious knowledge derived through the body; imagination is a notion in the soul; art is a habit of cooperating with reason. The words "with reason" are here added, for even a spider operates, but it lacks reason. Deliberation is a habit selective of the rightness of planning deeds; science is a habit of those things which remain ever the same, with Sameness; wisdom is a knowledge of the first causes; while Mind is the principle and fountain of all good things.

18. Docility is divided into three parts: shrewdness, memory and acuteness. Memory guards the things which have been learned; acuteness is quickness of understanding, and shrewdness is the ability of deducing the unlearned from what one has learned to investigate.

19. Heaven may be interpretted in three ways: first, as the outermost sphere; second, the space from the fixed sphere to the moon; third, the whole world, heaven and earth.*

20. The extreme elements, the best and worst, operate constantly. There is no intermission in activity with God, and things near him in Mind and Reason; and plants are continuously nourished by day and night. But man is not always active, nor are irrational animals, which rest and sleep most of the time.

21. The Greeks always surpassed the Barbarians in manners and habits, on account of the mild climate in which they live. The Scythians are troubled by cold, and the Aethiopians by heat, which determines a violent interior heat and moisture, resulting in violence and audacity. Analogously, those who live near the middle zone and the mountains participate in the mildness of the country they inhabit.† That is why, as Plato says, the Greeks, and especially the Athenians, improved the disciplines that they had derived from the Barbarians.‡

22. [From them had come] stratagems, painting, mechanics, polemics, oratory, and physical culture. But the sciences of these were developed by the Athenians, owing to the favorable natural conditions of light, and purity of air, which had the double effect of not only drying out the earth, as it is in Attica, but also making subtle the minds of men. So a rarified atmosphere is unfavorable to the fertility of the earth, but is favorable to mental development.

---

* From Aristotle, *On the Heavens,* I. 9. 278b.

† Cf. Aristotle, *Politics,* VII. 7. 1327b.

‡ Plato, *Epinomis,* 987d.

DIOGENES LAERTIUS:

THE LIFE OF PYTHAGORAS

DIOGENES LAERTIUS, who flourished during the third century of the common era, is best known for his remarkable compilation, *Lives of the Eminent Philosophers*, in which this *Life of Pythagoras* appears.

In compiling his biographical encyclopedia of Greek philosophy, Diogenes drew on a great many sources of varying quality. His work is especially valuable because, like Iamblichus and Porphyry, he quotes many earlier writers, often verbatim.

A convenient edition of the entire *Lives of the Eminent Philosophers* appears in two volumes, in the Loeb Classical Library, published by Harvard University Press. The divisions of the following text are those of Guthrie.

THE LIFE OF PYTHAGORAS

1. Early Life

SINCE WE have now gone through the Ionian philosophy, which was derived from Thales, and the lives of the several illustrious men who were the chief ornaments of that school, we will now proceed to treat the Italian School, which was founded by Pythagoras, the son of Mnesarchus, a gem-engraver, as he is recorded to have been by Hermippus, a native of Samos, or, as Aristoxenus asserts, a Tyrrhenian, and a native of one of the islands which the Athenians, after they had driven out the Tyrrhenians, had occupied. But some authors say that he was the son of Marmacus, the son of Hippasus, the son of Euthyphron, the son of Cleonymus, who was an exile from Phlious; and that Marmacus settled in Samos, and that from this this circumstance Pythagoras was called a Samian. After that, he migrated to Lesbos, having come to Pherecydes, with letters from his uncle Zoilus. Then he made three silver goblets, and carried them to Egypt as a present for each of the three priests. He had brothers, the eldest of whom was named Eunomus, the second one Tyrrhenus, and a slave named Zalmoxis, to whom the Getae sacrifice, believing him to be the same as Kronos, according to the account of Herodotus (iv. 93).

2. Studies

HE WAS A PUPIL, as I have already mentioned, of Pherecydes the Syrian, and after his death he came to Samos, and became a pupil of Hermodamas, the descendant of Creophylus, who was already an old man now.

3. Initiations

AS HE WAS a youth devoted to learning, he left his country, and had himself initiated into the Grecian and barbarian sacred mysteries. Accordingly he went to Egypt, on which occasion Polycrates gave him a letter of introduction to Amasis; and he learned the Egyptian language as Antiphon tells us, in his treatise *On Those Men Who Have Become Conspicuous for Virtue*, and he also associated with the

Chaldeans and Magi.

Afterwards he went to Crete, and in company with Epimenides, he descended into the Idaean cave—and in Egypt too he had entered into the holiest parts of their temples, and learned all the most secret mysteries that relate to their Gods. Then he returned again to Samos, and finding his country under the absolute dominion of Polycrates, he set sail, and fled to Croton in Italy. Having given laws to the Italians, he there gained a very high reputation, together with his followers, who were about three hundred in number, and governed the republic in a most excellent manner, so that the constitution was very nearly an aristocracy.

4. Transmigration

HERACLEIDES OF PONTUS says that he was accustomed to speak of himself in this manner: that he had formerly been Aethalides, and had been accounted to be the son of Hermes, and that Hermes had desired him to select any gift he pleased except immortality. Accordingly, he had requested that, whether living or dead, he might preserve the memory of what had happened to him. While, therefore, he was alive, he recalled everything, and when he was dead he retained the same memory. At a subsequent period he passed into Euphorbus, and was wounded by Menelaus. While he was Euphorbus, he used to say that he had formerly been Aethalides; and that he had received as a gift from Hermes the perpetual transmigration of his soul, so that it was constantly transmigrating and passing into whatever plants or animals it pleased, and he had also received the gift of knowing and recollecting all that his soul had suffered in Hades, and what sufferings too are endured by the rest of the souls.

But after Euphorbus died, he said that his soul had passed into Hermotimus, and when he wished to convince people of this, he went into the territory of the Branchidae, and going into the temple of Apollo, he showed his shield which Menelaus had dedicated there as an offering. For he said that he, when he sailed from Troy, had offered up his shield which was already getting worn out, to Apollo, and that nothing remained but the ivory face which was on it. He said that when Hermotimus died he had become Pyrrhus, a fisherman of Delos, and that he still recollected everything, how he had formerly been Aethalides, then Euphorbus, then Hermotimus, and then Pyrrhus. When Pyrrhus died, he became Pythagoras, and still recollected all the circumstances I have been mentioning.

5. Works of Pythagoras

NOW THEY SAY that Pythagoras did not leave behind him a single book, but they talk foolishly for Heraclitus, the natural philosopher, speaks plainly enough of him saying, "Pythagoras, the son of Mnesarchus, practiced inquiry beyond all other men, and making selections from these writings he thus formed a wisdom of his own, an extensive learning, and cunning art."* Thus he speaks, because Pythagoras, in the beginning of his treatise *On Nature*, writes in the following manner: "By the air which I breathe, and by the water which I drink, I will not endure to be blamed on account of this discourse."

---

*Heraclitus didn't care very much for polymaths, hence his disapproval of Pythagoras.

There are three volumes extant written by Pythagoras, one *On Education*, one *On Politics*, and one *On Nature*. The treatise which is now extant under the name of Pythagoras is the work of Lysis of Tarentum, a philosopher of the Pythagorean school, who fled to Thebes and became the teacher of Epaminondas. Heracleides, the son of Serapion, in his *Abridgement of Sotion*, says that he wrote a poem in epic verse *On the Universe*, and secondly the *Sacred Poem* which begins thus:

> Dear youths, I warn you cherish peace divine,
> And in your hearts lay deep these words of mine.

Thirdly he wrote *On the Soul*; fourthly *On Piety*; fifthly *Helothales, the Father of Epicharmus of Cos*; sixthly, *Croton*, and other works too. But the mystic discourse which is extant under his name, they say is really the work of Hippasus, having been composed with a view to bring Pythagoras into disrepute. There were also many other books composed by Aston of Croton, and attributed to Pythagoras.

Aristoxenus asserts that Pythagoras derived the greater part of his ethical doctrines from Themistoclea, the priestess at Delphi. Ion of Chios, in his *Triagmi*, says that he wrote some poems and attributed them to Orpheus. His also, it is said, is the poem called *Scopiads,* which begins thus:

> Behave not shamelessly to any one.

6. General Views of Life

SOSICRATES, in his *Successions of Philosophers*, relates that when asked who he was by Leon, the tyrant of the Phliasians, Pythagoras replied, "A philosopher." He adds that Pythagoras used to compare life to the Greater Games where some people come to contend for the prizes, and others for the purposes of traffic, but the best as spectators. So also in life the men of slavish dispositions are born hunters after glory and covetousness, but philosophers are seekers after the truth. Thus he spoke on this subject.

But in the three treatises above mentioned, the following principles are laid down by Pythagoras. He forbids men to pray for anything in particular for themselves, because they do not know what is good for them. He terms drunkenness an expression identical with ruin, and rejects all superfluity, saying that no one ought to exceed the proper quantity of meat and drink. On the subject of venereal pleasures, he says, "One ought to sacrifice to Aphrodite in the winter, not in the summer, and in autumn and spring in a lesser degree. But the practice is pernicious at every season, and is never good for the health." And once, when he was asked when a man might indulge in the pleasures of love, he replied, "Whenever you wish to be weaker than yourself."

7. Ages of Life

THUS DOES HE divide the ages of life: "A boy for twenty years, a young man for twenty years, a middle aged man for twenty years, and an old man for twenty. These different ages correspond proportionately to the seasons; boyhood answers to the spring, youth to the summer, middle age to autumn, and old age to winter," meaning by youth one not yet grown, and by young man one of mature age.

8. Social Customs

TIMAEUS says that he was the first person to assert that "The property of friends is common," and that "Friendship is equality." His disciples used to put all their possessions together into one store, and use them in common. For five years they kept silence, doing nothing but listening to discourses, and never once seeing Pythagoras, until they were approved; after that time they were admitted into his house and allowed to see him. They also abstained from the use of cypress coffins, because the sceptre of Zeus is made of that wood, as Hermippus tells us in the second book of his account *On Pythagoras*.

9. Distinguished Appearance

HE IS SAID to have been a man of the most dignified appearance, and his disciples adopted an opinion that he was Apollo who had come from the Hyperboreans. It is also said that once when he was stripped naked he was seen to have a golden thigh, and many people affirmed that when he was crossing the river Nessus it addressed him by name.

10. Women Deified by Marriage

TIMAEUS, in the tenth book of his *Histories*, tells us that he used to say that women who were married to men had the names of divinities, being successively called Virgins, Nymphs, and then Mothers.

11. Scientific Culture

ALSO it was Pythagoras who carried geometry to perfection, after Moeris had first found out the principles of the elements of that science, as Auticlides tells us in the second book of his *History of Alexander*, and that the part of that science to which Pythagoras applied himself above all others was arithmetic. He discovered the numerical relation of sounds on the monochord, and he also studied medicine. Apollodorus the logician says of him that he sacrificed a hecatomb, when he had discovered that the square of the hypotenuse of a right-angled triangle was equal to the squares of the sides containing the right angle. There is an epigram which is couched in the following terms:

> When the great Samian sage his noble problem found,
> A hundred oxen with their life-blood dyed the ground.

12. Diet and Sacrifices

HE is also said to have been the first man who trained athletes on meat. Eurymenes was the first man, according to the statement of Favorinus, in the third book of his *Commentaries*, who ever did submit to this diet, as before that time men used to train themselves on dry figs, and moist cheese and wheaten bread, as the same Favorinus informs us in the eight book of his *Miscellaneous History*. But some authors state that a trainer of the name of Pythagoras certainly did train his athletes on this system, but that it was not our philosopher, for as he even forbade men to kill animals at all, much less would he have allowed his disciples to eat them, since they have a right to live in common with mankind. And this was his pretext, but in reality he prohibited the eating of animals because he wished to train and accustom men to simplicity of life, so that all their food should be easily procurable, as it would be if they ate only such things as required no fire to cook them, and if they drank plain water; for from this diet they would derive health of body and acuteness of intellect.

The only altar at which he worshipped was that of Apollo the Giver of Life, at Delos, which is at the back of the Altar of Horns, because wheat and barley, and cheese cakes are the only offerings laid upon it, as it is not dressed by fire, and no victim is ever slain there, as Aristotle tells us, in his *Constitution of the Delians*. It is also said that he was the first person who asserted that the soul, revolving around the circle of necessity, is transformed and confined at different times in different bodies.

13. Measures and Weights

HE was also the first person who introduced measures and weights among the Greeks, as Aristoxenus the musician informs us.

14. Hesperus as Phosphorus

PARMENIDES assures us too that he was the first person who asserted the identity of Hesperus and Phosphorus [the Evening and Morning Star].

15. Students and Reputation

HE was so greatly admired that it used to be said that his disciples looked on all his sayings as the oracles of God. In his writings he himself said that he had come among men after having spent two hundred and seven years among the shades below. Therefore the Lucanians, Peucetians, Messapians and Romans flocked around him, coming with eagerness to hear his discourses. But until the time of Philolaus no doctrines of Pythagoras were ever divulged, and he was the first person who published the three celebrated books which Plato wrote to have purchased from him for a hundred minas. The students who used to come to his nightly lectures were no less than six hundred. Whenever any one of them was permitted to see him, he wrote of it to his friends, as if they had achieved something wonderful.

The people of Metapontum used to call his house the Temple of Demeter, and the street leading to it was called that of the Muses, as we are informed in the *Miscellaneous History* of Favorinus.

According to the account given by Aristoxenus in his tenth book of his *Rules of Education*, the rest of the Pythagoreans used to say that his precepts ought not to be divulged to all the world; and Xenophilus the Pythagorean, when he was asked what was the best way for a man to educate his son, said, "That he must first of all take care that he is born in a city which enjoys good laws."

Pythagoras formed many excellent men in Italy, by his precepts, and among them the lawgivers Zaleucus and Charondas.

16. Friendship Founded on Symbols

PYTHAGORAS was famous for his power of attracting friendships; and among other things, if he ever heard that any one had adopted his symbolic precepts, he at once made him a companion and a friend.

17. Symbols and Maxims

NOW WHAT HE CALLED his symbols were such as these. Do not poke the fire with a sword. Do not violate the beam of a balance. Do not sit down on a bushel. Do not devour your heart. Do not aid men in discarding a burden, but in increasing one. Always have your bed packed up. Do not bear the image of God on a ring. Efface the traces of a pot in the ashes. Do not wipe a seat with a lamp. Do not urinate towards the sun. Do not walk in the main street. Do not offer your hand lightly. Do not cherish swallows under your roof. Do not cherish birds with crooked talons. Do not urinate or stand upon the parings of your nails, or the cuttings of your hair. Avoid a sharp sword. When travelling abroad, do not look back at your own borders.

Now the precept not to poke the fire with a sword meant not to provoke the anger or swelling pride of powerful men; do not violate the beam of the balance meant not to transgress fairness and justice; not to sit on a bushel is to have an equal care for the present and the future, for by the bushel is meant one's daily food. By not devouring one's heart, he intended to show that we ought not to waste away our souls with grief and sorrow. In the precept that a man when travelling abroad should not turn his eyes back, he recommended those who were departing this life not to be desirous to live, and not to be too much attracted by the pleasures here on earth. And the other symbols may be explained in a similar manner, that we may not be too long-winded here.

18. Personal Habits

ABOVE ALL THINGS, he used to prohibit the eating of the red mullet and the blacktail; also the hearts of animals, and beans. Aristotle informs us that to these prohibitions he sometimes added tripe and gurnard. Some authors assert that he himself used to be contented with honey, honey-comb and bread, and that he never drank wine during the day. He usually ate vegetables, either boiled or raw, and he very rarely ate fish. His dress was white, very clean; his bed-clothes also were white, and woollen, for linen had not yet been introduced in that country. He was never known to have eaten too much, or to have drunk too much, or to indulge in the pleasures of love. He abstained wholly from laughter, and from all such indulgences as jests and idle stories. He never chastised anyone, whether slave or free man, while he was angry. Admonishing he used to call "feeding storks."

He used to practice divination, as far as auguries and auspices, but not by means of burnt offerings, except only the burning of frankincense. All the sacrifices which he offered consisted of inanimate things. But some, however, assert that he did sacrifice animals, limiting himself to cocks, and sucking kids, which are called *apalioi*, but that he never offered lambs. Aristoxenus, however, affirms that he permitted the eating of all other animals, and abstained only from oxen used in agriculture, and from rams.

19. Various Teachings

THE SAME AUTHOR tells us, as I have already mentioned, that he received his doctrines from Themistoclea, [the priestess] at Delphi. Hieronymus says, that when he descended into the shades below, he saw the soul of Hesiod bound to a brazen pillar, and gnashing its teeth, and that of Homer suspended from a tree, with snakes around it, as a punishment for the things that they said of the Gods. Those who refrained from commerce with their wives also were punished, and that on account of this he was greatly honored at Croton.

Aristippus of Cyrene, in his *Account of Natural Philosophers*, says that Pythagoras derived his name from the fact of his speaking (*agoreuein*) truth no less than the God at Delphi (*tou Pythiou*).*

He used to admonish his disciples to repeat these lines to themselves whenever they returned home to their houses:

> In what have I transgressed? What have I done?
> What that I should have done have I omitted?

He used to forbid them to offer sacrificial victims to the Gods, ordering them to worship only at those altars which were unstained with blood. He also forbade them to swear by the Gods, saying that every man ought so to exercise himself as to be worthy of belief without an oath. He also taught men that it behooves them to honor their elders, thinking that most honorable which is prior in time, just as in the world, the rising of the sun is more so than the setting, in life, the beginning more so than the end, and in animals, production more so than destruction.

Another of his rules was that men should honor the Gods above the daimons, and heroes above men, and that of all men, parents are those entitled to more honor. He held that people should associate with each other in such a way as not to make their friends enemies, but to render their enemies friends. Another rule was that they should not think anything exclusively their own. Another was to assist the law, and to make war upon lawlessness. He said not to destroy or to injure a cultivated tree, nor any animal which does not injure man. Modesty and decorum consist in never yielding to laughter, without looking stern. Men should avoid eating too much flesh, and in travelling should let rest and exertion alternate; that they should exercise memory, nor ever say or do anything in anger; to respect every kind of divination, to sing songs accompanied by the lyre, and to display a reasonable gratitude to the Gods and eminent men by hymns.

His disciples were forbidden to eat beans because, as they are flatulent, they greatly partake of animal properties; and besides, the stomach is kept in much better order by avoiding them, and such abstinence makes the visions that appear in one's sleep gentle and free from agitation.

---

*Pythios is the name of Apollo at Delphi. Iamblichus also alludes in chapter 1 of his biography to the etymological connection between the name Pythagoras and the Delphic Apollo.

Alexander, in his *Successions of Philosophers*, reports the following doctrines as contained in the Pythagorean memoirs. The Monad is the beginning of everything. From this proceeds the Indefinite Dyad, which is subordinate to the Monad, as to its cause. From the Monad and the Indefinite Dyad proceed numbers. From numbers proceed points. From these, lines, of which plane figures consist. From these plane figures are derived solid bodies. From solid bodies are derived sensible bodies, of which there are four elements, fire, water, earth, and air. The world, which is endued with life and intellect, and which is of a spherical figure, in its center containing the earth, which is also spherical, and inhabited all over, results from a combination of these elements, and from them derives its motion. There are also antipodes, and what to us is below, is to them above.

He also taught that light and darkness, cold and heat, dryness and moisture, are equally divided in the world; and that, while heat is predominant in summer, so when cold prevails, it is winter; when dryness prevails, it is spring; and when moisture preponderates, autumn. The loveliest season of the year is when all these qualities are equally balanced, of which the flourishing spring is the most wholesome, and the autumn the most pernicious. Of day, the most flourishing period is the morning, while the evening is the fading one, and the least healthy.

Another of his theories was that the air around the earth is immovable, and pregnant with disease, and that in it everything is mortal, while the upper air is in perpetual motion, and salubrious; and that in it everything is immortal, and on that account divine. The sun, moon and the stars are all Gods; for in them dominates the principle which is the cause of living things. The moon derives its light from the sun. There is a relationship between men and the Gods, because men partake of the divine principle, on which count, therefore, God exercises his providence for our advantage. Fate is the cause of the arrangement of the world, both in general and in particular. From the sun a ray penetrates both the cold aether, which is the air, *aer*, and the dense aether, *pachun aithera*, which is the sea and moisture. This ray descends into the depths and in this way vivifies all things. Everything which partakes of the principle of heat lives, by which account, also, plants are animated beings, but not all living beings necessarily have souls. The soul is something torn off from the aether, both warm and cold, for it partakes of the cold aether too. The soul is something different from life. It is immortal, because of the immortality of that from which it was torn.

Animals are born from one another by seeds [sperm], and it is impossible for there to be any spontaneous generation by the earth. Sperm is a drop from the brain which in itself contains a warm vapor, and when this is applied to the womb, it transmits moisture, virtue, and blood from the brain, from which flesh, sinews, bones and hair, and the whole body are produced. From the vapor is produced the soul and also sensation. The infant first becomes a solid being at the end of forty days, but, according to the principles of harmony, it is not perfect till seven, or perhaps nine, or at most ten months, and then it is brought forth. In itself it contains all the principles of life, which are all connected together, and by their union and combination form a harmonious whole, each of them developing itself at the appointed time.

In general the senses, and especially sight, are a vapor of intense heat, on which account a man is said to see through air, or through water. For the hot principle is opposed by the cold one; since, if the vapor in the eyes were cold, it would have the same temperature as the air, and so would be dissipated. As it is, in some passages he calls the eyes the gates of the sun. In a similar manner he speaks of hearing, and of the other senses.

He also says that the soul of man is divided into three parts: into intelligence, reason, and passion; and that the first and last divisions are found also in other animals, but that the middle one, reason, is found in man only. The chief abode of the soul is in those parts of the body which are between the heart and the brain. Passion abides in the heart, while intelligence and reason reside in the brain.

The senses are distillations of these, and the reasoning sense is immortal, while the others are mortal. The soul is nourished by the blood, and the faculties are the winds of the soul. The soul is invisible, and so are its faculties, inasmuch as the aether itself is invisible. The bonds of the soul are the arteries, veins and nerves. When the soul is vigorous, and is by itself in a quiescent state, then its bonds are words and actions. When it is cast forth upon the earth, it wanders about, resembling the body. Hermes is the steward of the souls, and that is the reason he is called Guide, Keeper of the Gate, and Subterranean, since it is he who conducts the souls from their bodies, and from earth, and sea. He conducts the pure souls to the highest region, and he does not allow the impure ones to approach them, nor to come near one another, committing them to be bound in indissoluble fetters by the Furies.

The Pythagoreans also assert that the whole air is full of souls, and that these are those that are accounted daimons or heroes. They are the ones that send down among men dreams, and tokens of disease and health; the latter not being reserved to human beings, but being sent also to sheep and cattle as well. They are concerned with purifications, expiations, and all kinds of divinations, oracular predictions, and the like.

Man's most important privilege is to be able to persuade his soul to be either good or bad. Men are happy when they have a good soul; yet [if bad] they are never quiet, never long retaining the same mind. An oath is justice; and on that account Zeus is God of Oaths. Virtue is harmony, health, universal good and God, on which account everything owes its existence and preservation to harmony. Friendship is a harmonious quality.

Honors to Gods and heroes should not be equal. The Gods should be honored at all times, extolling them with praises, clothed in white garments, and keeping one's body chaste; but, to the heroes, such honors should not be paid till after noon.

A state of purity is brought about by purifications, washings and lustrations, by a man's purifying himself from all deaths and births, or any kind of pollution, by abstaining from all animals that have died, from mullets, from gurnards, from eggs, from such animals as lay eggs, from beans, and from other things that are prohibited by those who have charge of the mysteries in the temples.

In his treatise *On the Pythagoreans*, Aristotle says that Pythagoras' reason for demanding abstention from beans on the part of his disciples, was that either they resemble genitals, or because they are like the gates of hell [...] they are the only plants without parts, or because they dry up other plants, or because they are representative of universal nature, or because they are used in elections in oligarchical governments.

He also forbade his disciples to pick up what fell from the table, for the sake of accustoming them to eat moderately, or else because such things belong to the dead. Aristophanes, indeed, said that what fell belonged to the heroes, in his *Heroes* singing,

> Never taste the things which fall,
> From the table on the floor.

He also forbade his disciples to eat white poultry, because a cock of that color was sacred to the Month, and was also a suppliant. Now white is an indication of a good nature, and black of a bad one. He was also accounted a good animal and he was sacred to the Month, for he indicates the time.

The Pythagoreans were also forbidden to eat of all fish that were sacred, on the grounds that the same animals should not be served up before both Gods and men, just as the same things do not belong to both freemen and slaves.

Another of the precepts of Pythagoras was never to break bread because in ancient times friends used to gather around the same loaf, as they even now do among the barbarians. Nor would he allow men to divide bread which united them. Some think that he laid down this rule in reference to the judgment which takes place in Hades, some because this practice engenders timidity in war. According to others, the reference is to the union which presides over the government of the universe.

Another one of his doctrines was that, of all solid figures, the sphere is the most beautiful, and of all plane figures, the circle. He held that old age and all diminution is similar, as is all increase and youth. Health, he said, is the permanence of form, and disease, its destruction. He thought salt should be set before people as a reminder of things just, for salt preserves everything which it touches, and comes from the purest sources, the sun and the sea.

These are the doctrines which Alexander asserts that he discovered in the Pythagorean treatises; what follows is Aristotle's.

20. Poetic Testimonies

TIMON, in his *Silli*, has not left unnoticed the dignified appearance of Pythagoras, though he attacks him on other points. Thus he speaks of:

> Pythagoras who often teaches
> Precepts of magic, and with speeches
> Of long high-sounding diction draws,
> From gaping crowds, a vain applause.

Referring to his having been different people at different times, Xenophanes says in an elegiac poem, that begins thus:

> Now will I upon another subject touch,
> And lead the way

And later,

> They say that once, as passing by he saw
> A dog severely beaten, he did pity him;
> And spoke as follows to the man who beat him:
> "Stop now, and beat him not; since in his body
> Abides the soul of a dear friend of mine,
> Whose voice I recognized as he was crying."

Cratinus also ridiculed him in his *Pythagorean Woman*, and in his *Tarentines* he speaks thus:

> They are accustomed, if by chance they see
> A private individual abroad,
> To try what powers of argument he has,
> How he can speak and reason; and they bother him
> With strange antitheses, and forced conclusions,
> Errors, comparisons, and magnitudes,
> Till they have filled, and quite perplexed his mind.

In his *Alcmaeon*, Mnesimachus says:

> As we do sacrifice to the Phoebus whom
> Pythagoras worships, never eating aught
> Which has the breath of life.

And Austophon says in his *Pythagorean*:

> He said that when he did descend below
> Among the shades in Hell, he there beheld
> All men who e'er had died; and there he saw,
> That the Pythagoreans differed much
> From all the rest; for that with them alone
> Did Pluto deign to eat, much honoring
> Their pious habits.

And:

> He's a civil God,
> If he likes eating with such dirty fellows.

And again in the same play he says,

> They eat nothing but herbs and vegetables, and drink
> Pure water only; but their lice are such,
> Their cloaks so dirty, and their unwashed
> So rank, that none of our younger men
> Will for a moment bear them.

21. The Death of Pythagoras

PYTHAGORAS died in this manner. When he was sitting with some of his companions in Milo's house, some of those whom he did not think worthy of admission into it, were by envy excited to set fire to it. But some say that the people of Croton themselves did this, being afraid lest he might aspire to the tyranny. Pythagoras was caught as he was trying to escape, and coming to a place full of beans, he stopped there, saying that it was better to be caught than to trample on the beans, and better to be slain than to speak; and so he was murdered by those who were pursuing him. In this way also, most of his companions were slain, being about forty in number, but a very few did escape, among whom were Archippus of Tarentum, and Lysis, whom I have mentioned before.

But Dicaearchus states that Pythagoras died later, having escaped as far as the temple of the Muses at Metapontum, where he died of [self-imposed] starvation after forty days. Heracleides, in his *Epitome of the Lives of Satyrus*, says that after he had buried Pherecydes at Delos, he returned to Italy, and there finding a superb banquet prepared at the house of Milo of Croton, he left that city for Metapontum, where, not wishing any longer to live, he put an end to his life by starvation. But Hermippus says that when there was war between the Agrigentines and the Syracusans, Pythagoras, with his usual companions, joined the Agrigentine army, which was put to flight. Coming up against a field of beans, instead of crossing it, he ran around it, and so was slain by the Syracusans, and the rest, about thirty-five in number, were burned at the stake in Tarentum, where they were trying to set up a new government against the prevailing magistrates.

Hermippus also relates another story about Pythagoras. When in Italy, he made a subterranean apartment, and charged his mother to write an account of everything that took place, marking the time of each on a tablet, then sending them down to him until he should ascend. His mother did so. Then after a certain time Pythagoras came up again, lean, and looking like a skeleton, he came into the public assembly, and said that he had arrived from Hades below, and then he recited to them all that had happened to them in the meanwhile. Being charmed with what he told them, they believed that Pythagoras was a divine being, so they wept and lamented, and even entrusted to him their wives, as likely to learn some good from him, and they took upon themselves the name of Pythagorean women. Thus far Hermippus.

22. Pythagoras' Family

PYTHAGORAS had a wife whose name was Theano, the daughter of Brontinus of Croton. Some say that she was the wife of Brontinus, and only Pythagoras' pupil. As Lysis mentions in his letter to Hipparchus, he had a daughter named Damo. Lysis' letter speaks of Pythagoras thus: "And many say that you philosophize in public, as Pythagoras deemed unworthy; for, when he had entrusted his commentaries to his daughter Damo, he charged her not to divulge them to any one outside of the house. Though she might have sold his discourses for much money, she did not abandon them; for she thought that obedience to her father's injunctions, even though this entailed poverty, was better than gold, and for all that she was a woman."

He had also a son, named Telauges, who was his father's successor in his school, and who, according to some authors, was the teacher of Empedocles. At least Hippobotus relates that Empedocles said,

> Telauges, noble youth, whom in due time
> Theano bore, to wise Pythagoras.

There is no book extant which is the work of Telauges, though there are some extant that are attributed to his mother Theano. Of her is told a story, that once, when asked how long it was before a woman becomes pure after intercourse, she said, "The moment she leaves her own husband, she is pure; but she is never pure at all, after she leaves anyone else." A woman who was going to her husband was by her told to put off her modesty with her clothes, and when she left him, to resume it therewith. When she was asked, "What clothes?" she replied, "Those which cause you to be called a woman."

23. Jesting Epigrams

NOW PYTHAGORAS, according to Heracleides, the son of Serapion, died when he was eighty years of age, according to his own account; by that of others, he was over ninety. On him we have written a sportive epigram, as follows:

> You are not the only man who has abstained
> From living food; for so have we;
> And who, I'd like to know, did ever taste
> Food while alive, most sage Pythagoras?
> When meat is boiled, or roasted well and salted,
> I do not think it well can be called living.
> Which, without scruple therefore then we eat it,
> And call it no more living flesh, but meat.

Another, which runs thus:

> Pythagoras was so wise a man, that he
> Never ate meat himself, and called it sin.
> Yet gave he good joints of beef to others;
> So that I marvel at his principles;
> Who others wronged, by teaching them to do
> What he believed unholy for himself.

Another, which follows:

> Should you Pythagoras' doctrine wish to know,
> Look on the center of Euphorbus' shield.
> For he asserts there lived a man of old,
> And when he had no longer an existence,
> He still could say that he had been alive,
> Or else he would not still be living now.

Another one follows:

> Alas! alas! why did Pythagoras hold
> Beans in such wondrous honor? Why, besides,
> Did he thus die among his choice companions?
> There was a field of beans; and so the sage,

> Died in the common road of Agrigentum,
> Rather than trample down his favorite beans.

24. The Last Pythagoreans

HE FLOURISHED about the sixtieth Olympiad (532-528 B.C.E.) and his system lasted for about nine or ten generations. The last Pythagoreans known to Aristoxenus were Xenophilus the Chalcidean, from Thrace, Phanton the Philiasian with his countrymen Echecrates, Diocles and Polymnastus, disciples of Philolaus and Eurytus of Tarentum.

25. Various Pythagorases

PYTHAGORAS was the name of four men, almost contemporaneous, and living close to each other. One was a native of Croton, a man with a tyrant's leanings; the second was a Phliasian, and as some say, a trainer of athletes. The third was a native of Zacynthus; the fourth was this our philosopher, to whom the mysteries of philosophy are said to belong, and in whose time the proverbial phrase, *ipse dixit* ("the Master said"), arose generally. Some also claim the existence of a fifth Pythagoras, a sculptor of Rhegium, who is believed to have been the first discoverer of rhythm and proportion. Another was a Samian sculptor. Another, an orator of small reputation. Another was a physician, who wrote a treatise on hernias, and some essays on Homer. Dionysius tells us there was another who wrote a history of the affairs of the Dorians.

Eratosthenes, quoted by Favorinus in the eighth book of his *Miscellaneous History*, tells us that this philosopher, of whom we are speaking, was the first man who ever practiced boxing in a scientific manner, in the forty-eighth Olympiad (588-584 B.C.E.), having long hair, and being robed in purple. From competition with boys he was rejected; but being ridiculed for his application for this, he immediately entered among the men, and was victorious. Among other things, this statement is confirmed by an epigram of Theaetetus:

> Stranger, if e'er you knew Pythagoras,
> Pythagoras, the man with flowing hair,
> The celebrated boxer, erst from Samos,
> I am Pythagoras. And if you ask
> A citizen of Elis of my deeds,
> You will surely think he is relating fables.

Favorinus says that he employed definitions on account of the mathematical subjects to which he applied himself. Socrates and his pupils did still more, and in this they were later followed by Aristotle and the Stoics.

He too was the first man who applied to the universe the name *kosmos*, and who first called the earth round, though Theophrastus attributes this to Parmenides, and Zeno to Hesiod. It is also said that he had a constant adversary, named Cylon, as Socrates' was Antilochus. This epigram was formerly repeated concerning Pythagoras the athlete:

Pythagoras of Samos, son of Crates,
Came while a child to the Olympic games;
Eager to battle for the prize in boxing.

26. Pythagoras' Letter

EXTANT is a letter of our philosopher's, which follows:

Pythagoras to Anaximenes.
You too, most excellent friend, if you were not superior to Pythagoras in birth
and reputation, would have migrated from Miletus, and gone elsewhere. But
now the reputation of your father keeps you back, which perhaps would have
restrained me too, if I had been like Anaximenes. But if you, who are the most
eminent men, abandon the cities, all their ornaments will disappear, and the Median power will be the more dangerous to them. Nor is it always seasonable
to be studying astronomy, but it is more honorable to exhibit a regard for one's
country. I myself am not always occupied about speculations of my own fancy,
but I am busied also with the wars which the Italians are waging one with another.

But since we have now finished our account of Pythagoras, we must also speak
of the most eminent of the Pythagoreans. After whom, we must mention those
who are spoken of more promiscuously in connection with no particular school,
and then we will connect the whole series of philosophers worth speaking of,
till we arrive at Epicurus. Now Telauges and Theano we have mentioned, so we
must now speak of Empedocles, in the first place, for according to some accounts,
he was a pupil of Pythagoras.

27. Empedocles as a Pythagorean

[Guthrie has omitted some genealogical material here.]

TIMAEUS, in the ninth book of his *Histories*, relates that Empedocles was a
pupil of Pythagoras, saying that he was afterwards convicted of having divulged
his doctrines, in the same way as Plato was, and that he was therefore henceforth
forbidden from attending his school. It is said that Empedocles had Pythagoras
in mind when he said:

And in that band there was a learned man
Of wondrous wisdom; one who of all men
Had the profoundest wealth of intellect.

But some say the philosopher was here referring to Parmenides.
Neanthes relates that until the time of Philolaus and Empedocles the
Pythagoreans used to admit all persons indiscriminately into their schools; but
when Empedocles by means of his poems publicized the doctrines, then they made
a law to admit no epic poet. They said that the same thing happened to Plato,
for that he too was excluded from the school. Empedocles' Pythagorean teacher
is not mentioned; and as for the letter of Telauges, in which he is stated to have

been a pupil of Hippasus and Brontinus, that is not worthy of belief. But Theophrastus says that he was an imitator and rival of Parmenides in his poems, for that he too had delivered his opinions on natural philosophy in epic verse.

Hermippus, however, says that he was an imitator not of Parmenides, but of Xenophanes with whom he lived; and that he imitated his epic style, and that it was at a later period that he fell in with the Pythagoreans. But Alcimadas, in his *Physics*, says that Zeno and Empedocles were pupils of Parmenides, about the same time, and that they subsequently left him. Zeno was said to have adopted a philosophical system peculiar to himself, but Empedocles became a pupil of Anaxagoras and Pythagoras, and he imitated the demeanor and way of life and gestures of the latter, and the natural philosophy of the other...

PART II:
THE PYTHAGOREAN LIBRARY

FIGURE 12. THE PYTHAGOREAN Y

The Pythagoric Letter two ways spread,
Shows the two paths in which Man's life is led.
The right hand track to sacred Virtue tends,
Though steep and rough at first, in rest it ends;
The other broad and smooth, but from its Crown
On rocks the Traveller is tumbled down.
He who to Virtue by harsh toils aspires,
Subduing pains, worth and renown acquires:
But who seeks slothful luxury, and flies,
The labor of great acts, dishonor'd dies.

—Maximinus

THE PYTHAGOREAN SYMBOLS OR MAXIMS

THE PYTHAGOREAN SYMBOLS are gnomic utterances whose meaning is not obvious on first glance. As Iamblichus observes, Pythagorean views were "not composed in popular or vulgar diction, or in a manner usual to all other writers, so as to be immediately understood, but in a way not easily apprehended by their readers."

"The result is that they who present these symbols without unfolding their meaning by a suitable exposition, run the danger of exposing them to the charge of being ridiculous and inane, trifling and garrulous. When, however, the meanings are expounded according to these symbols, and made clear and obvious even to the crowds, then they will be found analogous to prophetic sayings, such as the oracles of the Pythian Apollo. Their admirable meaning will inspire those who unite intellect and scholarliness."

The Pythagorean symbols are excellent examples of *akousmata* or "things heard," representing for the most part basic teachings on the proper conduct of life. A number of scholars have suggested that some of the Symbols represent archaic taboos to which Pythagoras gave spiritual or ethical interpretations.

In the following collection of 52 Symbols, many of the interpretations are traditional, but Guthrie has added some of his own. Most of the Symbols have more than one traditional interpretation. Iamblichus gives in-depth interpretations to 39 Pythagorean Symbols in his *Exhortation to Philosophy,* Phanes Press, 1988. Another good collection of Symbols, giving many variant interpretations and their sources, is the section on Pythagoras from Thomas Stanley's *History of Philosophy*, 1687, reprinted by the Philosophical Research Society, 1970.

THE PYTHAGOREAN SYMBOLS OR MAXIMS

1. Go not beyond the balance. (Transgress not Justice).
2. Sit not down on the bushel. (Do not loaf on your job).
3. Tear not to pieces the crown. (Do not be a joy-killer).
4. Eat not the heart. (Do not grieve over-much).
5. Do not poke the fire with a sword. (Do not further inflame the quarrelsome).
6. Having arrived at the frontiers, turn not back. (Do not wish to live your life over).
7. Go not by the public way. (Go not the broad popular way that leads to destruction).
8. Suffer no swallows around your house. (Associate not with those who chatter vainly).
9. Wear not the image of God on your ring. (Profane not the name of God).
10. Do not unload people, but load them up. (Encourage not idleness, but virtue).
11. Do not easily shake hands with a man. (Make no ill-considered friendship).
12. Leave not the least mark of the pot on the ashes. (After reconciliation, forget the disagreement).
13. Sow mallows, but never eat them. (Be mild to others, but not to yourself).
14. Wipe not out the place of the torch. (Let not all the lights of reason be extinguished).
15. Wear not a narrow ring. (Seek freedom, avoid slavery).

16. Feed not the animals that have crooked claws. (To your family admit no thief or traitor).

17. Abstain from beans. (Avoid food causing flatulence; avoid democratic voting).

18. Eat not fish whose tails are black. (Frequent not the company of men without reputation).

19. Never eat the gurnard.* (Avoid revenge).

20. Eat not the womb of animals. (Avoid that which leads to generation; avoid lust).

21. Abstain from flesh of animals that die of themselves. (Avoid decayed food).

22. Abstain from eating animals. (Have no conversation with unreasonable men).

23. Always put salt on the table. (Always use the principle of Justice to settle problems).

24. Never break the bread. (When giving charity, do not pare too close).

25. Do not spill oil upon the seat. (Do not flatter princes, praise God only).

26. Put not meat in a foul vessel. (Do not give good precepts to a vicious soul).

27. Feed the cock, but sacrifice him not; for he is sacred to the sun and the moon. (Cherish people who warn you, sacrifice them not to resentment).

28. Break not the teeth. (Do not revile bitterly; do not be sarcastic).

29. Keep far from you the vinegar-cruet. (Avoid malice and sarcasm).

30. Spit upon the parings of your nails, and on the clippings of your hair. (Abhor desires).

31. Do not urinate against the sun. (Be modest).

32. Speak not in the face of the sun. (Make not public the thoughts of your heart).

33. Do not sleep at noon. (Do not continue in darkness).

34. Stir up the bed as soon as you are risen; do not leave in it any print of the body. (When working, hanker not for luxurious ease).

35. Never sing without harp-accompaniment. (Make of life a whole).

36. Always keep your things packed up. (Always be prepared for all emergencies).

37. Quit not your post without your general's order. (Do not commit suicide).

38. Cut not wood on the public road. (Never turn to private use what belongs to the public).

39. Roast not what is boiled. (Never complicate that which is done in simplicity; mildness has no need of anger.)

40. Avoid the two-edged sword. (Have no conversation with slanderers).

41. Pick not up what is fallen from the table. (Always leave something for charity).

42. Abstain even from a cypress chest. (Avoid going to funerals).

43. To the celestial Gods sacrifice an odd number, but to the infernal, an even. (To God consecrate the indivisible soul; offer the body to hell).

44. Offer not to the Gods the wine of an unpruned vine. (Agriculture is a great piece of piety).

45. Never sacrifice without meal. (Encourage agriculture; offer bloodless

* A type of fish.

offerings).

46. Adore the Gods, and sacrifice barefoot. (Pray and sacrifice in humility of heart).

47. Turn round when you worship. (Adore the immensity of God, who fills the universe).

48. Sit down when you worship. (Never worship in a hurry).

49. Pare not your nails during the sacrifice. (In the temple behave respectfully).

50. When it thunders, touch the ground. (Appease God by humility).

51. Do not primp by torch-light. (Look at things in the light of God).

52. One, Two. (God and Nature; all things are known in God).

53. Honor marks of dignity, the Throne, and the Ternary. (Worship magistrates, Kings, Heroes, Geniuses and God).

54. When the winds blow, adore echo. (During revolts, flee to deserts).

55. Eat not in the chariot. (Eat not in the midst of hurried, important business).

56. Put on your right shoe first, and wash your left foot first. (Prefer an active life, to one of ease and pleasure).

57. Eat not the brain. (Wear not out the brain; refresh yourself).

58. Plant not the Palm-tree. (Do nothing but what is good and useful).

59. Make thy libations to the Gods by the ear. (Beautify thy worship with music).

60. Never catch the cuttle-fish. (Undertake no dark, intricate affairs that will wound you).

61. Stop not at the threshold. (Be not wavering, but choose your side).

62. Give way to a flock that goes by. (Oppose not the multitude).

63. Avoid the weasel. (Avoid tale-tellers).

64. Refuse the weapons a woman offers you. (Reject all suggestions revenge inspires).

65. Kill not the serpent that chances to fall within your walls. (Harm no enemy who becomes your guest or suppliant).

66. It is a crime to throw stones into fountains. (It is a crime to persecute good men).

67. Feed not yourself with your left hand. (Support yourself by honest toil, not by robbery).

68. It is a horrible crime to wipe off the seat with iron. (It is criminal to deprive a man by force of what he earned by labor).

69. Stick not iron into the footsteps of a man. (Mangle not the memory of a man).

70. Sleep not on a grave. (Live not in idleness on the parents' inherited estates).

71. Lay not the whole faggot on the fire. (Live thriftily, spend not all at once).

72. Leap not from the chariot with your feet close together. (Do nothing inconsiderately).

73. Threaten not the stars. (Be not angry with your superiors).

74. Place not the candle against the wall. (Persist not in enlightening the stupid).

75. Write not in the snow. (Trust not your precepts to persons of an inconstant character).

THE GOLDEN VERSES OF PYTHAGORAS

IN MANY WAYS the so-called Golden Verses of Pythagoras epitomize the Pythagorean way of life, outlining the principles of daily conduct leading to the divinization of the soul.

Concerning their authorship and date of composition there have been varying opinions. The French scholar Armand Delatte has argued in some depth that a large portion of the Golden Verses may go back in essence to an hexameter poem by Pythagoras, *The Sacred Discourse,* in which he set out a rule of life for members of his school. According to this theory the teaching was transmitted orally, only to be recorded when the few surviving Pythagoreans were expelled from Italy and threatened with extinction.

The Neoplatonic philosopher Hierocles of Alexandria was apparently the first to refer to these lines as the Golden Verses, explaining that as gold is the best and purest of metals, so are these the most divine of verses. The very interesting *Commentaries of Hierocles on the Golden Verses of Pythagoras* was first rendered into English in 1707 by N. Rowe and has been reprinted several times since.

THE GOLDEN VERSES OF PYTHAGORAS

FIRST HONOR THE IMMORTAL GODS, as the law demands;
Then reverence thy oath, and then the illustrious heroes;
Then venerate the divinities under the earth, due rites performing;
Then honor your parents, and all of your kindred.
Among others make the most virtuous thy friend!
Love to make use of his soft speeches, and learn from his deeds that are useful;
But alienate not the beloved comrade for trifling offences,
Bear all you can, what you can, for power is bound to necessity.
Take this well to heart: you must gain control of your habits;
First over stomach, then sleep, and then luxury, and anger.
What brings you shame, do not unto others, nor by yourself.
The highest of duties is honor of self.
Let justice be practiced in words as in deeds;
Then make the habit, never inconsiderately to act;
Neither forget that death is appointed to all;
That possessions here gladly gathered, here must be left;
Whatever sorrow the fate of the Gods may here send us
Bear, whatever may strike you, with patience unmurmuring;
To relieve it, so far as you can, is permitted,
But reflect that not much misfortune has Fate given to the good.
The speech of the people is various, now good, and now evil;
So let them not frighten you, nor keep you from your purpose.
If false calumnies come to your ears, support it in patience;
Yet that which I now am declaring, fulfil it faithfully:
Let no one with speech or with deeds e'er deceive you
To do or to say what is not the best.

Think, before you act, that nothing stupid results;
To act inconsiderately is part of a fool;
Yet whatever later will not bring you repentance, that you should carry through.
Do nothing beyond what you know,
Yet learn what you may need: thus shall your life grow happy.
Do not neglect the health of the body;
Keep measure in eating and drinking, and every exercise of the body.
By measure, I mean what later will not induce pain.
Follow clean habits of life, but not the luxurious;
Avoid all things which will arouse envy.
At the wrong time, never be a prodigal, as if you did not know what was proper,
Nor show yourself stingy, for a due measure is ever the best.
Do only those things which will not harm thee, and deliberate before you act.
Never let slumber approach thy wearied eyelids,
Ere thrice you review what this day you did:
Wherein have I sinned? What did I? What duty is neglected?
All, from the first to the last, review; and if you have erred grieve in your spirit,
    rejoicing for all that was good.
With zeal and with industry, this, then, repeat; and learn to repeat it with joy.
Thus wilt thou tread on the paths of heavenly virtue.
Surely, I swear it by him who into our souls has transmitted the Sacred
    Quaternary,*
The spring of eternal Nature.
Never start on your task until you have implored the blessing of the Gods.
If this you hold fast, soon will you recognize of Gods and mortal men
The true nature of existence, how everything passes and returns.
Then will you see what is true, how Nature in all is most equal,
So that you hope not for what has no hope, nor that anything should escape you.
Men shall you find whose sorrows they themselves have created,
Wretches who see not the Good that is too near, nothing they hear;
Few know how to help themselve in misfortune.
That is the Fate that blinds humanity; in circles,
Hither and yon they run in endless sorrows;
For they are followed by a grim companion, disunion within themselves;
Unnoticed, ne'er rouse him, and fly from before him!
Father Zeus, O free them all from sufferings so great,
Or show unto each the Genius, who is their guide!
Yet, do not fear, for the mortals are divine by race,
To whom holy Nature everything will reveal and demonstrate;
Whereof if you have received, so keep what I teach you;
Healing your soul, you shall remain insured from manifold evil.
Avoid foods forbidden; reflect that this contributes to the cleanliness
And redemption of your soul. Consider all things well:
Let reason, the gift divine, be thy highest guide;

* I.e., the Tetraktys.

Then should you be separated from the body, and soar in the aether,
You will be imperishable, a divinity, a mortal no more.

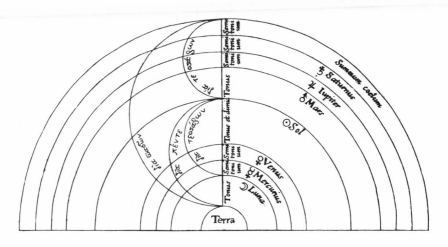

FIGURE 13. THE MUSIC OF THE SPHERES

THE FRAGMENTS OF PHILOLAUS

PHILOLAUS OF TARENTUM (latter half of fifth century B.C.E.) was educated by Lysis, one of the two Pythagoreans who escaped the persecution of the school at Croton. He was the first member of the school to record Pythagorean teachings in writing and it appears that these writings influenced the thought of Plato. Moreover, Plato's nephew Speusippus who took over the leadership of the Academy, drew on the work of Philolaus in compiling his treatise *On Pythagorean Numbers*, which dealt primarily with the properties of the Decad.

The fragments of Philolaus assembled here deal with the Pythagorean theory of the Limited and Unlimited, the principle of Harmonia through which they are conjoined, and the primacy of Number in the nature of Harmonia, and also the importance of Number in the pursuit of knowledge.

The Philolaic fragments are generally accepted as being authentic and their significance is not to be underestimated. This is because of all surviving Pythagorean writings the fragments of Philolaus are the earliest and most faithfully reflect the teachings of the original Pythagorean school.

For a good discussion of Philolaus see section 44 in Kathleen Freeman's *Companion to the Presocratic Philosophers*. The numbers following the fragments (e.g., DK 1) refer to the numeration in Diels-Kranz, *Fragmente der Vorsokratieker,* and are translated in Kathleen Freeman's *Ancilla to the Pre-Socratic Philosophers.*

THE LIFE OF PHILOLAUS

FROM DIOGENES LAERTIUS

PHILOLAUS OF CROTON, a Pythagorean, was he from whom Plato, in some of his Letters, begged Dion to purchase Pythagorean books. He (Dion) died under the accusation of having had designs on the tyranny. I have made about him the following epigram: "I advise everybody to take good care to avoid suspicion; even if you are not guilty but seem so, you are ruined. That is why Croton, the homeland of Philolaus, destroyed him, because he was suspected of wishing to establish autocracy."

Philolaus teaches that all things are produced by necessity and harmony, and he is the first who said that the earth has a circular movement; others, however, insist this was due to Hicetas of Syracuse. He had written a single book which the philosopher Plato, visiting Dionysius in Sicily, bought, according to Hermippus, from Philolaus' parents, for the sum of 40 Alexandrian minae, whence he drew his *Timaeus*. Others state that he received them as a present for having obtained the liberty of one Philolaus' disciples, whom Dionysius had imprisoned. In his *Homonyms*, Demetrius claims that he is the first of the Pythagorean philosophers who made a work *On Nature* public property. This book begins as follows: "The world's being is the harmonious compound of Unlimited and Limiting principles; such is the totality of the world and all it contains."

THE FRAGMENTS OF PHILOLAUS

1. (Stobaeus, 21. 7; Diogenes Laertius, 8. 85) The world's nature is a harmonious compound of Limited and Unlimited elements; similar is the totality of the world in itself, and of all it contains (DK 1).

B. All beings are necessarily Limited or Unlimited, or simultaneously Limited and Unlimited; but they could not all be Unlimited only.

2. Now, since it is clear that the beings cannot be formed either of elements that are all Unlimited, it is evident that the world in its totality, and its included beings are a harmonious compound of Limited and Unlimited elements. That can be seen in existing things. Those that are composed of Limiting elements, are Limited themselves; those that are composed of both Limiting and Unlimited elements, are both Limited and Unlimited; and those composed of Unlimited elements are Unlimited (DK 2).

B. All things, at least those we know, contain Number; for it is evident that nothing whatever can either be thought or known, without Number (DK 4). Number has two distinct kinds: the odd, and the even, and a third, derived from a mingling of the other two kinds, the even-odd. Each of its subspecies is susceptible of many very numerous varieties, which each manifests individually (DK 5).

3. (Nicomachus, *Arith. Intr.*, 2. 509) Harmony is generally the result of contraries; for it is the unity of multiplicity, and the agreement of discordances (DK 10).

4. This is the state of affairs concerning Nature and Harmony. The Being of things is eternal; it is a unique and divine nature, the knowledge of which does not belong to man. Still it would not be possible that any of the things that exist, and that are known by us, should arrive to our knowledge if this Being was not the internal foundation of principles of which the world was founded—that is, of the Limited and Unlimited elements. Now since these principles are not mutually similar, nor of similar nature, it would be impossible that the order of the world should have been formed by them in any manner whatever unless harmony had intervened. Of course, the things that were similar, and of similar nature, did not need harmony; but the dissimilar things, which have neither a similar nature, nor an equivalent function, must be organized by the harmony, if they are to take their place in the connected totality of the world.

5. The extent of the Harmony [octave] is a fourth, plus a fifth. The fifth is greater than the fourth by 8:9; for from the lowest string to the second lowest there is a fourth; and from this to the higher a fifth; but from this to the next, or third string, a fourth; and from this third string to the lowest, a fifth. The interval between the second lowest and the third [from the bottom] is 8:9 [a tone]; the interval of the fourth is 3:4; that of the fifth, 2:3; that of the octave, 1:2. Thus the Harmony contains five whole tones plus two semitones; the fifth, three tones, plus one semitone; the fourth, two whole tones, plus one semitone (DK 6).

6. (Boethius, *De. Inst. Mus.*, 3. 5). Nevertheless the Pythagorean Philolaus has tried to divide the tone otherwise; his tone's starting-point is the first uneven number which forms a cube, and you know that the first uneven number was

an object of veneration among these Pythagoreans. Now the first odd number is three; thrice three is nine, and nine times three is 27, which differs from the number 24 by the interval of one tone, and differs from it by this very number 3. Indeed, 3 is one eight of 24, and this eighth part of 24, added to 24 itself, produces 27, the cube of 3. Philolaus divides this number 27 in two parts, the one greater than half, which he calls *apotome* the other one smaller than half he calls sharp, but which latterly has become known as minor half-tone. He supposes that this sharp contains thirteen unities, because 13 is the difference between 256 and 243, and that this same number is the sum of 9, 3, and unity, in which the unity plays the part of the point, 3 of the first odd line, and 9 of the first odd square. After having, for these reasons, expressed by 13 the sharp, which is called a semitone, out of 14 unities he forms the other part of the number 27, which he calls *apotome*, and as the difference between 13 and 14 is the unity, he insists that the unity forms the comma, and that 27 unities form an entire tone, because 27 is the difference between 216 and 243, which are distant by one tone.*

7. (Boethius, *De. Inst. Mus.*, 3. 8). These are the definitions that Philolaus has given of these intervals, and of still smaller intervals. The comma, says he, is the interval whose eight-ninths relation exceeds the sum of two sharps, namely, the sum of two minor semitones. The schisma is half the comma, the diaschisma is half the sharp, namely, of the minor semitone.

8. (Claudianus Mamertus, *De Statu Animae*, 2. 3). Before treating of the substance of the soul, Philolaus, according to geometrical principles, treats of music, arithmetic, measures, weights, and numbers, insisting that these are the principles which support the existence of the universe.

9. (Nicomachus, *Arithm. Intr.*, 2. p. 72). Some, in this following Philolaus, think that this kind of a proportion is called harmonic, because it has the greatest analogy with what is called geometrical harmony; which is the cube, because all its dimensions are mutually equal, and consequently in perfect harmony. Indeed this proportion is revealed in all kinds of cubes which always have 12 sides, 8 angles, and 6 surfaces.†

B. (Cassiodorus, *Exp. in Ps.*, 9, p. 36). The number 8, which the arithmeticians call the first actual cube, has been given by the Pythagorean Philolaus the name of geometrical harmony, because he thinks he recognizes in it all the harmonic relations.

10 A. (Stobaeus, *Eclog. Physic.*, 1. 15. 7. p. 360). The world is single and it came into being from the center outwards. Starting from this center, the top is entirely identical to the base; still you might say that what is above the center is opposed to what is below it; for the base, lowest point would be the center, as for the top, the highest point would still be the center; and likewise for the other parts; in fact, in respect to the center, each one of the opposite points is identical, unless the whole be moved (DK 17).

B. (Stobaeus, *Eclog. Physic.*, 1. 21. 1. p. 468). The prime composite, the One

* This fragment concerns itself with musical intervals smaller than a whole tone. For a good discussion, which also relates to the next fragment, see McClain, *The Pythagorean Plato*, 159-62.
† 8 is the harmonic mean between 6 and 12.

placed in the center of the sphere, is called Hestia (DK 7).

11. A. (Stobaeus, *Eclog. Physic.*, 1. 22. 1. p. 488). Philolaus has located the fire in the middle, the center; he calls it Hestia, of the All, the Guardpost of Zeus, the Mother of the Gods, the Altar, the Link, and the Measure of Nature. Besides, he locates a second fire, quite at the top, surrounding the world. The center, says he, is by its nature the first; around it, the ten different bodies carry out their choral dance. These are: the heaven, the planets, lower the sun, and below it the moon; lower the earth, and beneath this, the counter-earth, then beneath these bodies the fire of Hestia, in the center, where it maintains order. The highest part of the Covering, in which he asserts that the elements exist in a perfectly pure condition, is called Olympus; the space beneath the revolution-circle of Olympus, and where in order are disposed the five planets, the sun and moon, forms the Cosmos; finally, beneath the latter is the sublunar region, which surrounds the earth, where are the generative things, susceptible to change. All that is the heaven. The order which manifests in the celestial phenomena is the object of science; the disorder which manifests in the things of becoming, is the object of virtue; the former is perfect, the latter is imperfect.

B. (ps.-Plutarch, *Plac. Phil.*, 3. 11). The Pythagorean Philolaus locates the fire in the center—it is the Hearth (Hestia) of the All—then the counter-earth, then the earth we inhabit, placed opposite the other, and moving circularly, which is the reason that its inhabitants are not visible to ours.

C. (Stobaeus, *Eclog. Physic.*, 1. 21. 6. p. 452). The directing fire, says Philolaus, is in the entirely central fire, which the Demiurge has placed as a sort of keel to serve as foundation to the sphere of the All.

12. (ps.-Plutarch, *Plac. Phil.*, 2. 5). Philolaus explains destruction by two causes: one is the fire which descends from heaven, the other is the water of the moon, which is driven away therefrom by the circulation of the air; the exhalations of these two stars nourish the world.

13. A. (Diogenes Laertius, 8.85). Philolaus was the first who said that the world moves in a circle; others attribute it to Hicetas of Syracuse.

B. (ps.-Plutarch, *Plac. Phil.*, 3. 7). Some insist that the earth is immovable; but the Pythagorean Philolaus says that it moves circularly around the central fire, in an oblique circle like the sun and moon.

14. (Stobaeus, *Eclog. Physic.*, 1. 25. 3. p. 530). The Pythagorean Philolaus says that the sun is a vitrescent body which receives the light reflected by the fire of the Cosmos, and sends it back to us, having filtered them, light and heat; so that you might say that there are two suns, the body of the fire which is in the heaven, and the igneous light which emanates therefrom, and reflects itself in a kind of mirror. Perhaps we might consider as a third light that which, from the mirror in which it is reflected, falls back on us in dispersed rays.

15. (Stobaeus, *Eclog. Physic.*, 1. 26. 1. p. 562). Some Pythagoreans, among whom is Philolaus, suggest that the moon's resemblance to the earth consists in its surface being inhabited, like our earth, but by animals and vegetation larger and more beautiful. For the lunar animals are fifteen times larger than ours, and do not evacuate excreta. The day is also fifteen times as long. Others say that the apparent form of the moon is only the reflection of the sea, which we inhabit

and which passes beyond the circle of fire.

16. (Censorinus, *De Die Natali*, 18). According to the Pythagorean Philolaus there is a year composed of 59 years and 21 intercalary months; he considers that the natural year has 364 and a half days.

17. (Iamblichus, *In. Nicom.*, 11). Philolaus says that Number is the sovereign and autogenic force which maintains the eternal permanence of cosmic things (DK 23).

18. A. (Stobaeus, 1. 3. 8). The power, efficacy and essence of Number is seen in the Decad; it is great, it realizes all its purposes, and it is the cause of all effects. The power of the Decad is the principle and guide of all life, divine, celestial, or human into which it is insinuated; without it everything is unlimited, obscure, and furtive. Indeed, it is the nature of Number which teaches us comprehension, which serves us as guide, and teaches us all things which would otherwise remain impenetrable and unknown to every man. For there is nobody who could get a clear notion about things in themselves, nor in their relations, if there was no Number or Number-essence. By means of sensation, Number instills a certain proportion, and thereby establishes among all things harmonic relations, analogous to the nature of the geometric figure called the gnomon; it incorporates intelligible reasons of things, separates them, individualizes them, both in limited and unlimited things. And it is not only in matters pertaining to daimons or Gods that you may see the force manifested by the nature and power of Number, but it is in all its works, in all human thoughts, everywhere indeed, and even in the productions of arts and music. The nature of Number and Harmony are numberless, for what is false has no part in their essence and the principle of error and envy is thoughtless, irrational, indefinite nature. Never could error slip into Number, for its nature is hostile thereto. Truth is the proper, innate character of Number (DK 11).

B. (ps.-Iamblichus, *Theologumena Arithmeticae*, 61). The Decad is also named Faith, because, according to Philolaus, it is by the Decad and its elements, if utilized energetically and without negligence, that we arrive at a solidly grounded faith about beings. It is also the source of memory, and that is why the Monad has been called Mnemosyne.

C. (Theon of Smyrna, *Plat. Math.*, p. 49). The Decad determines every number, including the nature of everything, of the even and the odd, of the mobile and immobile, of good and evil. It has been the subject of long discussions by Archytas, and of Philolaus in his work *On Nature*.

D. (Lucian, *Pro Lapsu Inter Salutandum*, 5). Some called the Tetraktys the great oath of the Pythagoreans, because they considered it the perfect number, or even because it is the principle of Health; among them is Philolaus.

19. A. (Theon of Smyrna, *Plat. Math.*, 4). Archytas and Philolaus use the terms Monad and Unity interchangeably.

B. (Syrianus, sub. init., *Comment. in Arist. Met.*, 1. xiv). You must not suppose that the philosophers begin by principles supposed to be opposite; they know the principle above these two elements, as Philolaus acknowledges when saying that it is God who hypostasizes the Limited and Unlimited. He shows that it is by Limit that every coordinate series of things further approaches Unity, and that it is by the Unlimited that the lower series is produced. Thus even above these two principles they posited the unique and separate cause distinguished by all of its excellence. This is the cause which Archinetus called the cause before the cause, and which Philolaus vehemently insists is the principle of all, and of which Brontinus says that in power and dignity it surpasses all reason and essence.

C. (Iamblichus, *In. Nicom.*, p. 109). In the formation of square numbers by addition, unity is as it were the starting-post from which one begins, and also the end whither one returns; for if one places the numbers in the form of a double procession, and you see them grow from unity to the root of the square, then the root is like the turning-point where the horses turn to go back through similar numbers to unity, as in the square of 5. For example:

$$\begin{array}{cccc} 1 & 2 & 3 & 4 \\ 1 & 2 & 3 & 4 \end{array} \ 5 = \text{added, } 25$$

It is not the same with rectangular numbers. If, just as in the gnomon, one adds to any number the sum of the even, then the number two will alone seem to receive and stand addition, and without the number two it will not be possible to produce rectangular numbers. If you set out the naturally increasing series of numbers in the order of the double race-track, then unity, being the principle of everything, according to Philolaus (for it is he who said, "unity, the principle of everything"), will indeed present itself as the barrier, the starting point which produces the rectangular numbers, but it will not be the goal or limit where the series returns and comes back; it is not unity, but the number 2, which will fulfill this function. Thus, 6 x 4:

$$\begin{array}{cccc} 1 & 2 & 3 & 4 \\ & 2 & 3 & 4 \end{array} \ 5 = \text{added, } 24$$

D. (Philo, *Mund. Opif.*, 24). Philolaus confirms what I have just said by the following words; "He who commands and governs everything is a God who is single, eternally existing, immutable, self-identical, and different from other things."

E. (Athenagoras, *Legat. Pro Christ.*, 6). Philolaus says that all things are by God kept as in captivity, and thereby implies the he is single and superior to matter. to matter.

20. (Proclus, *In Eucl.*, I. 36). Even among the Pythagoreans we find different angles consecrated to the different divinities, as did Philolaus, who attributed to some the angle of the triangle, to others the angle of the rectangle, to others other angles, and sometimes the same to several.

The Pythagoreans say that the triangle is the absolute principle of generation of begotten things, and of their form; that is why Timaeus says that the reasons of physical being, and of the regular formation of the elements are triangular; indeed, they have the three dimensions, in unity they gather the elements which in themselves are absolutely divided and changing; they are filled with the infinity characteristic of matter, and above the material beings they form bonds that indeed are frail. That is why triangles are bounded by straight lines, and have angles which unite the lines, and are their bonds. Philolaus was therefore right in devoting the angle of the triangle to four divinities, Kronos, Hades, Mars, and Bacchus, under these four names combining the fourfold disposition of the elements, which refers to the superior part of the universe, starting from the sky, or sections of the zodiac. Indeed, Kronos presides over everything humid and cold in essence; Mars, over everything fiery; Hades contains everything terrestrial, and Dionysius directs the generation of wet and warm things, represented by wine, which is liquid and warm. These four divinities divide their secondary operations, but they remain united; that is why Philolaus, by attributing to them one angle only, wished to express this power of unification.

The Pythagoreans also claim that, in preference to the quadrilateral, the tetragon bears the divine impress, and by it they express perfect order. For the property of being straight imitates the power of immutability, and equality represents that of permanence; for motion is the result of inequality, and rest, that of equality. Those are the causes of the organization of the being that is solid in its totality, and of its pure and immovable essences. They were therefore right to express it symbolically by the figure of the tetragon. Besides, Philolaus, with another stroke of genius, calls the angle of the tetragon that of Rhea, of Demeter, and of Hestia.... For considering the earth as a tetragon, and noting that this element possesses the property of continuousness, as we learned from Timaeus, and that the earth receives all that drips from the divinities, and also the generative powers that they contain, he was right in consecrating the angle of the tetragon to these divinities which procreate life. Indeed, some of them call the earth Hestia and Demeter, and claim that it partakes of Rhea, in its entirety, and that Rhea contains all the begotten cause. That is why, in obscure language, he says that the angle of the tetragon contains the single power which produces the unity of these divine creations.

And we must not forget that Philolaus assigns the angle of the triangle to four divinities, and the angle of the tetragon to three, thereby indicating their penetrative faculty, whereby they influence each other mutually, and showing how all things participate in all things, the odd things in the even and the even in the odd. The triad and the tetrad, participating in the generative and creative beings, contain the whole regular organization of begotten things. Their product is the dodecad, which ends in the single monad, the sovereign principle of Zeus, for Philolaus says that the angle of the dodecagon belongs to Zeus, because in unity Zeus contains the entire number of the dodecad.

21 A. (ps.-Iamblichus, *Theologumena Arithmeticae,* p. 56). After the mathematical magnitude which by its three dimensions or intervals realizes the number Four, Philolaus shows us the being manifesting in number Five quality and color; in the number Six, the soul and life; in the number Seven, reason, health, and what he calls light; then he adds that love, friendship, prudence and reflection are communicated to beings by the number Eight.

B. (ps.-Iamblichus, *Theologumena Arithmeticae,* p. 22). There are four principles of the reasonable animal, as Philolaus says in his work *On Nature:* the skull, the heart, the navel, and the sexual organs. The head is the seat of reason; the heart, that of the soul or life, and sensation; the navel, the principle of the faculty of striking roots and reproducing the first being; the sexual organs, of the faculty of projecting the sperma, and procreating. The skull contains the principle of man, the heart that of the animal, the navel that of the plant, the sexual organs that of all living beings, for these grow and produce offspring (DK 13).

C. (Stobaeus, *Eclog. Physic.*, 1. 2. 3. p. 10). There are five bodies in the sphere: fire, water, earth, air, and the circle of the sphere which makes the fifth (DK 12).*

22. (Stobaeus, *Eclog. Physic.*, 1. 20. 2. p. 418). This is from the Pythagorean Philolaus, drawn from his book *On the Soul*. He insists that the world is indestructible. Here is what he says in his book *On the Soul*:

That is why the world remains eternally, because it cannot be destroyed by any other, nor spontaneously destroy itself. Neither within it, nor without it can be found a force greater than itself, able to destroy it. The world has existed from all eternity, and will remain eternally, because it is One, governed by a principle whose nature is similar to its own, and whose force is omnipotent and sovereign. Besides, the single world is continuous, and endowed with a natural respiration, moving eternally in a circle, having the principle of motion and change; one of its parts is immovable, the other is changing. The immovable part extends from the soul, that embraces everything, to the moon; and the changing part from the moon to the earth; or, since the Mover has been acting since eternity, and continues his action eternally, and since the changeable part receives its manner of being from the Mover who acts thereon, it necessarily results thence that one of the parts of the world ever impresses motion, and that the other ever receives it passively. The one is entirely the domain of Mind and Soul, the other of Generation and Change; the one is anterior in power, and superior, the other is posterior and subordinate. The composite of these two things, the divine eternally in motion, and of generation ever changing, is the World. That is why one is right in saying that the world is the eternal energy of God, and of becoming which obeys the laws of changing nature. The one remains eternally in the same state, self-identical; the remainder constitutes the domain of plurality, which is born and perishes. But nevertheless, the things that perish transmit their essence and form, thanks to generation, which reproduces the identical form of the father who has begotten and fashioned them (DK 21).

23 A. (Claudianus Mamertus, *De Statu Animae,* 2. p. 7). The soul is introduced and associated with the body by Number, and by a harmony simultaneously immortal and incorporeal....the soul cherishes its body, because without it the soul cannot feel; but when death has separated the soul therefrom, the soul lives an incorporeal existence in the cosmos (DK 22).

B. (Macrobius, *Commentariorum in Somnium Scipionis,* 1. 14). Plato says that the soul is a self-moving essence; Xenocrates defines the soul as a self-moving number; Aristotle called it an entelechy; and Pythagoras and Philolaus, a harmony.

C. (Olympiodorus, *In. Plat. Phaed.,* p. 150). Philolaus opposed suicide because it was a Pythagorean precept not to lay down the burden, but to help others carry theirs; namely, that you must assist, and not hinder it.

---

* There is reason to believe that the "five bodies" referred to in this fragment are the so-called regular polyhedra or "Platonic solids" which are described for the first time in Plato's *Timaeus*. It is quite likely that the earlier Pythagoreans were aware of the regular solids. If this fragment is genuine, Plato followed their lead in associating these "molecular" forms with the "elements" of Greek physics, the latter of which actually represent states of matter rather than specific substances.

D. (Clement of Alexandria, *Stromateis,* 3. p. 433). It will help us to remember the Pythagorean Philolaus' utterance that the ancient theologians and divines claimed that the soul is bound to the body as a punishment, and is buried in it as in a tomb (DK 14).

24. A. (Aristotle, *Eth. Eud.,* 2. 9). As Philolaus has said, there are some reasons (*logoi*) stronger than us (DK 16).

B. (Iamblichus, *In Nicom.,* 1. 25). I shall later have a better opportunity to consider how, in raising a number to its square, by the position of the simple component unities, we arrive at very evident propositions, naturally, and not by any law, as says Philolaus.

25. (Sextus Empiricus, *Adversus Mathematicos,* 7. 92. p. 388). Anaxagoras has said how reason in general is the faculty of discerning and judging; the Pythagoreans also agree that it is Reason, not reason in general, but the Reason that develops in men by the study of mathematics, as Philolaus used to say, and they insist that if this Reason is capable of understanding All, it is only because its essence is kindred with this nature, for it is in the nature of things that the similar be understood by the similar.

26 A. (Laurentius Lydus, *De Mens.,* p. 16; Cedrenus, 1. 169b). Philolaus was therefore right in calling it a Decad, because it receives (*dechomai*) the Infinite, and Orpheus was right in calling it the Branch, because it is the branch from which issue all the numbers, as so many branches.

B. (Cedrenus, 1. p. 72). Philolaus was therefore right to say that the number seven was motherless (DK 20).

C. (Cedrenus, 1. p. 208). Philolaus was therefore right to call the Dyad the spouse of Kronos (DK 20A).

THE FRAGMENTS OF ARCHYTAS

ARCHYTAS OF TARENTUM (first half of the fourth century B.C.E.) was a student of Philolaus and a personal friend of Plato, who came to visit him in 388 B.C.E. He made a major contribution to harmonic theory, was engaged in mathematical studies, and was the first to solve the geometrical problem of doubling the volume of the cube.

Like Pythagoras himself, Archytas was also involved in political affairs; he was quite well liked in this capacity, being elected chief magistrate of Tarentum for seven terms though the law, which was waived in his favor, allowed for a maximum of one term. Archytas also seems to have had a knack for practical inventions: he is said to have created a mechanical pigeon, made of wood, which flew, and Aristotle refers to another well-known invention, Archytas' rattle, "which they give to children so that by using it they may refrain from breaking things about the house; for young things cannot keep still."

With the exception of the mathematical fragments and a few others, the fragments of Archytas are not considered genuine. For example, "The Ten Categories of Archytas" are obviously indebted to Aristotelian thought rather than vice versa. Nonetheless, even though not written by Archytas himself, some of the other fragments are quite valuable, especially the ethical ones. The correspondence between Plato and Archytas, reproduced below in the biography from Diogenes Laertius, is thought to be spurious.

For more on Archytas see Freeman's *Companion to the Pre-Socratic Philosophers,* section 47, and Guthrie's *History of Greek Philosophy,* vol. 1, 333 ff.

THE LIFE OF ARCHYTAS

FROM DIOGENES LAERTIUS

ARCHYTAS OF TARENTUM, son of Mnesagoras, or of Hestius, according to Aristoxenus, also was a Pythagorean. It was he who, by a letter, saved Plato from the death threatened by Dionysius. He possessed all the virtues, so that, being the admiration of the crowd, he was seven times named general, in spite of the law which prohibited reelection after one year. Plato wrote him two letters, in response to this one of Archytas:

"Greetings. It is fortunate for you that you have recovered from your illness, for I have heard of it not only from you, but also from Lamiscus. I have busied myself about those notes, and took a trip into Lucania, where I met descendants of Ocellus. I have in my possession the treatises *On Law* and *On Kingship, On Sanctity,* and *On the Origin of All Things,* and I am sending them to you. The others could not be discovered. Should they be found, they will be sent to you."

Plato answered:

"Greetings. I am delighted to have received the works which you have sent me, and I acknowledge a great admiration for him who wrote them. He seems to be worthy of his ancient and glorious ancestors, who are said to be from Myra, and among the number of those Trojans who emigrated under the leadership of

Laomedon, all worthy people, as the legend proves. Those works of mine about which you wrote me are not in a sufficient state of perfection, but I send them such as they are. Both of us are in perfect agreement on the subject of protecting them. No use to renew the request. May your health improve!''

Such are these two letters.

There were four Archytases: the first, of whom we have just spoken; the second, from Mytilene, was a musician; the third wrote *On Agriculture*; the fourth is an author of epigrams. Some mention a fifth, an architect, who left a treatise *On Mechanics*, beginning as follows: "This book contains what I have been taught by Teucer of Carthage." The musician is said to have made this joke: on being reproached for not advertising himself more, he said "It is my instrument which speaks for me."

Aristoxenus claims that the philosopher Archytas was never defeated during his command. Once, overcome by envy, he had been obliged to resign his command, and his fellow-citizens were immediately conquered. He was the first who methodically applied the principles of mathematics to mechanics; who imparted an organic motion to a geometric figure, by the section of the semi-cylinder seeking two means that would be proportional, in order to double the cube.* He also first, by geometry, discovered the properties of the cube, as Plato records in the *Republic* (528 B).

THE FRAGMENTS OF ARCHYTAS

1. Metaphysical Fragments

1. There are necessarily two principles of beings: the one contains the series of beings organized, and finished; the other, contains unordered and unfinished beings. That one which is susceptible of being expressed, by speech, and which can be explained, embraces both beings, and determines and organizes the non-being.

For every time that it approaches the things of becoming, it orders them, and measures them, and makes them participate in the essence and form of the universal. On the contrary, the series of beings which escapes speech and reason, injures ordered things, and destroys those which aspire to essence and being; whenever it approaches them, it assimilates them to its own nature.

But since there are two principles of things of an opposite character, the one the principle of good, and the other the principle of evil, there are therefore also two reasons, the one of beneficent nature, the other of maleficent nature.

That is why the things that owe their existence to art, and also those which owe it to nature, must above all participate in these two principles: form and substance.

The form is the cause of essence; substance is the substrate which receives the form. Neither can substance alone participate in form, by itself; nor can form by itself apply itself to substance; there must therefore exist another cause which

---

* See Heath, *A History of Greek Mathematics,* vol. 1, 246-49.

moves the substance of things, and forms them. This cause is primary, as regards substance, and the most excellent of all. Its most suitable name is God.

There are therefore three principles: God, the substance of things, and form. God is the artist, the mover; the substance is the matter, the moved; the essence is what you might call the art, and that to which the substance is brought by the mover. But since the mover contains forces which are self-contrary, those of simple bodies, and as the contraries are in need of a principle harmonizing and unifying them, it must necessarily receive its efficacious virtues and proportions from numbers, and all that is manifested in numbers and geometric forms, virtues and proportions capable of binding and uniting into form the contraries that exist in the substance of things. For, by itself, substance is formless; only after having been moved towards form does it become formed and receive the rational relations of order. Likewise, if movement exists, besides the thing moved, there must exist a prime mover; there must therefore be three principles: the substance of things, the form, and the principle that moves itself, and which by its power is the first; not only must this principle be an intelligence, it must be above intelligence, and we call it God.

Evidently the relation of equality applies to the being which can be defined by language and reason. The relation of inequality applies to the irrational being, and cannot be fixed by language; it is substance, and that is why all begetting and destruction take place in substance and do not occur without it.

2. In short, the philosophers began only by so to speak contrary principles; but above these elements they knew another superior one, as is testified to by Philolaus, who says that God has produced, and realized the Limited and Unlimited, and shown that at the Limit is attached the whole series which has a greater affinity with the One, and to the Unlimited, the series that is below. Thus, above these two principles thay have posited a unifying cause, superior to everything; which, according to Archenetus, is the cause before the cause, and, according to Philolaus, the universal principle.

3. A. Which One are you referring to? The supreme One, or the infinitely small One that you can find in the parts? The Pythagoreans distinguish between the One and the Monad, as says Archytas: the One and the Monad have a natural affinity, yet they differ.

B. Archytas and Philolaus indiscriminately call the One a Monad, and Monad a One. The majority, however, add to the name Monad, the distinction of first Monad, for there is a Monad which is not the first, and which is posterior to the Monad in itself, and to the One.

C. Pythagoras said that the human soul was a tetragon with right angles. Archytas, on the contrary, instead of defining the soul by the tetragon, did so by a circle, because the soul is a self-mover, and consequently, the prime mover, and this is a circle or a sphere.

D. Plato and Archytas and the other Pythagoreans claim that there are three parts in the soul: reason, courage and desire.

4. The beginning of knowledge of beings is in the things that produce themselves. Of these some are intelligible, and others sensible; the former are immovable, the latter are moved. The criterion of intelligible things is the world; that of sen-

sible things is sensation.

Of the things that do not manifest in things themselves, some are science, the others, opinion; science is immovable, opinion is movable.

We must, besides, admit these three things: the subject that judges, the object that is judged, and the rule by which that object is judged. What judges is the mind, or sensation; what is judged is the *logos*, or rational essence; the rule of judgement is the act itself which occurs in the being, whether intelligible or sensible. The mind is the judge of essence, whether it tends towards an intelligible being or a sensible one. When reason seeks intelligible things, it tends towards an intelligible element; when it seeks things of sense, it tends towards their element. Hence come those false graphic representations in figures and numbers seen in geometry, those researches in causes and probable ends, whose object are beings subject to becoming, and moral acts, in physiology or politics. It is while tending toward the intelligible element that reason recognizes that harmony is in the double relation [the octave] but sensation alone attests that this double relation is concordant. In mechanics, the object of science is figures, numbers, proportions—namely, rational proportions; the effects are perceived by sensation, for you can neither study nor know them outside of the matter or movement. In short, it is impossible to know the reason of an individual thing, unless you have preliminarily by the mind grasped the essence of the individual thing; the knowledge of the existence, and of quality, belongs to reason and sensation: to reason, whenever we effect a thing's demonstration by a syllogism whose conclusion is inevitable; to sensation, when the latter is the criterion of a thing's essence.

5. Sensation occurs in the body, reason in the soul. The former is the principle of sensible things, the latter, of intelligible ones. Popular measures are number, length, the foot, weight, equilibrium, and the scales, while the rule and the measure of straightness in both vertical and longitudinal directions is the right angle.

Thus sensation is the principle and measure of the bodies; reason is the principle and measure of intelligible things. The latter is the principle of beings that are intelligible and naturally primary; the former is the principle of sense-objects, and is naturally secondary. Reason is the principle of our soul; sensation is the principle of our body. The mind is the judge of the noblest things; sensation is the judge of the most useful. Sensation was created in view of our bodies, and to serve them; reason was created in view of the soul, and to initiate wisdom therein. Reason is the principle of science; sensation is that of opinion. The latter derives its activity from sensible things; the former, from intelligible forms. Sensible objects participate in movement and change; intelligible objects participate in immutability and eternity. There is analogy between sensation and reason; for sensation's object is the sensible, which moves, changes, and never remains self-identical; therefore, as you can see, it improves or deteriorates. Reason's object is the intelligible, whose essence is immobility; wherefore in the intelligible we cannot conceive of either more or less, better or worse; and just as reason sees the primary being, and the [cosmic] model, so sensation sees the image, and the copied. Reason sees man in himself; sensation sees in them the circle of the sun, and the forms of artificial objects. Reason is perfectly simple and indivisible, as unity, and the point; it is the same with intelligible beings.

The idea is neither the limit nor the frontier of the body; it is only the figure of being, that by which the being exists, while sensation has parts, and is divisible.

Some beings are perceived by sensation, others by opinion, others by science, and others by reason.

The bodies that offer resistance are sensible; opinion knows those that participate in the ideas, and are its images, so to speak. Thus some particular man participates in the idea of man, and this triangle, in the triangle-idea. The objects of science are the necessary accidents of ideas; thus the object of geometry is the properties of the figures; reason knows the ideas themselves, and the principles of the sciences and of their objects, for example, the circle, the triangle, and the pure sphere in itself. Likewise, in us, in our souls, there are four kinds of knowledge: pure thought, science, opinion and sensation; two are principles of knowledge [thought and sensation], two are its purpose, science and opinion.

It is always the similar which is capable of knowing the similar: reason knows intelligible things; science understands knowable things; opinion knows conjecturable things; sensation knows sensible things.

That is why thought must rise from things that are sensible, to the conjecturable, and from these to the knowable, and on to the intelligible; and he who wishes to know the truth about these objects, must in a harmonious grouping combine all these means and objects of knowledge. This being established, you might represent them under the image of a line divided into two equal parts, each of which would be similarly divided; if we separate the sensible, dividing it into two parts, in the same proportion, the one will be clearer, the other obscurer. One of the sections of the sensible contains images of things, such as you see reflected in water, or mirrors; the second represents the plants and animals of which the former are images. Similarly dividing the intelligible, the different kinds of sciences will represent the images; for the students of geometry begin by establishing by hypothesis the odd and the even, figures, three kinds of angles, and from these hypotheses deduce their science. As to the things themselves, they leave them aside, as if they knew them, though they cannot account for them to themselves or to others; they employ sensible things as images, but these things are neither the object nor the end proposed in their researches and reasonings, which pursue only things in themselves, such as the diameter, or square. The second section is that of the intelligible, the object of dialectics. It really makes no hypotheses, positing principles whence it rises to arrive at the unconditioned, universal principle; then, by an inverse movement, grasping that principle, it descends to the end of the reasoning, without employing any sensible object, exclusively using pure ideas. By these four divisions, you can also analyze the soul-states, and give the highest the name of thought, reasoning to the second, faith to the third, and imagination to the fourth.

6. Archytas, at the beginning of his book *On Wisdom* gives this advice: in all human things, wisdom is as superior as sight is to all the other senses of the body, as mind is superior to soul, as the sun is superior to the stars. Of all the senses, sight is the one that extends furthest in its sphere of action, and gives us the most ideas. Mind, being supreme, accomplishes its legitimate operation by reason and

reasoning; it is like sight, and is the power of the noblest objects. The sun is the eye and soul of natural things, for it is through it that they are all seen, begotten, and thought; through it the plants produced by root or seed are fed, developed, and endowed with sensation.

Of all beings, man is the wisest by far. For he is able to contemplate beings, and to acquire knowledge and understanding of all. That is why divinity has engraved in him, and has revealed to him the system of speech, which extends to everything, a system in which are classified all the beings, kinds of beings, and the meanings of nouns and verbs. For the specialized seats of the voice are the pharynx, the mouth and the nose. As man is naturally organized to produced sounds, through which nouns and verbs are expressed and formed, likewise he is naturally destined to contemplate the notions contained in visible objects. Such, in my view, is the purpose for which man has been created, and was born, and for which he received from God his organs and faculties.

Man is born and was created to know the essence of universal nature; and precisely the function of wisdom is to possess and contemplate the intelligence manifested in [all] beings.

The object of wisdom is no particular being, but all the beings, absolutely; and it should not begin to seek the principles of an individual being, but the principles common to all. The object of wisdom is all the beings, as the object of sight is all visible things. The function of wisdom is to see all the beings in their totality, and to know their universal attributes, and that is how wisdom discovers the principles of all beings.

He who is capable of analyzing all the species, and tracing and grouping them, by an inverse operation, into one single principle, seems to me the wisest, and the closest to the truth; he seems to have found that sublime observatory from the peak of which he may observe God, and all the things that belong to the series and order of divine things. Being master of this royal road, his mind will be able to rush forwards, and arrive at the end of the career, uniting principles to the purposes of things, and knowing that God is the principle, the middle and the end of all things made according to the rules of justice and right reason.

2. Physical and Mathematical Fragments

7. As Eudemus reports, Archytas used to ask this question: "If I was situated at the extreme and immovable limit of the world, could I, or could I not, extend a wand outside of it?" To say I could not, is absurd; but if I can, there must be something outside of the world, be it body or space; and in whatever manner we reason, by the same reasoning we will ever return to this limit. I will still place myself there, and ask, "Is there anything else on which I may place my wand?" Therefore, the Unlimited exists; if it is a body, our proposition is demonstrated; if it is space, place is that in which a body could be; and if it exists potentially, we will have to place it and classify it among the eternal things, and the Unlimited will then be a body and a place.

8. The essence of place is that all other things are in it, while itself is not in anything. For if it was in a place, there would be a place in a place, and that would continue to infinity. All other beings must therefore be in place, and place

in nothing. Its relation to things is the same as Limit to limited things; for the place of the entire world is the Limit of all things.

9 A. Some say that time is the sphere of the world; such was the sentiment of the Pythagoreans, according to those who had heard Archytas give this general definition of time: "Time is the interval of the nature of all."

B. The divine Iamblichus, in the first book of his *Commentaries on the Categories,* said that Archytas thus defined time: "It is the number of movement, or in general the interval of the nature of all."

C. We must combine these two definitions, and recognize time as both continuous and discrete, though it is properly continuous. Iamblichus claims that Archytas taught the distinction of physical time, and psychic time. So at least Iamblichus interpreted Archytas, but we must recognize that there, and often elsewhere, he adds his own commentaries to explain matters.

10. The general proper essence of "when-ness" and time is to be indivisible and unsubstantial. For, being indivisible, the present time has passed, while expressing it and thinking of it; nothing remains of it, and so becoming continuously the same it never subsists numerically, but only specifically. In fact, the actually present time and the future are not identical with former time. For the one has past, and is no more; the other one passes while being produced and thought. Thus the present is never but a bond; it perpetually becomes, changes, and perishes, but nevertheless it remains identical in its own kind.

In fact, every present is without parts, and indivisible; it is the term of past time, the beginning of time to come; just as in a broken line, the point where the break occurs becomes the beginning of a line, and the end of the other. Time is continuous, and not discrete as are number, speech and harmony.

In speech, the syllables are parts, and distinct parts; in harmony, they are the sounds; in number, the unities. The line, place and space are continuous; if they are divided, their parts form common sections. For the line divides into points, the surface into lines, the solid into surfaces. Therefore time is continuous. In fact there was no time when time was not; and there was no moment when the present was not. But the present has always been, it will always be, and will never fail; it changes perpetually, and becomes another according to the number, but remains the same according to kind. The line differs from the other continua, in that if you divide the line, place, and space, its parts will subsist; but in time, the past has perished, and the future will. That is why either time does absolutely not exist, or it hardly exists, and has but an insensible existence. For of its parts one, the past, is no more, and the future is not yet; how then could the present, without parts and indivisible, possess true reality?

11. Plato says that the movement is the great and small, the non-being, the unusual, and all that reduces to these; like Archytas, we had better say that it is a cause.

12. Why do all natural bodies take the spherical form? Is it, as said Archytas, because in the natural movement is the proportion of equality? For everything moves in proportion; and this proportion of equality is the only one which, when it occurs, produces circles and spheres, because it returns on itself.

13. He who knows must have learned from another, or have found his knowledge

by himself. The science that you learn from another, is as you might say, exterior; what you find by yourself, belongs to ourselves individually. To find without seeking is something difficult and rare; to find what one is seeking is commodious and easy; to ignore, and seek what you ignore, is impossible (DK 3).

14. The Pythagorean opinion about sciences to me seems correct, and they seem to show an exact judgment about each of them. Having known how to form a just idea of the nature of a ball, they should have likewise seen the essential nature of the parts. They have left us certain and evident theories about arithmetic, geometry and spherics, also about music, for all these sciences seem to be kindred. In fact, the first two kinds of being are indistinguishable.

15. A. First they have seen that it was not possible that noise should exist unless there was a shock of one body against another; they said there is a shock when moving bodies meet and strike each other. The bodies moved in the air in an opposite direction and those that are moved with an unequal swiftness—in the same direction—the first, when overtaken, makes a noise, because struck. Many of these noises are not susceptible of being perceived by our organs; some because of the slightness of the shock, the others because of their too great distance from us, some even because of the very excess of their intensity, for noises too great do not enter into our ears, as we cannot introduce anything into jars with too narrow an opening when one pours in too much at a time.

Of the sounds that fall within the range of our senses, some—those that come quickly from the bodies struck—seem shrill; those that arrive slowly and feebly, seem of low pitch. In fact, when one agitates some object slowly and feebly, the shock produces a low pitch; if the waving is done quickly, and with energy, the sound is shrill. This is not the only proof of the fact, which we can prove when we speak or sing; when we wish to speak loud and high, we use a great force of breath. So also with something thrown; if you throw them hard, they go far; if you throw them without energy, they fall near, for the air yields more to bodies moved with much force, than to those thrown with little. This phenomenon is also reproduced in the sound of the voice, for the sounds produced by an energetic breath are shrill, while those produced by a feeble breath are weak and low in pitch. This same observation can be seen in the force of a signal given from any place: if you pronounce it loud, it can be heard far; if you pronounce the same signal low, we do not hear it even when near. So also in flutes, the breath emitted by the mouth and which presents itself to the holes nearest the mouthpiece, produces a shriller sound, because the impulsive force is greater; farther [down], they are of lower pitch. It is therefore evident that the swiftness of the movement produces shrillness, and slowness, lower pitch. The same thing is seen in the bull roarers which are spun in the Mysteries; those that move slowly produce a low pitch, while those that move quickly with force make a shrill noise. Let us yet adduce the reed: if you close the lower opening, and blow into it, it will produce a certain sound; and if you stop it in the center, or in the front, the sound will be shrill. For the same breath traversing a long space weakens, while traversing a shorter, it remains of the same power. After having developed this opinion that the movement of the voice is measured by intervals, he resumes his discussion, saying, that the shrill sounds are the result of a swifter movement, the lower sounds, of a slower movement. This is a fact which numerous experiments demonstrate clearly.

B. Eudoxus and Archytas believed that the reasons of the agreement of the sounds was in the numbers; they agree in thinking that these reasons consist in the movements, the shrill movement being quick, because the agitation of the air is continuous, and the vibration more rapid; the low pitch movement being slow, because it is calmer.

16. Explaining himself about the means, Archytas writes: In music there are three means: the first is the arithmetical mean, the second is the geometrical, the third is the subcontrary mean, which is called harmonic. The mean is arithmetical, when the three terms are in a relation of analogical excess, that is to say, when the difference between the first and second is the same as between second and third; in this proportion, the relation of the greater terms is smaller, and the relation of the smaller is greater. The geometric mean exists when the first term is to the second as the second is to the third; here the relation of the greater is identical with the relation of the smaller terms. The subcontrary mean, which we call harmonic, exists when the first term exceeds the second by a fraction of itself, identically with the fraction [of the third] by which the second exceeds the third; in this proportion the relation of the greater terms is greater, and that of the smaller, smaller.

3. Ethical Fragments

17. A. We must first know that the good man is not thereby necessarily happy, but that the happy man is necessarily good; for the happy man is he who deserves praise and congratulations; the good man deserves only praise.

We praise a man because of his virtue, we congratulate him because of his success. The good man is such because of the goods that proceed from virtue; the happy man is such because of the goods that come from fortune. From the good man you cannot take his virtue; sometimes the happy man loses his good fortune. The power of virtue depends on nobody; that of happiness, on the contrary, is dependent. Long diseases, the loss of our senses, cause to fade the flower of our happiness.

B. God differs from the good man in that God not only possesses a perfect virtue, purified from all mortal affection, but enjoys a virtue whose power is faultless and independent, as suits the majesty and magnificence of his works.

Man, on the contrary, not only possesses an inferior virtue, because of the mortal constitution of his nature, but even sometimes by the very abundance of his goods, now by the force of habit, by the vice of nature, or from other causes, he is incapable of attaining the perfection of the good.

C. The good man, in my opinion, is he who knows how to act properly in serious circumstances and occasions. He will therefore know how to support good and bad fortune; in a brilliant and glorious condition, he will show himself worthy of it, and if fortune happens to change, he will know how to accept properly his actual fate. In short, the good man is he who, in every occasion, and according to the circumstances, well plays his part, and knows how to fit to it not only himself, but also those who have confidence in him, and are associated with his fortunes.

D. Since amidst the goods, some are desirable for themselves, and not for anything else, and others are desirable for something else, and not for themselves, there must necessarily exist a third kind of goods, which are desirable both for themselves and for other things. Which are the goods naturally desirable for themselves, and not for anything else? Evidently they include happiness, for it is the end on account of which we seek everything else, while we seek it only for itself, and not in view of anything else. Secondly, which are the goods chosen for something else, and not for themselves? Evidently those that are useful, and which are the means of procuring the real goods, which thus become the causes of the goods desirable for themselves; for instance: the bodily fatigues, the exercises, the tests which procure health; reading, meditation, the studies which procure virtues, and the quality of honesty. Finally, which are those goods which are both desirable for themselves, and for something else? The virtues, and the habitual possession of virtues, the resolutions of the soul, the actions, and in short anything pertaining to the possession of the beautiful. That which is to be considered for itself, and not for anything else, that is the only good.

Now what we seek for itself and for something else is divided into three classes: the one whose object is the soul, the body, and external goods. The first contains the virtues of the soul; the second contains the advantages of the body; the third consists in friends, glory, honor and wealth. Likewise with the goods that are desirable only for something else: one part of them procures goods for the soul, the other which regards the body, procures goods for it; the external goods furnish wealth, glory, honor and friendship.

We can prove that it is the characteristic of virtue to be desirable for itself, as follows: in fact, if the naturally inferior goods, I mean those of the body, are by us sought for themselves, and if the soul is better than the body, it is evident that we like the goods of the soul for themselves, and not for the result that they might produce.

E. In human life there are three circumstances: prosperity, adversity, and intermediary comfort. Since the good man who possesses virtue and practices it, practices it in these three circumstances—either in adversity, or prosperity, or comfort, since besides in adversity he is unhappy, in prosperity he is happy, and in comfort he is not happy—it is evident that happiness is nothing else than the use of virtue in prosperity. I speak here of human happiness. Man is not only a soul, he is also a body. The living being is a composite of both, and man also; for if the body is an instrument of the soul, it is as much a part of the man as the soul. That is why, among the goods, some belong to the man, and others belong to his component parts. The good of man is happiness amidst its integral parts. The soul's goods are prudence, courage, justice, and temperance; the body's are beauty, health, good disposition of its members, and the perfect condition of its senses. The external goods—wealth, glory, honor, nobility—are naturally superfluous advantages of man, and are naturally subordinate to the superior goods.

The inferior goods serve as satellites to the superior goods. Friendship, glory, and wealth are the satellites of the body and soul. Health, strength and sense-perfection are satellites of the body. Prudence, courage, justice and temperance are the satellites of the reason of the soul. Reason is the satellite of God; he is omnipotent, the supreme master. It is for these goods that the others must exist; for the army obeys the general, the sailors heed the pilot, the world obeys God, the soul heeds reason, the happy life is contingent on prudence. For prudence is nothing more than the science of the happy life, or the science of the goods which belong to human nature.

F. To God belongs happiness and the happy life; man cannot possess but a grouping of science, virtue and prosperity forming a single body. I call wisdom the science of the Gods and geniuses, and term prudence the science of human things, the science of life. For science should be the name of virtues which rest upon reasons and demonstrations, and moral virtue, the excellent habit of the irrational part of the soul, which makes you give the name of certain qualities corresponding to our habits, namely the names of liberal, just and temperate people. And I call prosperity this affluence of goods which we receive without reason being their cause. Then since virtue and science depend on us, and prosperity does not depend thereon, since happiness consists in the contemplation and practice of good things, and since contemplation and action when they meet obstacles, lend us a necessary support, when they go by an easy road, they bring us distraction and happiness. Since after all it is prosperity that gives us these benefits, it is evident that happiness is nothing else than the use of virtue in prosperity.

G. Man's relations with prosperity resemble a healthy and vigorous human body; he also can stand heat and cold, can raise a great burden, and can easily bear many other miseries.

H. Since happiness is the use of virtue in prosperity, let us speak of virtue and prosperity, the former first. Some goods, such as virtue, are not subject to excess; for excess is impossible in virtue, for one can never be too decent a man. Indeed, virtue's measure is duty, and is the habit of duty in practical life. But prosperity is subject to excess and lack, which excesses produce certain evils, disturbing man from his usual mood, so as to oppose him to virtue; this is not only the case with prosperity, but other more numerous causes also produce this effect. You need not be surprised at seeing in the hall certain impudent artists, who neglect true art, misleading the ignorant by a false picture; but do you suppose that this race does not exist as regards virtue? On the contrary, the greater and more beautiful virtue is, the more do people feign to adorn themselves with it. There are indeed many things which dishonor the appearance of virtue: first are the deceivers who simulate it, others are the natural passions which accompany it, and sometimes twist the dispositions of the soul into a contrary direction. Others are the bad habits which the body has rooted in us, or which have been ingrained in us by youth, age, prosperity, adversity, or by a thousand other circumstances. Wherefore we must not at all be surprised at entirely wrong judgments, because the true nature of our soul has been falsified within us. Just as we see an artist who is excellent make errors in works we are examining—or the general, the pilot or the painter and like may make errors without our detracting from their talent—so we must not call unworthy him who has had a moment of weakness, nor among the worthy a man who has done no more than a single action; but in respect to the evil, we must consider chance, and for the good, error, and to make an equitable and just judgment, and not regard a single circumstance, or a single period of time, but the whole life.

Just as the body suffers from both excess and lack, but as nevertheless the excess and so-called superfluities naturally produce the greatest diseases, so the soul suffers from both prosperity and adversity when they arrive at wrong times, and yet the greatest evils come from so-called absolute prosperity—which is absolute because like wine it intoxicates the reason of the worthy.

I. That is why it is not adversity but prosperity which is the hardest to stand properly. All men, when they are in adversity, at least the greater part of them, seem moderate and modest; but in good fortune, ambitious, vain and proud. For adversity is apt to moderate the soul, and concentrate it, while on the contrary prosperity excites it and puffs it up. That is why wretches are docile to advice, and prudent in conduct, while the happy are bold and venturesome.

J. Thus there is a measure and limit of prosperity that the worthy man should desire to have as auxiliary in the accomplishment of his actions, just as there is a measure in the size of the ship, and in the length of the tiller, which permits the experienced pilot to traverse an immense extent of sea, and to carry through a great voyage.

The result of excess of prosperity, even among worthy people, is that the soul loses leadership to prosperity; just as too bright a light dazzles the eyes so too great a prosperity dazzles the reason of the soul. Enough about prosperity.

18. I insist that virtue is sufficient to preclude unhappiness, that badness precludes happiness, if we know how properly to judge of the genuine condition of the soul in these two conditions. For the evil reason is necessarily always unhappy, whether in abundance—which he does not know how properly to judge or use—or in poverty, just as a blind man is always wondering whether he is in brilliant light, or in darkness. But the worthy man is not always happy, for happiness does not consist in the possession of virtue, but in its use, just as a man who sees does not see all the time will not see without light.

Life is as it were divided into two roads: the rougher one, followed by patient Ulysses, and the more agreeable one followed by Nestor. I mean that virtue desires the one, but can also follow the other. But nature cries aloud that happiness is life desirable in itself, whose state is assured, because one can realize one's purposes in it, so that if life is traversed by things one has not desired, one is not happy, without however being absolutely unhappy. Therefore be not so bold as to insist that the worthy man is exempt from sickness, and suffering; dare not to say that he does not know pain, for if the body is allow some causes of pain, the soul should also be allowed some. The griefs of the insane lack reason and measure, while those of the wise are contained within the measure which reason gives to everything. But this so advertised insensitivity to sorrow enervates the character of generosity of virtue, when it stands trials, great sorrows, when it is exposed to death, suffering, and poverty, for it is easy to support small sorrows. You must therefore practice *metriopathy* or sorrow-standardization so as to avoid the insensitivity just as much as the over-sensibility of pain, and not in words to boast about our strength above the measure of our human nature.

19. We might define philosophy as the desire of knowing and understanding

things in themselves, joined with practical virtue, inspired and realized by the love of science.

The beginning of philosophy is the science of nature, the middle, practical life, and the end, science itself. It is fortunate to have been well born, to have received a good education, to have been accustomed to obey a just rule, and to have habits conformable to nature. One must also have been exercised in virtue, and have been educated by wise parents, governors and masters. It is fine to impose the rule of duty on oneself, to have no need of constraint, to be docile to those who give us good advice about life and science. For a fortunate disposition of nature, and a good education are often more powerful than lessons to bring us to the good; its only lack would be the efficacious light of reason, which science gives us. Two rival directions of life contend for mastery, these being practical and philosophical life. By far the most perfect life unites them both, and in each different path adapts itself to circumstances. We are born for rational activity, which we call practical. Practical reason leads us to politics; the theoretical reason, to the contemplation of the universality of things. Mind itself, which is universal, embraces these two powers necessary to happiness, which we define as the activity of virtue in prosperity; it is not exclusively either a practical life which would exclude science, nor a speculative life which would exclude the practical. Perfect reason inclines towards these two omnipotent principles for which man is born, the principles of society and science. For if these opposite principles seem mutually to interfere in their development, the political principles turning us away from speculation, and the speculative principles turning us from politics, to persuade us to live at rest, nevertheless nature, uniting the ends of these two movements, shows them fused; for virtues are not contradictory and mutually antipathetic. Indeed, no harmony is more constant than the harmony of virtues. If from his youth man has subjected himself to the principles of virtues, and to the divine law of the world harmony, he will lead an easy life; and if, by his own inclination, he inclines towards evil and has the luck of meeting better guides, he will, by rectifying his course, arrive at happiness, like passengers favored by chance, finishing a fortunate sea-passage—thanks to the pilot—and the fortunate passage of life is happiness. But if by himself he cannot know his real interests, and if he does not have the luck of meeting prudent directors, what benefit would it be if he did have immense treasures? For the fool, even if he had for himself all the other elements of luck, is eternally unhappy. And since, in everything, you must first consider the end—for that is what is done by the pilots ever meditating over the harbor whither they are to land the ship, by the drivers who keep their eye on the goal of their trip, and by the archers and slingers who consider their objective, for it is the objective towards which all their efforts must tend—virtue must necessarily undertake an objective, which should become the art of living, and that is the name I give it in both directions it can take. For practical life this objective is improvement; for the philosophical life, the perfect good, which, in their human affairs the sages call happiness. Those who are in misery are not capable of judging of happiness according to exact ideas, and those who do not see it clearly would not know how to choose it. Those who consider that pleasure is the sovereign good are punished therefore by foolishness; those who above all seek the absence of pain, also receive their punishment. In summary: to define life-happiness as the enjoyment of the body, in an unreflective state of soul, is to expose oneself to all the whirlwinds of the tempest. Those who suppress moral beauty, by avoiding all discussion, all reflection about the matter, and seeking pleasure, absence of pain, simple and primitive physical enjoyments, and the irreflective inclinations of body and soul, are not more fortunate, for they commit a double fault by reducing the good of the soul and its superior functions to the level of that of the body, and in raising the good of the body to the high level due to the good of the soul. For an exact discernment of these goods, we should outline its proper part for the divine element, and for nature; yet some do not observe this relation of dignity from the better to the worse. But we do so when we say that if the body is the organ of the soul, then reason is the guide of the entire soul, the mistress of the body, this tent of the soul, and that all the other physical advantages should serve only as instruments to the intellectual activity, if you wish it to be perfect in power, duration and wealth.

20. These are the most important conditions to become a sage: first, you must have received from fate a mind endowed with facility to understand, memory, and industry. You must then from youth on exercise your intelligence by the practice of argumentation, by mathematical studies, and by the exact sciences. Then you must study healthful philosophy, after which you may undertake the knowledge of the Gods, of laws, and of human life. For there are two means of arriving at this state known as wisdom. The first is to acquire the habit of work that is intellectual, and the taste for knowledge; the other is to seek to see many things, to undertake business frequently, and to know them, either directly at first hand, or indirectly. For he who from youth on has exercised reason by dialectic reasonings, mathematical studies, and exact sciences, is not yet ready for wisdom, any more than he who has neglected these labors, and has only listened to others, and has immersed himself in business. The one has become blind, when the business is to judge particular facts; the other, when he is to judge of general deductions. Just as in calculations you obtain the total by combining the parts, so also, in business practice, reason can vaguely sketch the general formula, but experience alone can enable us to grasp the details and individual facts.

21. Age is in the same relation to youth. Youth makes men energetic, age makes them prudent. Never by imprudence does it let a thought escape. It reflects on what it has done, it considers maturely what it ought to do, in order that this comparison of the future with the present, and of the present with the future lead it to good conduct. To the past it applies memory, to the present, sensation, and to the future, foresight; for our memory has always as object the past, foresight the future, and sensation the present. He who therefore wishes to lead an honest and beautiful life must not only have senses and memory, but foresight.

4. Political Fragments

22 A. The laws of the wicked and atheists are opposed by the unwritten laws of the Gods, who inflict evils and terrible punishments on the disobedient. It is these divine laws which have developed and directed the laws and written max-

ims given to men.

B. The relation of law to the soul and human life is identical to that of harmony to the sense of hearing, and the voice; for the law instructs the soul, and thereby, the life, as harmony regulates the voice through education of the ear. In my opinion, every society is composed of the commander, the commanded, and the laws. Among the latter, one is living, namely the king, and the other is inanimate, this being the written letter. The law is therefore the most essential; only through it is the king legitimate, the magistrate regularly instituted, the commanded free, and the whole community happy. When it is violated, the king is no more than a tyrant, the magistrate is illegitimate, the commanded becomes a slave, and the whole community becomes unhappy. Human acts are like a mingled tissue, formed of command, duty, obedience, and force sufficient to overcome resistance. Essentially, the command belongs to the better, being commanded to the inferior, and force belongs to both. For the reasonable part of the soul commands, and the irrational part is commanded. Both have the force to conquer the passions. Virtue is born from the harmonious cooperation of both and leads the soul to rest and indifference by turning it away from pleasures and sorrows.

C. Law must conform to nature, and exercise an efficient power over things, and be useful to the social community; for if it lacks one, two, or all of these characteristics, it is no longer a law, or at least it is no longer a perfect law. It conforms to nature if it is the image of natural right, which fits itself, and distributes to each according to his deserts. It prevails if it harmonizes with the men who are to be subject thereto; for there are many people who are not apt to receive what by nature is the first of goods, and who are fitted to practice only the good which is in relation with them, and possible for them, for that is how the sick and the suffering have to be nursed. Law is useful to the political society if it is not monarchical, if it does not constitute privileged classes, if it is made in the interest of all, and is equally imposed on all. Law must also regard the country and the lands, for not all soils can yield the same returns, neither all human souls the same virtues. That is why some establish the aristocratic constitution, while others prefer the democratic or oligarchic. The aristocratic constitution is founded on the subcontrary proportion,* and is the most just, for this proportion attributes the greatest results to the greatest terms, and the smallest to the smallest. The democratic constitution is founded on the geometrical proportion, in which the results of the great and small are equal [in ratio]. The oligarchic and tyrannic constitutions are founded on the arithmetical proportion, which, being the opposite of the subcontrary, attributes to the smallest terms the greatest results, and vice versa.

Such are the kinds of proportions, and you can observe their image in families and political constitutions; for either the honors, punishments and virtues are equally attributed to the great and small, or they are so attributed unequally, according to superiority, in virtue, wealth or power. Equal distribution is the characteristic of democracy; and the unequal, that of aristocracy and oligarchy.

D. The best law and constitution must be a composite of all other constitutions,

* I.e., the harmonic mean.

and contain something democratic, oligarchic, monarchic and aristocratic, as in Lacedaemon; for in it the kings formed the monarchic element, the elders the aristocracy, the magistrates the oligarchy, while the cavalry generals and the youths formed the democracy. Law must therefore not only be beautiful and good, but its different parts must mutually compensate. This will give it power and durability, and by this mutual opposition I mean that the same magistracy command and be commanded, as in the wise laws of Lacedaemon. For the power of its kings is balanced by the magistrates, this by the elders, and between these two powers are the cavalry generals and the youths, who, as soon as they see any one party acquire the preponderance, throw themselves on the other side.

The law's first duty is to decide about the Gods, the geniuses, the parents—in short, on all that is estimable and worthy—and later decide about utility. It is proper that the secondary regulations should follow the best, and that the laws be inscribed, not on the houses and doors, but in the depths of the souls of the citizens. Even in Lacedaemon, which has excellent laws, the State is not administered by manifold written ordinances. Law is useful to the political community, if it is not monarchical, and does not serve private interests, if it is useful to all, if it extends its obligation to all, and if it aims its punishments to shame the guilty, and to brand him with infamy, rather than to deprive him of his wealth. If, indeed, you are seeking to punish the guilty by ignominy, the citizens will try to lead a wiser and more honest life, so as to avoid the law's punishment; if it is only by money fines, they will rate above everything wealth, understanding that it is their best means to repair their faults. The best would be that the State should be organized in a manner such that it would need nothing from strangers, neither for virtue, power, or anything else. In the same way the right constitution of a body, a house, or an army is to contain, and not to depend on outside sources for the principle of its safety; for in that way the body is more vigorous, the house better ordered, and the army will be neither mercenary nor badly drilled.

Beings that are thus organized are superior to others; they are free and liberated from servitude unless, for their conservation, they need many things, but have only few needs easily satisfied. In that way the vigorous man becomes able to bear heavy burdens, and the athlete, to resist cold, for men are exercised by events and misfortunes. The temperate man, who has tested his body and soul, finds any food, drink, even a bed of leaves, delectable. He who has preferred to live like a Sybarite among delights, would finally scorn and reject the magnificence of the great [Persian] king. Law must therefore deeply penetrate into the souls and habits of the citizens; it will make them satisfied with their fate, and distribute to each his deserts. Thus the sun, in traversing the zodiac, distributes to everything on the earth growth, food, life, in the proper measure, and institutes this wise legislation which regulates the succession of the seasons. That is why we call Zeus *nomios*, law-giver, from *Nomeios*, and we call *nomeus* he who distributes their food to the sheep; that is why we call the verses sung by the lyre players *nomoi*,* for these verses impart order to the soul because they are sung accord-

---

* Nomoi, in addition to meaning "laws," is also the term used for the various modes of Greek music. Each Greek mode or "scale" was associated with a distinctive style of playing and affect.

ing to the laws of harmony, rhythm, and measure.

23. The true chief must not only possess the science and power of commanding well, but he must also love men; for it is absurd that a shepherd should hate his flock, and feel hostile towards those he is educating. Besides, he must be legitimate; only thus can he sustain a chief's dignity. His science will permit him to discern well, his power to punish, his kindness to be beneficent, and the law to do everything according to reason. The best chief would be he who would closest approach the law, for he would never act in his own interest, and always in that of others, since the law does not exist for itself, but for its subjects.

24. See 21 A.

25. When the art of reflection was discovered, dissension diminished and concord increased; those who possess it feel the pride of predominance yielding to the sentiment of equality. It is by reflection that we succeed in adjusting our affairs in a friendly fashion; through it the poor receive riches, and the rich give to the poor, each possessing the confidence that he possesses the equality of rights.

26. Reflection is like a rule which hinders and turns aside the people who know how to reflect from committing injustices, for it convinces them that they cannot remain hidden if they carry out their purposes, and the punishment which has overtaken those who have not known how to abstain makes them reflect and not become back-sliders.

5. Logical Fragments

27. Logic, compared with the other sciences, is by far the most successful and succeeds in demonstrating its objectives even better than geometry. Where geometric demonstration fails, logic succeeds; and logic deals not only with general classes, but also with their exceptions.

28. In my opinion it is a complete error to insist that about every subject there are two contrary opinions which are equally true. To begin with, I consider it impossible that, if both opinions are true, they should contradict each other, and that beauty should contradict beauty, and whiteness whiteness. It cannot be so, for beauty and ugliness, whiteness and blackness are contraries. Likewise, the true is contrary to the false, and you cannot produce two contrary opinions either true or false; the one must be true, at the expense of the falseness of the other. For instance, he who praises the soul of man and accuses his body is not speaking of the same object, unless you claim that speaking exclusively of the heaven you are speaking exclusively of the earth. Why no—they are not one, but two propositions. What am I trying to demonstrate? That he who says that the Athenians are skillful and witty and he who says they are not grateful, are not supporting contradictory propositions, for contradictories are opposed to each other on the same points, and here the two points are different.

29. *Archytas' Ten Universal Categories.* First, all kinds of arts deal with five things: the matter, the instrument, the part, the definition, the end. The first notion, the substance, is something self-existent and self-subsistent. It needs nothing else for its essence, though it is subject to growth if it happens to be something that is born, for only the divine is uncreated, and veritably self-subsistent. The other notions are considered in relation to substance when the latter by opposi-

tion to them is termed self-subsisting, but such is not the case in relation to the divine. The nine notions appear and disappear without implying the ruin of the subject, the substrate, and that is what is called the universal accident. For the same subject does not lose its identity by being increased or diminished in quantity. Thus, excessive feeding creates excessive size and stoutness; sobriety and abstinence make men lean, but it is always the same body, the same substrate. Thus also human beings passing from childhood to youth remain the same substance, differing only in quantity. Without changing essence, the identical object may become white or black, changing only as regards quality. Again, without changing essence, the identical man may change disposition and relation, as he is friend or enemy, but being today in Thebes, and tomorrow in Athens changes nothing in his substantial nature. Without changing essence, we remain the same today that we were yesterday; the change affected only time. The man standing is the same as the man sitting; he has changed only in situation. Being armed or unarmed is a difference only of possession; the striker and the cutter are the same man in essence, though not in action. He who is cut or struck—which belongs to the category of suffering—still retains his essence.

The differences of the other categories are clearer. Those of quality, possession, and suffering present some difficulties in the differences, for we hesitate about the question of knowing if having fever, shivering or rejoicing belong to the category of quality, possession or suffering. We must distinguish: if we say it is fever, it is shivering, it is joy, it is quality; if we say he has fever, he shivers, he rejoices, it is possession. Possession again differs from suffering, in that the latter can be conceived without the agent. Suffering is a relation to the agent, and is understood only by him who produces it. If we say he is cut, he is beaten, we express the patient; if we say he suffers, we express possession.

We say that Archytas has ten, and no more universal notions, of which we may convince ourselves by the following division: the being is in a subject [a substance], or is not in a subject. That which is not in a subject, forms the substance. That which is in a subject is conceived by itself, or is not conceived by itself. That which is not conceived by itself constitutes relation, for relative beings, which are not conceived by themselves, but which forcibly import the idea of another being, are what is called *scheseis*, conditions; thus the term son is associated with the term father, that of slave, master. Thus all relative beings are conceived in a necessary bond together with something else, and not by themselves. The self-conceivable being is either divisible—when it is quantity— or indivisible, when it constitutes quality. The six other notions are produced by combination of the former. Substance mingled with quantity, if seen in space, constitutes the category of where; if seen in time, constitutes that of when. Mingled with quality, substance is either active, and forms the category of action, or when passive, forms that of suffering or passivity. Combined with relation, it is either posited in another, and that is what is called situation, or it is attributed to somebody else, and then it is possession.

As to the order of the categories, quantity follows substance and precedes quality because, by a natural law, everything that receives quality also receives mass, and that it is only by means of something so determinate that quality can be so affirmed and expressed. Again, quality precedes relation, because the former is self-sufficient, and the latter [subsists] through a relation; we first have to conceive and express something by itself before in a relation.

After these universal categories follow the others. Action precedes passivity, because its force is greater; the category of situation precedes that of possession, because being situated is something simpler than being possessed, and you cannot conceive something attributed to another, without conceiving the former as situated somewhere. That which is situated is also in a position, such as standing, seated, or lying. The characteristic of substance is more-or-lessness; for we say that a man is no more of an animal than a horse, by substance, and do not admit the contraries. The characteristic of quality is to admit more or less; for we say, more or less white, or black. The characteristic of quantity is to admit equality or inequality; for a square foot is not equal to an acre, and 144 square inches equals a square foot; five is not equal to ten, and twice five is equal to ten. The characteristic of relation is to join contraries; for if there is a father, there is a son, and if there is a master, there is a slave. The characteristic of whereness is to include, and of whenness not to remain, of situation to be located, and of possession to be attributed. The composite of substance and quantity is anterior to the composite of quality; the composite of substance and quality in its turn precedes that of substance and relation. Whereness precedes whenness because whereness presupposes the place that is fixed and permanent; whenness relates to time, and time, ever in movement, has no fixity, and rest is anterior to movement. Action is anterior to passivity, and situation to possession.

A. *Category of Substance.* Substance is divided into corporeal and incorporeal; the corporeal may be divided into bodies animate and inanimate. Animated bodies are divisible into those endowed with sensation, and without sensation. Sensebodies can be divided into animals and zoophytes, which do not further divide into opposite distinctions. The animal is divided into rational and irrational; the rational is divisible into mortal and immortal; the mortal can be divided into differences of genus, such as man, ox, horse, and the rest. The species are divided into individuals who have no abiding value. Each of the sections that we obtained above by opposite divisions is susceptible of being in turn divided equally, until we arrive at the indivisible individuals who are of no value.

B. *Category of Quantity.* This is divided into seven parts: the line, surface, the body, the place, the time, the number, and language. Quantity is either continuous or discrete: of continuous quantities there are five; of the discrete, number and language. In quantity, you may distinguish that which is composed of parts having position relative to each other, such as line, surface, body, and space; and of those whose parts have no position, such as number, language, and time. For although time is a continuous quantity, nevertheless its parts have no position because it is not permanent, and that which has no permanence could not have any position. Quantity has produced four sciences: immovable continuous quantity, geometry; movable continuous quantity, astronomy; immovable discrete quantity, arithmetic; and the movable discrete, music.

C. *Category of Quality.* This is divided into *hexis*, or habit, and *diathesis*, or affection, passive quality and passivity, power and impotence, figure and form.

Habit is affection in a state of energetic tension. It is the permanence and fixity derived from continuity and the energy of affection; it is affection become [second] nature, a second enriched nature. Another explanation of habit is the qualities given us by nature, and which are derived neither from affection, nor from the natural progress of the being; as sight and the other senses; both passive quality and passivity are increase, intensity, and weakening. To both of these are attributed anger, hate, intemperance, the other vicious passions, the affections of sickness, heat and cold; but these are classified at will under habit and affection, or under passive quality and passivity. You might say that so far as affection is communicable it might be called habit; so far as it causes a passion, it might be called a passive quality, which refers both to its permanence and fixity. For a modification contained in the measure is called passion. Thus from the one to whom it is communicated, heat may be called a habit. From the cause which produces the modification, we may say that it is either the passive quality, or the power of the passion; as when we say of a child that he is potentially a runner or a philosopher, and, in short, when at a given moment the being does not have the power to act, but it is possible that after the lapse of a certain period of time this power may belong to him. Impotence is when nature refuses itself to the possibility of accomplishing certain actions, as when the man is impotent to fly, the horse to speak, the eagle to live in water, and all the natural impossibilities.

Figure is a conformation of a determined character. Form is the quality showing itself exteriorly by color, or beauty or ugliness showing itself on the surface by color, and in short any form that is apparent, determinate, and striking. Some limit figure to inanimate things reserving form to living beings. Some say that the word figure gives the idea of the dimension of depth, and that the word form is applied only to the superficial appearance; but you have been taught all of that.

D. *Category of Relation.* Generally the relatives are divided into four classes: nature, art, chance and will. The relation of father to son is natural; that of master to disciple, that of art; that of master to slave, that of chance; and that of friend to friend, and enemy to enemy, that of will, although you might say that these are all natural relations.

E. *Category of Whereness.* The simplest division is into six: up, down, forwards, backwards, right and left. Each of these subdivisions contains varieties. There are many differences in upness: in the air, in the stars, to the pole, or beyond the pole, and such differences are repeated below. The infinitely divided spaces themselves are further subject to an infinity of differences, but this very ambiguous point will be explained later.

F. *Category of Whenness.* This is divided into present, past and future. The present is indivisible, the past is divided into nine subdivisions, the future into five. We have already spoken of them.

G. *Category of Action.* This is divided into action, discourse and thought. Action is in work of the hands, with tools, and with the feet, and each of these divisions is subdivided into technical divisions which also have their parts. Language is divided into Greek or barbarian, and each of these divisions has its varieties, namely, its dialects. Thought is divided into an infinite world of thoughts, whose objects are the world, other people, and the hypercosmic. Language and thought really belong to action, for they are acts of the reasonable nature; in fact, if we are asked, "What is Mr. X doing?" we answer that he is chatting, conversing, thinking, reflecting, and so on.

H. *Category of Passivity.* Passivity is divided into suffering of the soul and of the body. Each of these is subdivided into passions which result from actions of somebody else, as for instance, when somebody is struck, and passions which arise without the active intervention of someone else which occur in a thousand different forms.

I. *Category of Situation.* This is divided into three: standing, sitting, and lying, and each of these is subdivided by differences of location. We may stand on our feet, or on the tips of our fingers, with the leg unflexed, or the knee bent. Further differences are equal or unequal steps or walking on one or two feet. Being seated has the same differences: one may be straight, bent, reversed; the knees may form an acute or obtuse angle; the feet may be placed over each other, or in some other way. Likewise with lying down prone or head forwards, or to the side, the body extended, in a circle, or angularly. Far from uniform are these divisions; they are quite various. Position is also subject to other divisions: for instance, an object may be spread out like corn, sand, oil, and like all the other solids that are susceptible to position, and like all the liquids that we know. Nevertheless, being extended belongs to position, as with cloth and nets.

J. *Category of Possession.* "Having" signifies things that we put on, such as shoes, arms, coverings; things which are put on others, such as a basket, a bottle, and other vases, for we say that the basket has oats, that the bottle has wine. The same is true also of wealth and estates; we say, he has a fortune, fields, cattle, and other similar things.

30. The order of the categories is the following: in the first rank is substance, because it alone serves as substrate to all the others. We can conceive it alone, and by itself, but the others cannot be conceived without it, for all attributes' subjects reside therein, or are affirmed thereof. The second is quality, for it is impossible for a thing to have a quality without an essence.

31. Every naturally physical and sensible substance must, to be conceived by man, be either classified within the categories, or be determined by them, and cannot be conceived without them.

32. Substance has three differences: the one consists in matter, the other in form, and the third in the mixture of both.

33. These notions, these categories, have characteristics that are common and individual. I say that they are characteristics common to substance, not to receive more-or-lessness; for it is not possible to be more or less man, God, or plant. The characteristics have no contraries, for man is not the contrary of man, neither God of a God; neither is it contrary to other substances, to exist by oneself, and not to be in another, as green or blue color is the characteristic of the eye, since all substance depends on itself. All the things that belong to it intimately, or the accidents in it, cannot exist without it; quality is suited by several characteristics of substance, for example, not to be subject to more-or-lessness.

34. It is the property to remain self-identical, one in number, and to be susceptible of the contraries. Waking is the contrary of sleep; slowness is contrary to

swiftness, sickness to health, and the same man is susceptible of all these differences. For he awakes, sleeps, moves slowly or quickly, is well or sick, and in short is able to receive all similar contraries, so long as they be not simultaneous.

35. Quantity has three differences: one consists in weight, like bullion; the other in size, as the yard; the other in multitude, as ten.

36. Including its accidents, substance is necessarily primary; that is how they [the categories] are in relation to something else. After the substance come the relations of accidental qualities.

37. A common property which must be added to quality is to admit certain contraries and privation. The relation is subject to more-or-lessness. For though a being remains ever the same, to be greater or smaller than anything else is moreness. But all the relations are not susceptible thereto, for you cannot be more or less father, brother, or son. I do not mean to express the sentiments of both parents, nor the degree of tenderness held mutually by beings of the same blood, and the sons of the same parents; I only mean the tenderness which is in the nature of these relations.

38. Quality has certain common charactersistics: for example, of receiving the contraries and privation, which more or less affect the passions. That is why the passions are marked by the characteristics of indetermination, because they are in a greater or less indeterminate measure.

39. Relation is susceptible to conversion, and this conversion is founded either on resemblance, as the equal, and the brother, or on lack of resemblance, the large and the small. There are relatives which are not converted, for instance, science and sensation; for we may speak of the science of the intelligible, and of the sensation of the sensible, and the reason is that the intelligible and the sensible can exist independently of science and sensation while science and sensation cannot exist without the intelligible and the sensible [...] The characteristic of relatives is to exist simultaneously in each other, for if we grant the existence of doubleness, the half must necessarily exist; and if the half exists necessarily must the double exist, as it is the cause of the half, as the half is the cause of the double.

40. Since every moved thing moves in a place, since action and passivity are actualized movements, it is clear that there must be a primary space in which exist the acting and the passive objects.

41. The characteristic of the agent is to contain the cause of the motion, while the characteristic of the thing done, which is passive, is to have it in some other. For the sculptor contains the cause of the making of the statue, the bronze possesses the cause of the modification it undergoes, both in itself and in the sculptor. So also with the passions of the soul, for it is in the nature of anger to be aroused as the result of something else—that it be excited by some other external thing, as for example by scorn, dishonor, and outrage—and he who acts thus towards another, contains the cause of his action.

42. The highest degree of the action is the act which contains three differences: it may be accomplished in the contemplation of the stars, or in doing, such as healing or constructing, or in action, as in commanding an army, or administering the affairs of state. An act may occur even without reasoning, as in irrational

animals. Those are the most general contraries.

43. Passion differs from the passive state, for passion is accompanied by sensation, like anger, pleasure and fear, while one can undergo something without sensation, such as the wax that melts, or the mud that dries. Then also the deed done differs also from the passive state, for the deed done has undergone a certain action, while everything that has undergone a certain action is not a deed done; for a thing may be in a passive state as a result of lack or privation.

44. On one side there is the agent, on the other the patient; for example, in nature, God is the being who acts, matter the being which undergoes, and the elements are neither the one nor the other.

45. The characteristic of possession is to be something adventitious, something corporeal, separated from essence. Thus a veil or shoes are distinct from the possessor; they are not natural characteristics, nor essential accidents, like the blue color of the eyes, and rarefaction. The latter are two incorporeal characteristics while possession relates to something corporeal and adventitious.

46. Since the signs and the things signified have a purpose, and because man uses these signs and signified things is to fulfill the perfect function of speech, let us finish what we have said by proving that the harmonious grouping of all these categories does not belong to man in general, but to a certain definite individual. Necessarily it must be a definite man existing somewhere who possesses quality, quantity, relation, action, passivity, location and possession, who is in a place and time. The man in himself receives only the first of these expressions, I mean essence and form. But he has no quality, no age, he is not old, neither does he suffer anything, he has no location, he possesses nothing, he exists neither in place nor time. All those are only accidents of the physical and corporeal being, but not of the intelligible, immovable, and indivisible being.

47. Among contraries, some are said to be mutually opposed by convention and nature, as good to evil, the sick to the well man, truth to error; the others, as possession is opposed to privation, such as life and death, sight and blindness, science and ignorance; others as relatives, as the double and the half, the commander and the commanded, the master and the slave; others, like affirmation and negation, as being man and not a man, being honest and not.

48. The relatives arise and disappear necessarily simultaneously; the existence of the double is impossible without implying that of the half and vice versa. If something becomes double, the half must arise, and if the double is destroyed, the half passes away with it.

49. Of the relatives, some respond to each other in two senses, as the greater, the smaller, the brother, the relative. Others again respond, but not in the two senses, for we say equally, the science of the intelligible, and the science of the sensible, but we do not say the reciprocal, the intelligible of science, and the sensible of sensation. The reason is that the object of judgment can exist independently of him who judges, for instance, the sensible can exist without sensation, and the intelligible without science, while it is not possible that the subject which bears a judgment exists without the object which he judges. For example, there can be no sensation without sensible object, nor science without intelligible object. Relatives which respond reciprocally are of two kinds: these

are those that respond indifferently, as the relative, the brother, the equal, for they are mutually similar and equal. Some respond reciprocally, but not indifferently, for this one is greater than that one, and that one is smaller than this one, and this one is the father of that one, and that one the son of this one.

50. These opposites divide into kinds which band together; for of the contraries some are without a middle term and the others have one. There is no middle term between sickness and health, rest and movement, waking and sleep, straightness and curvedness, and other such contraries. But between the much and the little, there is a just medium; between the shrill and the low, there is the unison; between the rapid and slow, there is the equality of movement; between the greatest and the smallest, the equality of measure. Of universal contraries there must be one that belongs to what receives them, for they do not admit any medium term. Thus there is no medium term between health and sickness, for every living being is necessarily sick or well; neither between waking and sleeping, for every living being is either awake or asleep; nor between rest and movement, for every human being is either at rest or moving. [Concerning the opposites of which neither belong to the subject which may receive them,] between black and white there is the fawn, and it is not necessary that an animal be black or white. Between the great and the small there is the equal, and it is not necessary that a living being be either great or small; between the rough and soft there is the gentle, and it is not necessary that a living being be either rough or soft. In the opposites there are three differences: some are opposed, as the good is to evil, for instance, or health to sickness; the others, like evil to evil, as for instance, avarice to lechery; the others, as being neither the one or the other, for instance, as white is opposed to black, and the heavy to the light. Of the opposites, some occur in genus or genera, for the good is opposed to evil, and the good is the genus of virtues, and evil that of the evils. Other occur in the genera of species; virtue is the opposite of vice, and virtue is the genus of prudence and temperance, and vice is the genus of foolishness and debauch. Others occur in the species: courage is opposed to cowardliness, justice to injustice, and justice and excellence are species of virtue, injustice and debauch species of vice. The primary genera, which we call genera of genera, can be divided; the last species, which are the immediate nearest to the object, that is sensible, could no longer be genera, and are only species. For the triangle is the genus of the rectangle, of the equilateral and of the scalene [...] the species of good [...]

51. The opposites differ from each other in that for some—the contraries—it is not necessary that they arise at the same time, and disappear simultaneously. For health is the contrary of sickness, and rest that of movement; nevertheless neither of them arises or perishes at the same time as its opposite. Possession and privation of production differ in this, that it is in the nature of contraries that one passes from one to the other, for instance, from sickness to health and vice versa. It is not so with possession and privation; you do indeed pass from possession to privation, but the privation does not return to possession: the living die, but the dead never return to life. In short, possession is the persistance of what is according to nature, while privation is its lack and decay. Relatives necessarily arise and disappear simultaneously; for it is impossible for the dou-

ble to exist without half, or vice versa. If some double happens to arise, it is impossible that the half should not arise, or if some double be destroyed, that the half be not destroyed. Affirmation and negation are forms of proposition, and they eminently express the true and the false. Being a man is a true proposition, if the thing exists, and false if it does not exist. You could say as much of negation: it is true or false according to the thing expressed.

Moreover, between good and evil there is a medium which is neither good nor evil; between much and little, the just measure; between the slow and the fast, the equality of speed; between possession and privation there is no medium. For there is nothing between life and death, and sight and blindness, unless indeed you say that the living who is not yet born, but who is being born, is between life and death, and that the puppy who does not yet see is between blindness and sight. In such an expression we are using an accidental medium and not one according to the true and proper definition of contraries.

Relatives have middle terms, for between the master and the slave there is the free man, and between the greatest and the smallest there is equality; between the wide and the narrow there is the proper width. One might likewise find between the other contraries a medium, whether or not it has a name.

Between affirmation [and negation] there are no contraries, for instance, between being a man and not being a man, being a musician and not being a musician. In short, we have to affirm or deny. Affirming is showing of something that it is a man, for instance, or a horse, or an attribute of these beings, as of the man that he is a musician, and of the horse that he is warlike. We call it denying when we show of something that it is not something, not man, not horse, or that it lacks an attribute of these beings, for instance, that the man is not a musician and that the horse is not warlike; and between this affirmation and this negation there is nothing.

52. Privation and being deprived is taken in three senses: one does not at all have the thing, as the blind man does not have sight, the mute does not have voice, and the ignorant does not have science; or that one does not have it but partially, as the man hard of hearing has hearing, and that the man with sore eyes has sight; or one can say that partially he does not have it, as one says that a man whose legs are [so] crooked that he has no legs, and of a man who has [such] a bad voice that he has no voice.

OCELLUS LUCANUS:

ON THE NATURE OF THE UNIVERSE

OCELLUS LUCANUS was an early Pythagorean as were other members of his family. This writing seems to be post-Aristotelian. As Holger Thesleff observes in his *Introduction to the Pythagorean Writings of the Hellenistic Period*, the work seems to be influenced by Peripatetic conceptions and demonstrations concerning the nature of generation and destruction; and the ending, on the generation of good offspring, may derive from Aristoxenus.

ON THE NATURE OF THE UNIVERSE

1. On the Eternity and Indestructibility of the Universe

OCELLUS LUCANUS HAS WRITTEN what follows concerning the nature of the universe, having learnt some things through clear arguments from Nature herself, but others from opinion in conjunction with reason, it being his intention [here] to derive what is probable from intellectual perception.

Therefore it appears to me that the universe is indestructible and unbegotten, since it always was and always will be; for if it had a temporal beginning, it would not always have existed. Thus therefore the universe is unbegotten and indestructible. For if some one should claim that it was once generated, he would not be able to find anything into which it can be corrupted and dissolved, since that from which it was generated would be the first part of the universe; and again, that into which it would be dissolved would be the last part of it.

But if the universe was generated, it was generated together with all things; and if it should be corrupted, it would be corrupted together with all things. This however is impossible. This universe is therefore without a beginning, and without an end; nor is it possible that it can have any other mode of subsistence.

It may be added that everything which has received a beginning of generation, and which ought also to participate in dissolution, receives two mutations. The first, indeed, proceeds from the less to the greater, and from the worse to the better; and that from which it begins to change is denominated generation, but that which at length it arrives is called climax. The other mutation, however, proceeds from the great to the less, and from the better to the worse; but the end of this mutation is called corruption and dissolution.

If therefore the whole and the universe were generated, and are corruptible, they must, when generated, have been changed from the less to the greater, and from the worse to the better; but when corrupted, they must be changed from the greater to the less, and from the better to the worse. Hence, if the world was generated, it would receive increase, and would arrive at its consummation; and again, it would afterwards decrease and end. For every thing which has a progression possesses three boundaries and two intervals: the three boundaries are generation, consummation and end, and the intervals are progression from generation to consummation, and from consummation to end.

The whole, however, and the universe affords as from itself no indication of anything of this kind; for neither do we perceive it rising into existence, or becoming to be, nor changing to the better and the greater, nor changing to worse or less, but it always continues to subsist in the identical manner, and perpetually remains self-identical.

Clear signs and indications of this are the orders of things, their symmetry, figurations, positions, intervals, powers, swiftness and slowness in respect to each other; and besides these, their numbers and temporal periods are clear signs and indications. For all such things as these change and diminish conformably to the course of generation; for things that are greater and better tend towards consummation through power, but those that are less and worse decay through the inherent weakness of nature.

The whole world is what I call the whole universe; for this word "cosmos" was given it as a result of its being adorned with all things. From itself it is a consummate and perfect system of all things, for there is nothing external to the universe, since whatever exists is contained in the universe, and the universe subsists together with this, comprehending in itself all things, both parts and superfluities.

The things contained in the world are naturally congruous with it; but the world harmonizes with nothing else, symphonizing with itself. Other things do not possess self-subsistence, but require adjustment with their environment. Thus animals require conjunction with air for the purpose of respiration, and with light in order to see, and similarly the other senses with other environments to function satisfactorily. A conjunction with earth is necessary for the germination of plants. The sun, moon, planets and fixed stars likewise integrate with the world, as part of its general arrangement. The world, however, has no conjunction with anything outside of itself.

The above is supported by the following. Fire which imparts heat to others is self-hot; honey which is sweet to the taste is self-sweet. The principles of demonstrations, which conclude to things unapparent, are self-evident. Therefore the cause of the perfection of other things is itself perfect. That which preserves and renders permanent other things must itself be preserved and permanent. What harmonizes must itself be self-harmonic. Now as the world is the cause of the existence, preservation and perfection of other things, the world must itself be perpetual and perfect; and because its duration is everlasting, it becomes the cause of the permanence of all other things.

In short, if the universe should be dissolved, it would be dissolved either into the existent or non-existent. It could not be dissolved into existence, for in this case the dissolution would not be a corruption, as being either the universe or some part of it. Nor can it be dissolved into non-entity, since being cannot possibly arise from non-being, or be dissolved into non-entity. Therefore the universe is incorruptible and never can be destroyed.

If, however, somebody should think that it can be corrupted, it must be corrupted either from something external to or contained in the universe; but it cannot be corrupted by anything external to it, for nothing such exists, since all other things are comprehended in the universe, and the world is *the whole* and *the all*.

Nor can it be corrupted by the things it contains, which would imply their greater power. This however is impossible, for all things are led and governed by the universe, and thereby are preserved and adjusted, possessing life and soul. But if the universe can neither be corrupted by anything external to it, nor by anything contained within it, the world must therefore be incorruptible and indestructible, for we consider the world identical with the universe.

Further, the whole of nature surveyed through its own totality, will be found to derive continuity from the first and most honorable bodies, proportionally attenuating this continuity, introducing it to everything mortal, and receiving the progression of its peculiar subsistence; for the first (and most honorable) bodies in the universe revolve according to the Same,* and similarly. The progression of the whole of nature, however, is not successive and continuous, nor yet local, but is subject to mutation.

When condensed, fire generates air, air water, and water earth. A return circuit of transformation extends backward from earth to fire, whence it originated. Likewise, fruits and most rooted plants, originate from seeds. When however they fruit and mature, they are again resolved into seed, nature producing a complete circular progression.

In a subordinate manner men and other animals change the universal boundary of nature, for in these there is no periodical return to the first age; nor is there a transfusion, such as between fire and air, and water and earth, but the mutations of their ages being accomplished in a four-cycled circle, they are dissolved and reformed.

These therefore are the signs and indications that the universe which comprehends [all things] will always endure and be preserved, but that its parts and its nonessential additions are corrupted and dissolved.

Further, it is credible that the universe is without a beginning, and without end, from its figure, motion, time and essence; and therefore it may be concluded that the world is unbegotten and incorruptible, for its figure is circular, and as a circular figure is similar and equal on all sides, it is therefore without a beginning or end. Circular is also the motion of the universe, but this motion is stable and without transition. Time, likewise, in which motion exists, is infinite, for neither had this a beginning, nor will it have an end of its revolution. The universe's essence also does not waste elsewhere, and is immutable, because it is not naturally adapted to change, either from worse to better, or from better to worse. From all these arguments, therefore, it is obviously credible that the world is unbegotten and incorruptible. So much about the world and the universe.

2. Creation of the Elements

SINCE, HOWEVER, IN THE UNIVERSE there is a difference between generation and the generated, and since generation occurs where there is a mutation and egress from things which rank as subjects, then must the cause of generation subsist as long as the generated matter. The cause of generation must be both efficient and motive, while the recipient must be passive and moved.

* The Same and the Other are Platonic terms for Limit and Unlimited.

The Fates themselves distinguish and separate the impassive part of the world from that which is perpetually in motion. For the course of the moon is the meeting-line of generation and immortality. The region above the moon, as well as the lunar domain, is the residence of divinities, while the sublunar regions are the abodes of strife and nature, for in this place there is a mutation of things that are generated and a regeneration of things which have perished.

In that part of the world, however, in which nature and generation predominate, it is necessary that the three following things be present. In the first place, there is the body which yields to the touch, and which is the subject of all generated natures. But this will be an universal recipient, and a characteristic of generation itself, having the same relation to the things that are generated from it, as water to taste, silence to sound, darkness to light, and the matter of artificial forms to the forms themselves. For water is tasteless and devoid of quality, yet is capable of receiving the sweet and the bitter, the tart and the salty. Air also, which is formless as regards sound, is the recipient of words and melody. Darkness, which is without color, and without form, becomes the recipient of splendor, and of the yellow color, and the white; but white pertains to the statuary's art and to the wax-sculptor's art. Matter's relation, however, is different from the sculptor's art, for in matter, prior to generation, all things exist in potential, but they exist in perfection when they are generated, and receive their proper nature. Hence matter [or universal recipient] is necessary to the existence of generation.

The second necessity is the existence of contrarieties, in order to effect mutations and changes in quality, matter for this purpose receiving passive qualities and an aptitude to the participations of form. Contrariety is also necessary in order that powers which are naturally mutually repugnant may not finally conquer or vanquish each other. These powers are hot and cold, dryness and moistness.

In the third place rank essences, and these are fire and water, air and earth, of which heat and cold, dryness and moistness, are powers. Yet essences differ from powers, for essences are locally corrupted by each power, but powers are neither corrupted nor generated, as their reasons [or forms] are incorporeal.

Of these four powers, however, heat and cold subsist as causes and things of an effective nature, but the dry and the moist rank as matter and things that are passive, though matter is the first recipient of things, for it is that which is spread under all things in common. Hence the body, whose capacity is the object of sense, and ranks as a principle, is the first thing; while contraries, such as heat and cold, moistness and dryness, rank as primary differences, and heaviness and lightness, density and rarity, are related as things produced from primary differences. All of them, however, amount to sixteen: heat and cold, moistness and dryness, heaviness and lightness, rarity and density, smoothness and roughness, hardness and softness, thinness and thickness, acuteness and obtuseness. Knowledge of all of these is had by touch, which forms a judgement; hence also any body whatever which contains capacity for these can be apprehended by touch.

Heat and dryness, rarity and sharpness are the powers of fire; coldness and moistness, density and obtuseness are those of water; those of air are softness, smoothness, light, and the quality of being attenuated; while those of earth are hardness and roughness, heaviness and thickness.

Of these four bodies, however, fire and earth are the intensities of contraries. Fire is the intensity of heat, as ice is of cold; and if ice is a concretion of moisture and frigidity, fire will be the fervor of dryness and heat. That is why neither fire nor ice generate anything.

Fire and earth, therefore, are the extremities of the elements, while water and air are the media, for they have a mixed corporeal nature. Nor is it possible that there could be only one of the extremes, a contrary thereto being necessary. Nor could there only be two, for it is necessary to have a medium, as media oppose extremes.

Fire therefore is hot and dry, but air is hot and moist; water is moist and cold, and earth is cold and dry. Hence heat is common to air and fire; cold is common to water and earth; dryness to earth and fire, and moisture to water and air. But with respect to the peculiarities of each, heat is the peculiarity of fire, dryness of earth, moisture of air, and frigidity of water. These essences remain permanent, through the possession of common properties, but they change through such as are peculiar, when one contrary overcomes another.

Hence, when the moisture in air overcomes the dryness in fire, or when water's frigidity overcomes air's heat, and earth's dryness overcomes water's moistness, and vice versa, then are effected the mutual mutations and generations of the elements.

The body, however, which is the subject and recipient of mutations, is a universal receptacle, and is in capacity the first tangible substance.

But the mutations of the elements are effected either from a change of earth into fire, or from fire into air, or from air into water, or from water into earth. Mutation is also effected in the third place, when each element's contrariness is corrupted, simultaneously with the preservation of everything kindred and coeval. Generation therefore is effected when one contrary quality is corrupted. For fire, indeed, is hot and dry, but air is hot and moist, and heat is common to both; and the peculiarity of fire is dryness, and of air, moisture. Hence when the moisture in air overcomes the dryness in fire, then fire is changed into air.

Again, since water is moist and cold, but air is moist and hot, moisture is common to both. Water's peculiarity is coldness, and that of air, heat. When therefore the coldness in water overcomes the heat in air, air is altered into water.

Further, earth is cold and dry, and water cold and moist, coldness being common to both. But earth's peculiarity is dryness, and water's moisture. When therefore earth's dryness overcome water's moisture, water is altered into earth.

Earth's mutation in the ascending alteration occurs in a contrary way. One alternate mutation is effected when one whole vanquishes another, and two contrary powers are corrupted, nothing being common to them, at the same time. For since fire is hot and dry, while water is cold and moist, when the moisture in water overcomes the dryness in fire, and water's coldness overcomes fire's heat, then fire is altered into water.

Again, earth is cold and dry, while air is hot and moist. When therefore earth's coldness overcomes air's heat, and earth's dryness overcomes air's moisture, then air is altered into earth.

When air's moisture corrupts fire's heat, then from both of them will be generated fire; for air's heat, and fire's dryness will remain, fire being hot and dry.

When earth's coldness is corrupted, and also water's moisture, then from both of them will be generated earth. For earth's dryness and water's coldness will be left, as earth is cold and dry.

But when air's heat and fire's heat are corrupted, no element will be generated; for in both of these will remain contraries, air's moisture and fire's dryness. Moisture is however contrary to dryness.

Again, when earth's coldness, and that of water are corrupted, neither thus will any generation occur, for earth's dryness, and water's moisture will remain. But dryness is contrary to moisture.

Thus we have briefly discussed the generation of the first bodies, and how and from what subjects it is effected.

Since, however, the world is indestructible and unbegotten, and neither had a beginning of generation, nor will have an end, it is necessary that the nature which produces generation in another thing, and also that which generates in itself, should be simultaneously present. That which produces generation in another thing is the whole superlunary region, though the more proximate cause is the sun, who by his comings and goings continually changes the air, from hot to cold, which again changes the earth, and alters all its contents.

The obliquity of the zodiac, also, is well placed in respect to the sun's motion, for it likewise is the cause of generation. This is universally accomplished by the universe's proper order, wherein some things are active, and others passive. Different therefore is the generator, which is superlunary, while that which is generated is sublunary; and that which consists of both of these—namely, an ever-running body, and an ever-mutable generated nature—is the world itself.

3. The Perpetuity of the World

MAN'S GENERATION did not originate from the earth, other animals, or plants, but the world's proper order being perpetual, the aptly arranged natures it contains should share with it never-failing subsistence. As primarily the world existed always, its parts must coexist with it, and by these I mean the heavens, the earth, and what is contained between them, and that which is on high and is called aerial, for the world does not exist without these, but with and from these.

As the world's parts are co-subsistent, their comprehended natures must coexist with them; with the heavens, indeed, the sun, moon, fixed stars and planets; with the earth, animals and plants, gold and silver; with the aerial region, pneumatic substances and wind, heating and cooling; for it is the property of the heavens to subsist in conjunction with the natures which it comprehends, of the earth to support its native plants and animals, and of the aerial regions to be co-subsistent with the natures it has generated.

Since therefore in each division of the world there is arranged a certain genus of animals which surpasses its fellows, the heavens are the habitat of the Gods, on the earth men, and in the space between, the geniuses. Therefore the race of men must be perpetual, since reason convinces us that not only are the world's parts co-subsistent with it, but so also are their comprehended natures.

Sudden destruction and mutations, however, take place in the parts of the earth;

the sea overflows on to the land, or the earth shakes and splits through the unobserved entrance of wind or water. But an entire destruction of the earth's whole arrangement never took place nor ever will.

Hence the story that Grecian history began with Inachus of Argos is false, if understood to be a first principle, but true as some mutation of Greek politics; for Greece has frequently been and will again be barbarous, not only from the influx of foreigners, but from Nature herself, which, although she does not become greater or less, yet is always younger, and has a beginning in reference to us.

So much about the *whole*, and the *universe*, the generation and corruption of natures generated in it, of how they subsist, and forever, one part of the universe consisting of a nature which is perpetually moved, and another part being passive; and of how the former governs and how the latter is ever governed.

4. The Generation of Men

LAW, TEMPERANCE AND PIETY conspire in explaining as follows the generation of men from each other, after what manner, from what particulars, and how it is effected. The first postulate is that sexual association should occur never for pleasure, but only for procreation of children.

Those powers and instruments and appetites ministering to copulation were implanted in men by divinity, not for the sake of voluptuousness, but for the perpetuation of the race. Since it was impossible that man, who is born mortal, should participate in a divine life were his race not immortal, divinity operated this immortality through individuals, and lent continuity to mankind's generation. This is the first essential, that cohabitation should not be effected for mere pleasure.

Next, man should be considered in connection with the social organism, a house or city, and especially that each human progeny should work at the completion of the world, unless he plans to be a deserter of either the domestic, political or divine Vestal hearth.

For those who are not entirely connected with each other for the sake of begetting children injure the most honorable system of convention. But if persons of this description procreate with libidinous insolence and intemperance, their offspring will be miserable and flagitious, and will be execrated by God and divinities, by men, families and cities.

Those therefore who deliberately consider these things ought not, in a way similar to irrational animals, to engage in venereal connection, but should think copulation a necessary good. For it is the opinion of worthy men that it is necessary and beautiful not only to fill houses with large families, and also the greater part of the earth, for man is the most mild and the best of all animals, and it is a thing of the greatest consequence to cause them to abound with the most excellent men.

For on this account men inhabit cities governed by the best laws, rightly manage their domestic affairs, and if they are able, impart to their friends such political employments as are conformable to the polities in which they live, since they not only provide for the multitude at large, but especially for worthy men.

Hence many men err who enter into the connubial state without regarding the magnitude of the power of fortune, or of public utility, but direct their attention to wealth, or to dignity of birth. For in consequence of this, instead of uniting with females who are young and in the flower of their age, they become connected with extremely old women; and instead of having wives with a disposition according with, and most similar to their own, they marry those who are of an illustrious family, or are extremely rich. On this account they procure for themselves discord instead of concord; and instead of unanimity, dissension, contending with each other for the mastery. For the wife who surpasses her husband in wealth, in birth, or in friends, is desirous of ruling over him, contrary to the law of nature. But the husband justly resisting this desire of superiority in his wife, and wishing not to be the second, but the first in domestic sway, is unable in the management of his family to take the lead.

This being the case, it happens that not only families, but cities become miserable. For families are parts of cities, while the composition of the whole and the universe derives its subsistence from its parts. It is therefore reasonable to admit that such as are the parts, such likewise will be the whole and the all which consists of things of this kind.

As in fabrics of a primary nature the first structures cooperate greatly to the good or bad completion of the whole work—as for instance the manner in which the foundation is laid in house-building, the structure of a keel in ship-building, and the utterance and closing of the voice in musical modulation—so the concordant condition of families greatly contributes to the well or ill establishment of a polity.

Those therefore who direct their attention to the propagation of the human species ought to guard against everything which is dissimilar and imperfect; for neither plants nor animals when imperfect are prolific, but their fructification demands a certain amount of time, so that when the bodies are strong and perfect they may produce seeds and fruits.

Hence it is necessary that boys and girls while they are virgin should be trained up in exercises and proper endurance, and that they be nourished with that kind of food which is adapted to a laborious, temperate and patient life.

Moreover, in human life there are many things of such a kind that it is better for the knowledge of them to be deferred for a certain time. Hence a boy should be so tutored as not to seek after venereal pleasures before he is twenty years of age, and then should rarely engage in them. This however will take place if he conceives that a good habit of body and continence are beautiful and honorable.

The following laws should be taught in Grecian cities: that connection with a mother, or a daughter, or a sister should not be permitted whether in temples or in a public place, for it would be well to employ numerous impediments to this energy.

All unnatural connections should be prevented, especially those attended with wanton insolence. But such as harmonize with nature should be encouraged, such as are effected with temperance for the purpose of producing a temperate and legitimate offspring.

Again, those who intend to beget children should providentially attend to the welfare of their future offspring. A temperate and salutary diet therefore is the first and greatest thing to be considered by the would-be begetter, so that he should neither be filled with unseasonable food, nor become intoxicated, nor subject himself to any other perturbation which may injure the body-habits. But above all things he should be careful that the mind, in the act of copulation, should remain in a tranquil state, for bad seed is produced from depraved, discordant and turbulent habits.

With all possible earnestness and attention we should endeavor that children be born elegant and graceful, and that when born they should be well educated. For it is foolish that those who rear horses, birds or dogs should with the utmost diligence render the breed perfect, doing what is proper when it is proper, and likewise consider how they ought to be disposed when they copulate with each other, that the offspring be not the result of chance—while men are inattentive to their progeny, begetting them by chance; and having begotten offspring, should neglect both their food and education. It is the disregard of these things that causes all vice and depravity, since those born will resemble cattle, and will be ignoble and vile.

OCELLUS LUCANUS:

A FRAGMENT ON LAWS

AS LIFE CONTAINS BODIES, whose cause is the soul, so harmony, connectedly, comprehends the world, whose cause is God. Likewise concord unites families, whose cause is the law. Therefore there is a certain cause and nature which perpetually adapts to each other the parts of the world, hindering their being disordered and unconnected. However, cities and families continue only for a short time, as the formers' constituent matter, and the latters' progeny—being causes of dissolution—derive their subsistence from a mutable and perpetually passive nature. For the destruction of things which are generated is the salvation of the matter from which they are generated. That nature, however, which is perpetually moved [the celestial region] governs, while that which is always passive [the sublunary region] is governed, the capacity of the former being prior, and of the latter posterior. The former is divine, possessing reason and intellect, the latter being generated, irrational and mutable.

HIPPODAMUS THE THURIAN:

ON FELICITY

AND

ON A REPUBLIC

ON FELICITY

OF ANIMALS some are capable of felicity while others are incapable. Felicity cannot subsist without virtue, and this is impossible to any lacking reason, so that those animals are incapable of felicity who are destitute of reason. The blind cannot exercise or practice sight, nor can the irrational attain to the work and virtue dependent on reason. To that which possesses reason, felicity is a work, and virtue an art. Of rational animals, some are self-perfect, in need of nothing external, either for their existence or artistic achievement. Such indeed is God. On the contrary, those animals are not self-perfect whose perfection is not due to themselves, or who are in need of anything external. Such an animal is man. Of not self-perfect animals some are perfect and others are not. The former derive their subsistence from both their own proper causes, and from the external. They derive it indeed from their own causes, because they obtain from thence both an excellent nature, and deliberate choice; but also from external causes, because they receive from thence equitable legislation, and good rulers. The animals which are not perfect are either such as participate of neither of these, or of some one of these, or whose souls are entirely depraved. Such will be the man who is of a description different from the above.

Moreover, of perfect men there are two kinds. Some of them are naturally perfect, while others are perfect only in relation to their lives. Only the good are naturally perfect, and these possess virtue. For the virtue of the nature of anything is a consummation and perfection. Thus the virtue of the eye is the eye's nature's consummation and perfection. So man's virtue is man's nature's consummation and perfection.

Those also are perfect according to life who are not only good but happy. For indeed felicity is the perfection of human life. But human life is a system of actions, and felicity completes actions. Virtue and fortune also complete life, but only partially: virtue, according to use, and good fortune according to prosperity. God, therefore, is neither good through learning virtue from any one, nor is he happy through being attended by good fortune. For he is good and happy by nature, and always was, is and never will cease to be, since he is incorruptible and naturally good. But man is neither happy nor good by nature, requiring discipline and providential care. To become good he requires virtue, but to become happy, good fortune. On this account, human felicity may be summarily said to consist of these two things: praise, and being called happy. Praise, indeed, because of virtue; but being called happy from prosperity. Therefore it possesses virtue through a divine destiny, but prosperity through a mortal allotment. But moral concerns depend on divine ones, and terrestrial on celestial. Likewise, subordinate things depend on the more excellent. That is why the good man who follows the Gods is happy, but he who follows mortal nature is unhappy. For to him who possesses wisdom, prosperity is good and useful, being good through his knowledge of the use of it; but it is useful through his cooperating with actions. It is beautiful therefore when prosperity is present with intellect, and when, as if we were sailing with a prosperous wind, actions are performed that tend towards virtue, just as a pilot watches the stars. Thus he who does this will not only follow God, but will also harmonize human good with the divine.

This also is evident, that human life becomes different from disposition and action. But it is necessary that the disposition should be either worthy or depraved, and that action should be attended with either felicity or misery. A worthy disposition indeed participates of virtue, while a bad one of vice. With respect to actions, also, those that are prosperous are attended with felicity [for they derive their completion from looking to reason], but those that are unfortunate are attended with misery, for they are disappointed of their end. Hence it is not only necessary to learn virtue, but also to possess and use it: either for security, or growth [of property when it is too small], or for the improvement of families and cities, which is the greatest thing of all. For it is necessary not only to have the possession of beautiful things, but also their use. All these things, however, will take place when a man lives in a city that enjoys equitable laws. This is what is signified by the horn of Amalthea, for all things are contained in equitable legislation. Without this, the greatest good of human nature can neither be effected, nor, when effected, be increased and become permanent. For this contains both virtue and [the] tendency towards it, because excellent natures are generated according to it. Likewise manners, studies and laws through this subsist in the most excellent condition; and besides these, rightly-deciding reason, and piety and sanctity toward the most honorable natures. Therefore he who wishes to be happy, and whose life is to be prosperous, should live and die in a country governed by equitable laws, relinquishing all lawlessness. All the above is necessary, for man is a part of society, and according to the same reasoning will become entire and perfect, if he associates with others, but that in a becoming manner. For some things are naturally adapted to subsist in many things, and not in one thing; others in one thing and not in many; others both in many and in one, and on this account in one thing because in many. For indeed harmony, symphony and number are naturally adapted to be infused into many things. Nothing which makes a whole from these parts is sufficient in itself. But acuteness of seeing and hearing, and swiftness of feet, subsist in one thing alone. Felicity, however, and virtue of soul, subsist in one thing and in many things, in a whole, and in the universe. On this account they subsist in one thing, because they also subsist in many; and they subsist in many because they inhere in the whole and the universe. For the orderly distribution of the whole nature of things methodically arranges each particular. The orderly distribution of particulars gives completion to the whole of things, and to the universe. But this follows from the whole being naturally prior to the part, and not the part to the whole. For if the Cosmos was not, neither the sun nor the moon would exist, nor the planets, nor the fixed stars. But the universe existing, each of these also exists.

The truth of this may also be seen in the nature itself of animals. For if the animal had no existence, there would be neither eye, mouth, nor ear. But the animal existing, each of these likewise exists. However, as the whole is to the part, so is the virtue of the whole to that of the part. For if harmony did not exist, nor a divine inspection of human affairs, things adorned with order would no longer remain in good condition. Were there no equitable legislation in a city, the citizen would be neither good nor happy. Did the animal lack health, neither foot nor hand could be in health. The world's virtue is harmony, the city's virtue is equitable legislation, and the body's virtue is health and strength. Likewise, each of the parts is adjusted to the whole and the universe. For the eye sees on account of the whole body, and the other parts and members are adjusted for the sake of the whole [body] and the universe.

ON A REPUBLIC

I SAY THAT THE WHOLE OF A POLITY is divided into three parts: the good men who manage public affairs, those who are powerful, and those who are employed in supplying and procuring the necessities of life. The first group is that of the counselors, the second the auxiliaries, and third that which pertains to the mechanical and sordid arts. The first two groups belong to the liberal condition of life; the third, of those who labor to procure subsistence. Of these the council is best, the laborers the worst, and the auxiliaries, a medium between the two. The council should govern, and the laborers should be governed, and the auxiliaries should both govern and be governed. For that which consults for the general good previously deliberates what ought to be done; while that which is of an auxiliary nature, so far as it is belligerent, rules over the whole mechanical tribe, but is itself governed in so far as it has previously received advice from others.

Of these parts, however, each again receives a triple division. For of that which consults, one part presides, another governs, and another counsels for the general good. With respect to the presiding part, it is that which plans, contrives and deliberates about what pertains to the community, prior to the other parts, and afterwards refers its counsels to the senate. But the governing part is either that which now rules [for the first time], or which has before performed that office. With respect to the third part, which consults for the general good, this receives the advice of the earlier parts, and by its suffrages and authority confirms whatever is referred to its decision. In short, those who preside should refer the community's affairs to that part which consults for the general good, while the latter part should refer these affairs through the presiding officers to the convention.

Likewise, of that part which is auxiliary, powerful and efficacious: one part is of a governing nature, another part is defensive, and the remaining, and greater part, is private and military. It is the governing part, therefore, from which the leaders of the armies, the officers of bands, the bands of soldiers, and the vanguard are derived, and universally all those who rank as leaders. The vanguard consists of the bravest, the most impetuous, and the most daring, the remaining military and multitude being gregarious.

Of the third part engaged in sordid occupations, and in laboring to procure the necessities of life: one part consists of husbandmen, and those employed in the cultivation of land; another are artisans, making such instruments and machines as are required by the occasions of life; and another part travels and bargains, exporting to foreign regions such things as are superabundant in the city, and importing into it other things from foreign countries. The systems of political society are organized in many such parts.

Next we must study their adaption and union. Since, however, the whole of political society may well be compared to a lyre, as it requires apparatus and mutual adjustment, and also because it must be touched and used musically; this being the case, I have sufficiently spoken above about the apparatus of a polity, and shown from what and from how many particulars it is constituted. I shall now, therefore, endeavor to speak of the organization and union of these. Political society is organized by disciplines, the study of customs, and laws; through these three man is educated and improved.

Disciplines are the source of erudition, and lead the desires toward virtue. The laws, both repelling man [from the commissions of crimes] and alluring them by honors and gifts, excite them [to virtue]. Manners and studies fashion the soul like wax, and through their continued energy impress thereon propensities that become second nature. These three [parts of society] should however cooperate with the beautiful, the useful and the just; each of these three should if possible aim at all these three, but if not all of them, it should at least have two or one of them as the goal, so that discipline, manners and laws may be beautiful, just and advantageous. In the first place, the beautiful in conduct should be preferred; in the second place the just, and in the third place the useful. Universally the endeavor should be that through these the city may become, in the most eminent degree, unanimous and concordant with its parts, and may be free from sedition, and hostile contention. This will happen if the passions in the youths' souls are disciplined, and in things pleasing and painful are led to moderation, and if the possessions of men are not superfluous, and they derive their subsistence from the cultivation of the earth. This will also be accomplished if good men rule over those that are in want of virtue, skillful men over those that are wanting in skill, and right men over those things that require a certain amount of generosity and expenditure, and also if appropriate honors are distributed to those who govern in all these in a becoming manner. But there are three causes which are incitements to virtue—fear, desire and shame. Law can produce fear, but custom shame; for those that are accustomed to act well will be ashamed to do anything that is base. Desire is produced by disciplines, for they simultaneously assign the causes of things, and attract the soul, and especially so when accompanied by exhortation. Hence the souls of young men should be sufficiently instructed in what pertains to senates, fellowship and association, both military and political. Moreover, the tribe of elderly men should be trained to things of this kind, since young men indeed require correction and instruction, but elderly men need benevolent associations and a mode of living unattended by pain.

Since therefore we have said that the worthy man is perfect through three things—customs, laws and disciplines—we must consider how customs or manners are corrupted usually, and how they grow permanent. We shall then find that customs are corrupted in two ways: through ourselves, or through foreigners. This occurs through ourselves, indeed, due to our flying from pain, whereby we fail to endure labor, or through the pursuit of pleasure, whereby we reject the good. For labors procure good, but pleasures evil. Hence through pleasure, becoming incontinent and remiss, men are rendered effeminate in their souls, and more prodigal in their expenses. Customs and manners are corrupted through foreigners when their numbers swamp the natives, and boast of the success of their mercantile employments, or when those who dwell in the suburbs, becoming lovers of pleasures and luxury, spread their manners to the simple neighbors. Therefore the legislators, officers and mass of the people should diligently take notice whether the customs of the city are being carefully preserved, and that throughout the whole people. Moreover, they should observe whether the genuine and indigenous multitude, of which the polity consists, remains pure and unmingled with any other nation, and whether the magnitude of possessions remains in the same state, and does not become excessive. For the possession of superfluities is accompanied by the desire of still more of the superfluous. In such ways the customs should be preserved.

With respect to disciplines, however, the same legislators and officers should diligently inspect and examine the sophists, whether they are teaching what is useful to the laws, to the established political principles, and to the local economy of life. For sophistic doctrines may infect men with no passing, but [with the] greatest infelicity when they dare make innovations in anything pertaining to human or divine affairs, contrary to the popular views. In this regard, nothing can be more pernicious either with respect to truth, security or renown. In addition to this, they introduce into the minds of the general people obscurity and confusion. Of this kind are all doctrines that teach either that there is no God, or if there is, that he is not affected towards the human race so as to regard it with providential care, but despises and deserts it. In men such doctrines produce folly and injustice to a degree that is inexpressible. Any anarchist who has dismissed fear of disobedience to the laws violates them with wanton boasts. Hence the necessity of political and traditionally venerable principles, adapted to the speakers' disposition, free from any insincerity. Thus what is said exhibits the speakers' manners. The laws will inevitably introduce security if the polity is organized on lines of natural laws and not on the unnatural. From a tyranny cities derive no advantage, and very little from an oligarchy. The first need, therefore, is a kingdom, and the second is an aristocracy.

For a kingdom, indeed, is as it were an image of God, and which is with difficulty preserved and defended by the human soul. For it rapidly degenerates into luxury and insolence. Hence it is not proper to employ a kingdom universally, but only so far as it may be useful to the state, and an aristocracy should be liberally mingled with it, as this consists of many rulers who emulate each other and often govern alternately. There must also be democratic elements, for as a citizen is part of the whole state he should receive a reward from it. Yet he must be sufficiently restrained, for the common people are bold and rash.

* * *

By a necessity of nature, everything mortal is subject to changes, some improving, others growing worse. Things born increase until they arrive at their consummation, whereafter they age and perish. Things that grow of themselves by the same nature decay into the hidden beyond and then return to mortality through transformation of growth; then, by repeated decay, retrograde into another cycle. Sometimes, when houses or cities have attained the peak of supreme happiness, in exuberant wealth, they have, through a welling up of insolent self-satisfaction, through human folly, perished together with their vaunted possessions.

Thus every human empire has shown three distinct stages of growth, fruition and destruction. For in the beginning, being destitute of goods, empires are engrossed in acquisition, but after they become wealthy they perish. Such things, therefore, as are under the dominion of the Gods, being incorruptible, are preserved through the whole of time by incorruptible natures; but such things as are under the government of men, being mortal, from mortals receive perpetual disturbance. The end of self-satisfaction and insolence is destruction, but poverty and narrow circumstances often result in a strenuous and worthy life. Not poverty alone, but many other things bring human life to an end.

DIOTOGENES:

ON SANCTITY

AND

CONCERNING A KINGDOM

ON SANCTITY

IT IS NECESSARY that the laws should not be enclosed in houses, or by gates, but in the manners of the citizens. What, therefore, is the basic principle of any state? The education of the youth. For vines will never bear useful fruit unless they are well cultivated; nor will horses ever excel, unless they are properly trained. Recently ripened fruit grows similar to its surroundings. With utmost prudence do men study how to prune and tend the vines, but to things pertaining to the education of their species they behave rashly and negligently, though neither vines nor wine govern men, but man and the soul of man. The nurture of a plant, indeed, we commit to an expert who is supposed to deserve no less then two minae a day, but the education of our youth we commit to some Illyrian or Thracian who is worthless. As the earliest legislators could not render the middle class of society stable, they prescribed [in the curriculum] dancing and rhythm, which instills motion and order, and besides these they added sports, some of which induced fellowship, but others truth and mental keenness. For those who through intoxication or guzzling had committed any crime, they prescribed the pipe and harmony, which by maturing and refining the manners so shaped the mind that it became capable of being adorned.

* * *

It is well to invoke God at the beginning and end both of supper and dinner, not because he is in want of anything of the kind, but in order that the soul may be transfigured by the recollection of divinity. For since we proceed from him, and participate in a divine nature, we should honor him. Since also God is just, we should act justly in all things.

In the next place, there are four causes which terminate all things and bring them to an end—namely nature, law, art and fortune. Nature is admittedly the principle of all things. Law is the inspective guardian and creator of all things that change manners into political concord. Art is justly said to be the mother and guide of things consummated through human prudence. But of things which accidentally happen to the worthy and unworthy, the cause is ascribed to fortune, which does not produce anything orderly, prudent, moderate or controlled.

CONCERNING A KINGDOM

A KING SHOULD BE ONE who is most just; and he will be most just who most closely attends to the laws. Without justice it is impossible to be a king, and without law there can be no justice. For justice is such only through law, justice's effective cause. A king is either animated by law, or a legal ruler, when he will be most just and observant of the laws. There are however three peculiar employments of a king: leading an army, administering justice, and worshipping the Gods. He will be able to lead an army properly only if he knows how to carry on war properly. He will be skilled in administering justice and in governing all his subjects, only if he has well learned the nature of justice and law. He will worship the Gods in a pious and holy manner only if he has diligently considered the nature and virtue of God. So a good king must necessarily be a good general, judge and priest, which things are inseparable from the goodness and virtue of a king. It is the pilot's business to preserve the ship, the charioteer's to preserve the chariot, and the physician's to save the sick; but it is a king's or a general's business to save those who are in danger in battle. For a leader must also be a provident inspector and preserver. While judicial affairs are in general everybody's interest, this is the special work of a king who, like a God, is a world-leader and protector. While the whole state should be generally organized in a unitary manner, under unitary leadership, individual parts should accord with the same harmony and be submissive to the supreme domination. Besides—though the king should oblige and benefit his subjects, this should not be in contempt of justice and law. The third characteristic of a king's dignity is the worship of the Gods. The most excellent should be worshipped by the most excellent, and the leader and ruler by that which leads and rules. Of naturally most honorable things, God is the best, but of things on the earth and human, a king is the supreme. As God is to the world, so is a king to his kingdom; and as a city is to the world, so is a king to God. For a city, indeed, being organized from things many and various, imitates the organization of the world and its harmony; but a king whose rule is beneficent, and who himself is animated by law, exhibits the form of God among men.

* * *

It is hence necessary that a king should not be overcome by pleasure, but that he should overcome it; that he should not resemble, but excel the multitude; and that he should not conceive his proper employment to consist in the pursuit of pleasure, but rather in the achievement of character. Likewise, he who rules others should be able first to govern his own passions.

As to the desire of obtaining great property, it must be observed that a king ought to be wealthy so as to benefit his friends, relieve those in want, and justly punish his enemies. Most delightful is the enjoyment of wealth in conjunction with virtue. So also concerning the preeminence of a king, for since he always surpasses others in virtue, a judgment of his empire might be formed with reference to virtue, and not to riches, power, or military strength. Riches he possesses in common with any one of his subjects; power, in common with animals; and military strength in common with tyrants. But virtue is the prerogative of good men; hence, whatever king is temperate with respect to pleasures, liberal with respect to money, and prudent and sagacious in government, he will in reality be a king. The people, however, have the same analogy with respect to the virtues and the vices, as the parts of the human soul. For the desire to accumulate the superfluous subsists with the irrational part of the soul, for desire is not rational. But ambition and ferocity cling to the irascible part, for this is the spirited and strenuous part of the soul. The love of pleasure clings to the passionate part, which is effeminate and yielding. Injustice, however, which is the supreme vice, is composite, and clings to the whole soul. The king should therefore organize the well-legislated city like a lyre, first in himself establishing the justest boundary and order of law, knowing that the people's proper arrangement should be organized according to this interior boundary, the divinity having given him dominion over them. The good king should also establish proper positions and habits in the delivery of public orations, behaving in a cultured manner, seriously and earnestly, lest he seem either rough or abject to the multitude, but showing agreeable and easy manners. These things he will obtain if in the first place his aspect and discourse are worthy of respect, and if he appears to deserve the sovereign authority which he possesses; in the second place, if he proves himself to be benign in behavior to those he may meet, from his countenance and beneficence; and in the third place, if his hatred of depravity is formidable, by the punishment he inflicts thereon, from his quickness in inflicting it, and in short from his skill and exercise in the art of government. For venerable gravity, being something which imitates divinity, is capable of winning for him the admiration and honor of the multitude. Benignity will render him pleasing and beloved. His formidableness will frighten his enemies and save him from being conquered, and make him magnanimous and confident to his friends.

His gravity, however, should have no abject or vulgar element; it should be admirable, and worthy of the dignity of rule and sceptre. He should never contend with his inferiors or equals, but with those greater than himself; and, conformably to the magnitude of his empire, he should count those pleasures greatest which are derived from beautiful and great deeds, and not those which arise from sensual gratifications, separating himself indeed from human passions and approximating the Gods—not through arrogance, but through magnanimity and the invincible preeminence of virtue. Hence he should invest his aspect and reasonings with such a gracefulness and majesty, and also in his mental conceptions and soul-manners, in his actions, and body motions and gestures, that those who observe him may perceive that he is adorned and fashioned with modesty and temperance, and a dignified disposition. A good king should be able to charm those who behold him, no less than the sound of a flute and harmony attract those that hear them. Enough about the venerable gravity of a king.

I must now mention his benignity. Generally, any king who is just, equitable and beneficent will be benign. Justice is a connective and collective communion, and is that disposition of the soul which adapts itself to those near us. As rhythm is to motion, and harmony to the voice, so justice is to diplomacy, since it is the governors' and the governed's common good, harmonizing political society.

But justice has two fell administrators, equity and benignity, the former soften-
ing severity of punishment, the latter extending pardon to the less guilty offenders.
A good king must extend assistance to those in need of it and be beneficent, and
this assistance should be given not in one way only, but in every possible manner. Besides, this beneficence should not be hypocritical regarding the honor to
be derived therefrom, but come from the deliberate choice of the giver. Towards
all men a king should conduct himself so as to avoid being troublesome to them,
especially to men of inferior rank and of slender fortune, for these, like diseased
bodies, can endure nothing of a troublesome nature. Good kings, indeed, have
dispositions similar to the Gods, especially resembling Zeus, the universal ruler,
who is venerable and honorable through the magnanimous preeminence of virtue. He is benign because he is beneficent, and the giver of good; hence, by the
Ionic poet [Homer], he is said to be father of men and Gods. He is also eminently
terrible, punishing the unjust, reigning and ruling over all things. In his hand
he carries thunder, as a symbol of his formidable excellence.

All these particulars remind us that a kingdom is something resembling the
divine.

ON THE VIRTUES

THE SOUL is divided into reasoning power, anger and desire. Reasoning power rules knowledge, anger deals with impulse, and desire bravely rules the soul's affections. When these three parts unite into one action, exhibiting a composite energy, then in the soul results concord and virtue. When sedition divides them, then discord and vice appear.* Virtue therefore contains three elements: reason, power, and deliberate choice. The soul's reasoning power's virtue is wisdom, which is a habit of contemplating and judging. The irascible part's virtue is courage, which is a habit of enduring dreadful things, and resisting them. The appetitive part's virtue is temperance, which is a moderation and detention of the pleasures which arise from the body. The whole soul's virtue is justice, for men indeed become bad either through vice, or through incontinence, or through a natural ferocity. They injure each other either through gain, pleasure or ambition. More appropriately therefore does vice belong to the soul's reasoning part. While prudence is similar to good art, vice resembles bad art, inventing contrivances to act unjustly. Incontinence pertains to the soul's appetitive part, as continence consists in subduing, and incontinence in failure to subdue, pleasures. Ferocity belongs to the soul's irascible part, for when someone activated by evil desires is gratified not as man should be, but as a beast would be, then this is called ferocity.

The effects of these dispositions also result from the things for the sake of which they are performed. Vice, hailing from the soul's reasoning part, ends in covetousness; the irascible part's fault is ambition, which results in ferocity; and as the appetitive part ends in pleasure, this generates incontinence. As unjust actions are the results of so many causes, so also are just deeds; for virtue is as naturally beneficent and profitable as vice is maleficent and harmful.

Since, however, one part of the soul leads while the others follow, and since the virtues and vices subsist about these and in these, it is evident that with respect to the virtues also, some are leaders and others followers, while others are compounds of these. The leaders are such as wisdom, the followers being courage and temperance, and their composites include justice. Now the virtues subsist in and about the passions, so we may call the latter the matter of the former. Of the passions, one is voluntary, and the other involuntary, pleasure being the voluntary, and pain the involuntary. Men who have the political virtues increase and decrease these, organizing the other parts of the soul to that which possesses reason. The desirable point of this adaptation is that intellect should not be prevented from accomplishing its proper work, either by lack or by excess. We adapt the less good to that which is more so, and in the world every part that is always passive subsists for the sake of that which is always moved. In the con-

* These initial lines are repeated at the beginning of the next fragment.

junction of animals, the female subsists for the sake of the male, for the latter sows, generating a soul, while the former also imparts matter to that which is generated. In the soul, the irrational subsists for the sake of the rational part. Anger and desire are organized in dependence on the first part of the soul; the former as a satellite and guardian of the body, the latter as a dispenser and provider of necessary wants. Intellect, being established in the highest summit of the body, and having a prospect in that which is on all sides splendid and transparent, investigates the wisdom of real beings. This indeed is its natural function, to investigate and obtain possession of the truth, and to follow those beings which are more excellent and honorable than itself. For the knowledge of things divine and most honorable is the principle, cause and rule of human blessedness.

* * *

The principles of all virtue are three: knowledge, power and deliberate choice. Knowledge indeed is that by which we contemplate and form a judgment of things; power is a certain strength of nature from which we derive our subsistence, and which gives stability to our actions; and deliberate choice is, as it were, the hand of the soul by which we are impelled to, and lay hold on, the objects of our choice.

The soul is divided into reasoning power, anger and desire. Reasoning power rules knowledge, anger deals with impulse, and desire bravely rules the soul's affections. When these three parts unite into one action, exhibiting a composite energy, then concord and virtue result in the soul. When sedition divides them, then discord and vice appear.

When the reasoning power prevails over the irrational part of the soul, then endurance and continence are produced; endurance indeed in the retention of pains, but continence in the absence of pleasures. But when the irrational parts of the soul prevail over the reasoning part of the soul, then are produced effeminacy in flying from pain, and incontinence in being vanquished by the pleasures. When however the better part of the soul prevails, the less excellent part is governed; the former leads, and the latter follows, and both consent and agree, and then in the whole soul is generated virtue and all the goods. Again, when the appetitive part of the soul follows the reasoning, then is produced temperance; when this is the case with the irascible, courage appears; and when it takes place in all the parts of the soul, then the result is justice. Justice is that which separates all the vices and all the virtues of the soul from each other. Justice is an established order and organization of the parts of the soul, and the perfect and supreme virtue; in this every good is contained, while the other goods of the soul cannot subsist without it. Hence Justice possesses great influence both among Gods and men. It contains the bond by which the whole and the universe are held together, and also that by which the Gods and men are connected.* Among the celestials it is called Themis, and among the terrestrials it is called Dike, while among men it is called the Law. These are but symbols indicative that justice is the supreme virtue. Virtue, therefore, when it consists in contemplating and judging, is called wisdom; when in sustaining dreadful things, is called courage; when in restrain-

* Cf. Plato, *Gorgias* 507E.

ing pleasure, it is called temperance; and when in abstaining from injuring our neighbors, justice.

Obedience to virtue according to, and transgression thereof contrary to right reason, tends toward decorousness, and its opposite. Propriety is that which ought to be. This requires neither addition nor detraction, being what it should be. The improper is of two kinds: excess and defect. The excess is over-scrupulousness, and its deficiency, laxity. Virtue however is a habit of propriety. Hence it is both a climax and a medium of which are proper things. They are media because they fall between excess and deficiency; they are climaxes because they endure neither increase nor decrease, being just what they ought to be.

* * *

Since however the virtue of manners consists in dealing the the passions, over which pleasure and pain are supreme, virtue evidently does not consist in extirpating the passions of the soul, pleasure and pain, but in regulating them. So too health, which is an adjustment of the bodily powers, does not consist in expelling the cold and the hot, the moist and the dry, but in adjusting them suitably and symmetrically. Likewise in music, concord does not consist in expelling the sharp and the flat, but in exterminating dissonance by concord arising from their adjustment. Therefore it is the harmonious adjustment of heat and cold, moisture and dryness, which produces health and destroys disease. Thus by the mutual adjustment of anger and desire the vices and other passions are extirpated, while virtues and good manners are induced. Now the greatest peculiarity of the virtue of manners in beauty of conduct is deliberate choice. Reasoning and power may be used without virtue, but deliberate choice cannot be used without it, for deliberate choice inspires dignity of manners.

When the reasoning power by force subdues anger and desire it produces continence and endurance. Again, when the reasoning force is dethroned violently by the irrational parts, then result incontinence and effeminacy. Such dispositions of the soul as these are half-perfect virtues and vices. For [according to its nature] the reasoning power of the soul induces health, while the irrational induces disease. So far as anger and desire are governed and led by the soul's rational part, continence and endurance become virtues; but in so far as this is affected by violence, involuntarily, thus become vices. For virtue must carry out what is proper not with pain but pleasure. So far as anger and desire rule the reasoning power, there is produced effeminacy and incontinence, which are vices; but in so far as they gratify the passions with pain, knowing that they are erroneous, in consequence of the eye of the soul being healthy—so far as this is the case, they are not vices. Hence it is evident that virtue must voluntarily do what is proper, as the involuntary implies pain and fear, while the voluntary implies pleasure and delight.

This may be corroborated by division. Knowledge and perception of things are the province of the rational part of the soul, while power pertains to the irrational part whose peculiarity is inability to resist pain or to vanquish pleasure. In both of these, the rational and the irrational, subsists deliberate choice, which consists of intention and appetite, intention pertaining to the rational part, and appetite to the irrational. Hence every virtue consists in a mutual adaptation of the soul's parts, while both will and deliberate choice subsist entirely in virtue.

* * *

In general, therefore, virtue is a mutual adaptation of the irrational part of the soul to the rational. Virtue, however, is produced through pleasure and pain, receiving the boundary of that which is fit. For true virtue is nothing else than the habit of that which is fit. But the fit, or the decorous, is that which ought to be, and the unfit, or the indecorous, it that which ought not to be. Of the indecorous, however, there are two species, excess and defect. And excess, indeed, is more than is fit, but defect is less than is fit. But since the fit is that which ought to be, it is both a summit and a middle. It is a summit, indeed, because it neither requires ablation nor addition; but it is a middle because it subsists between excess and defect. The fit and the unfit are to each other as the equal and the unequal, as the ordered and the disordered, of which the two former are limited, and the two later unlimited. On this account the parts of the unequal are referred to the middle, but not to each other. An angle greater than a right angle is called obtuse, the acute one being less than it. [In a circle] also, the right line is greater than the radius drawn from the center. Any day beyond the equinox is greater than it. Too much heat or cold produce diseases. Overheatedness exceeds the mean, which frigidity does not attain.

This same analogy holds good in connection with the soul. Audacity is an excess of propriety in the endurance of things of a dreadful nature, while timidity is a deficiency. Prodigality is an excess of proper expenditure of money, while illiberality is its deficiency. Rage is an excess of the proper use of the soul's irascible part, while insensibility is the corresponding deficiency. The same reasoning applies to the opposition of the other dispositions of the soul.

Since however virtue is a habit of propriety, and a medium of the passions, it should be neither wholly impassive, nor immoderately passive. Impassivity causes unimpelledness of the soul and lack of enthusiasm for the beautiful in conduct, while immoderate passivity perturbs the soul, and makes it inconsiderate. We should then, in virtue, see passion as shadow and outline in a picture which depends on animation and delicacy, imitating the truth, in conjunction with goodness of coloring. The soul's passions are animated by the natural incitation and enthusiasm of virtue, which is generated from the passions, and subsisting with them. Similarly, harmony includes the sharp and the flat, and mixtures consist of heat and cold, and equilibrium results from weight and lightness. Therefore, neither would it be necessary nor profitable to remove the passions of the soul; but they must be mutually adjusted to the rational part, under the direction of propriety and moderation.

The Preface to the Laws

of Zaleucus the Locrian

ALL INHABITANTS OF CITY OR COUNTRY should in the first place be firmly persuaded of the existence of divinities as result of their observation of the heavens and the world, and the orderly arrangement of the beings contained therein. These are not the productions of chance or of men. We should reverence and honor them as causes of every reasonable good. We should therefore prepare our souls so they may be free from vice, for the Gods are not honored by the worship of a bad man, nor through sumptuosity of offerings, nor with the tragic expense of a depraved man, but by virtue and the deliberate choice of good and beautiful deeds. All of us, therefore, should be as good as possible, both in actions and deliberate choice, if we wish to be dear to divinity. We should not fear the loss of money more than that of renown; such people should be considered the better citizens.

Those who do not easily feel so impelled, and whose soul is easily excited to injustice, are invited to consider the following. They and their fellow-residents of a house should remember that there are Gods who punish the unjust, and should remember that no one escapes the final liberation from life. For in the supreme moment they will repent, from remembering their unjust deeds, and wishing that their deeds had been just. Every one in every action should be mindful of this time as if it were present, which is a powerful incentive to honesty and justice.

Should anyone feel the presence of an evil spirit, tempting him to injustice, he should go into a temple, remain at the altar, or into sacred groves, flying from injustice as from an impious and harmful mistress, supplicating the divinities to cooperate with him in turning it away from himself. He should also seek the company of men known for their virtue, in order to hear them discouse about a blessed life and the punishment of bad men, that he may be deterred from bad deeds, dreading none but the avenging divinities.

Citizens should honor all the Gods according to the particular country's legal rites, which should be considered as the most beautiful of all. Citizens should, besides obeying the laws, show their respect for the rulers by rising before them and obeying their instructions. Men who are intelligent and wish to be saved should, after the Gods, divinities and heroes, most honor parents, laws and rulers.

Let none love his city better than his country, the indignation of whose Gods he would thus be exciting; for such conduct is the beginning of treachery. For a man to leave his country and reside in a foreign land is something most afflicting and unbearable; for nothing is more kindred to us than our native land. Nor let any one consider a naturalized citizen an implacable enemy; for a person who thinks thus can neither judge nor govern properly, for his anger predominates over his reason. Likewise, let no one speak ill either of the whole city or of a private citizen.

Let the guardians of the laws keep a watchful eye over offenders, first by admonishing them, and if that is not sufficient, by punishment. Should any established law seem unsatisfactory, let it be changed into a better one; but whichever remain should be universally obeyed, for the breaking of established laws is neither beautiful nor beneficial, though it is both beautiful and beneficial to be restrained by a more excellent law, as if vanquished thereby.

Transgressors of established laws should however be punished, as promoting anarchy, which is the greatest evil. The magistrates should neither be arrogant, nor judge insultingly, nor in passing sentence regard friendship or hate, being partial, thus deciding more justly and being worthy of the magistracy. Slaves should do what is just through fear, but free men through shame, and for the sake of beauty in conduct. Governors should be men of this kind to arouse reverence.

Any one who wishes to change any one of the established laws, or to introduce another law, should put a halter around his neck and address the people. And if from the suffrages it should appear that the established law should be dissolved, or that a new law should be introduced, let him not be punished. But if it should appear that the preexisting law is better, or that the new proposition is unjust, let him who wishes to change an old or introduce a new law be executed by the halter.

THE PREFACE TO THE LAWS

OF CHARONDAS THE CATANEAN

FROM THE GODS should begin any deliberation or performance, for according to the old proverb, "God should be the cause of all our deliberation and works." Further, we should abstain from base actions, especially if we desire to consult with the Gods, for there is no communication between God and the unjust.

Next, everyone should help himself, inciting himself to the undertaking and performance of such things as are conformable to his abilities, for it seems sordid and illiberal for a man to extend himself similarly to small and great undertakings. You should carefully avoid rushing into things too extensive, or of too great an importance. In every undertaking you should measure your own desert and power, so as to succeed and gain credit.

A man or woman condemned by the city should not be assisted by anybody; anyone who should associate with him should be disgraced, as similar to the condemned. But it is well to love men who have been voted approved, and to associate with them to imitate and acquire similar virtue and honor, thus being initiated in the greatest and most perfect of the mysteries, for no man is perfect without virtue.

Assistance should be given to an injured citizen whether he is in his own or in a foreign country. But let every stranger who was venerated in his own country, and conformably to the proper laws of that country, be received or dismissed with auspicious cordiality, calling to mind hospitable Zeus as a God who is established by all nations in common, and who is the inspective guardian of hospitality and inhospitality.

Let the older men preside over the younger so that the latter may be deterred from, and be ashamed of vice, through reverence and fear of the former. For where the elders are shameless, so also are their children and grandchildren. Shamelessness and impudence result in insolence and injustice, and of this the end is death.

Let none be impudent, but rather modest and temperate; for he will thus earn the propitiousness of the Gods, and for himself achieve salvation. But no vicious man is dear to divinity. Let everyone honor probity and truth, hating what is base and false. These are the indications of virtue and vice. From their very youth children should therefore be accustomed [to worthy manners] by punishing those who love falsehood and delighting those who love the truth, so as to implant in each what is most beautiful, and most prolific of virtue.

Each citizen should be more anxious for a reputation for temperance than for wisdom, the pretense of which often indicates ignorance of probity and is also a sign of cowardliness. The pretense to temperance should lead to a possession of it; for no one should feign with his tongue that he performs beautiful deeds when destitute of worthiness and good intentions.

Men should preserve kindness towards their rulers, obeying and venerating them as if they were parents; for whoever cannot see the propriety of this will suffer the punishment of bad counsels from the divinities who are the inspective guardians of the seat of the empire. Rulers are the guardians of the city, and of the safety of the citizens.

Governors must preside justly over their subjects in a manner similar to that over their own children, in passing sentences on others, and in propitiating hatred and anger.

Praise and renown is due the rich who have assisted the indigent; they should be considered saviors of the children and defenders of their country. The wants of those who are poor through bad fortune should be relieved, but not the wants resulting from indolence or intemperance. While fortune is common to all men, indolence and intemperance is peculiar to bad men.

Let it be considered as a worthy deed to point out anyone who has acted unjustly, in order that the state may be saved, having many guardians of its proprieties. Let the informer be considered a pious man, though his information affect his most familiar acquaintance; for nothing is more intimate or kindred to a man than his country. However let not the information regard things done through involuntary ignorance, but of such crimes as have been committed from a previous knowledge of their enormity. A criminal who shows enmity to the informer should be generally despised, that he may suffer the punishment of ingratitude, through which he deprives himself of being cured of the greatest of diseases, namely injustice.

Further, let contempt of the Gods be considered as the greatest of iniquities, including voluntary injury to parents, neglecting of rulers and laws, and voluntary dishonoring of justice. Let him be considered as a most just and holy citizen who honors these things, and indicates to the rulers and the citizens those that despise them.

Let it be esteemed more honorable for a man to die for his country than, through a desire of life, to desert it, along with honor; for it is better to die well than to live basely and disgracefully.

We should honor each of the dead not with tears or lamentations, but with good remembrance, and with an oblation of annual fruits. For when we grieve immoderately for the dead we are ungrateful to the terrestrial divinities.

Let no one curse him by whom he has been injured; praise is more divine than defamation.

He who is superior to anger should be considered a better citizen than he who thereby offends.

Not praiseworthy, but shameful is it to surpass temples and palaces in the sumptuousness of one's expense. Nothing private should be more magnificent and venerable than things of a public nature.

Let him who is a slave to wealth and money be despised as cowardly and illiberal, being impressed by sumptuous possessions yet leading a tragic and vile life. The magnanimous man foresees all human concerns and is not disturbed by any accident of fortune.

Let no one speak obscenely, lest his thoughts lead him to base deeds and defile his soul with impudence. Proper and lovely things it is well and legal to advertise, but such things are honored by being kept silent. It is base even to mention something disgraceful.

Let everyone dearly love his lawful wife and beget children by her. But let none shed the seed due his children into any other person, and let him not disgrace that which is honorable by both nature and law. For nature produced the seed for the sake of producing children, and not for the sake of lust.

A wife should be chaste and refuse impious connection with other men, for otherwise she will subject herself to the vengeance of the daimons, whose office it is to expel those to whom they are hostile from their houses, and to produce hatred.

He who gives a step-mother to his children should not be praised, but disgraced as the cause of domestic dissension.

As it is proper to observe these mandates, let him who transgresses them be subjected to political execration.

The law also orders that these introductory suggestions be known by all the citizens, and should be read in the festivals after the hymns to Apollo called paeons, by him who is appointed for this purpose by the master of the feast, so that the precepts may germinate in the minds of all who hear them.

CALLICRATIDAS:

ON THE FELICITY OF FAMILIES

THE UNIVERSE MUST BE CONSIDERED as a system of kindred communion or association. But every system consists of certain dissimilar contraries, and is organized with reference to one particular thing, which is the most excellent, and also with a view to benefit the majority. What we call a choir is a system of musical communion in view of one common thing, a concert of voices. Further, a ship's construction plan contains many dissimilar contrary things which are arranged with reference to one thing which is best—the pilot, and the common advantage of a prosperous voyage.

Now a family is also a system of kindred communion, consisting of dissimilar proper parts organized in view of the best thing, the father of the family, the common advantage being unanimity. In the same manner as a zither, every family requires three things: apparatus, organization, and a certain manner of practice or musical use. An apparatus—being the composition of all its parts—is that from which the whole, and the whole system of kindred communion, derives its consummation. A family is divided into two divisions, man and the possessions, which latter is the thing governed which affords utility. Thus also, an animal's first and greatest parts are soul and body: soul being that which governs and uses, the body being that which is governed and affords utility. Possessions indeed are the advantageous instruments of human life, while the body is a tool born along with the soul, and kindred to it. Of the persons that complete a family, some are relatives and others only attracted acquaintances. The former are born from the same blood or race, but the latter are of an accidental alliance commencing with the communion of wedlock. These are either fathers or brothers, or maternal and paternal grandfathers, or other relatives by marriage. But if the good arising from friendship is also to be referred to a family—for thus it will become greater and more magnificent, not only through an abundance of wealth and many relations, but also through numerous friends—in this case it is evident that the family will thus become more ample, and that friendship is a social relation essential to a family. Possessions are either necessary or desirable. The necessary subserve the wants of life; the desirable produce an elegant and well-ordered life. However, whatever exceeds what is not needed for an elegant and well-ordered life are the roots of wantonness, insolence and destruction. Great possessions swell out with pride and this leads to arrogance and fastidiousness, conceiving that their kindred, nation and tribe do not equal them. Fastidiousness leads to insolence, whose end is destruction. Wherever then in family or city there is a superfluity of possessions, the legislator must cut off and amputate the superfluities, as a good husbandman prunes luxurious leafage.

In the family's domestic part there are three divisions: the governor (the husband), the governed (the wife), and the auxiliary (the offspring).

* * *

With respect to practical and rational domination, one kind is despotic, another protective, and another political. The despotic is that which governs with a view to the advantage of the governor, and not of the governed, as a master rules his slaves or a tyrant his subjects. But the guardian domination subsists for the sake of the governed and not the governor, as the masseurs rule the athletes, physicians rule over the sick, and instructors rule over their pupils. Their labors are not directed to their own advantage but to the benefit of those they govern: those of the physician being undertaken for the sake of the sick, that of the masseurs for the sake of exercising somebody else's body, and those of the erudite for the ignorant. Political domination, however, aims at the common benefit of both governors and governed. For in human affairs, according to this domination, are organized both a family and a city: just as the world and divine affairs are in correspondence, a family and a city stand in relation analogous to the government of the world. Divinity indeed is the principle of nature, and his attention is directed neither to his own advantage, nor to private good, but to that of the public. That is why the world is called *cosmos,* from the orderly disposition of all things, which are mutually organized with reference to the most excellent thing—God—who, according to our notions of him, is a celestial living being, incorruptible, and the principle and cause of the orderly disposition of wholes.

Since therefore the husband rules over the wife, he rules with a power either despotic, protective, or political. Despotic power is out of the question, as he diligently attends to her welfare; nor is it protective entirely, for he has to consider himself also. It remains therefore that he rules over her with a political power, according to which both the governor and the governed seek the common advantage. Hence wedlock is established with a view to the communion of life. Those husbands that govern their wives despotically are by them hated; those that govern them protectively are despised, being as it were mere appendages and flatterers of their wives. But those that govern them politically are both admired and beloved. Both these will be effected if he who governs exercises his power so that it may be mingled with pleasure and veneration: pleasure being produced from his fondness, but veneration from his doing nothing vile or abject.

* * *

He who wishes to marry ought to take for a wife one whose fortune is conformable to his own, neither above nor beneath, but of equal property. Those who marry a woman above their condition have to contend for the mastership; for the wife, surpassing her husband in wealth and lineage, wishes to rule over him, but he considers it to be unworthy of him and unnatural to submit to his wife. But those who marry a wife beneath their condition subvert the dignity and reputation of their family. One should imitate the musician who, having learned the proper tone of his voice, moderates it so as to be neither sharp nor flat, nor broken, nor strident. So wedlock should be adjusted to the tone of the soul, so that the husband and wife may accord, not only in prosperity, but also in adversity. The husband should be his wife's regulator, master and preceptor: regulator, in paying diligent attention to his wife's affairs; master, in governing and exercising authority over her; and preceptor in teaching her such things as are fitting for her to know. This will be specially effected by him who, directing his attention to worthy parents, from their family marries a virgin in the flower of her youth. Such virgins are easily fashioned and docile, and are naturally well disposed to be instructed by, and to fear and love their husbands.

PERICTYONE:

ON THE HARMONY OF A WOMAN

A WOMAN SHOULD BE A HARMONY of thoughfulness and temperance. Her soul should be zealous to acquire virtue so that she may be just, brave, prudent, frugal, and hating vainglory. Furnished with these virtues she will, when she becomes a wife, act worthily towards herself, her husband, her children and her family. Frequently also such a woman will act beautifully towards cities if she happens to rule over cities and nations, as we see is sometimes the case in a kingdom. If she subdues desire and anger there will be produced a divine symphony. She will not be pursued by illegal loves, being devoted to her husband, children and family. Women fond of connection with outside men come to hate their families, both the free members and the slaves. They also plot against their husbands, falsely representing them as the slanderers of all their acquaintances so that they alone may appear benevolent; and they govern their families in such a way as may be expected from lovers of indolence. Such conduct leads to the destruction of everything common to husband and wife.

The body should also be trained to moderation in food, clothes, baths, massage, hair dressing and jewelry adornment. Sumptuous eating, drinking, garments and keepsakes involve them in every crime, and faithlessness to their husbands and to everybody else. It is sufficient to satisfy hunger and thirst, and this from easily accessible things, and to protect themselves from the cold by garments of the simplest description. It is quite a vice to feed on things brought from distant countries and bought at a great price. It is also great folly to search after excessively elegant garments, made brilliant with purple or other precious colors.

The body itself demands no more than to be saved from cold and nakedness, for the sake of propriety, and that is all it needs. Men's opinions, combined with ignorance, demand inanities and superfluities. No woman should be decorated with gold, nor with gems from India or any other country, nor plait her hair artistically, nor be perfumed with Arabian perfumes, nor paint her face so that it may be more white or more red, nor give a dark tinge to her eyebrows and her eyes, nor artificially dye her gray hair, nor bathe continually. A woman of this sort is hunting a spectator of female intemperance. The beauty produced by thoughtfulness, and not by these particulars, pleases women that are well born. Neither should she consider it necessary to be noble, rich, to be born in a great city, have glory, and the friendship of renowned or royal men. The presence of such should not cause her any annoyance, but should they be absent she should not regret them; their absence will not hinder the prudent woman from living properly. Her soul should not anxiously dream about them, but ignore them. They are really more harmful than beneficial, as they lead to misfortune; inevitable are treachery, envy and calumny, so that their possessor cannot be free from perturbation.

She should venerate the Gods, thereby hoping to achieve felicity, also by obeying the laws and sacred institutions of her country. After the Gods, she should honor and venerate her parents, who cooperate with the Gods in benefiting their children.

Moreover she ought to live with her husband legally and kindly, claiming nothing as her own property but preserving and protecting his bed, for this protection contains all things. In a becoming manner she should bear any stroke of fortune that may strike her husband, whether he is unfortunate in business, or makes ignorant mistakes, is sick, intoxicated, or has connection with other women. This last error is granted to men, but not to women, since they are punished for this offence. She must submit to the law with equanimity, without jealousy. She should likewise patiently bear his anger, his parsimony, complaints he may make of his destiny, his jealousy, his accusations of her, and whatever other faults he may inherit from his nature. All these she should cheerfully endure, conducting herself towards him with prudence and modesty. A wife who is dear to her husband, and who truly performs her duty towards him, is a domestic harmony, and loves the whole of her family, to which also she conciliates the benevolence of strangers.

If however she loves neither her husband nor her children, nor her servants, nor wishes to see any sacrifice preserved, then she becomes the herald of every kind of destruction, which she likewise prays for, as being an enemy, and also prays for the death of her husband, as being hostile to him, in order that she may be connected with other men; and in the last place she hates whatever her husband loves.

But a wife will be a domestic harmony if she is full of prudence and modesty. For then she will love not only her husband, but also her kindred, her servants, and the whole of her family among with which she numbers her possessions, friends, fellow-citizens, and strangers. Their bodies she will adorn without any superfluous ornaments, and will both speak and hear such things only as are beautiful and good. She should conform to her husband's opinion as regards their common life, and be satisfied with those relatives and friends as meet his sanction. Unless she is entirely devoid of harmony she will consider pleasant or disagreeable such things which are thought so by her husband.

* * *

Parents ought not to be injured either in word or deed; and whatever their rank in life, great or small, they should be obeyed. Children should remain with them, and never forsake them, and almost submit to them even when they are insane, in every allotted condition of soul or body, or external circumstances, in peace, war, health, sickness, riches, poverty, renown, ignominy, class, or magistrate's rank. Such conduct will be wisely and cheerfully adopted by the pious. He who despises his parents will both among the living and the dead be condemned for this crime by the Gods, will be hated by men, and under earth will, together with the impious, be eternally punished in the same place by Justice, and the subterranean Gods, whose province it is to inspect things of this kind.

The aspect of parents is a thing divine and beautiful, and a diligent observance of them is attended by a delight such that neither a view of the sun, nor of all the stars, which swing around the illuminated heavens, is capable of producing any spectacle greater than this. The Gods are not envious in a case like this.

We should reverence parents both while living and dead, and never oppose them in anything they say or do. If ignorant of anything through deception or disease, their children should console and instruct, but by no means hate them on this account. For no greater error or injustice can be committed by men than to act impiously towards their parents.

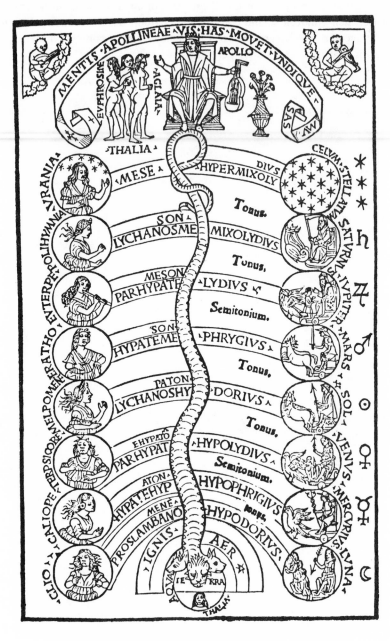

FIGURE 14. THE MUSIC OF THE SPHERES. Shown in this engraving from Renaissance Italy are Apollo, the Muses, the planetary spheres and musical ratios.

ARISTOXENUS OF TARENTUM:

APOTHEGMS

ARISTOXENUS OF TARENTUM (latter half of the 4th century B.C.E.) was a music theorist and student of Aristotle. He had connections with the last surviving members of the Pythagorean school at Phlious and has been categorized as actually being one of the Pythagorean *mathematikoi*. His writings on Pythagoras were used by Porphyry and Iamblichus. The second fragment is based on the 4th book of Plato's *Laws*.

APOTHEGMS

AFTER DIVINITY AND DIVINE SPIRITS, the greatest respect should be paid to parents and the laws; not fictitiously, but in reality preparing ourselves to an observance of, and perseverance in, the manners and laws of our country, though they should be in a small degree worse than those of other countries.

* * *

But after these things follow the honors which should be paid to living parents, it being right to discharge the first, greatest, and the most ancient of debts. Everyone, likewise, should think that all which he possesses belongs to those who begot and nurtured him, in order that he may be ministrant to their want to the utmost of his ability, beginning from his property; in the second place, discharging his debt to them from things pertaining to his body; and in the third place, from things pertaining to his soul, thus with usury repairing the cares and pains which his now very aged parents bestowed on him when he was young. Through the whole of life, likewise, he should particularly employ the most respectful language in speaking to his parents, because there is a most severe punishment for light and winged words and Nemesis, the messenger of Justice, is appointed to be the inspector of everything of this kind.

When parents are angry, therefore, we should yield to them and appease their anger, whether it is seen in words or deeds, acknowledging that a father may reasonably be very much enraged with his son when he thinks that he has been injured by him.

On the parents' death the most appropriate and beautiful monuments should be raised to them, not exceeding the usual magnitude, nor yet less than those which our ancestors erected for their parents. Every year, also, attention ought to be paid to the decoration of their tombs. They should likewise be continually remembered and reverenced, and this with a moderate but appropriate expense.

By always acting and living in this manner we shall each of us be rewarded according to our deserts, both by those Gods and those natures that are superior to us, and shall pass the greatest part of our life in good hope.

EURYPHAMUS:

CONCERNING HUMAN LIFE

THE PERFECT LIFE OF MAN falls short indeed of the life of God because it is not self-perfect, but surpasses that of irrational animals, participating as it does of virtue and felicity. For neither is God in want of external causes—as he is naturally good and happy, and is perfect from himself—nor is he in want of any irrational animal. For beasts being destitute of reason, they are also destitute of the sciences pertaining to actions. But the nature of man partly consists of his own proper deliberate choice, and partly is in want of the assistance derived from divinity. For that which is capable of being fashioned by reason, which has an intellectual perception of things beautiful and base, can from earth erect itself and look to heaven, and with the eye of intellect can perceive the highest Gods—that which is capable of all this likewise receives assistance from the Gods.

But in consequence of possessing will, deliberate choice, and a principle of such a kind as enables it to study virtue, and to be agitated by the storms of vice, to follow, and also to apostatize from the Gods—it is likewise able to be moved by itself. Hence it may be praised or blamed, partly by the Gods, and partly by men, according as it applies itself zealously either to virtue or vice.

For the whole reason of the thing is as follows: Divinity introduced man into the world as a most exquisite being, to be honored reciprocally with himself, and as the eye of the orderly systematization of everything. Hence also man gave things names, himself becoming the character of them. He also invented letters, through these procuring a treasury of memory. He imitated the established order of the universe, by laws and judicial proceedings, organizing the communion of cities. For no human work is more honorable in the eyes of the world, nor more worthy of notice by the Gods, than proper constitution of a city governed by good laws, distributed in an orderly fashion throughout the state. For though by himself no man amounts to anything, and by himself is not able to lead a life conforming to the common concord, and to the proper organization of a state; yet he is well adapted to the perfect system of society.

Human life resembles a properly tuned and cared-for lyre. Every lyre requires three things: apparatus, tuning, and musical skill of the player. By apparatus we mean preparation of all the appropriate parts: the strings, the plectrum and other instruments cooperating in the tuning of the instrument. By tuning we mean the adaptation of the sounds to each other. The musical skill is the motion of the player in consideration of the tuning. Human life requires the same three things. Apparatus is the preparation of the physical basis of life, riches, renown, and friends. Tuning is the organizing of these according to virtue and the laws. Musical skill is the mingling of these according to virtue and the laws, virtue sailing with a prosperous wind and no external resistance. For felicity does not consist in being driven from the purpose of voluntary intentions, but in obtaining them; nor in virtue lacking attendants and servers, but in completely possessing its own proper powers which are adapted to actions.

For man is not self-perfect, but imperfect. He may become perfect partly from himself, and partly from some external cause. Likewise, he may be perfect either according to nature or to life. According to nature he is perfect if he becomes a good man, as the virtue of everything is the climax and perfection of the nature of that thing. Thus the virtue of the eyes is the climax and perfection of their nature, and this is also true of the virtue of the ears. Thus too the virtue of man is the climax and perfection of the nature of man. But man is perfect according to life when he becomes happy. For felicity is the perfection and completion of human goods. Hence, again, virtue and prosperity become parts of the life of man.

Virtue, indeed, is a part of him so far as he is soul; but prosperity, so far as he is connected with body; but both parts of him, so far as he is an animal. For it is the province of virtue to use in a becoming manner the goods which are conformable to nature, but of prosperity to impart the use of them. The former, indeed imparts deliberate choice and right reason, but the latter imparts energies and actions. For to wish what is beautiful in conduct, and to endure things of a dreadful nature, is the proper business of virtue. But it is the work of prosperity to render deliberate choice successful, and to cause actions to arrive at the desired end. For a general conquers in conjunction with virtue and good fortune. The pilot sails well in conjunction with art and prosperous winds; the eye sees well in conjunction with acuteness of vision and light. So the life of man reaches its perfection through virtue and prosperity.

HIPPARCHUS:

ON TRANQUILITY

SINCE MEN LIVE for but a very short period, if their life is compared to the whole of time, they will, as it were, make a most beautiful journey if they pass through life with tranquility. This they will best possess if they will accurately and scientifically know themselves—namely, that they are mortal and of a fleshy nature, and that they have a body which is corruptible, and can be easily injured, and which is exposed to everything most grievous and severe, even to their last breath.

In the first place, let us observe those things which happen to the body, such as pleurisy, pneumnonia, phrensy, gout, stranguary, dysentery, lethargy, epilepsy, ulcers, and a thousand other diseases. But the diseases that can happen to the soul are much greater and more dire. For all the iniquitous, evil, lawless and impious conduct in the life of man originates from the passions of the soul. Through unnatural immoderate desires many have become subject to unrestrained impulses and have not refrained from the most unholy pleasures, arising from connection with daughters and even mothers. Many have even destroyed their fathers and offspring. But what is the use to continue detailing externally impending evils, such as excessive rain, drought, violent heat and cold, so that frequently from the anomalous state of the air, pestilence and famine arise, followed by manifold calamities making whole cities desolate? Since therefore many such calamities impend, we should neither be elated by the possession of worldly goods, which might rapidly be consumed by the irruption of some small fever, nor with what are conceived to be prosperous external circumstances, which from their own nature frequently decay quicker than they arose. For all these are uncertain and unstable, and are found to have their existence in many and various mutations, and no one of them is permanent, or immutable, or stable or indivisible. Considering these things well, and also being persuaded that if what is present and is imparted to us is able to remain for the smallest portion of time, it is as much as we ought to expect; we shall then live in tranquility, and with humor, generously bearing whatever may befall us.

How many people imagine that all they have and what they receive from fortune and nature is better than it is, not realizing what it is in reality. But such as it is able to become when it has arrived at its highest excellence, they then burden the soul with many and great and nefarious stupid evils when they are suddenly deprived of these transitory goods. That is how they lead a most bitter and miserable life. But this takes place in the loss of riches, or the death of friends and children, or in the privation of certain other things, which by them are conceived to be possessions most honorable. Afterwards, weeping and lamenting, they assert of themselves that they alone are most unfortunate and miserable, not remembering that these things have happened, and even now happen to many others, nor are they able to understand the life of those that are now in existence, and of those that have lived in former times, nor to see in what great calamities and waves of evils of which many of the present times are, and of which the past have been, involved. Therefore considering with ourselves that many who have lost their property have afterwards on account of this very loss been saved, since thereafter they might either have fallen into the hands of robbers or into the power of a tyrant; that many also who have loved certain persons, and have been extremely benevolently disposed towards them, but have afterwards hated them extremely—considering all these things of which history informs us, and learning likewise that many have been destroyed by their own children, and by those they have most dearly loved, and comparing our own life with that of those who have been more unhappy than we have been, and taking into account general human vicissitudes that happen to others besides ourselves, we shall pass through life with greater tranquility.

A reasonable man will not think the calamities of others easy to be borne, but not his own, since he sees that the whole of life is naturally exposed to many calamities. Those however who weep and lament, besides not being able to recover what they have lost, or recall to life those that are dead, impel the soul to still greater perturbations, in consequence of its being filled with much depravity. Being washed and purified, we should do our best to wipe away our inveterate stains by the reasoning of philosophy. This we shall accomplish by adhering to prudence and temperance, being satisfied with our present circumstances and not aspiring after too many things. Men who gather a great abundance of external things do not consider that enjoyment of them terminates with this present life. We should therefore use the present goods, and by the assistance of the beautiful and venerable results of philosophy we shall be liberated from the insatiable desire of depraved possessions.

Metopus:

Concerning Virtue

MAN'S VIRTUE IS THE PERFECTION of his nature. By the proper nature of his virtue every being becomes perfect, and arrives at the summit of its excellence. Thus the virtue of the horse is that which makes the best of the horse's nature. The same reasoning also applies to details. Thus the virtue of the eyes is acuteness of vision, and this is the summit of the eyes' nature. The virtue of the ears is the acuteness of hearing, and this is the aural nature's summit. The virtue of the feet is swiftness, and this is the locomotive nature's climax.

Every virtue, however, should include these three things: reason, power, and deliberate choice. Reason indeed judges and contemplates, power prohibits and vanquishes, and deliberate choice loves and enjoys propriety. Therefore to judge and contemplate pertain to the intellectual part of the soul; to prohibit and vanquish are the peculiarity of the irrational part of the soul; and to love and enjoy propriety includes both the rational and irrational parts of the soul, for deliberate choice consists of the discursive energy of reason and appetite. Intention, therefore, pertains to the rational, but appetite to the irrational parts of the soul.

We may discern the multitude of the virtues by observing the parts of the soul; also, the growth and nature of virtue. Of the soul's parts two rank first: the rational and the irrational. It is by the rational that we judge and contemplate, by the irrational we are impelled and desire. These are either concordant or discordant [with one another], their strife and dissonance being produced by excess or defect. The rational part's victory over the irrational produces endurance and continence. When the rational leads, the irrational follows; both accord and produce virtue. That is why endurance and continence are generally accompanied by pain; for endurance resists pain, and continence pleasure. However, incontinence and effeminacy neither resist nor vanquish pleasure. That is why men fly from good through pain, but reject it through pleasure. Likewise praise and blame and everything beautiful in human conduct are produced in these parts of the soul. This explains the nature of virtue.

Let us study virtue's kinds and parts. Since the soul is divided into two parts, the rational and the irrational, the latter is also divided into two, the irascible and appetitive part. By the rational we judge and contemplate; by the irrational we are impelled and desire. The irascible part defends us and revenges incidental molestations; the appetitive directs and preserves the body's proper constitution. So we see that the numerous virtues with all their differences and peculiarities do little more than conform to the distinctive parts of the soul.

CRITO:

ON PRUDENCE AND PROSPERITY

SUCH IS THE MUTUAL RELATION of prudence and prosperity: prudence is explainable and reasonable, orderly and definite; prosperity is unexplainable and irrational, disorderly and indefinite. In origin and power, prudence is prior to prosperity, the former governing and defining, the latter being governed and defined; but they are mutually adjusting, concurring in the same thing. For that which limits and adjusts must be explainable and reasonable, while that which is limited and adjusted is naturally unexplainable and irrational. That is how the principles of the Indefinite nature and Limit subsist in all things. Indefinites are always naturally disposed to be limited and adjusted by things possessing reason and prudence, for in relation to the latter the former stands as matter and essence. But finite things are self-adjusted and self-limited, being causal and energetic.

The mutual adjustment of these natures in different things produces a variety of adjusted substances. For in the comprehension of the whole of things, the mutual adjustment of both the motive and the passive is the world. There is no other possible way of salvation for the whole and the universe other than through the adjustment of the things generated to the divine, and of the ever passive to the ever motive. The similar adjustment in man, of the irrational to the rational part of the soul, is virtue, for this cannot exist in cases of mutual strife between the two. So also in a city, the mutual adjustment of the governors to the governed produces strength and concord. Governing is the specialty of the better nature, while being governed is more suited to the subordinate part. To both are common strength and concord. A similar mutual adjustment exists in the universe and in the family, for allurements and erudition concur with reason, and likewise pains and pleasures, prosperity and adversity.

Man's constitution is such that he needs work and rest, sorrow and gladness, prosperity and adversity. Some things draw the intellect towards wisdom and industry and keep it there; others relax and delight, rendering the intellect vigorous and prompt. Should one of these elements prevail then man's life becomes one-sided, exaggerating sorrow and difficulty or levity and smoothness. Now all these should be mutually adjusted by prudence, which discerns and distinguishes in actions the elements of the Limited and the Indefinite. That is why prudence is the mother and leader of the other virtues. For it is prudence's reason and law which organizes and harmonizes all other virtues.

In summary: the irrational and explicable are to be found in all things; the latter defines and limits, the former is defined and bounded. That which consists of both is the proper organization of the whole and the universe.

* * *

God fashioned man in a way such as to declare, not through the want of power or deliberate choice, that man is incapable of impulsion to beauty of conduct.

In man was implanted a principle such as to combine the possible with the desirable; so that while man is the cause of power and of the possession of good, God causes reasonable impulse and incitation. So God made man tend to heaven, gave him an intellective power, implanted in him a sight called Intellect, which is capable of beholding God. For without God, it is impossible to discover what is best and most beautiful; and without Intellect we cannot see God, since every mortal nature's establishment implies a progressive loss of [immortal] Intellect. It is not God, however, who effected this, but generation, and that impulse of the soul which lacks deliberate choice.

POLUS:

ON JUSTICE

I THINK THAT JUSTICE which subsists among men may be called the mother and nurse of the other virtues. Without it no man can be temperate, brave, or prudent. In conjunction with elegance it is the harmony and peace of the whole soul. This virtue's strength will become more manifest if we compare it to the other habits. They have a partial utility, and refer to one thing only, while this refers to a multitude and to whole systems. It conducts the whole world-government and is called providence, harmony, and Dike by the decrees of a certain genus of Gods. In a city it is justly called peace, and equitable legislation. In a house, it is the concord between husband and wife, the kindliness of the servant towards his master, and the anxious care of the master for his servant. In the body, likewise, which to all animals is the first and dearest thing, it is the health and wholeness of each part. In the soul it is the wisdom that depends from science and justice. As therefore this virtue disciplines and saves both the whole and parts of everything, mutually tuning and familiarizing all things, it surely deserves, by universal consensus, to be called the mother and nurse of all things.

STHENIDAS THE LOCRIAN:

ON A KINGDOM

A KING SHOULD BE a wise man; thus will he be honored in the same manner as the supreme divinity, whose imitator he will be. As the Supreme is by nature the first king and potentate, so will a king be by birth and imitation. As the former rules in the universe and in the whole of things, so does the latter in the earth. While the former governs all things eternally and has a never-failing life, possessing all wisdom in himself, so the latter acquires science through time. But a king will imitate the First God in the most excellent manner if he acquires magnanimity, gravity, the restriction of his wants to but few things, and to his subjects exhibits a paternal disposition.

For it is because of this especially that the First God is called the father of both Gods and men, because he is mild to everything that is subject to him and never ceases to govern with providential regard. Nor is he satisfied with being the Maker of all things, but he is the nourisher and preceptor of everything beautiful, and the legislator to all things equally. Such also ought to be a king who on earth rules over men.

Nothing is beautiful that lacks a director or ruler. Again, no king or ruler can exist without wisdom and science. He therefore who is both a sage and a king will be an imitator and legitimate minister of God.

ECPHANTUS THE CROTONIAN:

ON KINGS

MANY ARGUMENTS apparently prove that every being's nature is adapted to the world and the things it contains. Every animal thus conspiring [in union and consent] and having such an organization of its parts, through the attractive flux of the universe around it, effects the general ornamentation of the world and the peculiar permanence of everything it contains. Hence it is called the *kosmos* and is the most perfect living thing.

When we study its parts we find them many and naturally different: First, a being who is the best, both from its native alliance to the world, and in its particular divinity [containing the stars called planets, forming the first and greatest series]. Second is the nature of the divinities, in the sublunary region, where bodies move in a straight line. Third, in the earth and with us, the best being is man, of whom the most divine is a king, surpassing other men in his general being. While his body resembles that of other men, being made of the same physical matter, he was molded by the best sculptors who used him as the archetype. Hence, in a certain respect, a king is one and alone, being the production of the supernal king with whom he is always familiar, being beheld by his subjects in his kingdom as in a splendid light.

A kingdom has been said to resemble an eagle, the most excellent of winged animals, who undazzled stares at the sun. A kingdom is also similar to the sun, because it is divine, and because its exceeding splendor cannot be seen without difficulty, except by piercing eyes that are genuine. For the numerous splendors that surround it, and the dark vertigos it produces in those that gaze at it, as if they had ascended into some foreign altitude, demonstrates that their eyes are spurious. Those however who can safely arrive thither, on account of their familiarity or alliance therewith, can use it properly.

A kingdom, therefore, is something pure, genuine, uncorrupted, and because of its preeminence, divine and difficult of access. He who is established therein should naturally be most pure and lucid in his soul, that by his personal stains he may not obscure so splendid an institution, as some persons defile the most sacred places, and the impure pollute those they meet. But a king, who associates with men should be undefiled, realizing how much more divine than other things are both himself and his prerogatives; and from the divine exemplar of which he is an image, he should treat both himself and his subjects worthily.

When other men are delinquents, their most holy purification causes them to imitate their rulers, whether laws or kings. But kings who cannot on earth find anything better than their own nature to imitate should not waste time in seeking any model other or lower than God himself. No one would long search for the world, seeing that he exists in it, as a part of it; so the governor of others should not ignore him by whom he also is governed. Being ruled is the supreme ornament, inasmuch as there is nothing rulerless in the universe.

A king's manners should also be the inspiration of his government. Thus its beauty will immediately shine forth, since he who imitates God through virtue will surely be dear to him who he imitates, and much more dear will he be to his subjects. No one who is beloved by the divinity will be hated by men, since neither do the stars nor the whole world hate God. For if they hated their ruler and leader they would never obey him. But it is because he governs properly that human affairs are properly governed. The earthly king, therefore, should not be deficient in any of the virtues distinctive of the heavenly ruler.

Now as an earthly king is something foreign and external, inasmuch as he descends to men from the heavens, so likewise his virtues may be considered as works of God and descending upon him from divinity. You will find this true if you study out the whole thing from the beginning.

An earthly king obtains possession of his subjects by an agreement which is the first essential. The truth of this may be gathered from the state of affairs produced by the destruction of the usual unanimity among citizens, which indeed is much inferior to a divine and royal nature. Such natures are not oppressed by any such poverty but, conforming to intellect, they supply the wants of others, assisting them in common, being perfect in virtue. But the friendship existing in a city, and possessing a certain common end, imitates the concord of the universe. No city could be inhabited without an institution of magistrates. To effect this, however, and to preserve the city, there is a necessity of laws, a political domination, a governor and the governed. All this happens for the general good, for unanimity and the consent of the people in harmony with organic efficiency. Likewise, he who governs according to virtue is called a king, and is so in reality, since he possesses the same friendship and communion with his subjects as divinity possesses with the world and its contained natures. All benevolence, however, ought to be exerted in the first place, indeed, by the king towards his subjects; second, by the subjects towards the king; and this benevolence should be similar to that of a parent towards his child, or a shepherd towards his flock, and of the law towards the law-abiding.

For there is one virtue pertaining to the government and to the life of men. No one should through indigence solicit the assistance of others when he is able to supply himself with what nature requires. Though [in the city] there is a certain community of goods, yet everyone should live so as to be self-sufficient, which requires the aid of no others in his passage through life. If therefore it is necessary to lead an active life, it is evident that a king, though he should also consume other things, will nevertheless be self-sufficient. For he will have friends through his own virtue, and in using these, he will not use them by any virtue other than that by which he regulates his own life. For he must follow a virtue of this kind since he cannot procure anything more excellent. God, indeed, needing neither ministers nor servants, nor employing any mandate, and neither crowning nor proclaiming those that are obedient to him, or disgracing those that are disobedient, thus administers so great an empire. In a manner to me appearing most worthy of imitation, he instills into all things a most zealous desire to participate in his nature. As he is good, the most easy possible communication thereof is his only work. Those who imitate him find that this imitation enables them to accomplish everything else better. Indeed the imitation of God is the self-sufficiency of everything else, for there is an identity, and no difference between the virtues that make things acceptable to God, and those that imitate him; and is not our earthly king in a similar manner self-sufficient? By assimilating himself to one, and that the most excellent nature, he will beneficently endeavor to assimilate all his subjects to himself.

Such kings, however, as towards their subjects use violence and compulsion, entirely destroy in every individual of the community a readiness to imitate himself. Without benevolence no assimilation is possible, since benevolence particularly effaces fear. It is indeed much to be desired that human nature should not be in want of persuasion, which is the relic of human depravity, of which the temporal being called man is not destitute. Persuasion, indeed, is akin to necessity inasmuch as it is chiefly used on persons flying from necessity. But persuasion is needless with beings such as spontaneously seek the beautiful and the good.

Again, a king alone is capable of effecting this human perfection, that through imitation of the excellent man may pursue propriety and loveliness, and that those who are corrupted as if by intoxication, and who have fallen into an ignorance of the good by a bad education, may be strengthened by the king's eloquence, may have their diseased minds healed, their depravity's dazedness expelled, and may become mindful of an intimate associate, whose influence may persuade them. Though originating from undesirable seeds, yet [this royal influence] is the source of a certain good to inhabitants of this terrestrial realm, where language supplies our deficiencies in our mutual converse.

* * *

He who has a sacred and divine conception of things will in reality be a king. Persuaded by this, he will be the cause of all good, but of no evil. Evidently, as he is fitted for society, he will become just. For communion or association consists in equality, and in its distribution. Justice indeed precedes, but communion participates. For it is impossible for a man to be unjust and yet distribute equality, or that we should distribute equality, and yet not be adapted to association.

How is it possible that he who is self-sufficient should not be continent? For sumptuousness is the mother of incontinence, and this of wanton insolence, and from this an innumerable host of ills. But self-sufficiency is not mastered by sumptuousness, nor by any of its derivative evils, but itself being a principle, it leads all things, and is not led by any. To govern is the province of God, and also of a king, on which account indeed he is called self-sufficient; so to both it pertains not to be governed by anyone.

Evidently, these things cannot be effected without prudence, and it is manifest that the world's intellectual prudence is God. For the world reveals graceful design which would be impossible without prudence. Nor is it possible for a king without prudence to possess these virtues—I mean justice, continence, sociability and kindred virtues.

PEMPELUS:

ON PARENTS*

NEITHER DIVINITY nor anyone possessing the least wisdom will ever advise anyone to neglect his parents. Hence we cannot have any statue or temple which will be considered by divinity as more precious than our fathers and grandfathers when grown feeble with age. For he who honors his parents by gifts will be recompensed by God, for without this the divinities will not pay any attention to the prayers of such parents for their children. Our parents' and progenitors' images should by us be considered much more venerable and divine than any inanimate images. For our parents, who are divine images that are animated, when they are continually adorned and worthily honored by us, pray for us, and implore the Gods to bestow on us the most excellent gifts, and do the contrary when we despise them, neither of which occurs with inanimate images. Hence he who behaves worthily towards his parents and progenitors, and other kindred, will possess the most worthy of all statues, and the best calculated to endear him to divinity. Every intelligent person, therefore, should honor and venerate his parents, and should dread their execrations and unfavorable prayers, knowing that many of them take effect.

Nature having disposed the matter thus, prudent and modest men will consider their living aged progenitors a treasure, to the extremity of life; and if they die before the children have arrived there, the latter will be longing for them. Moreover, progenitors will be terrible in the extreme to their depraved or stupid offspring. The profane person who is deaf to these considerations will by all intelligent persons be considered as odious to both Gods and men.

* Cf. Plato, *Laws,* Book 11.

PHYNTIS, DAUGHTER OF CALLICRATES:

ON WOMAN'S TEMPERANCE

A WOMAN OUGHT TO BE WHOLLY GOOD AND MODEST; but she will never be a character of this kind without virtue, which renders precious whatever contains it. The eye's virtue is sight, the ear's hearing. A horse's virtue makes it good, while the virtue of man or woman makes them worthy. A woman's principal virtue is temperance, by means of which she will be able to honor and love her husband.

Some, perhaps, may not think that it becomes a woman to philosophize, any more than it is suitable for her to ride on horseback, or to harangue in public. But I think that while there are certain employments specialized to each sex, that there are some common to both man and woman. Male avocations are to lead an army, to govern, and to harangue in public. Female avocations are to guard the house, to stay at home, to receive and minister to her husband. Her particular virtues are fortitude, justice and prudence. Both husband and wife should achieve the virtues of the body and the soul; for as bodily health is beneficial to both, so also is health of the soul. The bodily virtues, however, are health, strength, vigor of sensation, and beauty. With respect to the virtues, also, some are peculiarly suitable to men, and some to women. Fortitude and prudence regard the man more than they do the woman both on account of the bodily habits and the power of the soul, but temperance peculiarly belongs to the woman.

It would be well to know the number and quality of the things through which this virtue is acquirable by women. I think that they are five. First, temperance comes through the sanctity and piety of the marriage bed. Second, through body-adornments; third, through trips outside the house. Fourth, through refraining from celebrating the rites and mysteries of the Mother of the Gods [i.e., Cybele]. Fifth, in being cautious and moderate in sacrifices to the divinities. Of these, however, the greatest and most comprehensive cause of temperance is undefiledness of the marriage bed and to have connexion with none but her husband.

By such lawlessness she acts unjustly toward the Gods who preside over nativities, changing them from genuine to spurious assisants to her family and kindred. In the second place, she acts unjustly towards the Gods who preside over Nature, by whom she and all her kindred solemnly swore that she would lawfully associate with her husband in the association of life and the procreation of children. Third, she injures her country in not observing its decrees. It is frivolous and unpardonable, for the sake of pleasure and wayward insolence, to offend in a matter where the crime is so great that the greatest punishment, death, is ordained. All such insolent conduct ends in death. Besides, for this offence there has been discovered no purifying remedy which might turn such guilt into purity beloved by divinity, for God is most averse to the pardoning of this crime. The best indication of a woman's chastity towards her husband is her children's resemblance to their father. This suffices about the marriage bed.

As to body-ornaments, a woman's garments should be white and simple and not superfluous. They will be so if they are neither transparent nor variegated, nor woven from silk, inexpensive, and white. This will prevent excess ornamentation, luxury, and superfluity of clothes, and will avoid the imitation of depravity by others. Neither gold nor emeralds should ornament her body for they are very expensive and exhibit pride and arrogance toward the vulgar. Besides, a city governed by good laws and well organized should adjust all its interests in an equable legislation, which therefore would expel from the city the jewelers who make such things.

A woman should, besides, illuminate her face, not by powder or rouge, but by the natural glow from the towel, adorning herself with modesty rather than by art. Thus she will reflect honor both on herself and her husband.

The lower class of women should chiefly go out of their houses to sacrifice to the municipal tutelary divinity for the welfare of her husband and her kindred. Neither should a woman go out from her house at dawn or dusk, but openly when the forum is full of people, accompanied by one or at the most two servants, to see something or to shop.

As to sacrifices of the Gods, they should be frugal and suited to her ability; she should abstain from celebration of the rites and the Cybelean sacrifice performed at home, for the municipal law forbids them to women. Moreover, these rites lead to intoxication and insanity. A family mistress, presiding over domestic affairs, should be temperate and undefiled.

A Fragment of Clinias

EVERY VIRTUE IS PERFECTED, as was shown in the beginning, by reason, deliberate choice, and power. Each of these, however, is by itself not a part of virtue, but its cause. Such, therefore, as have the intellective and gnostic part of virtue [i.e., the contemplative virtues], are called skillful and intelligent; but such as have its ethical and preparatory parts are called useful and equitable. Since, however, man is naturally adapted to act unjustly from exciting causes, these are three: the love of pleasure of corporeal enjoyments, avarice in the accumulation of wealth, and ambition in surpassing equals or fellows. Now it is possible to oppose to these such things as procure fear, shame, or desire in men: fear through the laws, shame through the Gods, and desire through the energies of reason. Hence youth should be taught from the very first to honor the Gods and the laws. Following these, every human work and every kind of human life, by the participation of sanctity and piety, will sail prosperously over the sea [of generation].

SELECT SENTENCES

OF SEXTUS THE PYTHAGOREAN

SHORT ETHICAL SAYINGS were quite popular among the Pythagoreans and the Sentences of Sextus were popular in Christian circles as well. It is possible that the Sentences were compiled in Alexandria in the second century of the common era, since the earliest mention of them is found in the writings of the church father Origin; however, any guess concerning the specific date and locale of their compilation is merely speculation.

For the Greek text and translation of all 451 Sentences, see *The Sentences of Sextus*, edited and translated by Richard A. Edwards and Robert A. Wild, Chico, CA, Scholars Press, 1981.

THE SENTENCES OF SEXTUS

1. To neglect things of the smallest consequence is not the least thing in human life.

2. The sage and the despiser of wealth most resemble God.

3. Do not investigate the name of God because you will not find it. For everything called by a name receives its appelation from that which is more worthy than itself, so that it is one person that calls and another that hears. Who is it, therefore, who has given a name to God? The word "God" is not a name of his, but an indication of what we conceive of him.

4. God is a light incapable of receiving its opposite.

5. You have in yourself something similar to God, and therefore use yourself as the temple of God, on account of that which in you resembles God.

6. Honor God above all things that he may rule over you.

7. Whatever you honor above all things, that which you so honor will have dominion over you.

8. The greatest honor which can be paid to God is to know and imitate him.

9. There is not anything, indeed, which wholly resembles God; nevertheless, the imitation of him as much as possible by an inferior nature is grateful to him.

10. God, indeed, is not in want of anything, but the wise man is in want of God alone. He, therefore, who is in want of but few things, and those necessary, emulates him who is in want of nothing.

11. Endeavor to be great in the estimation of divinity, but among men avoid envy.

12. The sage whose estimation with men was but small while he was living will be renowned when he is dead.

13. Consider lost all the time in which you do not think of divinity.

14. A good intellect is the choir of divinity.

15. A bad intellect is the choir of evil spirits.

16. Honor that which is just on this very account that it is just.

17. You will not be concealed from divinity when you act unjustly, nor even when you think of acting so.

18. The foundation of piety is continence, but the summit of piety is to love God.

19. Wish that what is expedient and not what is pleasing may happen to you.

20. Such as you wish your neighbor to be to you, such also be to your neighbors.

21. That which God gives you none can take away.

22. Neither do nor even think of that which you are unwilling God should know.

23. Before you do anything think of God, that his light may precede your energies.

24. The soul is illuminated by the recollection of God.

25. The use of animal food is indifferent, but it is more rational to abstain from it.

26. God is not the author of any evil.

27. You should not possess more than the use of the body requires.

28. Possess those things that no one can take away from you.

29. Bear that which is necessary, as it is necesary.

30. Ask God of things such as it is worthy of God to bestow.

31. The reason that is in you is the light of your life.

32. Ask from God those things that you cannot receive from man.

33. Wish that those things which labor ought to precede may be possessed by you after labor.

34. Be not anxious to please the multitude.

35. It is not proper to despise those things of which we shall be in want after the dissolution of the body.

36. Do not ask of divinity that which, when you have obtained, you cannot perpetually possess.

37. Accustom your soul after [it has conceived all that is great of] divinity, to conceive something great of itself.

38. Esteem precious nothing which a bad man can take from you.

39. He is dear to divinity who considers those things alone precious which are esteemed to be so by divinity.

40. Everything superfluous is hostile.

41. He who loves that which is not expedient will not love that which is expedient.

42. The intellect of the sage is always with divinity.

43. God dwells in the intellect of the wise man.

44. The wise man is always similar to himself.

45. Every desire is insatiable and therefore is always in want.

46. The knowledge and imitation of divinity are alone sufficient to beatitude.

47. Use lying as poison.

48. Nothing is so peculiar to wisdom as truth.

49. When you preside over men remember that divinity presides over you also.

50. Be persuaded that the end of life is to live conformably to divinity.

51. Depraved affections are the beginnings of sorrows.

52. An evil disposition is the disease of the soul, but injustice and impiety is the death of it.

53. Use all men in a way such as if, after God, you were the common curator of all things.

54. He who uses mankind badly uses himself badly.

55. Wish that you may be able to benefit your enemies.

56. Endure all things in order that you may live conformably to God.

57. By honoring a wise man you will honor yourself.

58. In all your actions keep God before your eyes.

59. You may refuse matrimony in order to live in incessant presence with God. If, however, you know how to fight and are willing to, take a wife and beget children.

60. To live, indeed, is not in our power; but to live rightly is.

61. Be unwilling to entertain accusations against a man studious of wisdom.

62. If you wish to live successfully, you will have to avoid much in which you will come out only second-best.

63. Sweet to you should be any cup that quenches thirst.

64. Fly from intoxication as you would from insanity.

65. No good originates from the body.

66. Estimate that you are suffering a great punishment when you obtain the object of corporeal desire; for desire will never be satisfied with the attainments of any such objects.

67. Invoke God as a witness to whatever you do.

68. The bad man does not think that there is a Providence.

69. Assert that the true man is he in you who possesses wisdom.

70. The wise man participates in God.

71. Wherever that which in you is wise resides, there also is your true good.

72. That which is not harmful to the soul does not harm the man.

73. He who unjustly expels from his body a wise man, by his iniquity confers a benefit on his victim; for he is thus liberated from his bonds.

74. Only through ignorance of his soul is a man saddened by fear of death.

75. You will not possess intellect till you understand that you have it.

76. Realize that your body is the garment of your soul and then you will preserve it pure.

77. Impure daimons let not the impure soul escape them.

78. Not to every man speak of God.

79. There is danger, and no negligible one, to speak of God even the things that are true.

80. A true assertion about God is an assertion of God.

81. You should not dare to speak of God to the multitude.

82. He who does not worship God does not know him.

83. He who is worthy of God is also a God among men.

84. It is better to have nothing than to possess much and impart it to no one.

85. He who thinks that there is a God, and that he protects nothing, is no better than he who does not believe that there is a God.

86. He best honors God who makes his intellect as like God as possible.

87. He who injures none has none to fear.

88. No one who looks down to the earth is wise.

89. To lie is to deceive, and be deceived.

90. Recognize what God is, and that in you which recognizes God.

91. It is not death, but a bad life, which destroys the soul.

92. If you know him by whom you were made, you would know yourself.

93. It is not possible for a man to live conformably to divinity unless he acts modestly, well and justly.

94. Divine wisdom is true science.

95. You should not dare to speak of God to an impure soul.

96. The wise man follows God, and God follows the soul of the wise man.

97. A king rejoices in those he governs, and therefore God rejoices in the wise man. He who governs likewise is inseparable from those he governs; and therefore God is inseparable from the soul of the wise man, which he defends and governs.

98. The wise man is governed by God, and on this account is blessed.

99. A scientific knowledge of God causes a man to use but few words.

100. To use many words in speaking of God obscures the subject.

101. The man who possesses a knowledge of God will not be very ambitious.

102. The erudite, chaste and wise soul is the prophet of the truth of God.

103. Accustom yourself always to look to the Divinity.

104. A wise intellect is the mirror of God.

SELECT PYTHAGOREAN SENTENCES

1. From the Exhortation to Philosophy of Iamblichus

105. As we live through soul, it must be said that by the virtue of this we do live well; just as because we see through the eyes, we see well through their virtues.

106. It must not be thought that gold can be injured by rust, or virtue by baseness.

107. We should betake ourselves to virtue as to an inviolable temple, so that we may not be exposed to any ignoble insolence of soul with respect to our communion with, and continuance in life.

108. We should confide in virtue as in a chaste wife, but trust to fortune as an inconstant mistress.

109. It is better that virtue should be received accompanied by poverty, than wealth with violence; and frugality with health, than voractiy with disease.

110. An overabundance of food is harmful to the body, but the body is preserved when the soul is disposed in a becoming manner.

111. It is as dangerous to give power to a depraved man as it is to give a sword to a madman.

112. As it is better for a part of the body that contains purulent decay to be burned than to continue as it is, thus also is it better for a depraved man to die than to continue to live.

113. The theorems of philosophy are to be enjoyed as much as possible, as if they were ambrosia and nectar. For the resultant pleasure is genuine, incorruptible and divine. They are also capable of producing magnanimity, and though they cannot make us eternal, yet they enable us to obtain a scientific knowledge of eternal natures.

114. If vigor of sensation is, as it is, considered to be desirable, so much more strenuously should we endeavor to obtain prudence; for it is, as it were, the sensitive vigor of the practical intellect, which we contain. And as through the former we are not deceived in sensible perceptions, so through the latter we avoid false reasonings in practical affairs.

115. We shall properly venerate Divinity if we purify our intellect from vice as from a stain.

116. A temple should, indeed, be adorned with gifts, but the soul with disciplines.

117. As the lesser mysteries are to be delivered before the greater, thus also discipline must precede philosophy.

118. The fruits of the earth, indeed, appear annually, but the fruits of philosophy ripen at all seasons.

119. As he who wishes the best fruit must pay most attention to the land, so must the greatest attention be paid to the soul if it is to produce fruits worthy of its nature.

2. From Stobaeus

120. Do not even think of doing what ought not to be done.

121. Choose rather to be strong in soul than in body.

122. Be sure that laborious things contribute to virtue more than do pleasurable things.

123. Every passion of the soul is most hostile to its salvation.

124. Pythagoras said that it is most difficult simultaneously to walk in many paths of life.

125. Pythagoras said that we must choose the best life, for custom will make it pleasant. Wealth is a weak anchor, glory still weaker, and similarly with the body, dominion, and honor. Which anchors are strong? Prudence, magnanimity and fortitude; these can be shaken by no tempest. This is the law of God: that virtue is the only thing strong, all else is a trifle.

126. All the parts of human life, just as those of a statue, should be beautiful.

127. As a statue stands immovable on its pedestal, so should stand a man on his deliberate choice, if he is worthy.

128. Incense is for the Gods, but praise for good men.

129. Men unfairly accused of acting unjustly should be defended, while those who excel should be praised.

130. It is not the sumptuous adornment of the horse that earns him praise, but rather the nature of the horse himself; nor is the man worthy merely because he owns great wealth, but rather because his soul is generous.

131. When the wise man opens his mouth the beauties of his soul present themselves to view as the statues in a temple.

132. Remind yourself that all men assert wisdom is the greatest good, but that there are few who strenuously endeavor to obtain this greatest good. —Pythagoras.

133. Be sober, and remember to be disposed to believe, for these are the nerves of wisdom. —Epicharmus.

134. It is better to live lying on the grass, confiding in divinity and yourself, than to lie on a golden bed with perturbation.

135. You will not be in want of anything, which is in the power of Fortune to give or take away. —Pythagoras.

136. Despise all those things which you will not want when liberated from the body; and exercising yourself in those things of which you will be in want when liberated from the body, be sure to invoke the Gods to become your helpers. — Pythagoras.

137. It is as impossible to conceal fire in a garment as a base deviation from rectitude in time. —Demophilus, rather than Socrates.

138. Wind increases fire, but custom increases love. —Demophilus, rather than Socrates.

139. Only those are dear to divinity who are hostile to injustice. —Democritus or Demophilus.

140. Bodily necessities are easily procured by anybody without labor or molestation; but those things whose attainment demands effort and trouble are objects of desire not to the body, but to depraved opinion. —Aristoxenus the Pythagorean.

141. Thus spoke Pythagoras of desire: This passion is various, laborious and very multiform. Of desires, however, some are acquired and artificial, while others are inborn. Desire is a certain tendency and impulse of the soul, and an appetite of fullness, or presence of sense, or of an emptiness and absence of it, and of non-perception. The three best known kinds of depraved desire are the improper, the unproportionate, and the unseasonable. For desire is either immediately indecorous, troublesome or illiberal; or if not absolutely so, it is improperly vehement and persistent. Or, in the third place, it is impelled at an improper time, or towards improper objects. —Aristoxenus.

142. Pythagoras said: Endeavor not to conceal your errors by words, but to remedy them by reproofs.

143. Pythagoras said: It is not so difficult to err, as not to reprove him who errs.

144. As a bodily disease cannot be healed, if it is concealed or praised, thus also can neither a remedy be applied to a diseased soul which is badly guarded and protected. —Pythagoras.

145. The grace of freedom of speech, like beauty in season, is productive of great delight.

146. To have a blunt sword is as improper as to use ineffectual freedom of speech.

147. Neither is the sun to be taken from the world, nor freedom of speech from erudition.

148. As one who is clothed with a cheap robe may have a good habit of body, thus also may he whose life is poor possess freedom of speech.

149. Pythagoras said: Prefer those that reprove to those that flatter; but avoid flatterers as much as enemies.

150. The life of the avaricious resembles a funeral banquet. For though it has all desirable elements no one rejoices.

151. Pythagoras said: Acquire continence as the greatest strength and wealth.

152. "Not frequently man from man," is one of the exhortations of Pythagoras, by which obscurely he signifies that it is not proper frequently to engage sexual connections.

153. Pythagoras said: A slave to his passions cannot possibly be free.

154. Pythagoras said that intoxication is the preparation for insanity.

155. On being asked how a wine-lover might be cured of intoxication Pythagoras said, "If he frequently considers what were his actions during intoxication."

156. Pythagoras said that unless you had something better than silence to say, you had better keep silence.

157. Pythagoras said that rather than utter an idle word you had better throw a stone in vain.

158. Pythagoras said, "Say not few things in many words, but much in few words."

159. Epicharmus said, "To men genius is a divinity, either good or evil."

160. On being asked how a man ought to behave towards his country when it had acted unjustly towards him, Pythagoras said, "As to a mother."

161. Traveling teaches a man frugality and self-sufficiency. The sweetest remedies for hunger and weariness are bread made of milk and flour, on a bed

of grass. —Attributed to Democritus, but probably Democrates or Demophilus.

162. Every land is equally suitable as a residence for the wise man; the worthy soul's fatherland is the whole world. *Ibid.*

163. Pythagoras said that into cities enter first, luxury; then being glutted; then lascivious insolence; and last, destruction.

164. Pythagoras said that the best city was that which contained the worthiest man.

165. "You should do those things that you judge to be beautiful, though in doing them you should lack renown, for the rabble is a bad judge of a good thing. Wherefore despise the reprehension of those whose praise you despise." — Pythagoras.

166. Pythagoras said that "Those who do not punish bad men are really wishing that good men be injured."

167. Pythagoras said, "Not without a bridle can a horse be governed, and no less riches without prudence."

168. The prosperous man who is vain is no better than the driver of a race on a slippery road. —Attributed to Socrates, but probably Democrates or Demophilus.

169. There is not any gate of wealth so secure which the opportunity of Fortune may not open. —Attributed to Democritus, but probably Democrates or Demophilus.

170. The unrestrained grief of a torpid soul may be expelled by reasoning. — Democrates, not Democritus.

171. Poverty should be born with equanimity by a wise man. —Democrates, not Democritus.

172. Pythagoras said: Spare your life, lest you consume it with sorrow and care.

173. Favorinus, in speaking of old age, said, "Nor will I be silent as to this particular, that both to Plato and Pythagoras it appeared that old age was not to be considered with reference to an egress from the present life, but to the beginning of a blessed one."

3. From Clement of Alexandria, Stromateis, Book 3.

174. Philolaus said that the ancient theologians and priests testified that the soul is united to the body as through a certain punishment, and that it is buried in this body as a sepulchre.

175. Pythagoras said that "Whatever we see when awake is death, and when asleep is a dream."

THE ETHICAL FRAGMENTS

OF HIEROCLES

HIEROCLES was a Neoplatonic philosopher of Alexandria during the fifth century of the common era. His *Commentaries on the Golden Verses of Pythagoras* survives intact, and fragments remain of a treatise *On Providence, Fate and Free Will*. The ethical fragments assembled here are preserved by Stobaeus.

The only thing known about his life is an anecdote preserved by Suidas. In the same way that some Romans mistreated the early Christians, so too did later Christians abuse others who did not share their faith. The story preserved by Suidas demonstrates that Hierocles maintained an admirable sense of humor even under the most adverse conditions: upon arriving in Byzantium he seems to have offended certain Christians and was therefore whipped in the presence of a Christian magistrate. Taking some of his blood into the cup of his hand, Hierocles sprinkled the judge with it, quoting the lines from the *Odyssey*: "Cyclops, since human flesh is thy delight / Now drink this wine."

As the following fragments and his *Commentaries* aptly demonstrate, Hierocles was greatly gifted as a writer and was especially adept in the realm of ethical matters. For a study of his thought see *Le Néo-Platonisme Alexandrin: Hieroclès d'Alexandre*, Leiden, E.J. Brill, 1987.

THE ETHICAL FRAGMENTS OF HIEROCLES

1. On How We Ought to Conduct Ourselves Towards the Gods

CONCERNING THE GODS we should assume that they are immutable and do not change their decrees; from the very beginning they never vary their conceptions of propriety. The immutability and firmness of the virtues we know, and reason suggests that it must transcendently be so with the Gods, and be the element which to their conceptions imparts a never-failing stability. Evidently no punishment which divinity thinks proper to inflict is likely to be remitted. For if the Gods changed their decisions, and omitted to punish someone whom they had designed to punish, the world could be neither beautifully nor justly governed; nor can we assign any probable reason for repentance on their part. Rashly, indeed, and without any reason, have poets written words such as the following:

> Men bend the Gods, by incense and libation,
> By gentle vows, and sacrifice and prayer,
> When they transgress, and stray from what is right!
> (Homer, *Iliad*, ix. 495-7)

And:

> Flexible are e'en the Gods themselves!
> (*ibid.*, verse 493)

Nor is this the only expression in poetry.

Nor must we omit to observe, that though the Gods are not the causes of evil, yet they connect certain persons with things of this kind, and surround those who deserve to be afflicted with corporeal and external hindrances; not through any malignity, or because they think it advisable that men should struggle with difficulties, but for the sake of punishment. For as in general pestilence and drought, rain storms, earthquakes and the like, are indeed for the most part produced by natural causes, yet they are sometimes caused by the Gods when the times are such that the multitude's iniquity needs to be punished publicly and in common; likewise the Gods sometimes afflict an individual with corporeal and external difficulties, in order to punish him and convert others to what is right.

The belief that the Gods are never the cause of any evil, it seems to me, contributes greatly to proper conduct towards the Gods. For evils proceed from vice alone, while the Gods are of themselves the causes of good, and of any advantage, though in the meantime we slight their beneficence, and surround ourselves with voluntary evils. That is why I agree with the poet who says,

> ————that mortals blame the Gods

as if they were the causes of their evils!

> ————though not from fate,
> But for their crimes they suffer woe!
> (Homer, *Odyssey,* i. 32-34)

Many arguments prove that God is never in any way the cause of evil, but it will suffice to read [in the first book of the *Republic*] the words of Plato "that as it is not the nature of heat to refrigerate, so the beneficent cannot harm; but the contrary." Moreover, God being good, and from the beginning replete with every virtue, cannot harm nor cause evil to anyone; on the contrary, he imparts good to all willing to receive it, bestowing on us also such indifferent things as flow from nature, and which result in accordance with nature. But there is only one cause of evil.

2. On How We Ought to Conduct Ourselves Towards Our Country

AFTER SPEAKING OF THE GODS it is most reasonable, in the second place, to show how we should conduct ourselves towards our country. For God is my witness that our country is a sort of secondary divinity, and our first and greatest parent. That is why its name is, for good reason, *patris,* derived from *pater,* a father, but taking a feminine termination, to be as it were a mixture of *father and mother.* This also explains that our country should be honored equally with our parents, preferring it to either of them separately, and not even to it preferring both of our parents; preferring it besides to our wife, children and friends, and in short to all things, under the Gods.

He who would esteem one finger more than five would be considered stupid, inasmuch as it is reasonable to prefer five to one; the former despising the most desirable, while the latter among the five preserves also the one finger. Likewise, he who prefers to save himself rather than his country, in addition to acting unlawfully, desires an impossibility. On the contrary, he who to himself prefers his country is dear to divinity and reasons properly and irrefutably. Moreover it has been observed that though someone should not be a member of an organized society, remaining apart therefrom, yet it it proper that he should prefer the safety of society to his own; for the city's destruction would demonstrate that on its existence depended that of the individual citizen, just as the amputation of the hand involves the destruction of the finger as an integral part. We may therefore draw the general conclusion that general utility cannot be separated from private welfare, both at bottom being identical. For whatever is beneficial to the whole country is common to every single part, inasmuch as without the parts the whole is nothing. Vice versa, whatever rebounds to the benefit of the citizen extends also to the city, the nature of which is to extend benefits to the citizen. For example, whatever is beneficial to a dancer must, in so far as he is a dancer, be so also to the whole choric ballet. Applying this reasoning to the discursive power of the soul, it will shed light on every particular duty, and we shall never omit to perform whatever may by us be due to our country.

That is the reason why a man who proposes to act honorably by his country should from his soul remove every passion and disease. The laws of his country should, by a citizen, be observed as precepts of a secondary divinity, conforming himself entirely to their mandates. He who endeavors to transgress or make any innovation in these laws should be opposed in every way, and be prevented therefrom in every possible way. By no means beneficial to the city is contempt of existing laws and preference for the new. Incurable innovators, therefore, should be restrained from giving their votes, and making hasty innovations. I therefore commend the legislator Zaleucus of Locri, who ordained that he who intended to introduce a new law should do it with a rope around his neck, in order that he might be immediately strangled unless he succeeded in changing the ancient constitution of the state to the very great advantage of the community.

But customs which are truly those of the country and which, perhaps, are more ancient than the laws themselves, are, no less than the laws, to be preserved. However, the customs of the present, which are but of yesterday, and which have been everywhere introduced only so very recently, are not to be dignified as the institutes of our ancestors, and perhaps they are not even to be considered as customs at all.* Moreover, because custom is an unwritten law, it has as sanction the authority of a very good legislator, namely common consent of all that use it, and perhaps on this account its authority is next to that of justice itself.

3. On Proper Conduct Towards Our Parents

AFTER CONSIDERING THE GODS AND OUR COUNTRY, what person deserves to be mentioned more than, or prior to our parents? That is why we turn towards them. No mistake, therefore, will be made by him who says that they are as it were secondary or terrestrial divinities, since, on account of their proximity they should, in a certain non-blasphemous sense, be by us more honored

---

* Hierocles is referring to the innovations of the Christians.

than the Gods themselves. To begin with, the only gratitude worthy of the name is a perpetual and unremitting promptness to repay the benefits received from them, since, though we do our very utmost, this would yet fall short of what they deserve. Moreover, we might also say that in one sense our deeds are to be counted as theirs, because we who perform them were once produced by them. If, for instance, the works of Phidias and other artists should themselves produce other works of art, we should not hesitate to attribute these latter deeds also to the original artists; that is why we may justly say that our performances are the deeds of our parents, through whom we originally derived our existence.

In order that we may the more easily apprehend the duties we owe them, we should keep in mind the underlying principle that our parents should by us be considered as the images of the Gods, and, by Zeus, images of the domestic Gods, who are our benefactors, our relatives, our creditors, our lords, and our most stable friends. They are indeed most stable images of the Gods, possessing a likeness to them which no artist could possibly surpass. They are the guardian divinities of the home, and live with us; they are our greatest benefactors, endowing us with benefits of the greatest consequence, and indeed bestowing on us not only all we possess, but also such things as they wish to give us, and for which they themselves pray. Further they are our nearest kindred, and the causes of our alliance with others. They are also creditors of things of the most honorable nature and repay themselves only by taking what we shall be benefited by returning. For to a child what benefit can be so great as piety and gratitude to his parents? Most justly, too, are they our lords, for of what can we be the possession of in a greater degree than of those through whom we exist? Moreover, they are perpetual and spontaneous friends and auxiliaries, affording us assistance at all times and in every circumstance. Since, besides, the name of parent is the most excellent of names which we apply even to the divinities, we may add something to this conception: namely, that children should be persuaded that they dwell in their father's house, as if they were ministers and priests in a temple, appointed and consecrated for this purpose by nature herself, who entrusted to their care a reverential attention to their parents. If we are willing to carry out the dictates of reason we shall readily attend to both kinds of affective regard, for both the body and the soul. Yet reason will show us that to the body is to be paid less regard than to the soul, although we shall not neglect the former very necessary duties. For our parents, therefore, we should obtain liberal food, and such as is adequate to the weakness of old age; besides this, a bed, sleep, massage, a bath, and proper garments, in short, the necessities of the body, that they may at no time experience the want of any of these, by this imitating their care for the nurture of ourselves when we were infants. Our attention to them should partake of the prophetic nature, whereby we may discover what special bodily necessity that they may be longing for without expressing it to us. Respecting us, indeed, they divined many things when our desires could be expressed by no more than inarticulate and distressful cries, unable to express the objects of our wants clearly. By the benefits they formerly conferred upon us, our parents became to us the preceptors of what we ought to bestow upon them.

With respect to our parents' souls, we should in the first place procure for them diversion, which will be obtained especially if we associate with them by night and day, taking walks, being massaged, and living by their side, unless something necessary interferes. For just as those who are undertaking a long journey desire the presence of their families and friends to see them off, as if accompanying a solemn procession, so also parents, verging on the grave, enjoy most of all the diligent and unremitting attention of their children. Moreover, should our parents at any time, as happens often, especially with those whose education was deficient, display conduct which is reprehensible, they should indeed be corrected, but not as we are accustomed to do with our inferiors or equals, but as it were with suggestiveness—not as if they had erred through ignorance, but as if they had committed an oversight through inattention, as if they would not have erred had they considered the matter. For reproof, especially if personal, is to the old very bitter. That is why their oversights should be supplemented by mild exhortation, as by an elegant artifice.

Children, besides, cause their parents to rejoice by performing for them servile offices such as washing their feet, making their bed, or ministering to their wants. These necessary servile attentions are all the more precious when performed by the dear hands of their children, accepting their ministrations. Parents will be especially gratified when their children publicly show their honor to those whom they love and very much esteem.

That is why children should affectionately love their parents' kindred and pay them proper attention, as also to their parents' friends and acquaintances. These general principles will aid us to deduce many other smaller filial duties which are neither unimportant nor accidental. For since our parents are gratified by the attention we pay to those they love, it will be evident that as we are in a most eminent degree beloved by our parents, we shall surely much please them by paying a proper attention to ourselves.

4. On Fraternal Love

THE FIRST ADMONITION, therefore, is very clear and convincing, and generally obligatory, being sane and self-evident. Here it is: Act by everyone in the same manner as if you supposed yourself to be him, and him to be you. A servant will be well treated by one who considers how he would like to be treated by him if he was the master, and himself the servant. The same principle might be applied between parents and children, and vice versa, and, in short, between all men. This principle, however, is peculiarly adapted to the mutual relation of brothers, since no other preliminary considerations are necessary, in the matter of conduct towards one's brother, than promptly to assume that equitable mutual relation. This therefore is the first precept, to act toward one's brother in the same manner in which he would think it proper for his brother to act towards him.

But someone will say, by Zeus, I do not transgress propriety and am equitable, but my brother's manners are rough and brusque. This is not right for, in the first place, he may not be speaking the truth, as excessive vanity might lead a man to extol and magnify his own manners and diminish and vilify what pertains to others. It frequently happens, indeed, that men of inferior worth prefer themselves to others who are far more excellent characters. Second, though the brother should indeed be of the rough character mentioned above, the course to take would be to prove oneself the better character by vanquishing his rusticity by your beneficence. Those who conduct themselves worthily towards moderate, gracious men are entitled to no great thanks; but to transform to graciousness the stupid vulgar man, he deserves the greatest applause.

It must not be thought impossible for exhortation to take marked effect, for in men of the most impossible manners there are possibilities of improvement, and of love and honor for their benefactors. Not even animals, and such as naturally are the most hostile to our race, who are captured by violence and dragged off in chains, and confined in cages, are beyond being tamed by appropriate treatment and daily food. Will not then the man who is a brother, or even the first man you meet, who deserves attention far greater than a beast, be rendered gentle by proper treatment, even though he should never entirely lose his boorishness? In our behavior, therefore, towards every man, and in a much greater degree towards our brother, we should imitate Socrates who, to a person who cried out against him, "May I die, unless I am revenged on you," answered, "May I die if I do not make you my friend!" So much then for external, fraternal relations.

Further, a man should consider that in a certain sense his brothers are part of him, just as my eyes are part of me; also my legs, my hands, and other parts of me. So are the relations of brother to a family social organism. If then the eyes and the hands should receive a particular soul and intellect, they would because of the above mentioned communion, and because they could not perform their proper offices without the presence of the other members who watch over the interests of the other members with the interest of a guardian spirit. So also, we who are men and who acknowledge that we have a soul should, towards our brothers, omit no proper offices. Indeed, more naturally adapted for mutual assistance than parts of the body are brothers. The eyes, being mutually adjusted, do see what is before them, and one hand cooperates with the other, but the mutual adaptation of brothers is far more various. For they accomplish things which are mutually profitable, though at the greatest intervening distance; and they will greatly benefit each other though their mutual differences be immeasurable. In short, it must be recognized that our life resembles nothing so much as a prolonged conflict which arises partly from the natural strife in the nature of things, and partly through the sudden unexpected blows of fortune, but most of all through vice itself, which abstains neither from violence, fraud, nor evil strategems. Hence nature, as not being ignorant of the purpose for which she generated us, produced each of us, as it were, accompanied by an auxiliary.

No one, therefore, is alone, nor does he derive his origin from an oak or a rock, but from parents, in conjunction with brothers, relatives, and other intimates. Here reason for us performs a great work, conciliating us to strangers who are no relatives of ours, furnishing us with many assistants. That is the very reason why we naturally endeavor to allure and make everyone our friend. How insane a thing it therefore is to wish to be united to those who naturally have nothing suitable to procure our love, and become as familiar as possible with them voluntarily, and yet neglect those willing helpers and associates supplied by nature herself, who are called brothers!

5. *On Marriage*

THE DISCUSSION OF MARRIAGE is most necessary as the whole of our race is naturally social, and the most fundamental social association is that effected by marriage. Without a household there could be no cities; and households of the unmarried are most imperfect, while on the contrary those of the married are most complete. That is why, in our treátise *On Families,* we have shown that the married state is to be preferred by the sage, while a single life is not to be chosen except under peculiar circumstances. Therefore, inasmuch as we should imitate the man of intellect so far as possible, and as for him marriage is preferable, it is evident it will be so also for us, except if hindered by some exceptional circumstance. This is the first reason for marriage.

Entirely apart from the model of the sage, Nature herself seems to incite us thereto. Not only did she make us gregarious, but adapted to sexual intercourse, and proposed the procreation of children and stability of life as the one and universal work of wedlock. Now Nature justly teaches us that a choice of such things as are fit should be made so as to accord with what she has procured for us. Every animal, therefore, lives in conformity to its natural constitution, and so also every plant lives in harmony with its laws of life. But there exists this difference, that the latter do not employ any reasoning or calculation in the selection of the things on which they lay hold, using nature along without participation in [rational] soul. Animals are drawn to investigate what may be proper for them by imagination and desires. To us, however, Nature gave reason to survey everything else and, together with all things—nay, prior to all things—to direct its attention to Nature itself, so as to tend towards her as a glorious aim, in an orderly manner, that by choosing everything consonant with her, we might live in a becoming manner. Following this line of argument, he will not error in saying that a family without wedlock is imperfect, for nature does not conceive of the governor without the governed, nor of the governed without a governor. Nature therefore seems to me to shame those who are adverse to marriage.

In the next place, marriage is beneficial. First, because it produces a truly divine fruit, the procreation of children who are, as partaking of our nature, to assist us in all our undertakings while our strength is yet undiminished; and when we shall be worn out, oppressed with old age, they will be our assistants. In prosperity they will be the associates of our joy and, in adversity, the sympathetic diminishers of our sorrows.

Marriage is beneficial not only because of procreation of children, but for the association of a wife. When we are wearied with our labors outside of the home, she receives us with officious kindness and refreshes us by her solicitous attentions. Next, she induces a forgetfulness of molestations outside of the house. The annoyances in the forum, the gymnasium, or the country, and in short all the vicissitudes of our intercourse with friends and acquaintances, do not disturb us so obviously, being obscured by our necessary occupations; but when released from these, we return home, and our mind has time to reflect, then availing themselves of this opportunity these cares and anxieties rush in upon us, to torment us, at the very moment when life seems cheerless and lonely. Then comes the wife as a great solace and, by making some inquiry about external affairs, or by referring to and together considering some domestic problem, she, by her sincere vivacity inspires him with pleasure and delight. It is needless to enumerate all the help a wife can be in festivals, when making sacrifice; or, during her husband's journeys, she can keep the household running smoothly, and direct at times of urgency; or in managing the domestics and in nursing her husband when sick.

In summary: in order to pass through life properly, all men need two things—the aid of relatives, and kindly sympathy. But nothing can be more sympathetic than a wife, nor anything more kindred than children. Both of these are afforded by marriage; how therefore could be found anything more beneficial?

Also beautiful is a married life, it seems to me. What relation can be more ornamental to a family that that between husband and wife? Not sumptuous edifices, nor walls covered with marble plaster, nor piazzas adorned with stones, which indeed are admired by those ignorant of true goods; nor paintings and arched myrtle walks, nor anything else which is the subject of astonishment to the stupid, is the ornament of a family. The beauty of a household consists in the conjunction of man and wife, united to each other by destiny, and consecrated to the Gods presiding over nuptial birth and houses, and who harmonize, and use all things in common for their bodies, or even their very souls; who likewise exercise a becoming authority over their house and servants; who are properly solicitous about the education of their children; and to the necessities of life pay an attention which is neither excessive nor negligent, but moderate and appropriate. For, as the the most admirable Homer says, what can be more excellent

> Than when at home the husband and wife
> Live in entire unanimity.
> *(Odyssey,* 7. 183).

That is the reason why I have frequently wondered at those who conceive that life in common with a woman must be burdensome and grievous. Though to them she appears to be a burden and molestation, she is not so; on the contary, she is something light and easy to be borne or, rather, she possesses the power of charming away from her husband things burdensome and grievous. No trouble so great is there which cannot easily be borne by a husband and wife who harmonize and are willing to endure it in common. But what is truly burdensome and unbearable is impudence, for through it things naturally light, and among others a wife, become heavy.

To many, indeed, marriage is intolerable, in reality not from itself, or because such an association as this with a woman is naturally insufferable, but when we marry the wrong person and, in addition to this, are ourselves entirely ignorant of life, and unprepared to take a wife in such a way as a free-born woman ought to be taken, then indeed it happens that this association with her becomes difficult and intolerable. Vulgar people do marry in this way, taking a wife neither for the procreation of children, nor for harmonious association, being attracted to the union by the magnitude of the dowry, or through physical attractiveness, or the like; and by following these bad counsellors, they pay no attention to the bride's disposition and manners, celebrating nuptials to their own destruction, and with crowned doors introduce to themselves instead of a wife a tyrant, whom they cannot resist, and with whom they are unable to contend for chief authority.

Evidently, therefore, marriage becomes burdensome and intolerable to many, not through itself, but through these causes. But it is not wise to blame things which are not harmful, nor to make our own deficient use of these things the cause of our complaint against them. Most absurd, besides, is it feverishly to seek the auxiliaries of friendship, and achieve certain friends and associates to aid and defend us in the vicissitudes of life, without seeking and endeavoring to obtain the relief, defence and assistance afforded us by Nature, by the Gods, and by the laws, through a wife and children.

As to a numerous offspring, it is generally suitable to nature and marriage that all, or the majority of the offspring be nurtured. Many dissent from this, for a not very beautiful reason, through love of riches, and the fear of poverty as the greatest evil. To begin with, in procreating children we are not only begetting assistants, nurses for our old age, and associates in every vicissitude of life—we do not however beget them for ourselves alone, but in many ways also for our parents. To them our procreation of children is gratifying because, if we should suffer anything calamitous prior to their decease we shall, instead of ourselves, leave our children as the support of their old age. Then for a grandfather is it a beautiful thing to be conducted by the hands of his grandchildren, and by them to be considered worthy of every attention. Hence, in the first place, we shall gratify our own parents by paying attention to the procreation of children. In the next, we shall be cooperating with the ardent wishes and fervent prayers of those who begot us. They were solicitous about our birth from the first, thereby looking for an extended succession of themselves, that they should leave behind them children of children, therefore paying attention to our marriage, procreation and nurture. Hence, by marrying and begetting children we shall be, as it were, fulfilling a part of their prayers; while, acting contrarily, we shall be destroying the object of their deliberate choice.

Moreover, it would seem that everyone who voluntarily, and without some prohibiting circumstance avoids marriage and the procreation of children, accuses his parents of madness, as having engaged in wedlock without the right conception of things. Here we see an unavoidable contradiction. How could that man live without dissension who finds a pleasure in living and willingly continues in life, as one who was properly brought into existence by his parents, and yet conceives that for him procreation of offspring is something to be rejected?

We must remember that we beget children not only for our own sake but, as we have already stated, for our parents'; but further also for the sake of our friends and kindred. It is gratifying to see children which are our offspring on account of human kindness, relatives, and security. Like ships which, though greatly agitated by the waves, are secured by many anchors, so do those who have children, or whose friends or relatives have them, ride at anchor in port in absolute security. For this reason, then, will a man who is a lover of his kindred and associates earnestly desire to marry and beget children.

Our country also loudly calls upon us to do so. For after all we do not beget children so much for ourselves as for our country, procuring a race that may follow us, and supplying the community with successors to ourselves. Hence the priest should realize that to the city he owes priests; the ruler, that he owes rulers; the orator, that he owes orators; and in short, the citizen, that he owes citizens. So it is gratifying to those who compose a choric ballet that it should continue perennially; and as an army looks to the continuance of its soldiers, so the perpetuation of its citizens is a matter of concern to a city. A city would not need succession were it only a temporary grouping, of duration commensurate with the lifetime of any one man; but as it extends to many generations, and if it invokes a fortunate genius may endure for many ages, it is evidently necessary to direct its attention not only to its present, but also to its future, not despising our native soil, nor leaving it desolate, but establishing it in good hopes from our prosperity.

6. On Conduct Towards Our Relatives

DUTIES TO RELATIVES depend on duties to our immediate families, the arguments of which apply also to the former. Each of us is, indeed, as it were circumscribed by many circles, larger and smaller, comprehending and comprehended, according to various mutual circumstances.

The first and nearest circle is that which everyone describes about the center of his own mind, wherein is comprehended the body and all its interests; this is the smallest circle, nearly touching the center itself. The second and further circle which comprehends the first is that which includes parents, brethren, wife and children. The third greater circle is the one containing uncles, aunts, grandfathers and grandmothers, and the children of brothers and sisters. Beyond this is the circle containing the remaining relatives. Next to this is the circle containing the common people, then that which comprehends our tribe, then that of all the citizens; then follow two further circles: that of the neighboring suburbs, and those of the province. The outermost and greatest circle is that which comprehends the whole human race.

In view of this, he who strives to conduct himself properly in each of these connections should, in a certain respect, gather together the circles into one center, and always endeavor to transfer himself from the comprehending circles to the several particulars to which they comprehend.

The lover of his kindred, therefore, should conduct himself in a becoming manner towards his parents and brother; also, according to the same analogy, towards the more elderly of his relatives of both sexes, such as grandfathers, uncles and aunts; towards those of the same age as himself, as his cousins; and towards his juniors, as the children of his cousins. This summarizes his conduct towards his kindred, having already shown how he should act towards himself, toward his parents and brothers, and besides these, toward wife and children. To which must be added that those who belong to the third circle should be honored similarly to these, and again, kindred similarly to those that belong to the third circle. For benevolence must somehow fade away from those who are more distant from us by blood, though at the same time we should endeavor to effect a mutual assimilation. This distance will moderate if through the diligent attention which we pay to them we shorten the bond connecting us with each. Such then are the most comprehensive duties towards our kindred.

It might be well to say a word about the general names of kindred, such as the calling of cousins, uncles and aunts by the names of brothers, fathers and mothers; while of the other kindred, to call some uncles, others the children of brothers and sisters, and others cousins, according to the difference in age, for the sake of the emotional extension derivable from names. This mode of appellation will manifest our sedulous attention to these relatives, and at the same time, will incite and extend us in a greater degree to the contraction of the above circles.

We should however remember the distinction between parents that we made above. Comparing parents, we said that to mother was due more love, but to the father more honor. Similarly, we should show more love to those connected with us by a maternal alliance, but more honor to those connected with us by an alliance that is paternal.

7. On Economics*

TO BEGIN WITH, we must mention the kind of labor which preserves the union of the father. To the husband are usually assigned rural, forensic and political activities, while to the mother belong spinning of wool, making of bread, cooking, and in short, everything of a domestic nature. Nevertheless, neither should be entirely exempt from the labors of the other. For sometimes it will be proper, when the wife is in the country, that she should superintend the laborers and act as master of the household; and that the husband should sometimes attend to domestic affairs, inquiring about and inspecting what is doing in the house. This joint participation of necessary cares will more firmly unite their mutual association.

We should not fail to mention the manual operations which are associated with the spheres of occupations. Why should the man meddle with agricultural labors? This is generally admitted, and though men of the present day spend much time in idleness and luxury, yet it is rare to find any unwilling to engage in the labor of sowing and planting, and other agricultural pusuits. Much less persuasive perhaps will be the arguments which invite the man to engage in those other occupations that belong to the woman. For such men as pay little attention to neatness and cleanliness will not conceive wool-spinning to be their business since, for the most part, vile diminutive men, delicate and effeminate, apply themselves to the elaboration of wool, through an emulation of feminine softness. But it does not become a man who is manly to apply himself to things of this kind, so perhaps neither shall I advise such employments to those who have not unmistakably demonstrated their modesty and virility. What therefore should hinder the man from sharing in the labors pertaining to a woman, whose past life has been such as to free him from all suspicion of absurd and effeminate conduct? For is it not thought that more domestic labors pertain to man than to women in other fields? For they are more laborious, and require corporeal strength such as to grind, to knead meal, to cut wood, to draw water from a well, to carry large vessels from one place to another, to shake coverlets and carpets and the like. It will

---

* The word "economy" is derived from *oikos* (house) and *nomos* (law).

be quite proper for men to engage in such occupations.

But it would be well if the legitimate work of a woman be enlarged in other directions so that she may not only engage with her maid-servants in the spinning of wool, but may also apply herself to other more virile occupations. It seems to me that bread-making, drawing water from a well, the lighting of fires, the making of beds, and such like are labors suited to a free-born woman.

But to her husband a wife will seem much more beautiful, especially if she is young, and not yet worn out by the bearing of children, if she becomes his associate in the gathering of grapes and collecting the olives; and if he is verging toward old age, she will render herself more pleasing to him by sharing with him the labor of sowing and plowing, and while he is digging or planting, extending to him the instruments he needs for his work. For when by the husband and wife a family is governed thus, in respect to necessary labors, it seems to me that it will be conducted in the best possible manner.

TIMAEUS OF LOCRI:

ON THE WORLD AND THE SOUL

TIMAEUS OF LOCRI is the central character of Plato's dialogue dealing with Pythagorean cosmology but it is uncertain whether or not there ever actually was a Timaeus of Locri who was a Pythagorean.

This particular writing may have gone through several stages of composition. It started out as an epitome of the cosmology of the Platonic dialogue. However, certain important details are not adequately treated and, in general, the cosmology is reduced to a series of statements while the underlying explanations and reasonings are omitted. At this stage the writing could well have been a summary of a student, and it seems likely that the attribution of the writing to Timaeus was added at a later date. Also added at a later date was a table of tone numbers which relate to the division of the world soul.

The best translation of this work is that of Thomas Tobin, published by Scholars Press in 1985, which features a good introduction and extensive notes. Tobin argues persuasively that this work may be seen as a Middle Platonic interpretation of the *Timaeus*; hence it was probably composed in the first century of, or before, the common era.

While Plato's *Timaeus* constitutes essential reading for anyone interested in Pythagorean cosmology, the writing reproduced here possesses more significance for the history of Middle Platonism than it does for the study of Pythagorean thought.

ON THE WORLD AND THE SOUL

1. Mind, Necessity, Form and Matter

TIMAEUS OF LOCRI said the following:

Of all the things in the universe there are two causes: Mind, of things existing according to reason; and Necessity, of things [existing] by force, according to the power of bodies. The former of these causes is the nature of the good, and is called God, and the principle of things that are best, but what accessory causes follow are referred to Necessity. Regarding the things in the universe, there exist Form, Matter and the Perceptible which is, as it were, an offspring of the two others. Form is unproduced, unmoved, stationary, of the nature of the Same, perceptible by the mind, and a pattern of such things produced as exist by a state of change: that is what Form is said to be.

Matter, however, is a recipient of impressions, is a mother and a nurse, and is procreative of the third kind of being; for receiving upon itself the resemblances of form, and as it were remoulding them, it perfects these productions. He asserted moreover that matter, though eternal, is not unmoved; and though of itself it is formless and shapeless, yet it receives every kind of form; and that which is around bodies is divisible and partakes of the nature of the Different; and that matter is called by the twin names of Place and Space.

These two principles then are opposite to each other, of which Form is analogous to a male power and a father, while matter is analogous to a female power and a mother. The third thing is their offspring. Being three, they are recognizable by three marks: Form, by mind, according to knowledge; Matter by a spurious kind of reasoning, because it cannot be mentally perceived directly, but by analogy; and their production by sensation and opinion.

2. Creation of the World

BEFORE THE HEAVENS, then, there existed through reason Form and Matter, and the God who develops the best. But since the older surpasses the younger, and the ordered surpasses the orderless, the deity, being good—on seeing that Matter receives Form, and is altered in every way, but without order—found the necessity of organizing it, altering the undefined to the defined, so that the differences between bodies might be proportionately related, not receiving various alterations at random. He therefore made this world out of the whole of Matter, laying it down as a limit to the nature of being, through its containing in itself the rest of things, being one, only-begotten, perfect, endowed with soul and reason—for these qualities are superior to the soulless and the irrational—and of a sphere-like body, for this is more perfect than the rest of forms.

Desirous then of making a very good production he made it a divinity, created and never to be destroyed by any cause other than the God who had put it in order, if indeed he should ever wish to dissolve it. But on the part of the good there is no rushing forward to the destruction of a very beautiful production. Such therefore being the world, it continues without corruption and destruction, being blessed. It is the best of things created, since it has been produced by the best cause, which looked not to patterns made by hand but to Form in the abstract, and to Existence, perceiving by the mind to which the created thing, having been carefully adjusted, has become the most beautiful. It is even perfect in the realm of sense because its pattern, containing in itself all the living things perceived by mind, left out nothing, being the limit of the things perceived by mind, as this world is of those perceived by sense.

Being solid and perceptible by touch and sight, the world has a share of earth and fire, and of the things between them, air and water; and it is composed of all perfect bodies, which are in it as wholes, so that no part might ever be left out, in order that the body of the Universe might be altogether self-sufficient, uninjured by corruption from without or within; for apart from these there is nothing else, and hence the things combined according to the best proportions and with equal powers, neither rule over, nor are ruled by each other in turn, so that some receive an increase, others a decrease, remaining indissolubly united according to the very best proportions.

3. Proportions of the World Combination

WHENEVER THERE ARE any three terms with mutually equal intervals that are proportionate, we then perceive that, after the matter of an extended string, the middle is to the first, as is the third to it, and this holds true inversely and alternately, interchanging places and order, so that it is impossible to arrange them numerically without producing an equivalence of results. Likewise the world's shape and movement are well arranged; the shape is a sphere, self-similar on all sides, able to contain all shapes that are similar, and the movement endlessly exhibits the change dependent on a circle. Now as the sphere is on every side equidistant from the center, it is able to retain its poise whether in movement or at rest, neither losing its poise nor assuming another. Its external appearance being exactly smooth, it needs no mortal organs such as are fitted to and present in all other living beings because of their wants. The world soul's element of divinity radiates out from the center entirely penetrating the whole world, forming a single mixture of divided substance with undivided form; and this mixture of two forces, the Same and the Different, became the origin of motion, which indeed was not accomplished in the easiest way, being extremely difficult.

Now all these proportions are combined harmonically according to numbers, which proportions were scientifically divided according to a scale which reveals the elements and the means of the soul's combination. Now seeing that the earlier is more powerful in power and time than the later, the deity did not rank the soul after the substance of the body, but made it older by taking the first of unities, 384. Knowing this first, we can easily reckon the double (square) and the triple (cube); and all the terms together, with the complements and eights, there must be 36 divisions, and the total amounts to 114,695.

These are the divisions:

	(1)	(2)	(3)	(4)	(5)	(6)	(7)
1	384	432	486	512 l.	576	648	729

	(8)	(9)	(10)	(11)
2	768 l.	864	972	1024 l.

	(12)	(13)	(14)
3	1152	1296	1458

	(15)	(16)	(17)	(18)	(19)	(20)	(21)	(22)
4	1536 l.	1728	1944	2048 l.	2187 ap.	2304	2592	2916

	(23)
8	3072 l.

	(24)	(25)	(26)	(27)	(28)	(29)	(30)	(31)
9	3456	3888	4374 l.	4608 l.	5184	5832	6144 l.	6561 ap.

	(32)	(33)	(34)	(35)
	6912 l.	7776	8748	9216 l.

	(36)
27	10368

FIGURE 15. A TABLE OF TONE NUMBERS. There is evidence that this table of tone numbers is a later addition to the text. The abbreviations l. and ap. represent the two types of semitones, the *leimma* and the *apotome* respectively.

4. *Planetary Revolutions and Time*

GOD THE ETERNAL, the chief ruler of the Universe and its creator, is beheld alone by the mind, but we may behold by sight all that is produced in this world in connection with those parts which are heavenly, and, being ethereal, must be divided into kinds: some relating to Sameness, others to Difference. Sameness draws onward all that is within, with the general motion of the entire sphere of the universe from east to west. Difference draws along all self-moved portions from west to east, fortuitously rolled around and along by the superior power of Sameness.*

The movement of the Different, being divided in harmonic proportion, assumes the order of seven circles. Nearest to the earth the Moon revolves in a month, while beyond her the Sun completes his revolution in a year. Two planets run co-equal with that of the sun: Mercury and the star of Hera, the latter of which is also called the star of Venus and the Lightbringer because shepherds and common people, generally not skillful in sacred astronomy, confuse the western and eastern risings. The same star may shine in the west when following the sun at a distance great enough to be viewed in spite of solar splendor; and at another time in the east when, as herald of the day, it rises before the sun, leading it. Because of its running together with the sun, Venus is the Lightbringer frequently but not always; for there are planets and stars of any magnitude seen above the horizon before sunrise, herald of the day. But the three other planets, Mars, Jupiter and Saturn have their peculiar velocities and different years, completing their course while making their periods of effulgence, of visibility, of obscuration and eclipse, accurately rising and setting. Moreover, they complete their appearances conspicuously in the east or west according to their position relative to the sun who, during the day, speeds westward, which during the night it reverses, under the influence of Sameness, while its annual revolution is due to its inherent motion. In consequence of these two kinds of motion it rolls out a spiral, moving one degree each day, but is whirled around under the sphere of the fixed stars according to each revolution of darkness and day.

Now these revolutions are by men called portions of time, which the deity arranged together with the world. For before the world the stars did not exist, and hence there was neither year, nor periods of season, by which this generated time is measured, and which is the representation of the ungenerated time called eternity. For as this heaven has been produced according to an eternal pattern, the world of ideas, so was our world-time created simultaneously according to the pattern of eternity.

5. *The World's Creation by Geometric Figures*

THE EARTH, fixed at the center, becomes the hearth of the Gods and the boundary of darkness and day, producing settings and risings according to the occulta-

---

* Plato identified the power of Sameness with the regular movement of the stars and the celestial sphere. The power of Difference is identified with the movements of the planets which, over the course of the year, wander in the opposite direction of the fixed stars.

tion produced by the things that form the boundary, just as we improve our sight by making a tube with our closed hand, to exclude refraction. Earth is the oldest body in the heavens. Water was not produced without earth, nor air without moisture, nor could fire continue without moisture and the materials that are inflammable, so that earth is fixed upon its balance at the root and base of all other substances.

Of produced things, the substratum is Matter, while the reason of each shape is abstract Form; of these two the offspring is Earth and Water, Air and Fire.

This is how they were created. Every body is composed of surfaces, whose elements are triangles, of which one is right-angled, and the other has all unequal sides, with the square of the longer side being thrice the size of the lesser, while its least angle is the third of a right angle. The middle one is the double of the least, for it is two-thirds of a right angle. The greatest is a right angle, being one-and-a-half times greater than the middle one, and the triple of the least. Now this unequal sided triangle is half of an equilateral triangle, cut into two equal parts by a line let down from the apex to the base. In each of these triangles there is a right angle; but in the one, the two sides about the right angle are equal, and in the other all the sides are unequal. Now let this be called a scalene triangle; while the other, the half of the square, is the principle of the constitution of Earth. For the square produced from this scalene triangle is composed of four half-squares and from such a square is produced the cube, the most stationary and steady form in every way, having six sides and eight angles. On this account Earth is the heaviest and most difficult elemental body to move, and its substance is inconvertible, because it has no affinity with the other type of triangle. Only Earth has a peculiar element of the square, while the other triangle is the element of the three other substances, Fire, Air and Water. For when the half triangle is put together six times it produces the solid equilateral triangle, the exemplar of the tetrahedron, which has four faces with equal angles, which is the form of Fire, as the easiest to be moved, and composed of the finest particles. After this ranks the octahedron, with eight faces and six angles, being the element of Air; and the third is the icosahedron, with twenty faces and twelve angles, being the element of Water, composed of the most numerous and heaviest particles.

These then, as being composed of the same element, are transmuted into one another. But the deity made the dodecahedron the image of the Universe, as being the nearest to the sphere. Fire then, by the fineness of its particles, passes through all things; and Air through the rest of things, with the exception of Fire; and Water through the Earth. All things are therefore full, and have no vacuum. They cohere by the revolving movement of the Universe, and are pressed against and rubbed by each other in turn, and produce the never-failing change from generation to destruction.

6. Concretion of the Elements

BY MAKING USE OF THESE THE DEITY put together this world, sensible to touch through the particles of Earth, and to sight through those of Fire, which two are the extremes. Through the particles of Air and Water he had conjoined the world by the strongest chain, namely proportion, which restrains not only itself but all its subjects. Now if the conjoined object is a plane surface one middle term is sufficient, but if a solid there will be need of two mean terms. With two middle terms, therefore, he combined two extremes, so that as Fire is to Air, Air is to Water; and as Air is to Water, so is Water to Earth; and by alternation, as Fire is to Water, Air might be to Earth. Now since all are equal in power, their ratios are in a state of equilibrium. This world then is one, through the bond of the deity, made according to proportion.

Now each of these substances possesses many forms. Fire has those of flame, burning and luminousness, through the inequality of the triangles in each of them. In the same manner Air is partly clear and dry, and partly turbid and foggy. Water can be partly flowing and partly congealed, as it is in snow, frost, hail or ice. That which is moist is in one respect flowing as honey and oil, but in another is compact as pitch and wax. Concerning solids some are fusible, as gold, silver, copper, tin, lead and copper, and some brittle as sulphur, asphalt, nitre, salt, alum, and similar materials.

7. Composition of the Soul

AFTER PUTTING TOGETHER THE WORLD, the deity planned the creation of mortal beings so that, himself being perfect, he might perfectly complete the world. Therefore he mixed up the soul of man out of the same proportions and powers, and after taking the particles and distributing them, he delivered them over to Nature, whose office is to effect change. She then took up the task of working out mortal and ephemeral living beings, whose souls were drawn in from different sources, some from the moon, others from the sun, and others from various planets, [from] that cycle within the Difference, with the exception of one single power which was derived from Sameness, which she mixed up in the rational portion of the soul, as the image of wisdom in those of a happy fate.

Now in the soul of man one portion is rational and intellectual, and another irrational and unintellectual. Of the logical part the best portion is derived from Sameness,while the worst comes from Difference, and each is situated around the head so that the other parts of the soul and body may minister to it, as the supreme part of the whole body. Of the irrational portion, that which represents passion hovers around the heart, while desire inhabits the liver. The principle of the body and root of the marrow is the brain, wherein resides the ruling power; and from this, like an effusion, through the back-bone flows what is left over from the brain, from which are separated the particles of semen and seed. The marrow's surrounding defenses are the bones, of which the flesh is the covering and concealment. To the nerves he united joints by tendons, suitable for their movement. Of the internal organs, some exist for the sake of nourishment and others for safety. Of exterior motions, some are conveyed to the interior intelligent places of perception while others, not falling under the power of apprehension, are unperceived, either because the affected bodies are too earth-like or because the movements are too feeble. The painful movements tend to arouse nature, while the pleasurable lull nature into remaining within herself.

8. *Sensations*

AMONG THE SENSES, the deity has in us lit sight to view the objects in the heavens and for the reception of knowledge, while to make us capable to receive speech and melody, he has implanted hearing in us, of which he who is deprived thereof from birth will become dumb, nor be able to utter any speech, and that is why this sense is said to be related closest to speech.

Many affections of the body that have a name are so called with reference to touch, and others from relation to their seat. Touch judges the properties connected with life such as warmth, coldness, dryness, moisture, smoothness, roughness, and of things that are yielding, opposing, hard or soft. Touch also judges heaviness or lightness. Reason defines these affections as being centripetal and centrifugal, which men mean to express when they say below and middle. For the center of a sphere is below, and that part lying above it and stretching to the circumference is called upwardness.

Now what is warm appears to consist of fine particles, causing bodies to separate, while coldness consists of the grossness of the particles, causing a tendency to condense.

The circumstances connected with the sense of taste are similar to those of touch. For substances grow either astringent or smooth through contraction and dilation, also by entering the pores and assuming shapes. For those that cause the tongue to melt away, or that scrape it, appear to be rough. Those that act moderately in scraping appear brackish. Those that inflame or separate the skin are acrid; while their opposites, the smooth and sweet, are reduced to a juicy state.

The kinds of odors have not been defined because they percolate through narrow pores that are too stiff to be closed or separated. Things seem to be sweet smelling or bad smelling from the putrefaction or concoction of the earth and of similar substances.

A vocal sound is a percussion in the air, arriving at the soul through the ears. The passages of the ears reach to the liver, and among them is *pneuma*, by the movement of which hearing exists. Now of the voice and hearing, that portion which is quick is acute, while that which is slow is grave, the medium being the most harmonious. What is much and diffused is great; what is little and compressed is small; what is arranged to musical proportions is in tune; while that which is unarranged and unproportionate is out of tune and not properly adjusted.

The fourth kind of things relating to the senses is the most uniform and various, and they are called objects of sight, in which are all kinds of colors and an infinity of colored substances. The principle ones are four: white, black, brilliant [blue] and red, out of a mixture of which all other colors are prepared. What is white dilates the eye, and what is black causes it to contract, just as warmth expands, and cold contracts, and what is rough contracts the tasting, and what is sharp dilates it.

9. *Respiration*

IT IS NATURAL for the covering of animals that live in the air to be nourished and kept together by the food being distributed in the veins through the whole mass, in the manner of a stream, conveyed as it were by channels, and moistened by the breath, which diffuses it, and carries it to the extremities. Respiration is produced because there is no vacuum in nature: the air, as it flows in, is inhaled in place of that which is exhaled through unseen pores, such as those through which perspiration drops appear on the skin, but a portion is excreted by the natural warmth of the body. It then becomes necessary for an equivalent portion to be reintroduced to avoid a vacuum.

Now in lifeless substances, according to the analogy of respiration, the same organization occurs. The cupping-glass and amber, for instance, bear resemblance to respiration.*

Now the breath flows through the body to an orifice outwards and is, in turn, introduced through respiration by the mouth and nostrils, and again after the manner of the flow of the Euripus, is in turn carried to the body which is extended according to the expiration. Also the cupping-glass, when the air within is expelled by fire, attracts moisture to itself; and amber, when the air is separated from it, attracts a nearby substance.

Now all nourishment comes as from a root from the heart, and from the stomach as a fountain, and is conveyed to the body to which, if it be moistened by more than what flows out, there is said to be an increase, but if more flows out it is known as a decay. The point of perfection is the boundary between these two, and is considered to exist in an equality of the efflux and influx; but when the joints of the system are broken, should there no longer exist any passage for the breath, or the nourishment should not be distributed, then the animal dies.

10. Disorders

THERE ARE MANY THINGS HURTFUL TO LIFE which are the causes of death. One kind is disease. Its beginning is disharmony of the functions when the simple powers such as heat, cold, moisture or dryness are excessive or deficient. Then come changes and alterations in the blood from corruption and the deterioration of the flesh, when changes in the blood or flesh take place according to the changes of what is acid, brackish, or pungent in the blood. Hence arise the production of bile and of phlegm, of diseased juices, and of rotten liquids. Their effects are weak indeed, unless deeply seated, but difficult to cure when their commencement is generated from the bones, and acute if located in the marrow. The last disorders are those of the breath, bile and phlegm, when they increase and flow into places inappropriate for them. For by taking the place of the better, and driving away what is congenial, they fix themselves there, injuring bodies, and resolving these into themselves.

These then are the sufferings of the body, and hence arise many diseases of the soul, some from one faculty, some from another. Of the perceptive soul the disease is a difficulty of perception; of the recollecting, a forgetfulness; of the

---

* As Thomas H. Tobin observes in his translation of this text, the cupping-glass was a device used in medicine. When heated the air inside was expelled and the device was placed on a wound to remove poison. Rubbing amber with a cloth was likewise thought to expel the air in it, causing the amber to attract small object to it as the vacuum was filled. The actual cause is static electricity.

appetitive part, a deficiency of desire and eagerness; of the affective, a violent suffering and excited madness; of the rational, an indisposition to learn and think.

But of wickedness the beginnings are pleasures and pains; desires and fears, inflamed by the body, mingled with the mind, and are called by different names. For there loves and desires let loose uncontrolled passions, heavy resentments, and appetites of various kinds, and immoderate pleasures. Plainly, to be unreasonably disposed towards the affections is the limit of virtue, and to be under their rule is that of vice; for to abound in them, or to be superior to them, places us in a good or bad position. Against such impulses the temperaments of our bodies are greatly able to cooperate whether quick or hot, or various, by leading us to melancholy or violent lewdness; and certain parts, when affected by a flux, produce itchings and forms of body more similar to a state of inflammation than one of health, through which a sinking of the spirits and a forgetfulness, delirium and a state of fear result.

11. Discipline

IMPORTANT, TOO, ARE THE HABITS in which persons are trained, in the city or at home, and their daily food, by luxury enervating the soul, or fortifying it for strength. For living out of doors, and simple fare, and gymnastic exercises, and the morals of companions, produce the greatest effect in the way of vice and virtue. These causes are derived from our parents and the elements, rather than ourselves, provided that on our part there be no remissness by keeping aloof from acts of duty. The animal cannot be in good condition unless the body possesses the better properties under its control, namely health and correct perception, and strength and beauty. Now the principles of beauty are a symmetry as regards its parts, and as regards the soul. For nature has arranged the body, like an instrument, to be subservient to and in harmony with the subjects of life. The soul must likewise be brought into harmony with its analogous good qualities, namely in the case of temperance, as the body is in the case of health; and in that of prudence, as in the case of correct perception; and in that of fortitude, as in the case of vigor and strength; and in that of justice, as in the case of beauty.

Nature, of course, furnishes their beginnings, but their continuation and maturation result from carefulness: those relating to the body from the gymnastic and medical arts, those to the soul through instruction and philosophy. For these are the powers that nourish and give a tone to the body and soul by means of labor and gymnastic exercise and pureness of diet; some through drug medication applied to the body, and others through discipline applied to the soul by means of punishments and reproaches, for by the encouragement they give strength and excite to an onward movement and exhort to beneficial deeds. The art of the gymnasium trainer and its nearest approximation, that of the medical man, do on application to the body reduce their powers to the utmost symmetry, purifying the blood and equalizing the breath so that, if there were any diseased virulence there, the powers of blood and breath may be made vigorous; but music and its leader philosophy which the Gods ordained as regulators for the soul, accustom, persuade, and partly compel the irrational to obey reason, and induce the spirited and appetitive parts of the soul to become one mild and the other quiet, so as not to be moved without reason, nor to be unmoved when the mind incites either to desire or enjoy something; for this is the definition of temperance, namely, docility and firmness. Intelligence and philosophy the highest in honor, after cleansing the soul from false opinions, have introduced knowledge, recalling the mind from excessive ignorance and setting it free for the contemplation of divine things, in which to occupy oneself with self-sufficiency, as regards the affairs of a man, and with an abundance, for the commensurate period of life, is a happy state.

12. Human Destiny

NOW HE WHOM THE deity has happened to assign somewhat of a good fate is, through opinion, led to the happiest life. But if he be morose and indocile, let the punishment that comes from law and reason follow him, bringing with it the fears ever on the increase, both those that originate in heaven or Hades, how that punishments inexorable are below laid up for the unhappy, as well as those ancient Homeric threats of retaliation for the wickedness of those defiled by crime. For as we sometimes restore bodies to health by means of diseased substances, if they will not yield to the more healthy, so if the soul will not be led by true reasoning, we restrain it by false. These are unusual since, by a change, we say that the souls of cowards enter into the bodies of women who are inclined to insulting conduct; and the souls of the blood-stained take on the bodies of wild beasts; the lascivious enter into the bodies of sows and boars; the light-minded and frivolous take on shapes of aeronautic birds; and those who neither learn nor think of anything enter into the bodies of idle fish.

On all these matters, however, there has at a second period been delivered a judgment by Nemesis, of Fate, together with the avenging deities that preside over murderers, and those under the earth in Hades, and the inspectors of human affairs to whom God, the leader of all, has entrusted the administration of the world, which is filled with Gods and men, and the rest of the living beings who have been fashioned according to the best model of an unbegotten, eternal and mentally-perceived form.

SELECT PASSAGES

FROM THE CHURCH FATHERS

IT WAS NOT UNCOMMON for the early church fathers to refer to the philosophers of Greece, even though for many the contact with their thought was only through outlines and handbooks rather than through primary sources.

For the most part the church fathers had positive things to say about the Pythagoreans. Clement of Alexandria, who had more than a passing aquaintance with Platonic thought, shows an interest in Pythagorean mathematics, and even applied the numbers of the harmonic ratio to the interpretation of scripture. Moreover, Justin Martyr sought entrance to a Pythagorean school but was rejected on account of inadequate mathemtical knowledge; he later became a Platonist and then a Christian. The fragments which follow, which were not included in Guthrie's original edition of this book, are representative of what the church fathers had to say.

NOTICES FROM THE CHURCH FATHERS

HERACLEIDES AND THE PYTHAGOREANS think that each of the stars is a world, including an Earth, and an atmosphere and an ether in the infinite space. These doctrines are introduced in the Orphic Hymns, for they make each star a world. —Ps.-Plutarch, *On the Opinions of the Philosophers*. Quoted by Eusebius, *Preparation for the Gospel,* 839b.

Then, in regular succession from another starting-point, Pythagoras the Samian, son of Mnesarchus, calls numbers, with their proportions and harmonies, and the elements composed of both, the first principles; and he includes also Unity and the Indefinite Dyad. —Justin Martyr, *Exhortatory Address to the Greeks,* IV.

For the Pythagorean Theano writes, "Life would indeed be a feast to the wicked, who, having done evil, then die; were not the soul immortal, death would be a godsend." —Clement of Alexandria, *Stromateis* IV, 7.

Did not Theano the Pythagorean make such progress in philosophy, that to him who looked intently at her, and said, "Your arm is beautiful," she answered "Yes, but it is not public." Characterized by the same propriety there is also reported the following reply. When asked when a woman after being with her husband may attend a religious festival, said, "From her own husband at once, from a stranger never." —Clement of Alexandria, *Stromateis,* IV, 19.

Pythagoras thus defined the being of God, "as a soul passing to and fro, and diffused through all parts of the universe, and through all nature, from which all living creatures which are produced derive their life." —Lactantius, *The Divine*

Institutes, I, 5.

And Pythagoras, son of Mnesarchus, who expounded the doctrines of his own philosophy mystically by means of symbols, as those who have written his life show, himself seems to have entertained thoughts about the unity of God not unworthy of his foreign residence in Egypt. For when he says that Unity is the first principle of all things, and that it is the cause of all good, he teaches by an allegory that God is one, and alone. And that this is so, is evident from his saying that unity and one differ widely from one another. For he says that unity belongs to the class of things perceived by the mind, but that one belongs to numbers. And if you desire to see a clearer proof of the opinion of Pythagoras concerning one God, hear his own opinion, for he spoke as follows: "God is one; and he himself does not, as some suppose, exist outside the world, but in it, he being wholly present in the entire circle, and beholding all generations, being the regulating ingredient of all the ages, and the administrator of his own powers and works, the first principle of all things, the light of heaven, and father of all, the intelligence and animating soul of the universe, the movement of all orbits." Thus, then, Pythagoras. —Justin Martyr, *Exhortatory Address to the Greeks,* XIX.

PASSAGES REFERRING TO THE PYTHAGOREANS

FROM PLATO AND ARISTOTLE

TRANSLATED BY ARTHUR FAIRBANKS

PASSAGES IN PLATO
REFERRING TO THE PYTHAGOREANS

Phaedo 62 B. The saying uttered in secret rites, to the effect that we men are in a sort of prison, and that one ought not to release himself from it nor yet to run away, seems to me something great and not easy to see through; but this at least I think is well said, that it is the Gods who care for us, and we men are one of the possessions of the Gods.

Cratylus 400 B. For some say that it [the body] is the tomb of the soul—I think it was the followers of Orpheus in particular who introduced this word—which has the soul enclosed like a prision in order that it may be kept safe.

Gorgias 493 A. I once heard one of the wise men say that now we are dead and the body (*soma*) is our tomb (*sema*), and that the part of the soul where desires are, it so happens, is open to persuasion, and moves upward or downward. And, indeed, a clever man—perhaps some inhabitant in Sicily or Italy—speaking allegorically, and taking the word from 'credible' (*pithanos*) and 'persuadable' (*pistikos*), called this a jar (*pithos*); and he called those without intelligence uninitiated, and that part of the soul of uninitiated persons where the desires are, he called its intemperatness, and said it was not water-tight, as a jar might be pierced with holes—using the simile because of insatiate desires.

Gorgias 507 E. And the wise men say that one community embraces heaven and earth and Gods and men and friendship and order and temperance and righteousness, and for that reason they call this whole a *kosmos*, my friend, for it is not without order nor yet is there excess. It seems to me that you do not pay attention to these things, though you are wise in regard to them. But it has escaped your notice that geometrical equality prevails widely among both Gods and men.

PASSAGES IN ARISTOTLE
REFERRING TO THE PYTHAGOREANS

Physics. iii. 4; 203 a 1. Some, like the Pythagoreans and Plato, have made the Unlimited a first principle existing by itself, not connected with anything else, but being the infinite itself in its essence. Only the Pythagoreans found it among all things perceived by sense (for they say that number is not an abstraction), and they held that what is outside the heavens is Unlimited.

iii. 4; 203 a 10. The Pythagoreans identify the Unlimited with the even. For this, they say, is cut off and shut in by the odd, and provides things with an element of infinity. An indication of this is what happens with numbers. If gnomons are place round the one, and without the one, in the one construction the figure that results is always the same [square], in the other it is always different [oblong].

iii. 4; 204 a 33. [The Pythagoreans] both hold that the infinite is substance, and divide it into parts.

iv. 6; 213 b 22. And the Pythagoreans say that there is a void, and that it enters into the heaven itself from the infinite air, as though it [the heaven] were breathing; and this void defines the natures of things, inasmuch as it is a certain separation and definition of things that lie together; and this is true first in the case of numbers, for the void defines the nature of these.

On the Heavens. i. 1; 268 a 10. For as the Pythagoreans say, the All and all things are defined by threes; for end and middle and beginning constitute the number of the All, and also the number of the Triad.

ii. 2; 284 b 6. And since there are some who say that there is a right and a left of the heavens, as, for instance, those that are called Pythagoreans (for such is their doctrine), we must investigate whether it is as they say.

ii. 2; 285 a 10. Wherefore one of the Pythagoreans might be surprised in that they say that there are only these two first principles, the right and the left, and they pass over four of them as not having the least validity; for there is no less difference up and down, and front and back than there is right and left in all creatures.

ii. 2; 285 b 23. And some are dwelling in the upper hemisphere and to the right, while we dwell below and to the left, which is the opposite to what the Pythagoreans say; for they put us above and to the right, while the others are below and at the left.

ii. 9; 290 b 15. Some think it necessary that noise should arise when so great bodies are in motion, since sound does arise from bodies among us which are not so large and do not move so swiftly; and from the sun and moon and from the stars in so great number, and of so great size, moving so swiftly, there must necessarily arise a sound inconceivably great. Assuming these things and that the swiftness has the principle of harmony by reason of the intervals, they say that the sound of the stars moving on in a circle becomes musical. And since it seems unreasonable that we also do not hear this sound, they say that the reason for this is that the sound exists in the very nature of things, so as not to be distinguishable from the opposite silence; for the distinction of sound and silence lies in their contrast with each other, so that as blacksmiths think there is no difference between them because they are accustomed to the sound, so the same thing happens to men.

ii. 9; 291 a 7. What occasions the difficulty and makes the Pythagoreans say that there is a harmony of the bodies as they move, is a proof. For whatever things move themselves make a sound and noise; but whatever things are fastened in what moves or exist in it as the parts in a ship, cannot make a noise, nor yet does the ship if it moves in a river.

ii. 12; 293 a 19. They say that the whole heaven is limited, the opposite to what those of Italy, called the Pythagoreans, say; for these say that fire is at the center and that the earth is one of the stars, and that moving in a circle about the center it produces night and day. And they assume yet another earth opposite this which they call the counter-earth (*antichthon*), not seeking reasons and causes for phenomena, but stretching phenomena to meet certain assumptions and opinions of theirs and attempting to arrange them in a system. ...And what is more, the Pythagoreans say that the most authoritative part of the All stands guard, because it is specially fitting that it should, and this part is the center; and this place that the fire occupies, they call the Guardpost of Zeus, as it is called simply the center, that is, the center of space and the center of matter and of nature.

Metaphysics. i. 5; 985 b 23 - 986 b 8. With these before them [Anaxagoras, Empedocles, Atomists] those called Pythagoreans, applying themselves to the sciences, first developed them; and being brought up in them they thought that the first principles of these [i.e., numbers] were the first principles of all things. And since of these [sciences] numbers are by nature the first, in numbers rather than in fire and earth and water they thought they saw many likenesses to things that are and that are coming to be, as, for instance, justice is such a property of numbers, and soul and mind are such a property, and another is opportunity, and of other things one may say the same of each one.

And further, discerning in numbers the conditions and reasons of harmonies also—since, moreover, other things seemed to be like numbers in their entire nature, and numbers were the first of every nature—they assumed that the elements of numbers were the elements of all things, and that the whole heavens were harmony and number. And whatever characteristics in numbers and harmonies they could show were in agreement with the properties of the heavens and its parts and with its whole arrangement, these they collected and adapted; and if there chanced to be any gap anywhere, they eagerly sought that the whole system might be connected with these [stray phenomena]. To give an example of my meaning: inasmuch as ten seemed to be the perfect number and to embrace the whole nature of numbers, they asserted that the number of bodies moving through the heavens were ten, and when only nine were visible, for the reason just stated they postulated the counter-earth as the tenth. We have given a more definite account of these thinkers in other parts of our writings. But we have referred to them here with this purpose in view, that we might ascertain from them what they asserted as the first principles and in what manner they came upon the causes that have been enumerated. They certainly seem to consider Number as the first principle and, as it were, the matter in things and in their conditions and states; and the odd and the even are elements of number, and of these the one is Limited and the other Unlimited, and unity is the product of both of them, for it is both odd and even, and Number arises from the one, and the whole heaven, as has been said, is numbers.

A different party in this same school says that the first principles are ten, named according to the following table: Limited and Unlimited, Odd and Even, One and Many, Right and Left, Male and Female, Rest and Motion, Straight and

Crooked, Light and Darkness, Good and Bad, Square and Oblong. After this manner Alcmaeon of Croton seems to have conceived them, and either he received this doctrine from them or they from him, for Alcmaeon arrived at maturity when Pythagoras was an old man, and his teachings resembled theirs. For he says that most human affairs are twofold, not meaning opposites reached by definition, as did the former party, but opposites by chance—as, for example, white-black, sweet-bitter, good-bad, small-great. This philosopher let fall his indefinite opinions about the other contraries, but the Pythagoreans declared the number of the opposites and what they were. From both schools one may learn this much: that opposites are the first principles of things—but from the latter he may learn the number of these, and what they are. Yet how it is possible to bring them into relation with the causes of which we have spoken they have not clearly worked out. They seem to range their elements under the category of matter, for they say that substance is compounded and formed from them, and that they inhere in it.

987 a 9-27. Down to the Italian philosophers, and with their exception, the rest have spoken more reasonably about these principles, except that, as we said, they do indeed use two principles, and the one of these, whence is motion, some regard as one and others as twofold. The Pythagoreans, however, while they in similar manner assume two first principles, add this which is peculiar to themselves: that they do not think that the Limited and the Unlimited and the One are certain other things by nature, such as fire or earth or any other such thing, but the Unlimited itself and Unity itself are the essence of things of which they are predicated, and so they make Number the essence of all things. So they taught after this manner about them, and began to discourse and to define what essence is, but they made it altogether too simple a matter. For they made their definition superficially, and to whatever first the definition might apply, this they thought to be the essence of the matter, as if one should say that twofold and two were the same, because the twofold subsists in the two. But undoubtedly the two and the twofold are not the same, otherwise one thing will be many—a consequence which they actually drew. So much then may be learned from the earlier philosophers and from their successors.

i. 6; 987 b 10. And Plato only changed the name, for the Pythagoreans say that things exist by 'imitation' of numbers, but Plato, by 'participation.'

i. 6; 987 b 22. Plato concurred with the Pythagoreans in saying that the One is the real essence of things, and not something else with unity as an attribute. In harmony with them he affirms that Numbers are the principles of being for other things. But it is peculiar to him that instead of a single Indefinite he posits a double Indefinite, an Infinite of greatness and of littleness; and it is also peculiar to him that he separates Numbers from things that are seen, while they say that Numbers are the things themselves, and do not interpose mathematical objects between them. This separation of the One and Numbers from things, in contrast with the position of the Pythagoreans, and the introduction of Forms, are the consequence of his investigation by definitions.

i. 8; 989 b 32-990 a 32. Those, however, who carry on their investigation with reference to all things, and divide things into what are perceived and what are not perceived by sense, evidently examine both classes, so one must delay a little longer over what they say. They speak correctly and incorrectly in reference to the questions now before us. Now those who are called Pythagoreans use principles and elements yet stranger than those of the physicists, in that they do not take them from the sphere of sense, for mathematical objects are without motion, except in the case of astronomy. Still, they discourse about everything in nature and study it; they construct the heaven, they observe what happens in its parts and their states and motions; they apply to these their first principles and causes, as though they agreed entirely with the other physicists in that being is only what is perceptible and all that which is called heaven includes. But their causes and first principles, they say, are such as to lead up to the higher parts of reality, and are in harmony with this rather than with the doctrines of nature. In what manner motion will take place when Limit and Unlimited, Odd and Even, are the only underlying realities, they do not say; nor how it is possible for genesis and destruction to take place without motion and change, or for the heavenly bodies to revolve. Further, if one grants to them that spatial magnitude arises from these principles, or if this could be proved, still, how will it be that some bodies are light and some heavy? for their postulates and statements apply no more to mathematical objects than to things of sense; accordingly they have said nothing at all about fire or earth or any such objects, because I think they have no distinctive doctrine about things of sense. What is more, how is it necessary to assume that Number and states of Number are the causes of what is in the heavens and what is taking place there from the beginning and now, and that there is no other number than that out of which the world is composed? For when opinion and opportune time are at a certain point in the heavens, and a little farther up or down are injustice and judgment or a mixture of them, and they bring forward as proof that each one of these is Number, and the result then is that at this place there is already a multitude of compounded qualities because those states of Number have each their place—is this Number in heaven the same which it is necessary to assume that each of these things is, or is it something different? Plato says it is different; still, he thinks that both these things and the cause of them are Numbers, but the one class are intelligible causes, and the others are sensible causes.

iii. 1; 996 a 4. And the most difficult and perplexing question of all is whether unity and being are not something different from things, as Plato and the Pythagoreans say, but their very essence, or whether the underlying substance is something different, such as Love, as Empedocles says, or as another says, fire, or water, or air.

iii. 4; 1001 a 9. Plato and the Pythagoreans assert that neither being nor unity is something different from things, but that it is the very nature of them, as though essence itself consisted in unity and existence.

vii. 10; 1036 b 17. So it turns out that many things of which the forms appear different have one Form, as the Pythagoreans discovered; and one can say that there is one Form for everything, and hold that others are not forms, and thus all things will be one.

x. 2; 1053 b 11. Whether the One itself is a sort of essence, as first the Pythagoreans and later Plato affirmed...

xii. 7; 1072 b 31. And they are wrong who assume, as do the Pythagoreans and Speusippus, that the most beautiful and the best is not in the beginning of things, because the first principles of plants and animals are indeed causes, but that which is beautiful and perfect is in what comes from these first principles.

xiii. 4; 1078 b 21. The Pythagoreans [before Democritus] only defined a few things, the concepts of which they reduced to numbers, as for instance opportunity or justice or marriage...

xiii. 6; 1080 b 16. The Pythagoreans say that there is but one number, the mathematical, but that things of sense are not separated from this, for they are composed of it; indeed, they construct the whole heaven out of numbers, but not out of abstract numbers, for they assume that the units have magnitude; but how the first unit was so constituted to have magnitude they seem at a loss to say.

xiii. 6; 1080 b 31. All, as many as regard the one as the element and first principle of things, except the Pythagoreans, assert that numbers are based on the unit; but the Pythagoreans assert, as has been remarked, that numbers have magnitude.

xiii. 8; 1083 b 9. The Pythagorean standpoint has on the one hand fewer difficulties than those that have been discussed, but it has new difficulties of its own. The fact that they do not regard number as separate removes many of the contradictions; but it is impossible that bodies should consist of numbers, and that this number should be mathematical. Nor is it true that indivisible elements have magnitude; but, granted that they have this quality of indivisibility, the units have no magnitude—for how can magnitude be composed of indivisible elements? But arithmetical number consists of units. For these say that things are number; at least, they adapt their speculations to bodies as if they consist of numbers.

xiv. 3; 1090 a 20. On the other hand the Pythagoreans, because they see many qualities of numbers in bodies perceived by sense, regard objects as numbers, not as separate numbers, but as derived from numbers. And why? Because the qualities of numbers exist in a musical scale, in the heaven and in many other things. But for those who hold that number is mathematical only, it is impossible on the basis of their hypothesis to say any such thing, and it has already been remarked that there can be no science of these numbers. But we say, as above, that there is a science of numbers. Evidently the mathematical does not exist by itself, for in that case its qualities could not exist in bodies. In such a matter the Pythagoreans are restrained by nothing; when, however, they construct out of numbers physical bodies—out of numbers that have neither weight nor lightness, bodies that have weight and lightness—they seem to be speaking about another heaven and other bodies than those perceived by sense.

Nicomachean Ethics. i. 6; 1096 b 5. And the Pythagoreans seem to speak more persuasively about it, putting unity in the column of good things.

ii. 6; 1106 b 29. Evil partakes of the nature of the Unlimited, Good of the Limited, as the Pythagoreans conjectured.

v. 5; 1132 b 21. Reciprocity seems to some to be absolutely just, as the Pythagoreans say; for these defined the just as that which is reciprocal to another.

Moralia. i. 1; 1182 a 11. First Pythagoras attempted to speak concerning virtue, but he did not speak correctly; for bringing virtues into correspondence with numbers, he did not make any distinct.

Passages Referring to the Pythagoreans

From the Doxographers

Translated by Arthur Fairbanks

THE WRITINGS of the doxographers, the *Vetusta Placita* of Aetius, the *Placita Philosophorum* attributed to Plutarch, and so on, ultimately derive from a work of Theophrastus, *Physikon Doxon,* "Opinions of the Natural Philosophers." In this work Theophrastus compiled information on the doctrines of different philosophers by subject, serving to compare and contrast them with one another.

The fragments of the doxographers were collected together and published by Hermann Diels as *Doxographi Graeci*, Berlin, 1879, and the corresponding numeration of Diels' edition is reproduced at the beginning of each fragment. These fragments relating to the Pythagoreans, like the preceding passages from Plato and Aristotle, are translated by Arthur Fairbanks and reproduced from his *The First Philosophers of Greece: An Edition and Translation of the Remaining Fragments of the Pre-Sokratic Philosophers, Together with a Translation of the More Important Accounts of their Opinions Contained in the Early Epitomes of their Works*, New York, Charles Scribner's Sons, 1898.

FRAGMENTS FROM THE DOXOGRAPHERS

Aetius, *Plac.* i. 3; *Dox.* 280. And again from another starting-point, Pythagoras, son of Mnesarchus, a Samian, who was the first to call this matter by the name of philosophy, assumed as first principles the numbers and the symmetries existing in them, which he calls harmonies, and the elements compounded of both, that are called geometrical. And again he includes the Monad and the Indefinite Dyad among the first principles; and for him one of the first principles tends toward the creative and form-giving cause, which is intelligence, that is God, and the other tends toward the passive and material cause, which is the visible universe. And he says that the starting-point of Number is the Decad; for all Greeks and all barbarians count as far as ten, and when they get as far as this they return to the monad. And again, he says, the power of ten is in four and the tetrad. And the reason is this: if anyone from the monad adds the numbers in a series as far as four, he will fill out the number ten [i.e., $1 + 2 + 3 + 4 = 10$], but if he goes beyond the number of the tetrad, he will exceed ten. Just as if one should add one and two and should add to these three and four, he will fill out the number ten; so that according to the monad number [actually] is in the ten, but potentially in the four. Wherefore the Pythagoreans were wont to speak as though the greatest oath were the Tetrad:

> By him that transmitted to our soul the Tetraktys,
> The spring and root of ever-flowing nature.

And our soul, he says, is composed of the Tetrad, for this is intelligence, understanding, opinion, and sense, from which things come every art and science, and we ourselves become reasoning beings. The Monad, however, is intelligence, for intelligence sees according to the Monad. As for example, men are made up of many parts, and part by part they are devoid of sense and comprehension and experience, yet we perceive that man as one alone, whom no being resembles, possessing these qualities; and we perceive that a horse is one, but part by part it is without experience. For these are forms and classes according to monads. Wherefore, assigning this limit with reference to each one of these, they speak of a reasoning being and a neighing being. On this account then the Monad is intelligence by which we perceive these things. And the Indefinite Dyad is fittingly science, for all proof and persuasion is part of science, and further every syllogism brings together what is questioned out of some things that are agreed upon, and easily proves something else; and science is the comprehension of these things, wherefore it would be the Dyad. And opinion as the result of comprehending them is fittingly the Triad, for opinion has to do with many things, and the Triad is quantity, as 'The thrice-blessed Danaoi.' On this account then he includes the Triad... And their sect is called Italic because Pythagoras taught in Italy, having left Samos, his fatherland, of dissatisfied with the tyranny of Polycrates.

i. 7; *Dox.* 302. Pythagoras held that one of the first principles, the Monad, is God and the Good, which is the origin of the One, and is itself Intelligence, but the Indefinite Dyad is a daimon and bad, surrounding which is the mass of matter.

i. 8; *Dox.* 307. Divine spirits (*daimones*) are psychical beings, and heroes are souls separated from bodies; good heroes are good souls, bad heroes are bad souls.

i. 9; *Dox.* 307. The followers of Thales and Pythagoras and the Stoics held that matter is variable and changeable and transformable and is in a state of flux, the whole through the whole.

i. 10; *Dox.* 309. Pythagoras asserted that the so-called forms and ideas exist in numbers and their harmonies, and in what are called geometrical objects, apart from bodies.

i. 11; *Dox.* 310. Pythagoras and Aristotle asserted that the first causes are immaterial, but that other causes involve a union or contact with material substance [so that the world is material].

i. 14; *Dox.* 312. The followers of Pythagoras held that the universe is a sphere according to the form of the four elements, but the highest, fire, alone is conical.

i. 15; *Dox.* 314. The Pythagoreans call color the manifestation of matter.

i. 16; *Dox.* 314. Bodies are subject to change of condition, and are divisible to infinity.

i. 18; *Dox.* 316. (After a quotation from Aristotle, *Physics*, iv. 4; 212 a 20.) And in his first book on the philosophy of Pythagoras he writes that the heaven is one, and that time and wind and the void which always defines the places of each thing, are introduced from the infinite. And among other things he says that place is the immovable Limit of what surrounds the world, or that in which bodies abide and are moved, and that it is full when it surrounds body on every side, and empty when it has absolutely nothing in itself. Accordingly it is necessary for place to exist, and body, and it is never empty except from the standpoint of thought, for the nature of it in perpetuity destroys the interrelation of things and the combination of bodies; motions arise according to the place of bodies that surround and oppose each other, and no infiniteness is lacking, either of quality or of extent.

i. 20; *Dox.* 318. Pythagoras said that time is the sphere which surrounds the world.

i. 21; *Dox.* 318. Pythagoras, Plato: Motion is a certain otherness or difference in matter.

i. 24; *Dox.* 320. Pythagoras, and all that assume matter is subject to change, assert that genesis and destruction in an absolute sense take place, for from change of the elements, modification and separation of them there takes place juxtaposition and mixture, and intermingling and melting together.

Aetius, *Plac.* ii. 1; *Dox.* 327. Pythagoras first named the circumference of all things the *kosmos* by reason of the order in it.

ii. 4; *Dox.* 330. Pythagoras, Plato, and the Stoics held that the universe is brought into being by God. And it is perishable so far as its nature is concerned, for it is perceived by sense, and therefore material; it will not however be destroyed in accordance with the foreknowledge and plan of God.

ii. 6; *Dox.* 334. Pythagoras: The universe is made from five solid figures which are also called mathematical; of these he says that earth has arisen from the cube, fire from the pyramid, air from the octahedron, and water from the icosahedron, and the sphere of the All from the dodecahedron.

ii. 9; *Dox.* 338. The followers of Pythagoras hold that there is a void outside the universe into which the universe breathes forth, and from which it breathes in.

ii. 10; *Dox.* 339. Pythagoras, Plato, Aristotle: The right hand side of the universe is the eastern part from which comes the beginning of motion, and the left hand side is the west. They say the universe has neither height nor depth, in which statement height means distance from below upwards, and depth from above downwards. For none of the distance thus described exists for the universe, inasmuch as it is disposed around the middle of itself, from which it extends toward the All, and with reference to which it is the same on every side.

ii. 12; *Dox.* 340. Thales, Pythagoras, and their followers: The sphere of the whole heaven is divided into five circles which they call zones; the first of these is called the arctic zone and is ever visible, the second the summer solstice, the third the equinoctial, the fourth the winter solstice, and the fifth the antarctic zone, which is invisible. And the ecliptic called the zodiac in the three middle ones is projected to touch the three middle ones. And the meridian crosses all these from the north to the opposite quarter at right angles. It is said that Pythagoras was the first to recognize the slant of the zodiacal circle which Oenopides of Chios appropriated as his own discovery.

ii. 13; *Dox.* 343. Heracleides and the Pythagoreans asserted that each world of the stars is air and aether surrounding earth in the infinite aether. And these doctrines are brought out in the Orphic writings, for they [likewise] construct each world of the stars.

ii. 22; *Dox.* 352. The Pythagoreans: The sun is spherical.

ii. 23; *Dox.* 353. Plato, Pythagoras, Aristotle: The solstices lie along the slant of the zodical circle, through which the sun goes along the zodiac, and with the accompaniment of the tropical circles, and all these things the globe also shows.

ii. 24; *Dox.* 354. An eclipse takes place when the moon comes past.

ii. 25; *Dox.* 357. Pythagoras: The moon is a mirror-like body.

ii. 29; *Dox.* 360. Some of the Pythagoreans (according to the Aristotelian account and Philip of Opus) said that an eclipse of the moon takes place sometimes by the interposition of the earth, sometimes by the interposition of the counter-earth (*antichthon*). But it seems to some more recent thinkers that it takes place by a spreading of the flame little by little as it is gradually kindled, until it gives the complete full moon, and again, in like manner, it grows less until the conjunction, when it is completely extinguished.

ii. 30; *Dox.* 361. Some of the Pythagoreans, among them Philolaus, said that the earthy appearance of the moon is due to its being inhabited by animals and by plants, like those on our earth, only greater and more beautiful; for the animals on it are fifteen times as powerful, not having any sort of excrement, and their day is fifteen times as long as ours. But others said that the outward appearance in the moon is a reflection on the other side of the inflamed circle of the sea that is on our earth.

ii. 32; *Dox.* 364. Some regard the greater year...as the sixty year period, among whom are Oenopides and Pythagoras.

Aetius, *Plac.* iii. 1; *Dox.* 364. Some of the Pythagoreans said that the Milky Way is the burning of a star that fell from its own foundation, setting on fire the region through which it passed in a circle, as Phaethon was burned. And others say that the course of the sun arose in this manner at the first. And certain ones say that the appearance of the sun is like a mirror reflecting its rays toward the heaven, and therefore it happens at times to reflect its rays on the rainbow in the clouds.

iii. 2; *Dox.* 366. Some of the followers of Pythagoras say that a comet is one of the stars which are not always shining, but which emit their light periodically through a certain definite time; but others say that it is the reflection of our vision into the sun, like reflected images.

iii. 14; *Dox.* 378. Pythagoras: The earth, after the analogy of the sphere of the All, is divided into five zones, arctic, antarctic, summer, winter and equinoctial; of these the middle one he defines to be the middle of the earth, called for this very reason the torrid zone, the inhabited one [the one between the arctic and the torrid zones] being well-tempered...

Aetius, *Plac.* iv. 2; *Dox.* 386. Pythagoras holds that number moves itself, and he takes number as an equivalent for intelligence.

iv. 4, *Dox.* 389. Pythagoras, Plato: According to a superficial account the soul is of two parts, the one possessing, the other lacking, reason; but according to close and exact examination, of three parts, for the unreasoning part they divide into the emotion and the desires.

Theodor. v. 20; *Dox.* 390. The successors of Pythagoras saying that the body is a mixture of five elements (for they ranked aether as a fifth along with the four), held that the powers of the soul are of the same number as these. And these they named intelligence and wisdom and understanding and opinion and sense-perception.

Aetius, *Plac.* iv. 5; *Dox.* 391. Pythagoras: The principle of life is about the heart, but the principle of reason and intelligence is about the head.

iv. 5; *Dox.* 392. Pythagoras, et al.: The intelligence enters from without.

iv. 7; *Dox.* 392. Pythagoras, Plato: The soul is imperishable.

iv. 9; *Dox.* 396. Pythagoras, et al.: The sense-perceptions are deceptive.

iv. 9; *Dox.* 397. Pythagoras, Plato: Each of the sensations is pure, proceeding from each single element. With reference to vision, it is of the nature of aether; hearing, of the nature of wind; smell, of the nature of fire; taste, of the nature of moisture; touch, of the nature of earth.

iv. 14; *Dox.* 405. The followers of Pythagoras and of the mathematicians on reflections of vision: For vision moves directly as it were against the bronze [of a mirror], and meeting with a firm, smooth surface, it is turned and bent back on itself, meeting some such experience as when the arm is extended and then bent back to the shoulder.

iv. 20; *Dox.* 409. Pythagoras, Plato, Aristotle: Sound is immaterial. For it is not air, but it is the form about the air and the appearance (*epiphaneia*) after some sort of percussion which becomes sound; and every appearance is immaterial, for it moves with bodies, but is itself absolutely immaterial, as in the case of a bent rod the surface appearance suffers no change, but the matter is what is bent.

Aetius, *Plac.* v. 1; *Dox.* 415. Pythagoras did not admit the sacrificial part alone (of augury).

v. 3; *Dox.* 417. Pythagoras: Sperm is foam of the best part of the blood, a secretion from the nourishment, like blood and marrow.

v. 4; *Dox.* 417. Pythagoras, Plato, Aristotle: The power of seed is immaterial, like intelligence, the moving power; but the matter that is poured forth is material.

v. 20; *Dox.* 432. Pythagoras, Plato: The souls of animals called unreasoning are reasonable, not however with active reasoning powers, because of an imperfect mixture of the bodies and because they do not have the power of speech, as is the case of apes and dogs, for these have intelligence but not the power of speech.

Ar. Did. *Ep. Fr.* 32; *Dox.* 467. Apollodorus in the second book *Concerning the Gods*: It is the Pythagorean opinion that the morning and the evening star are the same.

Theophr. *Phys. Op.* Fr. 17; *Dox.* 492. Favorinus says that he [Pythagoras] was the first to call the heavens a *kosmos* and the earth spherical.

Cic., *de Deor. Nat.,* i. 11; Philod., *Piet.* Fr. c 4 b; *Dox.* 533. For Pythagoras, who held that soul is extended through all the nature of things and mingled with them, and that from this our souls are taken, did not see that God would be separated and torn apart by the separation of human souls; and when souls are wretched, as might happen to many, then part of God would be wretched—a thing which could not happen.

Hippol., *Phil.* 2; *Dox.* 555. There is a second philosophy not far distant from the same time, of which Pythagoras, whom some call a Samian, was the first representative. And this they call the Italian philosophy because Pythagoras fled the rule of Polycrates over the Samians and settled in an Italian city where he spent his life. The successive leaders of this sect shared the same spirit. And he in his studies of nature mingled astronomy and geometry and music [and arithmetic]. And thus he asserted that God is a monad, and examining the nature of number with especial care, he said that the *kosmos* produces melody and is put together with harmony, and he first proved the motion of the seven stars to be rhythm and melody. And in wonder at the structure of the universe, he decreed that at first his disciples should be silent, as if they were *mystae* who were coming into the order of the All; then when he thought they had sufficient education in the principles of truth, and had sought wisdom sufficiently in regard to stars and in regard to nature, he pronounced them pure and then bade them to speak. He separated his disciples into two groups, and called one esoteric, and the other exoteric. To the former he entrusted the more perfect sciences, to the latter the more moderate. And he dealt with magic, as they say, and himself discovered the art of physiognomy. Postulating both numbers and measures he was wont to say that the first principle of arithmetic embraced philosophy by combination, after the following manner:

Number is the first principle, a thing which is undefined, incomprehensible, having in itself all numbers which could reach infinity in amount. And the first principle of numbers is in substance the first Monad, which is a male monad, begetting as a father all other numbers. Secondly the Dyad is a female number, and the same is called by the arithmeticians even. Thirdly the Triad is a male number; this the arithmeticians have been wont to call odd. Finally, the Tetrad is a female number, and the same is called even because it is female.

All numbers, then, taken by classes are four—but number is undefined in reference to class—of which is composed the perfect number, the Decad. For the series one, two, three and four becomes ten, and its own name is kept in its essence by each of the numbers. Pythagoras said that this sacred Tetraktys is "the spring having the roots of ever-flowing nature" in itself, and from this numbers have their first principle. For the eleven and the twelve and the rest derive from the ten the first principle of their being. The four parts of the Decad, this perfect number, are called number, monad, power and cube. And the interweavings and minglings of these in the origin of growth are what naturally completes nascent number; for when a power is multiplied upon itself, it is the power of a power; and when a power is multiplied on a cube, it is the power of a cube; and when a cube is multiplied on a cube, the cube of a cube; thus all numbers, from which arise the genesis of what arises, are seven: number, monad, power, cube, power of a power, power of a cube, and cube of a cube.

He said that the soul is immortal, and that it changes from one body to another; so he was wont to say that he himself had been born before the Trojan war as Aethalides, and at the time of the Trojan war as Euphorbus, and after that as Hermontimus of Samos, then as Pyrrhos of Delos, fifth as Pythagoras. And Diodorus of Eretria and Aristoxenus the musician say that Pythagoras had come unto Zaratas of Chaldaea [i.e., Zoroaster]; and he set forth that in his view there were from the beginning two causes of things: father and mother. The father is light and the mother darkness; and the parts of light are warm, dry, light, swift;

and of darkness are cold, moist, heavy, slow; and of all these the universe is composed, of male and female. And he says that the universe exists in accordance with musical harmony, so the sun also makes an harmonious period. And concerning the things that arise from the earth and the universe they say Zaratas spoke as follows: There are two divinities, one of the heavens and the other of the earth; the one of the earth produces things from the earth, and it is water; and the divinity of the heavens is fire with a portion of air, warm, and cold; wherefore he says that none of these things will destroy or even pollute the soul, for these are the essence of all things. And it is said that Zaratas forbade men to eat beans because he said that at the beginning and composition of all things when the earth was still a whole, the bean arose. And he says that the proof of this is that if one chews a bean to a pulp and exposes it to the sun for a certain time (for the sun will affect it quickly), it gives off the odor of human seed. And he says that there is another and clearer proof: if when a bean is in flower we were to take the bean and its flower, and putting it into a pitcher moisten it and then bury it in the earth, and after a few days dig it up again, we should see in the first place that it had the form of a womb, and examining it closely we should find the head of a child growing with it.

Pythagoras perished in a conflagration with his disciples in Croton in Italy. And it was the custom when one became a disciple to burn one's property and to leave one's money under a seal with Pythagoras, and one remained in silence sometimes three years, and sometimes five years, and studied. And immediately on being released from this one mingled with the others and continued as a disciple and made one's home with them; otherwise one took one's money and was sent off. The esoteric class were called Pythagoreans, and the others Pythagoristians. And those of the disciples who escaped the conflagration were Lysis and Archippus and Zalmoxis the slave of Pythagoras, who is said to have taught the Pythagorean philosophy to the Druids among the Celts. It is said that Pythagoras learned numbers and measures from the Egyptians. Astonished at the wisdom of the priests, which was deserving of belief and full of fancies and difficult to grasp, he imitated it and himself also taught his disciples to be silent, and obliged the student to remain quietly in rooms underneath the earth.

Epiph. *Pro.* i; *Dox.* 587. Pythagoras laid down the doctrine of the Monad and of foreknowledge and the prohibition on sacrificing to the Gods then believed in, and he bade men not to partake of beings that had life, and to refrain from wine. And he drew a line between the things from the moon upwards, calling these immortal, and those below, which he called mortal; and he taught the transmigration of souls from bodies into bodies even as far as animals and beasts. And he used to teach his followers to observe silence for a period of five years. Finally he named himself a God.*

Epiph. *Haer.* iii. 8; *Dox.* 390. Pythagoras the Samian, son of Mnesarchus,

---

* While Pythagoras may have thought of himself as having some type of special relationship with the God Apollo, there is no reason to believe that he ever thought of himself as being a God. In fact, other church fathers attributed to Pythagoras a statement which challenged any man who thought himself a God to create a universe.

THE DOXOGRAPHERS

said that the Monad is God, and that nothing has been brought into being apart from this. He was wont to say that wise men ought not to sacrifice animals to the Gods, nor yet to eat what had life, nor beans, nor to drink wine. And he was wont to say that all things from the moon downward were subject to change, while from the moon upward they were not. And he said that the soul goes at death into other animals. And he bade his disciples to keep silence for a period of five years, and finally he named himself a God.

Herm. *I.G.P.* 16; *Dox.* 655. Others then from the ancient tribe, Pythagoras and his fellow tribesmen, revered and taciturn, transmitted other dogmas to me as mysteries, and this is the great and unspeakable *ipse dixit:* the Monad is the first principle of all things. From its forms and from numbers the elements arose. And he declared that the number, form and measure of each of these is somehow as follows: Fire is composed of twenty-four right-angled triangles, surrounded by four equilaterals. And each equilateral consists of six right-angled triangles, whence they compare it to the pyramid. Air is composed of forty-eight triangles, surrounded by eight equilaterals. And it is compared to the octahedron, which is surrounded by eight equilateral triangles, each of which is separated into six right-angled triangles so as to become forty-eight in all. And water is composed of one hundred and twenty triangles, surrounded by twenty equilaterals, and it is compared to the icosahedron, which is composed of one hundred and twenty equilateral triangle. And aither is composed of twelve equilateral pentagons, and is like a dodecahedron. And earth is composed of forty-eight triangles, and is surrounded by six equilateral tetragons, and it is like a cube. For the cube is surrounded by six tetragons, each of which is separated into eight triangles, so that they become in all forty-eight.

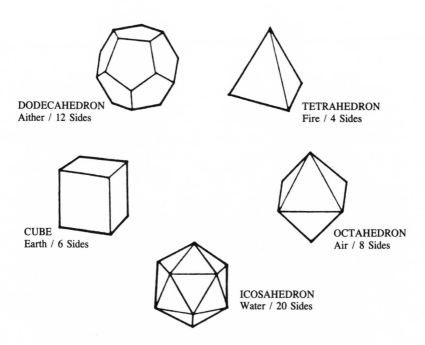

DODECAHEDRON
Aither / 12 Sides

TETRAHEDRON
Fire / 4 Sides

CUBE
Earth / 6 Sides

OCTAHEDRON
Air / 8 Sides

ICOSAHEDRON
Water / 20 Sides

FIGURE 16. THE REGULAR SOLIDS. The regular solids, also known as the Platonic solids, were first described by Plato in his *Timaeus*. Plato identified the dodecahedron with the cosmic sphere (later identified with aither), and the four other solids with the four elements. Each one of the elemental "molecules" is constructed out of the triangular "atoms" shown below. The five regular solids are the only polyhedra that can be constructed out of the same regular polygons. The archetypal ratios and geometries with which they are associated underlie the structure and divisions of three-dimensional space.

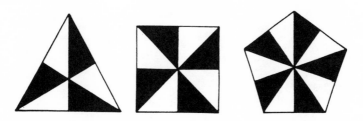

HOW MANY TETRAKTYS ARE THERE?

BY THEON OF SMYRNA

THE IMPORTANCE OF THE QUATERNARY obtained by addition (that is to say 1 + 2 + 3 + 4) is great in music because all the consonances are found in it. But it is not only for this reason that all Pythagoreans hold it in highest esteem: it is also because it seems to outline the entire nature of the universe. It is for this reason that the formula of their oath was: "I swear by the one who has bestowed the Tetraktys to the coming generations, source of eternal nature, into our souls." The one who bestowed it was Pythagoras, and it has been said that the Tetraktys appears indeed to have been discovered by him.

The first quaternary is the one of which we've just spoken: it is formed by addition of the first four numbers.

The second is formed by multiplication, of even and odd numbers, starting from unity. Of these numbers, unity is the first because, as we have said, it is the principle of all the even numbers, the odd numbers and of all the odd-even numbers, and its essence is simple. Next comes three numbers from the odd as well as the even series. They allow for the unification of odd and even because numbers are not only odd or even. For this reason, in multiplication, two quaternaries are taken, one even, the other odd; the even in double ratio, the first of the even numbers being 2 which comes from unity doubled; the odd in triple ratio, the first of the odd numbers being the number 3 which arise from unity being tripled, so that unity is odd and even simultaneously and belongs to both. The second number in the even and double [series] is 2 and in the odd and triple is 3. The third of the order of even numbers is 4, and in the odd series, 9. The fourth among the even numbers is 8, and among the odd numbers, 27.

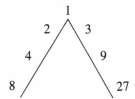

FIGURE 17. THE PLATONIC LAMBDA

The ratios of the most perfect consonances are found in these numbers; even the tone is included. However unity contains the principle of ratio, of limit and of point. The second numbers, 2 and 3, have the side ratio, being prime, incomposite numbers, and measured only by the unit, and are consequently linear numbers. The third terms, 4 and 9, have the power of the squared surface, being equally equal (that is to say square numbers). The fourth terms, 8 and 27, have the power of the cubic solid, being equally equal equally (that is to say, cubic numbers). In this way, by virtue of the numbers from this tetraktys, growth proceeds from the limit and the point up to the solid. In fact, after the limit and the point comes the side, then the surface and finally the solid. It is with these numbers that Plato, in the *Timaeus*, constitutes the [world] soul.* The last of these seven numbers is equal to the sum of all the preceding, as we have $1+2+3+4+8+9=27$.

There are then two quaternaries of numbers, one which is made by addition, the other by multiplication; and these quaternaries encompass the musical, geometric and arithmetic ratios of which the harmony of the universe is composed.

The third quaternary is that which, following the same proportion, embraces the nature of all magnitudes, for the place taken by unity, in the preceding quaternary, is that of the *point* in this one; and that of the numbers 2 and 3, having lateral (or linear) power, is here that of the *line*, through its double form, straight or circular, the straight line corresponding to the even number because it terminates at two points (the line and circle are given as examples here), and the circular to the odd, because it is composed of a single line without terminus.

And what, in the preceding quaternary, are the numbers 4 and 9, having the power of the *surface*, the two types of surface, the planar and the curved, are so (surface) in this one. Finally, what, in the preceding are the numbers 8 and 27, which have the power of the cube and of which one is even and the other odd, is constituted by the *solid* in this one. There are two kinds of solids, one with a curved surface, like the sphere or the cylinder, the other with a plane surface, such as the cube and the pyramid. This is the third tetraktys then, the one having the property of constituting any magnitude, through the point, the line, the surface and the solid.

The fourth quaternary is that of the simple bodies, fire, air, water and earth, and it offers the same proportion as the quaternary of numbers. The place occupied by unity in the quaternary of numbers is taken by fire in this one, air corresponds to the number 2, water to the number 3, earth to the number 4; such is indeed the nature of the elements according to their fineness or density, in such a way that fire is to air as 1 is to 2, to water as 1 is to 3, and to earth as 1 is to 4. The other relationships are also equal (that is to say, that air is to water as 2 is to 3, and so forth for the others).

The fifth quaternary is that of the shapes of simple bodies, for the pyramid is the figure of fire, the octahedron the figure of air, the icosahedron the figure of water and the cube the figure of earth.

The sixth is that of the created things, the seed being analogous to unity and the point. A growth in length is analogous to the number 2 and the line, and a growth in width is analogous to the number 3 and to the surface, and finally a growth in thickness is analogous to the number 4 and to the solid.

The seventh quaternary is that of societies. Man is principle and is thus unity. The family corresponds to the number 2, the village to the number 3 and the city to the number 4; for these are the elements which comprise the nation.

All of these quaternaries are material and perceptible.

* Plato, *Timaeus* 36BC.

The eighth contains faculties by which we are able to form judgment on the preceding, and which are its intellectual part, namely: thought, science, opinion and feeling. And certainly thought, in its essence, must be assimilated to unity; science is the number 2, because it is the science of all things; opinion is like the number 3, because it is something between science and ignorance; and finally feeling is like the number 4 because it is quadruple, the sense of touch being common to all, all the senses being motivated through contact.

The ninth quaternary is that which composes the living things, body and soul, the soul having three parts, the rational, the emotional and the willful; the fourth part is the body in which the soul resides.

The tenth quaternary is that of the of the seasons of the year, through the succession of which all things take birth, that is, spring, summer, autumn and winter.

The eleventh is that of the ages: childhood, adolescence, maturity and old age.

There are thus eleven quaternaries. The first is that of the numbers which are formed by addition, the second is that of the numbers formed by multiplication, the fourth is that of magnitudes, the fifth is that of simple bodies, the sixth is that of created things, the seventh is that of societies, the eighth is that of the faculties of judgment, the ninth is that of the living things, the tenth is that of the seasons, and the eleventh is that of the ages. They are proportional to one another, since what is unity in the first and the second quaternary, the point is in the third, fire is in fourth, the pyramid in the fifth, the seed in the sixth, man in the seventh, thought in the eighth, and so forth with the others following the same proportion.

Thus the first quaternary is 1, 2, 3, 4. The second is unity, the side, the square, the cube. The third is the point, the line, the surface, the solid. The fourth is fire, air, water, earth. The fifth is the pyramid, the octahedron, the icosahedron, the cube. The sixth is the seed, the length, the width, the height. The seventh is man, the family, the village, the city. The eighth is thought, science, opinion, sense. The ninth is the rational, the emotional and the willful parts of the soul, and the body. The tenth is spring, summer, autumn, and winter. The eleventh is childhood, adolescence, maturity and old age. And the perfect world which results from these quaternaries is geometrically, harmonically and arithmetically arranged, containing in power the entire nature of number, every magnitude and every body, whether simple or composite. It is perfect because everything is part of it, and it is itself a part of nothing else. This is why the Pythagoreans used the oath whose formula we have reported, and through which all things are assimilated to number.

From Theon of Smyrna: *Mathematics Useful for Understanding Plato*, Chapter 38. Translated by Robert and Deborah Lawlor. San Diego, Wizards Bookshelf, 1979. Reproduced with permission of the publisher.

THE PYTHAGOREAN TITLES
OF THE FIRST TEN NUMBERS

FROM THE THEOLOGY OF NUMBERS BY IAMBLICHUS

TRANSLATED BY DAVID R. FIDELER

PLUTARCH AND PLOTINUS inform us that the Pythagoreans called the One Apollo because of its lack of multiplicity—this is both a clever pun and a revealing statement, for *a-pollon* in Greek means literally "not of many."

Such, then, was the Greek style of "theological arithmetic." This form of number symbolism became quite popular in late antiquity and much of it was transmitted by Christian writers through Medieval times. The symbolism finds its basis in the Pythagorean observation that the primary numbers represent far more than quantitative signs: each one of the primary numbers is a qualitative, archetypal essence, possessing a distinct, living *personality*. This personality can be directly intuited by studying the archetypal manifestations of these principles in the realms arithmetic (number in itself), geometry (number in space) and harmonics (number in time).

The following list represents a compilation of the titles from the anonymous *Theology of Arithmetic* which was based closely on a work by Iamblichus. Since the first printing of this volume, however, a complete, fully annotated translation of *The Theology of Arithmetic* has appeared, which represents the first translation of this work into any European language (*The Theology of Arithmetic*, translated by Robin Waterfield, Phanes Press, Grand Rapids, 1988.) In the text, explanations are given for the various appellations. For more on arithmology also see book three of Thomas Taylor's *Theoretic Arithmetic of the Pythagoreans* and the section on number symbolism in Thomas Stanley's *Pythagoras*.

THE MONAD

Instrument of Truth
Obscure
Not-Many
A Chariot
Male-Female
Immutable Truth and Invulnerable Destiny
A Seed
Fabricator (*demiurge*)

True Happiness (*eudaimonia*)
Zeus
Life
God
The Equality in Increase and Decrease
Memory
A Ship
Essence (*ousia*)
The Inkeeper (*pandokeus*), "that which takes in all"
The Pattern or Model (*paradeigma*)
The Moulder
Prometheus
The First (*Proteus*)
Darkness
Blending
Commixture

Harmony (*symphonia*)
Order (*taxis*)
Materia
A Friend
Infinite Expanse (*chaos*)
Space-Producer

THE TRIAD

Proportion (*analogia*)
Harmonia
Marriage
Knowledge (*gnosis*)
Peace
Every Thing
Hecate
Good Counsel
Piety
The Mean Between Two Extremes
Oneness of Mind
The All
Perfection
Friendship
Purpose

THE DYAD

Inequality
Indefinite (*aoristos*)
The Unlimited (*apeiron*)
Without Form or Figure
Growth
Birth
Judgment
Appearance
Anguish
The Each of Two
Falling Short, Defect
Erato
Equal
Isis
Movement
The Ratio (*logos*) in Proportion (*analogia*)
Revolution
Distance
Impulse
Excess
The Thing with Another
Rhea (the wife of Kronos, but also "flow")
Selene
Combination
That Which is To Be Endured; Misery, Distress
Boldness, Audacity (*tolma*)
Matter
Obstinacy
Nature

THE TETRAD

Nature of Change
Righteousness
Hercules
Holding the Key of Nature

THE PENTAD

Alteration
Immortal
Androgyny

Lack of Strife
Aphrodite
Boubastia (named after the Egyptian divinity Boubastis)
Wedding
Marriage
Double
Manifesting Justice
Justice
Demigod
Nemesis
Pallas
Five-Fold
Forethought
Light

THE HEXAD

Resembling Justice
The Thunder-Stone
Amphitrite (Poseidon's wife; a verbal pun: on both sides [*amphis*] three [*trias*])
Male-Female
Marriage
Finest of All
In Two Measures
Form of Forms
Peace
Far-Shooting (name of Apollo)
Thaleia
Kosmos
Possessing Wholeness
Cure-All (*panacea*)
Perfection
Three-Fold
Health
Reconciling

THE HEPTAD

The Forager (epithet of Athena)
Athena
Citadel (*akropolis*)
Reaper
Hard to Subdue Defence
Due Measure (*kairos*)
Virgin (*parthenos*)
Revered Seven (*septas* + *sebomai* = *heptas*)
Bringing to Completion (*Telesphorus*)
Fortune, Fate
Preserving

THE OCTAD

Untimely Born
Steadfast
Seat or Abode
Euterpe
Cadmia
Mother
All Harmonious

THE ENNEAD   THE DECAD

Brother and Consort of Zeus   Eternity (*aeon*)
Helios   Untiring
Absence of Strife   Necessity
Far-Working (epithet of Apollo)   Atlas
Hera   Fate
Hephaestus   Helios
Maiden (*kore*)   God
Of the Kouretes   Key-Holding
Assimilation   Kosmos
Oneness of Mind   Strength
Horizon (because it limits the series of   Memory
units before returning to the Decad)   Ourania
Crossing or Passage   Heaven
Prometheus   All
Consort and Brother   All Perfect
Perfection   Faith
Bringing to Perfection (*Telesphorus*) Phanes
Terpsichore
Hyperion
Oceanus

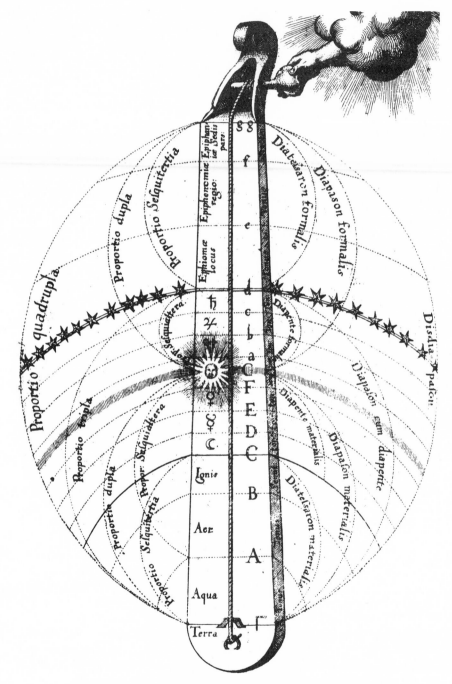

FIGURE 18. THE DIVINE MONOCHORD. This particular monochord is tuned in the key of G, while the examples on the right and in the introduction use the key of C. The three top notes on this monochord are incorrectly placed.

Appendix III:

The Formation and Ratios

of the Pythagorean Scale

by David R. Fideler

Notes	"Musical Proportion"	Tone Numbers	Tone Ratios	Tone Fractions		String Length
c¹	24	768	4	4	4	.25
b		729	3.796875	$243/64$	$35\tfrac{1}{64}$	.2633744
a		648	3.375	$27/8$	$3\tfrac{3}{8}$	.296296
g	18	576	3	3	3	.3333
f	16	512	2.6666	$8/3$	$2\tfrac{2}{3}$	.375
e		486	2.53125	$162/64$	$2\tfrac{34}{64}$	.3950617
d		432	2.25	$18/8$	$2\tfrac{2}{8}$	.4444
c	12	384	2	2	2	.5
B		364.5	1.8984375	$243/128$	$1\tfrac{115}{128}$	.5267489
A		324	1.6875	$27/16$	$1\tfrac{11}{16}$	.5925925
G	9	288	1.5	$3/2$	$1\tfrac{1}{2}$	.6666
F	8	256	1.3333	$4/3$	$1\tfrac{1}{3}$	.75
E		243	1.265625	$81/64$	$1\tfrac{17}{64}$	.7901234
D		216	1.125	$9/8$	$1\tfrac{1}{8}$	.8888
C	6	192	1	1	1	1

Figure 19. The Ratios of the Pythagorean Scale

AS NOTED in the introductory essay, the structure of the musical scale possesses a great deal of significance in Pythagorean thought as it is an excellent example of the principle of mathematical *harmonia* at work. In the case of the scale, the "opposites" of the high (2) and the low (1)—the two extremes of the octave— are united in one continuum of tonal relationships through the use of a variety of forms of proportion which actively mediate between these two extremes.

The best way to understand the mathematical principles of harmonic mediation involves actually charting out and playing out the ratios of the scale on the monochord. In constructing a monochord, it is best to make it as long as possible, perhaps in the region of 4—5 feet, as that makes it easier to differentiate between the harmonic nodal points at the high end of the spectrum (see fig. 6).

It is useful at first to play out the harmonic overtone series. Measure the exact length of the string and then mark off the overtone intervals: ½ the string length, ⅓ the string length, ¼ the string length, etc. It is possible to play out the overtone series without the use of the bridge; simply pluck the string about 1 inch from either end while simultaneously touching the nodal point with the other hand. It will be noted that there is an inverse relationship between the vibrational frequency of the tone and the string length. This is also illustrated in the above chart: hence a tone with a vibration of 2 is associated with a string division of .5 or ½. It is also useful at this point to play out the harmonic "Tetraktys," or the perfect consonances: 1:2 (octave), 2:3 (perfect fifth), and 3:4 (perfect fourth). Listen carefully to these ratios and reflect on the fact that you are actually hearing the relationships between these primary whole numbers.

To "tune" the monochord to the ratios of the Pythagorean scale use the string length ratios in the above chart, multiplying these ratios by the length of the string. Mark off these intervals, along with the corresponding notes, on the sounding board as they are carefully measured out.

Having marked out the Pythagorean scale, it might be useful at this point to review the material in the introductory essay relating to the harmonic proportion and then to play out these relations:

1) Play out the relationship of the octave (1:2). These are the two tonal extremes which must be united.

2) Play out the arithmetic mean linking together the extremes: C—G—c, or 6—9—12. This is the perfect fifth, the strongest musical relationship (2:3).

3) Play out the harmonic mean linking together the two extremes: C—F—c, or 6—8—12. This is the perfect fourth, the next strongest musical relationship (3:4).

4) Now play out the harmonic or musical proportion which is the basis of the musical scale: C—F—G—c, or 6:8::9::12. Play this out as a continued proportion and then the individual parts. Play out the two perfect fifths 6:9 and 8:12. Play out the two perfect fourths 6:8 and 9:12. Then play out the whole tone 8:9.

5) Having played out the harmonic foundation of the scale, now "fill in" the remaining 8:9 whole tone intervals. Play out C—D, D—E, G—A, and A—B. Along with F—G, these are all in the 8:9 ratio.

6) Play out the ratio of the leimma or the semitone: E—F and B—c. The leimma is the relationship between the perfect fourth and three whole tones.

7) Finally play out the entire scale: C—D—E—F—G—A—B—c. Through the use of arithmetic, harmonic and geometric proportion the two extremes have been successfully united.

A SUMMARY OF PYTHAGOREAN

MATHEMATICAL DISCOVERIES

BY SIR THOMAS HEATH

NOT ONLY did the early Pythagoreans make many contributions in the realm of philosophy, but their mathematical studies laid the foundation for the development of Greek geometry, and many portions of Euclid's *Elements* can be traced back to mathematical discoveries of the Pythagorean school.

This listing of early Pythagorean mathematical discoveries is excerpted from Thomas Heath's *History of Greek Mathematics,* vol. I, pp. 166-169.

A SUMMARY OF PYTHAGOREAN MATHEMATICAL DISCOVERIES

1. They were acquainted with the properties of parallel lines, which they used for the purpose of establishing by a general proof the proposition that the sum of the three angles of any triangle is equal to two right angles. This latter proposition they again used to establish the well-known theorems about the sums of the exterior and interior angles, respectively, of any polygon.

2. They originated the subject of equivalent areas, the transformation of an area of one form into another of different form and, in particular, the whole method of *application of areas*, constituting a *geometrical algebra*, whereby they effect the equivalent of the algebraical processes of addition, subtraction, multiplication, division, squaring, extraction of the square root, and finally the complete solution to the mixed quadratic equation $x^2 \pm pxq = 0$ so far as its roots are real. Expressed in terms of Euclid, this means the whole content of Book I. 35-48 and Book II. The method of *application of areas* is one of the most fundamental in the whole of later Greek geometry; it takes its place by the side of the powerful method of proportion; moreover, it is the starting point of Apollonius' theory of conics, and the three fundamental terms, *parabole, ellipsis,* and *hyperbole* used to describe the three separate problems in 'application' were actually employed by Apollonius to denote the three conics, names which, of course, are those which we use to-day. Nor was the use of the geometrical algebra for solving *numerical* problems unknown to the Pythagoreans; this is proved by the fact that the theorems of Eucl. II. 9, 10 were invented for the purpose of finding successive integral solutions of the indeterminate equations

$$2x^2\text{-}y^2 = \pm 1$$

3. They had a theory of proportion pretty fully developed. We know nothing of the form in which it was expounded; all we know is that it took no account of incommensurable magnitudes. Hence we conclude that it was a numerical

theory, a theory on the same lines as that contained in Book VII of Euclid's *Elements*.

They were aware of the properties of similar figures. This is clear from the fact that they must be assumed to have solved the problem, which was, according to Plutarch, attributed to Pythagoras himself, of describing a figure which shall be similar to one given figure and equal in area to another given figure. This implies a knowledge of the proposition that similar figures (triangles or polygons) are to one another in the duplicate ratio of corresponding sides (Eucl. VI. 19, 20). As the problem is solved in Eucl. VI. 25, we assume that, subject to the qualification that their theorems about similarity, &c., were only established of figures in which corresponding elements are commensurable, they had theorems corresponding to a great part of Eucl., Book VI.

Again, they knew how to cut a straight line in extreme and mean ratio (Eucl. VI. 30);* this problem was presumably solved by the method used in Eucl. II. 11, rather than by that of Eucl. VI. 30, which depends on the solution of a problem in the application of areas more general than the methods of Book II enable us to solve, the problem namely of Eucl. VI. 29.

4. They had discovered, or were aware of the existence of, the five regular solids. These they may have constructed empirically by putting together squares, equilateral triangles, and pentagons. This implies that they could construct a regular pentagon and, as this construction depends upon the construction of an isosceles triangle in which each of the base angles is double of the vertical angle, and this again on the cutting of a line in extreme and mean ratio, we may fairly assume that this was the way in which the construction of the regular pentagon was actually evolved. It would follow that the solution of problems by *analysis* was already practised by the Pythagoreans, notwithstanding that the discovery of the analytical method is attributed by Proclus to Plato. As the particular construction is practically given in Eucl. IV. 10, 11, we may assume that the content of Eucl. IV was also partly Pythagorean.

5. They discovered the existence of the irrational in the sense that they proved the incommensurability of the diagonal of a square with reference to its side; in other words, they proved the irrationality of $\sqrt{2}$. As a proof of this is referred to by Aristotle in terms which correspond to the method used in a proposition interpolated in Euclid, Book X, we may conclude that this proof is ancient, and therefore that it was probably the proof used by the discoverers of the proposition. The method is to prove that, if the diagonal of a square is commensurable with the side, then the same number must be both odd and even; here then we probably have of early Pythagorean use of the method of *reductio ad absurdum*.

Not only did the Pythagoreans discover the irrationality of $\sqrt{2}$; they showed, as we have seen, how to approximate as closely as we please to its numerical value.

After the discovery of this one case of irrationality, it would be obvious that

---

* The extreme and mean division of the line is an important mathematical and geometrical ratio which underlies various universal forms. This is the so-called "Divine Proportion," "Golden Section," or Phi ratio. On the properties and significance of this principle see Ghyka, *The Geometry of Art and Life*, and other titles on sacred geometry listed in the bibliography.

propositions theretofore proven by means of the numerical theory of proportion, which was inapplicable to incommensurable magnitudes, were only partially proved. Accordingly, pending the discovery of a theory of proportion applicable to incommensurable as well as commensurable magnitudes, there would be an inducement to substitute, where possible, for proofs employing the theory of proportion other proofs independent of that theory. This substitution is carried rather far in Euclid, Books I-IV; it does not follow that the Pythagoreans remodelled their proofs to the same extent as Euclid felt bound to do.

GLOSSARY OF SELECT PYTHAGOREAN TERMS

Analogia—Literally, "through proportion." Hence, continued geometrical proportion or ratio. See *logos*.

Apeiron—Boundless; Unlimited; Infinite; Indefinite. One of the Pythagorean first principles in the Table of Opposites. See *peras* and Indefinite Dyad.

Harmonia—A "joint" or "fitting together;" hence, the musical scale comprised within the octave. Also, music per se; philosophically, the principle of Union, opposite Strife. Also, a Pythagorean name of the number Three, because a third element must be introduced to mediate between or join together two separate principles or numerical values.

Indefinite Dyad—Plato's term for the Pythagorean principle of Apeiron, as contrasted with the One, the principle of Limit.

Kosmos—"Order." Also, "ornament." First applied to the universe by Pythagoras, hence cosmos means world-order. Also, a Pythagorean name of the numbers Six and Ten.

Logos—Usually translated "Word" or "Reason." In the mathematical and Pythagorean sense, the same as the Latin *ratio*, i.e. "proportion;" hence also, a principle of mediation. Can also mean "principle;" the plural *logoi* can be translated as "principles," "reasons" or "causes," or (mathematical) "ratios."

Mean or **median**—The middle term in a mathematical proportion which links two extreme terms together in harmonia. The three most important are the Arithmetic, Harmonic, and Geometric means, which underlie the structure of the musical scale in Pythagorean tuning. In the following equations, the two extremes are A and C, and the mean term is B.

$$\text{Arithmetic Mean: } B = (A + C) / 2$$
$$\text{Harmonic Mean: } B = 2AC / A + C$$
$$\text{Geometric Mean: } B = \sqrt{A \times C}$$

Monochord (*kanon*)—A one-stringed musical instrument with a movable bridge used for dividing the string at any length. The monochord is used to demonstrate the harmonic overtone series and the principles on which the musical scale is based.

Peras—The principle of Limit or Boundary. The opposite of Apeiron, the Unlimited.

Symphonia—Literally, "sounding together." "Harmony," agreement or concord. The term applies to the perfect intervals or consonance of the octave, fifth, and fourth, par excellence. This is the *modern* meaning of the word "harmony," but not the ancient one.

Tetraktys—(from *tetras*, four). "Fourness." Also, the first four numbers, especially when arranged in an equilateral triangle, the sum of which is the number Ten. Hence also, the Decad.

The Tetraktys symbolizes the perfection of Number and the elements which comprise it. The Tetraktys also contains the symphonic ratios which make possible the musical scale, i.e., 1:2, the octave; 2:3, the perfect fifth; and 3:4, the perfect fourth.

A SELECT BIBLIOGRAPHY OF WORKS

RELATING TO PYTHAGORAS

AND PYTHAGOREAN PHILOSOPHY

COMPILED BY DAVID R. FIDELER

AND JOSCELYN GODWIN

WHILE THE FOLLOWING BIBLIOGRAPHY of 400 titles cannot be considered as constituting the final word on writings which relate to Pythagorean studies, it does include all the important works that we are familiar with, and some works that are less frequently cited.

To make this bibliography more useful, the listing has been divided into several categories: Pythagorean Texts, Secondary Sources, Classical Philosophy, Mathematics, Music, Astronomy, Medieval and Renaissance, Sacred Geometry, and Whole Systems. A few words of explanation have been added underneath each category heading, and titles are arranged alphabetically by author under each category. The major problem with this format is that certain works could fall into more than one category. Despite this potential shortcoming, it was decided that the virtues of this arrangement outweigh any potential drawbacks.

For individuals who are beginning a study of Pythagorean thought, the best starting point is probably the lengthy and very well written section on the Pythagoreans to be found in W.K.C. Guthrie's *History of Greek Philosophy*, vol. 1. While his conclusions are not universally accepted, another excellent study is Cornford's article "Science and Mysticism in the Pythagorean Tradition." In terms of general histories of Greek philosophy, the accounts of Pythagorean thought given by John Burnet in *Early Greek Philosophy* and John Robinson in *An Introduction to Early Greek Philosophy* are better than most. The topic of Neopythagorean thought in the late Hellenistic period has yet to receive the full scale treatment that it deserves, but good accounts of Neopythagorean philosophers can be found in Dillon's *The Middle Platonists*. No account of Pythagorean scholarship would be complete without mentioning the massive, though perhaps hypercritical, study of Walter Burkert, *Lore and Science in Ancient Pythagoreanism*. Two other significant and delightful studies, which approach the topic from somewhat different angles, are Vogel's *Pythagoras and Early Pythagoreanism: An Interpretation of Neglected Evidence on the Philosopher Pythagoras* and Heninger's *Touches of Sweet Harmony: Pythagorean Cosmology and Renaissance Poetics*. Finally, Holger Thesleff has made very important contributions to Pythagorean studies in two volumes, *An Introduction to the Pythagorean Writings of the Hellenistic Period* and *The Pythagorean Writings of the Hellenistic Period*. In the latter volume Thesleff has collected together and edited the Greek texts of the Hellentistic Pythagorica.

PYTHAGOREAN TEXTS

The writings in this section are individual Pythagorean or Neopythagorean writings. If these writings appear in this volume, that fact is noted and the page number is given.

Anonymous. Accounts of Pythagorean thought in Sextus Empiricus, Vol. 1, 429-39; Vol. 2, 49-57; Vol. 3, 331-61, Loeb Classical Library, Harvard University Press, 1933.

Anonymous. *The Golden Verses of the Pythagoreans.* Brook, Surrey, Shrine of Wisdom, n.d.

Anonymous. *The Golden Verses of Pythagoras.* In this volume, 163-65.

Anonymous. *The Life of Pythagoras* preserved by Photius. In this volume, 137-40.

Anonymous. *Pythagorean Symbols or Maxims.* In this volume, 159-61.

Apollonius of Tyana. *The Letters of Apollonius of Tyana: A Critical Text with Prolegomena, Translation and Commentary* by R. J. Penella. Leiden, E.J. Brill, 1979.

Archytas. *The Fragments of Archytas.* In Chaignet, *Pythagore et la philosophie pythagoricienne,* Paris, 1874, vol. 1, 256-331; in this volume, 177-201.

Aristoxenus of Tarentum. *Apothegms.* In Taylor, *Political Fragments,* 65; in this volume, 243.

Boeckh. *Philolaus des Pythagoreer's Lehren, nebst den Bruchstucken seiner Werke.* Berlin, 1819.

Brown, Hellen Ann. *Philosophorum Pythagoreorum collectionis specimen.* Diss., University of Chicago, 1944. (Greek texts.)

Callicratidas. *On the Felicity of Families.* In Taylor, *Political Fragments,* 50-57; in this volume, 235-37.

Cardini, Maria Timpanaro, ed. *Pitagorici: Testimonianze e frammenti.* 3 vols. Florence, La Nuova Italia, 1958-64. (Greek texts.)

Chaignet, A.E. *Pythagore et la philosophie pythagoricienne.* 2 vols. Paris, Librairie Académique, 1874. (Contains the fragments of Philolaus and Archytas).

Charondas the Catanean. *Preface to the Laws of Charondas the Catanean.* In Taylor, *Political Fragments,* 38-45; in this volume, 231-33.

Clinias. *A Fragment of Clinias.* In Taylor, *Life of Pythagoras,* 167; in this volume, 265.

Crito. *On Prudence and Prosperity.* In Taylor, *Life of Pythagoras,* 177-79; in this volume, 251-52.

Delatte, A. *La Vie de Pythagore de Diogène Laërce: édition critique avec introduction et commentaire.* Brussels, Lamertin, 1922.

Demophilus. "The Pythagoric Sentences of Demophilus," in *Sallust on the Gods and the World.* Trans. by Thomas Taylor. (1793) Los Angeles, Philosophical Research Society, 1976.

Diehl, E., and Young, David, eds. *Theognis, ps.-Pythagoras, ps.-Phocylides.* Leipzig, Teubner, 1961.

Diels, H. and Kranz, W. *Die Fragmente der Vorsokratiker.* 6th ed., 3 vols. Berlin, Weidmann, 1951-2. (Greek texts, translated in Freeman, *Ancilla to the Pre-Socratic Philosophers,* Harvard University Press, 1983.)

Diogenes Laertius. *Lives of the Eminent Philosophers.* 2 vols. Trans. by R.D. Hicks. Harvard University Press, 1925.

Diogenes Laertius. *Life of Pythagoras.* In this volume, 141-56.

Diotogenes. *Concerning a Kingdom.* In Taylor, *Political Fragments,* 18-26; in this volume, 222-24.

Diotogenes. *On Sanctity.* In Taylor, *Political Fragments,* 10-11, 37-38; in this volume, 221.

Ecphantus the Crotonian. *On a Kingdom.* In Taylor, *Poltical Fragments,* 27-37; in this volume, 257-59.

Euryphamus. *Concerning Human Life.* In Taylor, *Life of Pythagoras,* 148-50; in this volume, 245-46.

Fabre d'Olivet, Antoine. *Les Vers Dorés de Pythagore.* (1813) Paris, L'Age d'Homme, n.d.

Fabre d'Olivet, Antoine. *The Golden Verses of Pythagoras.* Trans. by N.L. Redfield. (1917) New York, Weiser, 1975.

Fairbanks, Arthur. *The First Philosophers of Greece: An Edition and Translation of the Remaining Fragments of the Pre-Sokratic Philosophers, Together with a Translation of the More Important Accounts of Their Opinions Contained in the Early Epitomes of Their Works.* New York, Charles Scribners, 1898.

Freeman, Kathleen. *Ancilla to the Pre-Socratic Philosophers.* (1948) Harvard University Press, 1983.

Hadas, Moses, and Smith, Morton. *Heroes and Gods: Spiritual Biographies in Antiquity.* New York, Harper & Row, 1965. (Contains a trans. of Porphyry's *Life of Pythagoras.*)

Hierocles. *Ethical Fragments.* In Taylor, *Political Fragments,* 71-115; in this volume, 275-86.

Hierocles. *Commentary of Hierocles on the Golden Verses of Pythagoras.* Translated by N. Rowe from the French version of Andre Dacier. (1907) London, Theosophical Publishing House, 1971.

Hipparchus. *On Tranquility.* In Taylor, *Life of Pythagoras,* 151-53; in this volume, 247-48.

Hippodamus the Thurian. *On a Republic.* In Taylor, *Political Fragments,* 1-10, 17; in this volume, 217-20.

Hippodamus the Thurian. *On Felicity.* In Taylor, *Life of Pythagoras,* 143-47; in this volume, 215-17.

Iamblichus. *Iamblichi De vita Pythagorica liber; accedit epimetrum De Pythagorae Aureo carmine.* St. Petersburg, 1884. (Greek text.)

Iamblichus. *De Vita Pythagorica.* Ed. by Deubner. Leipzig, Teubner, 1937. (Greek text.)

Iamblichus. *De vita Pythagorica liber.* Edited by August Nauck. (1884) Amsterdam, 1965.

Iamblichus. *The Life of Pythagoras.* Trans. by Thomas Taylor. (1818) London, J.M. Watkins, 1965; in this volume, 57-122.

Iamblichus. *Exhortation to Philosophy.* Trans. by Thomas M. Johnson. Grand Rapids, Phanes Press, 1988. (Part of Iamblichus' "Pythagorean Encyclopedia;" contains his commentary on the Pythagorean Maxims.)

Iamblichus. (Pseudo-Iamblichus) *Theologumena Arithmeticae*. Edited by V. de Falco. Leipzig, Teubner, 1922. (Greek text.)

Maddalena, A. I Pitagorici: raccolta delle testimonianze e dei frammenti pervenutici. Bari, 1954. (Italian trans. of texts in DK with essays and notes.)

Metopus. *Concerning Virtue*. In Taylor, *Life of Pythagoras*, 164-66; in this volume, 249.

Ocellus Lucanus. *On the Nature of the Universe*. (1831) Trans. by Thomas Taylor. Los Angeles, Philosophical Research Society, 1976.

Ocellus Lucanus. *On the Nature of the Universe*. In this volume, 203-11.

Pempelus. *On Parents*. In Taylor, *Political Fragments*, 67-69; in this volume, 261.

Perictyone. *On the Harmony of a Woman*. In Taylor, *Political Fragments*, 57-65; in this volume, 239-41.

Philolaus. *The Fragments of Philolaus*. In Chaignet, *Pythagore et la philosophie pythagoricienne*, Paris, 1874, vol. 1, p. 226-54; in this volume, 167-75.

Philostratus. *The Life of Apollonius of Tyana*. 2 vols. Trans. by F.C. Conybeare. Harvard University Press, 1912.

Phyntis. *On Woman's Temperance*. In Taylor, *Political Fragments*, 69-74; in this volume, 263-64.

Polus. *On Justice*. In Taylor, *Life of Pythagoras*, 182; in this volume, 253.

Porphyrius. "Vita Pythagorae" in *Porphyrii Opuscula Selecta*, ed. A. Nauck, 2nd edn. (1886) Hildesheim, Olms, 1963.

Porphyry. *The Life of Pythagoras*. In this volume, 123-35.

Sextus Pythagoreus. *The Sentences of Sextus*. Ed. and trans. by R. Edwards and R. Wild. Chico, Scholars Press, 1981.

Sextus. *Select Sentences of Sextus the Pythagorean*. In Taylor, *Life of Pythagoras*, 192-200; in this volume, 267-70.

Speusippus. Fragments from his work *On Pythagorean Numbers* in Thomas, *Greek Mathematical Works*, vol. 1, Harvard University Press, 1939.

Sthenidas the Locrian. *On a Kingdom*. In Taylor, *Political Fragments*, 26-27, in this volume, 255.

Taylor, Thomas, trans. *Political Fragments of Archytas, Charondas, Zaleucus and Pythagoreans, preserved by Stobaeus; and also Ethical Fragments of Hierocles, the celebrated Commentator on the Golden Pythagoric Verses, preserved by the same author*. London, 1822.

Theages. *On the Virtues*. In Taylor, *Life of Pythagoras*, 161-63, 168-73; in this volume, 225-28.

Thesleff, Holger. *The Pythagorean Writings of the Hellenistic Period*. Abo, Abo Akademi, 1965. (A complete collection of the Hellenistic Pythagorean writings in the original Greek.)

Timaeus Locrus. *De natura mundi et animae*. Überlieferung, Testimonia, Text und Übersetzung von W. Marg. Editio maior. Leiden, E.J. Brill, 1972.

Timaeus Locrus. *Über die Natur des Kosmos und der Seele*. Kommentiert von M. Baltes. Leiden, E.J. Brill, 1972.

Timaios of Locri. *On the Nature of the World and the Soul*. Trans. by T.H. Tobin. Chico, Scholars Press, 1985.

Timaeus of Locri. *On the World and the Soul.* In this volume, 287-96.

Zaleucus the Locrian. *Preface to the Laws of Zaleucus the Locrian.* In Taylor, *Political Fragments,* 46-50; in this volume, 229-30.

SECONDARY SOURCES

The writings in this section, while not actual Pythagorean writings, are all specific studies of Pythagoras, Pythagorean thought, or Pythagorean writings.

Balch, L. "The Neo-pythagorean Moralists and the New Testament," in H. Temporini and W. Haase (ed.), *Aufstieg und Niedergang der roemischen Welt,* Berlin, de Gruyter, 1983, Teil II, Band 26.

Bamford, Christopher. "Homage to Pythagoras," in *Lindisfarne Letter* 14.

Bindel, Ernst. *Pythagoras.* Stuttgart, Freies Geistesleben, 1962.

Bömer, F. *Der Lateinische Neuplatonismus und Neupythagoreismus.* Leipzig, Harrassowitz, 1936.

Boehm, F. *De Symbolis Pythagoreis.* Diss., Berlin, 1905.

Boyancé, Pierre. "Note sur la Tétractys," *L'Antiquite Classique* 20 (1951), 421-5.

Boyancé, Pierre. "Sur l'Abaris d'Héraclide le Pontique," *Revue des études anciennes* 36 (1934) 321-52.

Boyancé, Pierre. "Sur la vie pythagoricienne," *Revue des études grecques* 52 (1939), 36-50.

Burkert, Walter. "Hellenistiche Pseudopythagorica," *Philologus* 105 (1961), 16-43, 226-246.

Burkert, W. *Lore and Science in Ancient Pythagoreanism.* Harvard University Press, 1972.

Burnet, John. "Pythagoras and Pythagoreanism," in *Encyclopedia of Religion and Ethics,* New York, 1919, vol. X, 520-530.

Bywater, J. "On the Fragments Attributed to Philolaus the Pythagorean," *Journal of Philology* 1 (1868), 20-53.

Cameron, Alister. *The Pythagorean Background of the Theory of Recollection.* Menasha, WI, George Banta, 1938.

Carcopino, Jérôme. *La basilique pythagoricienne de la Porte Majeure.* Paris, L'artisan du livre, 1927.

Carcopino, Jérôme. *Aspects Mystiques de la Rome Paienne.* Paris, L'Artisan du Livre, 1941.

Carcopino, Jérôme. *De Pythagore aux Apotres.* Paris, Flammarion, 1956.

Casa, Adriana della. *Nigidio Figulo.* Rome, Ateneo, 1962.

Chaignet, A.E. *Pythagore et la philosophie pythagoricienne.* 2 vols. Paris, Librairie Académique, 1874.

Cornford, F.M. "The Earliest Pythagorean Cosmology," in his *Plato and Parmenides.* London, Paul, Trench, Trubner, 1939.

Cornford, F.M. "The Invention of Space," in *Essays in Honor of Gilbert Murray*. London, Allen and Unwin, 1936.

Cornford, Francis M. "Mysticism and Science in the Pythagorean Tradition," *Classical Quarterly* 16 (1922), 137-150; 17 (1923), 1-12.

Dacier, Andre. *The Life of Pythagoras*. (Trans. from French, London, 1707.) York Beach, Samuel Weiser, 1981.

Delatte, Armand. *Etudes sur la littérature pythagoricienne*. Paris, Champion, 1915.

Delatte, Armand. *Essai sur la politique pythagoricienne*. Paris, Champion, 1922.

Dillon, John. *The Middle Platonists*. Cornell University Press, 1977. (Contains a good account of the Neopythagoreans.)

Eliade, Mircea. "Orpheus, Pythagoras, and the New Eschatology," chapter 22 in *A History of Religious Ideas*, vol. 2, University of Chicago Press, 1982.

Festugière, A. "Les mémoires pythagoriques cités par Alexandre Polyhistor," *Revue des études grecques* 58 (1945), 1-65.

Frank, Erich. *Plato und die sogenannten Pythagoreer*. Halle, 1923.

Freeman, Kathleen. *Companion to the Pre-Socratic Philosophers: A Companion to Diels' Fragmente Der Vorsokratiker*. Oxford University Press, 1946.

Fritz, Kurt von. "Pythagoras of Samos," in *The Dictionary of Scientific Biography*, New York, Charles Scribner's Sons, 1975, vol. 9, 214-25.

Fritz, Kurt von. *Pythagorean Politics in Southern Italy: An Analysis of the Sources*. (1940) New York, Octagon Books, 1977.

Fritz, K. von, Dorrie, H., and van der Waerden, B.L. "Pythagoras" and "Pythagoreer" in Pauly-Wissowa *Realencyclopädie der classischen Altertumswissenschaft*, vol. 27 (1963), and suppl. vol. 10 (1965).

Godwin, Joscelyn. "Pythagoreans, Today?", in *Lindisfarne Letter* 14.

Goettling, C.W. "Die Symbole des Pythagoras," *Gesammelte Abhändlungen*, vol. 1, Halle, 1851.

Goodenough, E.R. "A Neo-Pythagorean Source in Philo Judaeus." *Yale Classical Studies* 3 (1932), 117-64.

Gorman, Peter. *Pythagoras, a Life*. London, Routledge & Kegan Paul, 1979.

Guthrie, W.K.C. *A History of Greek Philosophy. Vol. 1: The Earlier Presocratics and The Pythagoreans*. Cambridge University Press, 1971.

Haase, Rudolf. "Literatur zur Geschichte des harmonikalen Pythagoreismus" [558 entries] in *Aufsätze zur harmonikalen Naturphilosophie*, Graz, Akademische Druck-und Verlagsanstalt, 1974.

Heidel, W.A. "*Peras* and *Apeiron* in the Pythagorean Philosophy," *Archiv für Geschichte der Philosophie* 14 (1901), 384-399.

Heidel, W.A. "Notes on Philolaus," *American Journal of Philosophy* 28 (1907), 77-81.

Jäger, Hans. *Die Quellen des Porphyrios in seiner Pythagoras-Biographie*. Diss., Zürich, Chur, 1919.

Kahn, Charles. "Pythagorean Philosophy before Plato," in Morelatos, *The Pre-Socratics: A Collection of Essays*, Garden City, Anchor Press, 1974, 161-85.

Kucharski, Paul. "Les principes des pythagoriciens et la dyade de Platon," *Archives de Philosophie* 22 (1959), 385-431.

Kucharski, Paul. "Aux frontières du Platonisme et du Pythagorisme," *Archives de Philosophie* 19.1 (1955-56), 7-43.

Lévy, Isidore. *La légend de Pythagore de Grèce en Palestine.* Paris, Champion, 1927.

Lévy, Isidore. *Recherches sur les sources de la legénd de Pythagoras.* Paris, Leroux, 1926.

Lindisfarne Letter 14, "Homage to Pythagoras." West Stockbridge, MA, Lindisfarne Press, 1982.

Long, H.S. *A Study of the Doctrine of Metempsychosis in Greece from Pythagoras to Plato.* Diss., Princeton, 1948.

Mallinger, Jean. *Pythagore et les mystères.* Paris, Niclaus, 1944.

Minar, Edwin L., Jr. "Pythagorean Communism," *Transactions of the American Philological Association* 75 (1944), 34-46.

Minar, E.L. *Early Pythagorean Politics in Practice and Theory.* Baltimore, Waverly Press, 1942.

Morrison, J.S. "Pythagoras of Samos," *Classical Quarterly* 50 (1956), 135-156.

Morrison, J.S. "The Origins of Plato's Philosopher-Statesman," *Classical Quarterly* 52 (1958), 198-218.

Oppermann, Hans. "Eine Pythagoraslegend," *Bonner Jahrbucher* 130 (1925), 284-301.

Philip, J.A. "Aristotle's Monograph On the Pythagoreans," *Transactions of the American Philological Association* 94 (1963), 185-198.

Raine, Kathleen. "Blake, Yeats and Pythagoras," in *Lindisfarne Letter* 14.

Raven, J.E. *Pythagoreans and Eleatics.* Cambridge University Press, 1948.

Richardson, Hilda. "The Myth of Er (Plato, *Republic,* 616B)," *Classical Quarterly* 20 (1926), 113-34.

Ridgeway, William. "What Led Pythagoras to the Doctrine that the World was Built of Numbers?" *Classical Review* 10 (March 1896), 92-95.

Rivaud, A. "Platon et la politique pythagoricienne," Mélanges Gustave Glotz, vol. 2. Paris, Presses Universitairs de France, 1932.

Rohde, Erwin. "Die Quellen des Iamblichus in seiner Biographie des Pythagoras," *Rheinisches Museum für Philologie* 26 (1871), 554-6; 27 (1872), 23-61.

Rosenthal, F. "Some Pythagorean Documents Transmitted in Arabic," *Orientalia* 10 (1941), 104-15; 383-95.

Rougier, Louis. *L' Origine astronomique de la croyance pythagoricienne en l'immortalité céleste des âmes.* Cairo, Institut français d'Archéologie orientale, 1933.

Rougier, L. *La Religion astrale des Pythagoriciens.* Paris, Presses Universitairs de France, 1959.

Rutherford, Ward. *Pythagoras: Lover of Wisdom.* Aquarian Press, Wellingborough, 1984.

Santillana, G. de and Pitts, W. "Philolaus in Limbo: or, What happened to the Pythagoreans?", *Isis* (42) 1951, 112-20.

Seltman, C.T. "The Problem of the First Italiote Coins," *Numismatic Chronicle,* 6th series, 9 (1949), 1-21.

Stanley, Thomas. "Pythagoras," from his *History of Philosophy.* (1687) Los Angeles, Philosophical Research Society, 1970.

Stapelton, H.E. "Ancient and Modern Aspects of Pythagoreanism," *Osiris* 13 (1958), 12-53.

Stocks, J.L. "Plato and the Tripartite Soul," *Mind,* n.s., 24 (1915), 207-21.

Swanson, R. A. "Ovid's Pythagorean Essay," *Classical Journal* 54 (1958), 21-24.

Taran, L. *Asclepius of Tralles: Commentary to Nicomachus' Introduction to Arithmetic.* (Transactions of the American Philosophical Society, n.s., 59, 4.) Philadelphia, American Philosophical Society, 1969.

Taylor, A.E. "Two Pythagorean Philosophemes," *Classical Review* 40 (1926), 149-51.

Thesleff, Holger. *An Introduction to the Pythagorean Writings of the Hellenistic Period.* Abo, Abo Akademi, 1961.

Vogel, Cornelia J. de. *Pythagoras and Early Pythagoreanism: An Interpretation of Neglected Evidence on the Philosopher Pythagoras.* Assen, Van Gorcum, 1966.

Waerden, B.L. van der. "Die Harmonielehre der Pythagoreer," *Hermes* 78 (1968), 163-199.

Watters, Hallie. *The Pythagorean Way of Life with a Discussion of the Golden Verses.* (Masters thesis.) Adyar, Theosophical Publishing House, 1926.

Wellmann, Max. "Eine pythagoreische Urkunde des IV. Jahrhunderts vor Christus," *Hermes* (1919), 225-48.

White, M. "The Duration of the Samian Tyranny," *Journal of Hellenic Studies* 74 (1954), 36-43.

Whittaker, John. "Epekeina nou kai ousias," *Vigilate Christianae* 23 (1969), 91-104. (On Moderatus.)

Whittaker, John. "Neopythagoreanism and Negative Theology," *Symbolae Osloenses* 44 (1969), 109-25.

Whittaker, John. "Neopythagoreanism and the Transcendent Absolute," *Symbolae Osloenses* 48 (1973), 77-86.

Zeller, Eduard. *A History of Greek Philosophy: From the Earliest Period to the Time of Socrates.* Trans. by S.F. Alleyne. Vol. I: Pre-Socratic Philosophy. London, 1881.

GREEK PHILOSOPHY

These works on early classical philosophy and Greek religion discuss Pythagorean thought.

Armstrong, A.H., ed. *Cambridge History of Later Greek and Early Medieval Philosophy.* Cambridge University Press, 1967.

Aujoulat, Noel. *Le Néo-Platonisme Alexandrin: Hiéroclès d'Alexandrie.* Leiden, E.J. Brill, 1987.

Baldry, H.C. "Embryological Analogies in Presocratic Cosmogony," *Classical Quarterly* 26 (1932), 27-34.

Booth, N.B. "Were Zeno's Arguments Directed Against the Pythagoreans?", *Phronesis* 2 (1957), 90-103.

Brommer, P. "De numeris idealibus," *Mnemosyne* 3.11 (1943), 263-295.

Brumbaugh, Robert S. *Plato's Mathematical Imagination: The Mathematical Passages in the Dialogues and Their Interpretation.* Bloomington, Indiana University Press, 1954.

Burnet, J. *Early Greek Philosophy: Part I, Thales to Plato.* London, Macmillan, 1914.

Burnet, John. *Early Greek Philosophy.* 4th ed. London, Macmillan 1930.

Capek, M. "The Theory of Eternal Recurrence," *Journal of Philosophy* (57) 1960, 289-96.

Copleston, S.J. *A History of Philosophy: Greece and Rome.* New York, Doubleday, 1962.

Cornford, F.M. "Mystery Religions and Pre-Socratic Philosophy," in *The Cambridge Ancient History,* Cambridge University Press, 1926, vol. 4, 522-78.

Cornford, F.M. *Principium Sapientiae: The Origins of Greek Philosophical Thought.* Cambridge University Press, 1952.

Cornford, F.M. *Plato's Cosmology.* London, Routledge, 1937.

Cornford, F.M. *The Laws of Motion in Ancient Thought.* Cambridge University Press, 1931.

Cornford, F.M. *From Religion to Philosophy.* London, Arnold, 1912

Critchlow, Keith. "The Platonic Tradition on the Nature of Proportion," in *Lindisfarne Letter 10.*

Gomperz, Theodor. *Greek Thinkers.* London, Murray, 1912.

Guthrie, W.K.C. "The Presocratic World-Picture," *Harvard Theological Review,* 45 (1952), 87-104.

Kirk, G.S., and Raven, J.E. *The Presocratic Philosophers: A Critical History with a Selection of Texts.* Cambridge University Press, 1957.

Merlan, Philip. *From Platonism to Neoplatonism.* The Hague, Nijhoff, 1960.

Onians, R.B. *The Origins of European Thought about the Body, the Mind, the Soul, the World, Time and Fate.* Cambridge University Press, 1951.

Porphyry. *On Abstinence from Animal Food.* Edited by E. Wynne-Tyson. London, Barnes & Noble, 1965.

Robinson, John. *An Introduction to Early Greek Philosophy.* New York, Houghton Mifflin, 1968.

Rohde, Erwin. *Psyche: The Cult of Souls and Belief in Immortality Among the Greeks.* London, Routledge, 1925.

Taran, L. *Speusippus of Athens: A Critical Study with a Collection of the Related Texts and Commentary.* Leiden, E.J. Brill, 1982.

Taylor, A.E. *A Commentary on Plato's Timaeus.* Oxford University Press, 1928.

Zeller, Eduard. *Outlines of the History of Greek Philosophy.* New York, Dover, 1980.

MATHEMATICS

These works contain information on the mathematical discoveries of the Pythagoreans. Also included are works dealing with Pythagorean arithmology and geometry.

Adam, James. *The Nuptial Number of Plato*. (1891) London, Kairos, 1985.

Allendy, René. *Le Symbolisme des nombres*. Paris, Charcornac, 1921.

Anatolius. (Edited by Heiberg.) *Anatolius sur les dix premiers nombres*. (On the Numbers Up to Ten.) Macon, Protat Frères, 1900. (Greek text.)

Butler, Christopher. *Number Symbolism*. New York, Barnes & Noble, 1970.

Fritz, Kurt von. "The Discovery of Incommensurability by Hippasos of Metapontum," *Annals of Mathematics* 46 (1945), 242-264.

Gardner, Martin. "Simple Proofs of the Pythagorean Theorem," *Scientific American* 211.4 (Oct. 1964), 118-125.

Guénon, René. "La Tetraktys et le carré de quatre," *Etudes Traditionnelles* 42 (May 1937).

Guénon, René. *Symboles fondamentaux de la Science sacrée*. Paris, Gallimard, 1962 (includes the above article).

Heath, Thomas. *A History of Greek Mathematics*. 2 vols. Oxford University Press, 1921.

Heath, T. L. *The Thirteen Books of Euclid's Elements*. 3 vols. Cambridge University Press, 1926.

Heidel, W.A. "The Pythagoreans and Greek Mathematics," *American Journal of Philology* 61 (1940), 1-33.

Hippocrates. *De Hebdomad. Classical Quarterly* 65 (1971), 365-88.

Hopper, V.F. *Medieval Number Symbolism: Its Sources, Meaning and Influence on Thought and Symbolism*. New York, Columbia University Press, 1938.

Junge, Gustave. "Die pythagoreische Zahlenlehre," *Deutsche Mathematik* 5 (1940), 341-57.

Junge, Gustave. "Von Hippasos bis Philolaus: das Irrationale und die geometrischen Grundbegriffe," *Classica et Medievalia* 19 (1958), 41-72.

Kleinhammes, Otto. *Die Quadratur des Kreises aus dem Geiste der Musik*. Wanger im Allgau, J. Kleinhammes, 1949.

Kozminsky, Isidore. *Numbers, Their Meaning and Magic*. New York, Putnam's Sons, 1927.

Kucharski, Paul. *Etude sur la doctrine pythagoricienne de la tétrad*. Paris, Les Belles Lettres, 1952.

Michel, P. *De Pythagore à Euclide*. Paris, Les Belles Lettres, 1950.

Neugebauer, O. *The Exact Sciences in Antiquity*. Princeton University Press, 1952.

Nicomachus of Gerasa. *Introduction to Arithmetic*. Trans. by Martin Luther D'Ooge. New York, MacMillan, 1926.

Oliver, G. *The Pythagorean Triangle*. (1875) San Diego, Wizards Bookshelf, 1975.

Pacioli, Luca. *Summa de arithmetica, geometria, proportioni & proportionalita.* Venice, 1494.

Pacioli, Luca. *De divina proportione.* Milan, 1956; and Paris, Librairie du Compagnonnage, 1984.

Robbins, Frank E. "The Tradition of Greek Arithmology," *Classical Philology* 16 (1921), 97-123.

Saint-Martin, Louis-Claude de. *Les Nombres.* Paris, Documents martinistes, 1983.

Schnitzler, Gunter, ed. *Musik und Zahl: Interdisziplinäre Beiträge zum Grenzbereich zwischen Musik und Mathematik.* Bonn, Verlag für systematische Musikwissenschaft, 1976.

Speusippus. Fragments from his work "On Pythagorean Numbers" in Thomas, *Greek Mathematical Works,* vol. 1, Harvard University Press, 1939.

Taylor, Thomas. *The Theoretic Arithmetic of the Pythagoreans.* (1816) New York, Samuel Weiser, 1978.

Theon of Smyrna. *Mathematics Useful for Understanding Plato.* Trans. by R. & D. Lawlor. San Diego, Wizards Bookshelf, 1979.

Thomas, Ivor. *Greek Mathematical Works. Vol. I: From Thales to Euclid.* Harvard University Press, 1951.

Waerden, B.L. van der. "Die Arithmetik der Pythagoreer," *Mathematische Annalen,* 1 (1948), 127-53; 2 (1948), 676-700.

Waerden, B.L. van der. *Science Awakening: Egyptian, Babylonian and Greek Mathematics.* New York, Science Editions, 1961.

Waerden, B.L. van der. *Geometry and Algebra in Ancient Civilizations.* New York, Springer-Verlag, 1983.

Wasserstein, A. "Theatetus and the Theory of Numbers," *Classical Quarterly* 52 (1958), 165-79.

Wedberg, A. *Plato's Philosophy of Mathematics.* Stockholm, Almquist and Wiksell, 1955.

Weiss, C.H. *Betrachtung des Dimensionsverhältnisse in den Hauptkörpern des sphäroidischen Systems und ihren Gegenkörpern, im Vergleich mitden harmonischen Verhältnissen der Töne.* Berlin, 1820.

Wescott, Wynn. *Numbers: Their Occult Power and Mystic Virtues.* (1902) London, Theosophical Publishing House, 1974.

MUSIC

These writings deal with Pythagorean musical and harmonic theory.

Abert, Hermann. *Die Musikanschauung des Mittelalters und ihre Grundlagen.* Halle, 1905, reprinted Tutzing, Schneider, 1964.

Amy-Sage, Fidèle. *La Musique et l'esprit.* Paris, Voile d'Isis, 1920.

Aristeides Quintilianus. *On Music* Trans. by T. Mathiesen. Yale University Press, 1983.

Bailly, Edmond. *Le Chant des Voyelles comme Invocation aux Dieux Planétaires.* (1911) Nice, Bélisae, 1976.

Barbour, J. Murray. "The Persistence of the Pythagorean Tuning System," *Scripta Mathematica* 1 (1932-33), 286-304.

Becker, Oskar. "Fruhgriechische Mathematik und Musiklehre," *Archiv fur Musikwissenschaft* 14 (1957), 156-164.

Boethius. *The Principles of Music.* Trans. by Calvin M. Bower. Diss., George Peabody College for Teachers, 1966.

Bonnaire, M.U. *De l'influence de la musique sur les moeurs.* Vienne, 1856.

Bower, Calvin. "Boethius and Nicomachus, an Essay Concerning the Sources of *De Institutione Musica*," Vivarium 16 (1978), 1-45.

Cazden, Norman. "Pythagoras and Aristoxenus Reconciled," *Journal of the American Musicological Society* 11.2-3 (1958), 97-105.

Chailley, Jacques. *Nombres et symboles dans le langage de la musique.* Paris, Académie des Beaux-Arts, 1982.

Chamberlain, David S. "Philosophy of Music in the Consolatio of Boethius," *Speculum* 45 (1970), 80-97.

Cornford, F.M. "The Harmony of the Spheres" in his *The Unwritten Philosophy and Other Essays.* Cambridge University Press, 1950.

Coste, Charles. *L'Influence de la musique.* Poligny, 1863.

Crocker, Richard L. "Pythagorean Mathematics and Music," *Journal of Aesthetics and Art Criticism*, 22.2 (1963), 189-98; 22.3 (1964), 325-36.

Dalberg, J.F.H. von. *Untersuchungen über die Ursprung der Harmonie.* Erfurt, 1800.

De Vismes du Valgay, A.-P.-J. *Pasilogie.* Paris, 1806.

Dénereáz, Alexandre. *Cours d'harmonie.* Paris, Gauthier-Villars, 1906.

Düring, I. *Ptolemaios und Porphyrios über die Musik.* Göteborg, 1934. (Göteborgs Högskolas Arsskrift 40)

Fabre d'Olivet, Antoine. *La Musique expliquée comme Science et comme Art.* (1842-50) Paris, Dorbon Ainé, 1928.

Gandillot, Maurice. *Essai sur la Gamme.* Paris, Cavel, 1937.

Godwin, Joscelyn. *Cosmic Music: Three Musical Keys to the Interpretation of Reality.* West Stockbridge, Mass., Lindisfarne Press, 1987.

Godwin, Joscelyn. *Music, Mysticism and Magic: A Sourcebook.* London, Routledge & Kegan Paul, 1986.

Godwin, Joscelyn. *Harmonies of Heaven and Earth.* London, Thames & Hudson, 1987.

Godwin, Joscelyn. "The Golden Chain of Orpheus: A Survey of Musical Esotericism in the West," *Temenos* 4 (1985), 7-25; 5 (1985), 211-39.

Henderson, Isobel. "Ancient Greek Music," *New Oxford History of Music,* Oxford University Press, 1957, 336-403.

Henry, Charles. "Conception psycho-physique de la Gamme," *Bull. de l'Inst. Gén. Psychologique* 21.1-3 (1921).

Ikhwan al-Safa. *Epistle on Music.* Trans. by A. Shiloah. Tel-Aviv University, Department of Musicology, 1978.

Junge, G. "Die Sphärenharmonie und die pythagorisch-platonische Zahlenlehre," *Classica et Medievalia* 8 (1947), 183-94.

La Borde, J.B. de. *Mémoire sur les Proportions Musicales, le genre enharmonique des grecs, et celui des modernes.* Paris, 1781.

Le Voile d'Isis, special number on "La Musique dans ses rapports avec l'Esotérisme," Apr. 1928.

Levarie, Siegmund and Levy, Ernst. *Musical Morphology.* Kent State University Press, 1983.

Levarie, Siegmund, and Levy, Ernst. *Tone: A Study in Musical Acoustics.* Kent State University Press, 1968.

Levin, Flora R. *The Harmonics of Nicomachus and the Pythagorean Tradition.* (American Classical Studies, No. 1.) New York, Interbook, 1975.

Liebard, Louis. *Anachronie Musicale, ou la pyramide inversèe.* Besançon, Résonances, 1979.

Lohmann, Johannes. "Die griechische Musik als mathematische Form," *Archiv fur Musikwissenschaft* 14 (1957), 147-155.

Lucas, Louis. *Une Revolution dans la Musique: essai d'application, à la musique, d'une théorie philosophique.* Paris, 1849.

McClain, Ernest G. "Plato's Musical Cosmology," *Main Currents in Modern Thought* 30.1 (1973), 34-42.

McClain, Ernest G. "Musical Marriages in Plato's Republic," *Journal of Music Theory* 18.2 (1974), 242-72.

McClain, Ernest G. "A New Look at Plato's Timaeus," *Music and Man* 1.4 (1975), 341-60.

McClain, Ernest G. *The Myth of Invariance.* New York, Nicolas-Hays, 1976.

McClain, Ernest G. *The Pythagorean Plato: Prelude to the Song Itself.* York Beach, Nicolas-Hays, 1984.

Meyer-Baer, Kathi. *Music of the Spheres and the Dance of Death.* Princeton University Press, 1970.

Millet, Yves. "La primauté de la gamme dite de Pythagore: son symbolisme cosmique," *Etudes Traditionnelles* 59 (1958), 37-44, 138-161.

Montargis, Frédéric. *De Platone Musico.* (1886) Utrecht, Joamchimsthal, 1976.

Mountford, J.F. "The Musical Scales of Plato's Republic," *Classical Quarterly* 17 (1923), 125-136.

Paul, Maela and Müxelhaus, Patrick. *Le Chant Sacré des Energies.* Paris, Présence, 1983.

Pfrogner, Hermann. *Lebendige Tonwelt: zur Phänomen Musik.* Munich, Langen Müller, 1976.

Portnoy, Julius. *Music in the Life of Man.* New York, Holt, Rinehart and Winston, 1963.

Provost, Prudent. *La Musique rénovée selon la synthèse acoustique.* Paris, Sociéte francaise d'éditions littéraires et techniques, 1931.

Reinach, Théodore. "La Musique des Spheres," *Revue de Etudes grecques* 13 (1900), 432-49.

Rice, Isaac. *What is Music?* New York, 1875.

Roussier, P.J. *Mémoire sur la Musique des Anciens.* (1770) New York, Broude, 1966.

Rudhyar, Dane. *The Magic of Tone and the Art of Music.* Boulder, Shambhala, 1982.

Scott, Cyril. *Music: Its Secret Influence throughout the Ages.* (1933) New York, Weiser, 1969.

Thamar, Jean. "Notion de la Musique Traditionnelle," *Etudes Traditionnelles* 48 (1947), 281-293, 336-349; 49 (1948), 58-67, 106-112, 240-253, 301-308, 348-356; 50 (1949), 216-227, 303-318.

Troupenas, E. "Essai sur la Théorie de la Musique déduite du principe métaphysique," *Revue musicale* 17 (1832), 129-31.

Vassiliadou, Maria. "Le pythagorisme et la musique," in *Musique et Philosophie,* Colloque de Dijon, 1983, 15-26.

Villoteau, G.A. *Mémoire sur la possibilité et l'utilité d'une théorie exacte des principes naturels de la Musique.* Paris, 1807.

Waerden. B.L. van der. "Die Harmonielehre der Pythagoreer," *Hermes* 78 (1943), 163-199.

Walker, D.P. "Kepler's Celestial Music," *Journal of the Warburg and Courtauld Institutes* 30 (1967), 228-50.

ASTRONOMY

These writings deal with Pythagorean astronomy and cosmology.

Azbel (= Emile Chizat). *Harmonie des mondes: Loi des distances et des harmonies planétaires.* Paris, Hugues-Robert, 1903.

Burch, G.B. "The Counter-Earth," *Osiris* (1954), 267-94.

Dicks, D.R. *Early Greek Astronomy to Aristotle.* Ithaca, Cornell University Press, 1970.

Dreyer, John Louis Emil. *History of the Planetary Systems from Thales to Kepler.* Cambridge University Press, 1906.

Guénon, René. "Le symbolisme du Zodiaque chez les pythagoriciens," *Etudes Traditionnelles* 43 (June 1938).

Guénon, René. *Symboles fondamentaux de la Science sacrée.* Paris, Gallimard, 1962 (includes the above article).

Heath, Thomas L. *Greek Astronomy.* New York, AMS Press, 1969.

Waerden, B.L. van der. *Die Astronomie der Pythagoreer.* Amsterdam, Royal Academy, 1951.

MEDIEVAL AND RENAISSANCE

These studies deal primarily with Pythagorean thought in the Medieval and Renaissance periods.

Africa, Thomas W. "Copernicus' Relation to Aristarchus and Pythagoras," *Isis* 52 (1961), 403-409.

Amman, P.J. "The Musical Theory and Philosophy of Robert Fludd," *Journal of the Warburg and Courtauld Institutes,* 30 (1967), 198-227.

Boethius. *De arithmetica.* Edited with commentary by Girardus Rufus. Paris, 1521.

Boethius. *De musica.* Oscar Paul, ed. Leipzig, 1872.

Bongo, Pietro. *Myticae numerorum significationis liber.* Bergamo, 1585. Expanded ed., Basel, 1618, entitled *De Numerorum Mysteria.*

Clulee, Nicholas. *The Glass of Creation: Renaissance Mathematics and Natural Philosophy.* Diss., University of Chicago, 1973.

Debus, Allen G. "Mathematics and Nature in the Chemical Texts of the Renaissance," *Ambix* 15 (1968), 1-28.

Fludd, Robert. *Utriusque cosmi historia scilicet et minoris metaphysica, physica atque technica historia.* Oppenheim, 1621.

Giorgio, Francesco. *De harmonia mundi.* Venice, 1525.

Godwin, Joscelyn. *Robert Fludd: Hermetic Philosopher and Surveyor of Two Worlds.* London, Thames & Hudson, 1979.

Hart, Thomas Elwood. "Calculated Casualties in Beowulf: Geometrical Scaffolding and Verbal Symbol," *Studia neophilologica* 53 (1981), 3-35.

Hart, Thomas Elwood. "Twelfth-Century Platonism and the Geometry of Textual Space in Hartman's Iwein: A 'Pythagorean' Theory," *Res publica litterarum* 2 (1979), 81-107.

Heninger, S.K., Jr. "Some Renaissance Versions of the Pythagorean Tetrad," *Studies in the Renaissance* 8 (1961), 7-35.

Heninger, S.K., Jr. "Pythagorean Cosmology and the Triumph of Heliocentrism," in *Le soleil à la renaissance.* Presses universitaires de Bruxelles, 1965, 33-53.

Heninger, S.K., Jr. *Touches of Sweet Harmony: Pythagorean Cosmology and Renaissance Poetics.* San Marino, CA, Huntington Library, 1974.

Heninger, S.K., Jr. *The Cosmographical Glass: Renaissance Diagrams of the Universe.* San Marino, CA, Huntington Library, 1977.

Hopper, V.F. *Medieval Number Symbolism: Its Sources, Meaning and Influence on Thought and Symbolism.* New York, Columbia University Press, 1938.

Ingpen, William. *The Secrets of Numbers.* London, 1624.

Kayser, Hans. *Ein harmonikaler Teilungskanon.* Zurich, Occident, 1946.

Kepler, Johannes. *Mysterium cosmographicum.* Tubingen, 1596.

Kepler, Johannes. *Harmonice mundi.* Linz, 1619.

Kircher, Athanasius. *Musurgia universalis sive ars magna consoni et dissoni in x libros digesta.* Rome, 1650.

Kircher, Athanasisus. *Arithmologia: sive de abditis numerorum mysteriis.* Rome, 1665.

Koyre, A. *Metaphysics and Measurement: Essays in the Scientific Revolution.* Harvard University Press, 1968.

Macrobius. *Commentary on the Dream of Scipio.* Trans. and ed. W. H. Stahl. New York, Columbia University Press, 1952.

Martianus Capella. *De Nuptiis Philologiae et Mercurrii.* Ed., A. Dick. Leipzig, 1925.

Münxelhaus, Barbara. *Pythagoras Musicus: zur Rezeption der pythagorischen Musiktheorie als quadrivialer Wissenschaft im Lateinischen Mittelalter.* Bonn, Verlag für systematische Musikwissenschaft, 1976.

Nasr, Seyyed Hossein. *An Introduction to Islamic Cosmological Doctrines.* (Rev. ed.) Boulder, Shambhala, 1978.

Patrides, C.A. "The Numerological Approach to Cosmic Order During the English Renaissance," *Isis* 49 (1958), 391-397.

Reuchlin, Johann. *On the Art of the Kabbalah.* (1516) Trans. by Martin & Sarah Goodman. New York, Abaris Books, 1983.

Rosen, Edward. "Was Copernicus a Pythagorean?" *Isis* 53 (1962), 504-509.

Walker, D.P. *Studies in Musical Science in the Late Renaissance.* London, Warburg Institute, 1978.

Yates, Francis A. *The Occult Philosophy in the Elizabethan Age.* London, Routledge & Kegan Paul, 1979.

SACRED GEOMETRY

The writings in this section are concerned with Pythagorean and Platonic geometry in a theoretic and practical sense. Also included are works dealing with the application of "Pythagorean" canons of proportion in sacred architecture.

Bond, F.B., and Lea, T.S. *Gematria: A Preliminary Investigation of the Cabala.* (1917) London, RILKO, 1977.

Bond, F.B., and Lea, T.S. *The Apostolic Gnosis.* London, RILKO, 1979. (On Greek gematria.)

Bouleau, Charles. *The Painter's Secret Geometry.* Trans. by J. Griffin. Paris, 1963.

Brunés, Tons. *Secrets of Ancient Geometry.* 2 vols. Copenhagen, Rhodos, 1967.

Caskey, L.D. *Geometry of the Greek Vases.* Boston, 1922.

Colman, Samuel. *Nature's Harmonic Unity.* (1912) New York, Blom, 1971.

Critchlow, Keith. "The Platonic Tradition on the Nature of Proportion," in *Lindisfarne Letter* 10.

Critchlow, Keith. *Islamic Patterns: An Analytical and Cosmological Approach.* New York, Schocken Books, 1976.

Critchlow, Keith. *Order in Space: A Design Sourcebook.* New York, Viking, 1965.

Critchlow, Keith. *Time Stands Still: New Light on Megalithic Science.* New York, St. Martins Press, 1982.

Doczi, György. *The Power of Limits: Proportional Harmonies in Nature, Art and Architecture.* Boulder, Shambhala, 1981.

Ghyka, Matila C. *Le Nombre d'Or.* 2 vols. Paris, Gallimard, 1931.

Ghyka, Matila C. *The Geometry of Art and Life.* New York, Dover, 1977.

Gougy, Charles. *L'Harmonie des proportions et des formes dans l'architecture d'après les lois de l'harmonie des sons.* Paris, Charles Massin, 1925.

Guénon, René. *The Symbolism of the Cross.* London, Luzac, 1975.

Hambridge, Jay. *Dynamic Symmetry: The Greek Vase.* 1920.

Hambridge, Jay. *The Parthenon and other Greek Temples: Their Dynamic Symmetry.* 1924.

Hambridge, Jay. *The Elements of Dynamic Symmetry.* Yale University Press, 1948.

Hudson, H.P., ed. *Ruler and Compass.* Longmans Green, 1915.

Huntley, H.E. *The Divine Proportion: A Study in Mathematical Beauty.* New York, Dover, 1970.

Iverson, E. *Canon and Proportions in Egyptian Art.* Warminster, Aris and Phillips, 1975.

Kielland, E.C. *Geometry in Egyptian Art.* London, Tiranti, 1955.

Lawlor, Robert. "Ancient Temple Architecture," in *Lindisfarne Letter* 10.

Lawlor, Robert. *Sacred Geometry: Philosophy and Practice.* London, Thames and Hudson, 1982.

Lesser, G. *Gothic Cathedrals and Sacred Geometry.* 3 vols. London, Tiranti, 1957.

Lindisfarne Letter No. 10, "Geometry and Architecture." West Stockbridge, MA, Lindisfarne Press, 1980.

Lund, F.M. *Ad Quatratum: A Study of the Geometrical Basis of Classical and Mediaevel architecture.* London, Batsford, 1921.

Macaulay, Anne. "Apollo: The Pythagorean Definition of God," in *Lindisfarne Letter* 14.

Michell, John. *City of Revelation.* London, Sphere, 1978. (On Greek gematria.)

Purce, Jill. *The Mystic Spiral: Journey of the Soul.* London, Thames & Hudson, 1974.

Saint-Yves d'Alveydre. *L'Archéometre.* (1912) Paris, Dorbon Ainé, 1979.

Scholfield, P.H. *The Theory of Proportion in Architecture.* Cambridge, 1958.

Schwaller de Lubicz, R.A. *The Temple in Man.* Trans. by R. & D. Lawlor. Brookline, MA, Autumn Press, 1977.

Simson, Otto von. *The Gothic Cathedral.* New York, Pantheon, 1956.

Stirling, William. *The Canon: An Exposition of the Pagan Mystery Perpetuated in the Cabala as the Rule of All the Arts.* (1897) London, RILKO, 1981 (On Greek gematria.)

Sunderland, Elizabeth R. "Symbolic Numbers and Romanesque Church Plans," *Journal of the Society of Architectural Historians* 18 (1959), 94-103.

Talemarianus, Petrus. *De L'Architecture Naturelle.* Paris, Véga, 1950.

Thompson, D.W. *On Growth and Form.* Cambridge University Press, 1917.

Williams, R. *The Geometrical Foundation of Natural Structure.* New York, Dover, 1979.

WHOLE SYSTEMS

Included here are works pertaining to the application of the Pythagorean approach, especially the principles of harmonics, to scientific, artistic or philosophical synthesis.

Arnoux, George. *Musique Platonicienne, Âme du Monde.* Paris, Dervy, 1960.

Azbel (=Emil Chizat). *Le Beau et sa Loi: Loi de l'Action et des Nombres, Loi de l'Harmonie, Loi de l'Intelligence.* Paris, Hugues-Robert, 1899.

Bailly, Edmond. *Le Son dans la Nature*. Paris, L'Art Independant, 1900.

Bindel, Ernst. *Die Zahlengrundlagen der Musik im Wandel der Zeiten*. 2 vols. Stuttgart, Freies Geistesleben, 1950, 1951.

Blair, Lawrence. *Rhythms of Vision*. New York, Schocken, 1975.

Briseux, C.E. *Traité du Beau essential dans les Arts*. Paris, 1752.

Britt, Ernest. "La Synthèse de la Musique," *Annales du XXe Siecle*, 2 (1914), reprinted Paris, Véga, 1938.

Britt, Ernest. *Gamme Sidérale et Gamme Musicale: Etude Paléosophique*. Paris, Aux Ecoutes, 1924.

Britt, Ernest. *La Lyre d'Apollon*. Paris, Véga, 1931.

Choisnard, Paul. *La Chaine des Harmonies et la Spirale dans la Nature*. (2nd augmented ed.) Paris, Ernest Leroux, 1926.

Dénéreaz, Alexandre. *La Gamme, ce problème cosmique*. Zürich, Hug, 1939.

"Francisque," *Le Secret de Pythagore dévoilé, ou le fond de la musique*. Rochefort, 1869.

Franz, Marie-Louise von. *Number and Time*. London, Rider, 1974.

Fuller, Buckminster. *Synergetics*. New York, Macmillan, 1975.

Fuller, Buckminster and Applewhite, Edgar. *Synergetics II*. New York, Macmillan, 1979.

Griveau, Maurice. *Programme d'une science idéaliste*. Paris, Revue Moderne d'Esthetique, 1896.

Griveau, Maurice. *La sphère de la beauté* Paris, Alcan, 1901.

Guyot, E. *La Boussole de l'harmonie universelle, esthétique applicable aux arts des sons, de la couleur et de la forme*. Albi, Corbière et Julien, 1894.

Hill, Clarence. *Harmonia Harmonica*. 3 vols. Bournemouth, Author, 1920-1935.

Kayser, Hans. *Akróasis: The Theory of World Harmonics*. Trans. by R. Lilienfeld. Boston, Plowshare, 1970.

Kayser, Hans. *Orphikon: eine harmonikale Symbolik*. Basel, Schwabe, 1973.

Kayser, Hans. *Lehrbuch der Harmonik*. Zürich, Occident, 1950.

Labat, J.B. *Les Nombres appliqués à la Science Musicale*.Bordeaux, 1861.

Lacuria, P.F.G. *Les Harmonies de l'Etre exprimées par les Nombres*. 2 vols. Paris, 1847.

Landsberg, G.F. "Essai Tentative d'adaptation des Lois Musicales à une clef des Lois Universelles," *Voile d'Isis*, 1914, 385-394.

Lange, Anny von. *Mensch, Musik und Kosmos*. 2 vols. Freiburg, Die Kommenden, 1960.

Lawlor, Robert. "Pythagorean Number as Form, Color and Light," in *Lindisfarne Letter* 14.

Levarie, Sigmund and Levy, Ernst. "The Pythagorean Table," *Main Currents in Modern Thought* 30.4 (1973), 117-29.

Levy, Ernst. "The Pythagorean Concept of Measure," *Main Currents in Modern Thought* 21.3, (1965), 51-57.

Malfatti de Montereggio, Johann. *Anarchie und Hierarchie des Wissens*. Leipzig, 1845.

Malfatti de Montereggio, Johann. *Etudes sur la mathèse* (= French trans. of the above). Paris, A. Frank, 1849.

Néroman, Dom. *La Leçon de Platon*. Paris, Arma Artis, 1983.

Pouyaud, Robert. "Astrologie et Harmonie colorée," *L'Atelier de la Rose,* 1951, 36-40.

Schmidt, Thomas Michael. *Musik und Kosmos als Schözpfungswunder*. Frankfurt, Schmidt, 1974.

Spitzer, L. *Classical and Christian Ideas of World Harmony*. Johns Hopkins Press, 1963.

Swiecianowski, Jules. *L'échelle musicale comme loi de l'harmonie dans l'universe et dans l'art*. Warsaw, 1881.

Thimus, Albert von. *Die harmonikale Symbolik des Alterthums*. 2 vols. (1868, 1876) Hildesheim, Olms, 1972.

Wagner, Johann Jacob. *Von der Natur der Dinge*. Leipzig, 1803.

Zajonc, Arthur G. "The Two Lights," in *Lindisfarne Letter* 14.

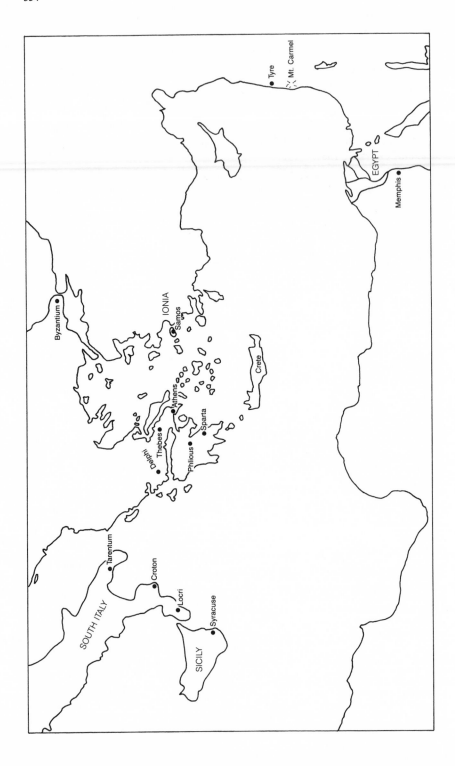

INDEX OF PROPER NAMES

INDEX OF SELECT TOPICS